PRAISE FOR
BEHIND THE SHADES

"To me, life consists of three phases. Learning who we are, learning about what we think we need in life, and finally, giving it all back. Sometimes life even seems unfair. It's not about the cards we are dealt in life but rather how we play our hand. Sheila Raye, you are the Royal Flush of all hands possible, and you give it all back in this amazing recollection of a tough hand gone good. *Behind the Shades: Hope Beyond the Darkness* is a must-read for anyone who feels alone, ashamed, and lonely for the journey traveled; it will bless those who want to feel the power and love of GOD as well as come to know God as their own source of power.

Love you, sister Sheila. Thank you for sharing . . . many will convert their house to a Full House as a result of this account."

— PAT MELFI, FOUNDER AND CEO
OF MUZART WORLD FOUNDATION

"Sheila Raye Charles is an outstanding talent and inspiration! From the first time I spoke with her, I found Ms. Charles to be sincere, driven, supportive, giving, and incredibly loving of humanity. Ms. Charles has an amazing story of hope to share that will inspire and motivate everyone she meets. She has touched my life, and I am proud to know her and call her friend."

—JOSIE PASSANTINO, HOST OF
THE JOSIE SHOW, WWW.JOSIESHOW.COM

"Sheila Raye Charles is a powerhouse vocalist, a lantern of light, and an inspiration of hope. She has the ability to stand among the weak and spread the word of the Gospel, to lift those broken and help them stand in awe of what God can do. It is a gift she humbly wears, knowing she was handpicked by God to spread the message of love, hope, faith, and charity among all human life. She has truly been the "RAYE" of hope in mine. Those blessed by her presence will leave knowing she was truly touched by God! Sheila's journey and testimony will certainly bless you and those who read about the amazing grace of our Lord and Savior."

—*MILLIEA TAYLOR MCKINNEY, AWARD-WINNING SONGWRITER AND CEO OF* **CONSCIOUS MUSIC ENTERTAINMENT**

"Listen to Sheila Raye; she knows what she's talking about."

—*JOHN LEGEND, NINE-TIME GRAMMY AWARD WINNER AND RECIPIENT OF STARLIGHT AWARD FROM THE SONGWRITERS HALL OF FAME*

BEHIND THE SHADES

HOPE BEYOND THE DARKNESS

SHEILA RAYE CHARLES
&
GLENN SWANSON

VOX DEI
An Imprint of Libertary

Cover Design by Greg Simanson
Proofread by Thomas Dean

Interior Photographs © Kevin McClellan
Back Cover Photograph © Doug Bryant

PRINT ISBN 978-1-62015-162-4

EPUB ISBN 978-1-62015-258-4

For further information regarding permissions, please contact info@booktrope.com.

Library of Congress Number: 2013913876

ACKNOWLEDGMENTS

Editor, Joel Swanson
A special thanks to tireless effort
and burning the candle

A grateful acknowledgement and
remembrance of
Wayne Swanson
(1954–2001)
For his writing efforts and assistance
with Sandra Betts and her manuscript
of *Behind the Shades* contained herein.
His brilliant light is remembered with
the greatest of love.

A special thank you to
Sole Soul Publishing
for the permission to print
excerpts from *shoes on the table*
©2007 Glenn Swanson/
Sole Soul Publishing
solesoul.net

DEDICATIONS

To my mother, Sandra Betts
Your greatness gave me hope
Your passion gave me knowledge
And your pain gave me love

To my father, Ray Charles Robinson
Your absence has made me strong
Your wisdom will never die
And your legacy paved the way

To my children, Jeanna, Jaymi, Kevin, Alicia, Jonnica:

There are no words to describe what is in my heart, so I will have to go forth with what I have from my limited catalog of words.

First and foremost, *I love you all very much!* Though my history would reflect something different, I solemnly promise my actions were never from any lack of love for you. I had truly lost love for myself. In a pool of lies, deceit, drugs, and more drugs, I was caught in a spiral that led to a place from which I thought there was no return, away from God's true intent for me. I wish I could have been a better mother to all of you. I can only pray God's healing love is where you find peace. My heart aches with an indescribable yearning for your presence in my life. The Bible says God will restore what the locust destroyed. I know this to be true, for he has blessed my life with all of you. God's perfect gift to us is that we are connected in spirit, and that may never be severed.

To apologize to you or say "sorry" just isn't enough, and by no means will I insult you by saying it. However, if I could take back every hour, minute, or second of pain caused by my afflictions, I would replace them with joy, love, and peace.

Kevin, Alicia, and Jonnica: because of your age, it may be some time before you read this, but I believe without question, we will be together again. I miss you. I know God's hand is on you. I thank God for your life daily.

Jaymi, Bubbling Brown Sugar, my precious child: it was prophesized you would be a huge part of carrying on your grandfather's musical legacy and the one I am attempting to create.

Jeanna-Bear, my rock, my angel, and my first-born; I believe your prayers were of the greatest powers spiritually for my return. You never stopped believing in me. *I loves ya, girl!* I hope when you read this book, it will further fill your heart, mind, body, and spirit with the deepest understanding of God's greatness. His love is unchanging, never-ending, and always forgiving. And for this purpose, I was born.

A prayer of God's blessings on all of you.

Love,
Your Mom

Matt and Becky:

God sent you to us as but a boy, and what a great man you grew up to be. I know God makes no mistakes. I am so grateful for the love, security, and hope you and Becky were willing and able to give *our* children. I pray for the day we come back full circle in our relationship. Thank you so much! How I love you so. Always have, always will.

—Sheila

To my brother Kevin:

Bro, we've made it through the fire. Don't you feel like Shadrach, Meshach, and Abednego? Whew, God's sooo good. The Three Musketeers: Mom, you, and me. Well, we always said we wanted to get caught up in the rapture together. You know Sandy, always jumping the gun! I'm so glad God put us together here on earth. *You da man!*

Love you always, your sis
—Sheila

Patty "Cakes" Maltz:

Girl, you have hung with this crazy chick through thick and thin, sick and sin. Talk about a true blessing from God. I'm proud to be able to say you're my friend.

I love you
—Sheila

Glenn Swanson:

From out of the basement, from the depths of Hell, your love has continually been without fail. When I think of Jesus and his walk here on earth, I think of you. If there is anyone who walks in the path of love such as Christ, it is surely you. I am who I am today in part because of your much-shared wisdom and undying, unconditional love.
Glenn, I love you forever.

—Sheila

A NOTE FROM SHEILA RAYE

I was raised by my mother with only limited contact with my father throughout my life; it wasn't until I was fourteen that I first met Dad in person. Prior to that meeting, most of my life had been spent in the small town of Cambridge, Ohio. During my childhood, I suffered sexual abuse and, consequently, disillusionment with the world, struggling to find my identity. I moved to Los Angeles at the age of thirteen to live with my Uncle Jerry and attended Anaheim High School with the hope to establish a relationship with my father.

Within a year, I found myself back with my mother in Cambridge and once again heading for trouble. I ran away to North Carolina, and on my sixteenth birthday, I became a victim in an auto accident that nearly cost me my life. I was hospitalized for six months, my right eye lodged at the back of my skull. Recovering from this over a period of years, I once again returned to Los Angeles, this time with my mother and brother, Kevin. At that time, my musical career was launched, and I had the opportunity to record with my band at my father's studio under his supervision.

I traveled with the DeBarge family and eventually found myself in Minneapolis to record at Paisley Park. Unable to generate a product that the music industry found marketable, I began writing with various local musicians and producers. I was voted New Artist of the Year at the 1990 Minnesota Black Music Awards, continuing to receive the counsel of my father on my musical career. For a variety of reasons, I was unable to break free from my troubled youth and fell further into a dependency on drugs. Ultimately I found myself in federal prison, which is where and when I finally was able to put the most troubling demons of my past to rest. Returning to Minneapolis, I began with earnest to build my musical career over the past several years, forming my own production company, assembling a band, and preparing to strategically enter onto the world's entertainment stage.

Circumstances of abandonment and neglect have a way of stealing the joy of your own being. It has been a painful and trying experience to relive them, but such sense of loss and hurt is nothing pushed up against the painful vision of your own abuses that steal joy from another. In the process of recovering this joy of self, it was easier to forgive others and far more difficult to forgive myself. Inexplicable as it is, such a transformation and return to the simple "joy of being" is possible. Though I yet remain within that process (of which the writing of this book is but a part), I stand confident as I open the door to the mystical journey of Spirit. Realizing I am free to enjoy the beauty of God's creation as nothing less than His child is the most empowering freedom.

A Note from Glenn Swanson

Within the first few weeks of Sheila arriving in Minneapolis, I met her and her brother Kevin at a recording studio to work on a music project together. Within those first moments, an unbreakable bond of friendship formed among the three of us. Shortly thereafter, I met their mother, Sandra Betts, and from that moment forward, a mutual embrace of family was shared. It was but several days later I began writing music with both of them. Years later, after several previous attempts left her dissatisfied, Sandra invited me to assist chronicling her life and relationship with Ray Charles within a book she entitled *Behind the Shades*. As is noted within the acknowledgments, my brother, Wayne Swanson, poured his energy into the effort once mutually invited to assist. The three of us came to know each other as family. As we worked together, Sandy and Wayne shared our home for several months. I remember those days of laughter and tears with the greatest of fondness. Though the work was never completed for a variety of reasons, I maintained countless hours of taped interviews and several hundred pages of text. After both had come to pass away, Sheila approached me with the proposal to assist her in a similar effort, and herein is revealed the result of that endeavor.

I regard it as a great privilege to have served in this capacity to both Sheila and her mother. That there is an Unseen Hand within the story of *Behind the Shades* is undeniable, and I approached the task of assisting this effort with an air of privilege—the depth of Sheila's story, coupled with her mother's voice and input to this story, is indeed panoramic, revealing the extremes of human tragedy and triumph. Revealed properly, it is a story that is bigger than life—the drama at times unbelievable. For that reason, it has been more than a humbling task; it has been a process of personal growth in Spirit. To reveal such a story requires of its presenter a degree of personal detachment few attain, and I applaud Sheila for her candor and frankness. It is nothing short of courageous.

To best serve Sheila in this effort, it was a conscious decision not to include our professional interaction in the attempt to personally detach from her story. There exists an extraordinary creative chemistry between us. Sheila kept her addiction and other aspects of her life distant from my experiences with her, though they undoubtedly influenced our relationship of some twenty years.

PREFACE

An aspect of *Behind the Shades: Hope Beyond the Darkness* is the voice of Sheila's mother, Sandra Betts, revealing the story of her life with Ray Charles. This story within a story is authentic, distilled from countless hours of taped conversations with Sandy sharing amazing accounts of her deeply meaningful, often bizarre affair with Ray, expressed in Sandy's magically unique, honestly warm, and vibrantly dynamic fashion. The manuscript revealed within this book is real, written more than ten years ago. It was intended to document facets of Ray Charles no one else had known. Though fate would postpone the work, its appearance within this book contributes and complements both narratives. Now, Sheila's story frames her mother's thirty-some-year relationship with music's pioneering power. This format adds meaning and clarity to both stories, as mother and daughter come full circle around the recollections of the one man who became an undeniable influence in the lives of both.

Sheila reveals her life story through the bars of federal prison. Her fifteen-month incarceration at Bryan FPC and Houston Federal Prison maximum security serves as the book's principal framework. During her incarceration, she begins to make peace with the demons that have haunted her. Also, within this time period, the most significant event of her life begins to bud, blossom, and flower: the unfolding of Spirit within.

The environment is devoid of family and past relationships, highly structured, and confined; these elements are naturally conducive to reflection and contemplation. Deep introspection of past events weaves the web for the reader by which Sheila had been ensnared and from which she ultimately and dramatically emerges.

The crux of her disillusionment revolves around her relationship, or lack thereof, with her father who, ironically, is the only family member she sees while incarcerated, as impersonal as ever, on the prison's television. The language contained herein at times is harsh and extreme. It was and is the reality of such an environment and experience. A conscious decision was made to preserve and accurately represent that reality within the story.

CHAPTER 1

ROCK BOTTOM

It is said that the farther one falls,
the higher we might again one day fly,
the degree of joy we may experience
inversely proportional
to the depth of our greatest misery.

I BEGIN MY STORY at the moment of my fall. On this day, when my father stood at the height of his career, adored by fans worldwide, I—his daughter, Sheila Raye Charles, at the age of 34—was entrenched within the darkest corridor of my life. Shackled and humiliated, delivered by my own actions, I found myself once again heading to federal prison, a two-time loser.

"03318-041." It was an authoritative voice, dispassionate and impersonal, one of the federal marshals overseeing my transfer from Elk River, Sherburne County Jail and Federal Holding Facility in Minnesota to Bryan Federal Prison Camp in Texas.

I responded to the numbers imprinted on the wristband I'd worn over the last four months. I felt like a dog picked off the street and thrown into the pound. It was not unfamiliar ground; I had been caught, tagged, and caged years before. This time, however, I was to be escorted by the "animal control officers" to a much bigger cage, housing much bigger dogs. Afraid and making every effort to conceal it, I was as alone as I had ever been.

Joint tenant with my fear and anxiety was an unexpected sense of relief. Soon, I would face the next phase of my sentence. Though I was not permitted to know the name of the prison to which I was being transferred, I knew better than most—there is nothing in a name. When there is no direction home, moving forward is all you have.

Between the shackles that bound both my ankles, there stretched a metal bar; at its center was affixed a chain that ran upward to handcuffs connecting to another chain encircling my waist. I advanced with the characteristic shuffle such restraints demand, ankle to wrist in bright federal orange.

There were the numerous directors of this jailhouse dance troupe: the federal agents, marshals, and guards with aviator sunglasses, dark suits and ties, black SUVs and vans with black-tinted windows, the stern all-about-business countenance, and the fraternal commitment never to question treating those in their charge as anything but animals that belonged in cages, chains, and shackles. Emotions had no place in this road show.

Vaguely, I understood I had earned my place on this stage, but I couldn't remember the audition. If life was a crapshoot, I had been throwing loaded dice. The house knew my number before I did.

"03318-041. Robinson."[1]

Directed to the elevator, a marshal and I descended to an underground garage and vehicle that would chauffeur me to a landing strip of unknown location. I was about to hop a flight on the not-so-friendly skies of Con Air. I tried to focus, to stay alert to my surroundings. Certainly the marshals were, and I could not attribute their anxiety to my presence within this small party of convicts. I was as docile as a lamb going to slaughter.

But I was angry beyond words—not at the justice system nor the society from which it sprang but at myself, at a heart that yet sought to love those who had so violently abused me, to yet care for those who had abandoned me, to forgive those who should have been there

---

[1] Sheila Raye Charles' full birth name was Sheila Jean Robinson, daughter of "Ray Charles" Robinson, the musician.

for me but hadn't been. Furthermore, I was disgusted for becoming the very thing that enraged me about others: wholly self-absorbed, unable to resolve the contradictions within me.

Like when I was escorted into my father's office at age fourteen for our first meeting, I was filled with debilitating anxiety. He had not suggested such a meeting, though Dad had many opportunities to do so during innumerable phone conversations over those years. It wasn't until that age that I asked it of him and of myself, a meeting that left many unanswered questions and raised new ones. That such a condition would remain with me throughout life whenever I was granted an opportunity to be in his presence was equally confusing. I would spend hours fixing my makeup and hair, searching for a new outfit, knowing full well he was blind. With outstretched hands simply asking for his embrace, I felt like a beggar off the street. I had lost faith and hope. Unable to break the chains of abuse inflicted upon me, I in turn inflicted it upon others. Federal prison was not the issue. I had been born imprisoned. I was angry with God.

Though the uniform I wore seemed to identify me as part of this group of criminals, seemed to engender a sense of camaraderie—a "we're all in this together" mentality—nothing could have been further from the truth. Inmates shared no togetherness, no "sense of the flock." No one led, no one followed, and there was nowhere to fly. The idea of bonding was ludicrous. Each inmate was on a solo flight and by definition antisocial. Unaware of how the others felt, if they felt at all, I knew I did not belong here.

Who were these people? Rapists? Kidnappers? Murderers? I had been raped many times as a child and held against my will, events that usher a slow and torturous death of hope, spawn the act of self-betrayal, a fate worse than death. I never knew where I belonged. I only knew where I did not belong, and I did not belong here! I was afraid of everyone around me, hadn't a solid belief to call my own, and through my veins pumped liquid fear and loneliness. If humanity is at its best when the situation is at its worst, then the very best I could do was nothing at all.

I took my place within a large black van with five rows of seats. Five male convicts were already seated inside, and, once aboard, I momentarily surveyed this mobile prison with a sixth sense, feeling the tone of the others, struggling for a sense of balance. The men were in the rear, segregated from the female convicts by a thick chain-link fence that ran floor to ceiling. A locked door was framed in the center, like the door to a kennel. They were serious about the separation of sexes, as if fornication were imminent without a physical barrier, and this was their most intelligent solution to prevent, at least during this short ride, a new generation of criminals. This wire-mesh diaphragm implied that seating such genetic material within the same vehicle was venturing a catastrophic social risk. Genetics 101. *Come on,* I thought. *We're all chained up, surrounded by guards tripped for a chance to explode, and they really think that somehow without the blasted fence we would dive right into a wild, violent orgy?*

The process by which this insane condom had been developed struck me as hilarious. There was no mistaking it: this was a boardroom decision, and the silly van had had to be retrofitted. Who would get that contract? Laughter began to rise within me. A smile crossed my face, and I caught myself. There was no etiquette on which I had been coached, no manual written on proper prison-transfer behavior, but I understood that feeling free enough to laugh was not cool. The humor faded more rapidly than it had risen, and I wanted to cry.

We were off. There were marshals in vehicles ahead of us, flanking us, and trailing us. I stared blankly out the window and relaxed. Instantly, before my mind's eye, the headlines from the *National Enquirer* flashed like a marquee: RAY CHARLES' GREATEST HEARTBREAK. Puh-lease! As if they would have some idea of what his heart was capable of! No one was asking me. I wondered if any of the marshals knew who I was, if anyone did. I could hear the voice of my mother saying, *Now, that's a question you should be asking yourself.*

At this point in life, I had no idea. That was self-evident. There were five who would call me their mother and knew little of me beyond that. I suspected most merely thought of me as the daughter of Ray Charles. I found that meaningless. Certainly, it impressed people who would frequently alter their position with me after its disclosure. Whenever I witnessed such a reaction, I wanted to vomit. It was inescapable: most people I had met were intoxicated by the idea of Ray Charles. Wherever I was going and whomever I was about to encounter, I vowed to honor a decision I had made long ago—to keep the name of my father to myself. It was to open a door to confusion and pain, something remarkably unreal and yet an undeniable part of me.

Without knowing the intentions and clandestine nature of the transport caravan I was a part of, an observer would have declared it a textbook case of the blind leading the blind. At one freeway cloverleaf, like a kiddie ride at the zoo, we took every exit only to end up traveling the same direction in which we had started, like a reenactment of some Warner Brothers cartoon—*Sylvester and Tweety, The Road Runner*. If God was within me, directing my path, I was convinced He saw the humor as well.

It was after a few more of the convoy's covert detours that I observed a car traveling parallel in the lane next to ours. It was of the same color, make, and model as the one I had recently purchased. I missed going whenever and wherever I wanted or needed—asphalt and concrete beneath my feet was the only "normal" I had ever known. I gazed blankly out the window, hypnotized by the blurred stream of concrete rushing below as the events that led to my incarceration played upon the screen of my memory.

*   *   *

It is around 3:00 a.m., and I am awakened by the sound of the hotel room door. It's Wayne (nicknamed Spud for his love of potatoes) finally returning from wherever he's been after abandoning me here for two days with his friend RJ, an older guy—I'd guess around sixty—who has the most sickening way of getting high. Immediately after taking a huge hit of crack, he says, "You just want another one!" It is too clear a mirror into myself and makes me sick. He sucks that pipe so hard, I'm always afraid he is going to drop dead with a heart attack or stroke. Because I'm on the run and have no car, I am stuck with him, as he is my only source of transportation.

RJ is asleep on the chair when Wayne enters and comes over to the bed. He starts shaking my leg. With contempt in my heart and fire in my eyes, I rise. "What in the world do you want?"

"Give me some money," he says.

"Are you crazy? You've been gone two days. You left me here with him, alone, and now you're asking for money? Oh no!"

Wayne becomes agitated, his temper beginning to spark. "I just let someone hold my pager for forty bucks' worth of crack. I need it back so I can keep up with my customers."

"Well, you are FULL of jokes today!" I know half his "customers" are his dealers, and that means he spends more time smoking their stuff than they do selling it.

Spud is having a hard time taking "NO" for an answer and is becoming unpredictable. I remove myself to the bathroom, ancient sanctuary for all females when things get too deep. I begin feeling light cramps in my lower stomach. I know this feeling. I had felt it on four other occasions. Knowing I am about to deliver a baby into this world, I pray, "Please, God, don't let this happen right now. Not now. Not this way. Please, God, I will do anything; just keep this from happening now. I promise You—I will do anything."

I have been smoking crack for three days. "Up" for seventy-two hours, no sleep, flooding my bloodstream with cocaine and alcohol, and, of course, I have eaten hardly anything at all. I do want this baby, and I darn sure don't want to struggle through the heartbreak of losing another child to the system again. Or do I?

The desire for crack cocaine has me in its death grip, caught in the stranglehold of a whispered euphoria only a crack pipe can promise. When you are pregnant, there comes a time in the pregnancy when the baby begins craving it, too. As a mother, I am aware of this, and—sick as it is— at that point, there is no turning back.

Can anyone who hasn't lived under crack cocaine's tyranny understand this unholy perversion of the unconditional maternal love for the unborn child in the sharing of such an addiction?

The cramps continue in spite of my prayers, so I exit the bathroom and start drinking whiskey in an effort to deaden the pain. I'm trying to think of a way to get at the $600 I have hidden in the mattress so Wayne won't be able to get it when I go to the hospital.

"You're faking it," Wayne says, "just playing me. Give me the money!"

My circumstance is so outrageous and Wayne's refusal to appreciate it so complete, I am paralyzed by what's becoming the unavoidable. I am frozen, inanimate— my tears are the only thing suggesting I have any life left in me. Looking at my baby's father, who was never my "man" in any way but one, I realize I am about to give birth to a baby only to lose it. Were it not for that child's life within me, I would end mine right now by any means possible.

"I'm not faking anything, you pitiful sucker!" I scream. "The pains are getting worse. THIS IS ABOUT TO HAPPEN!"

Amazingly, R.J. is still asleep, oblivious to the situation. "R.J. Get up! You've got to take me to the hospital. The baby's coming."

"Oh man!" R.J. says. "Can't you wait? What's wrong? I'm tired. Spud, take my car. You take her!"

"Heck no," Wayne says. "Man, I ain't taking her nowhere. I'm telling you, this girl is tripping. She probably don't even need to go." Turning to me, he repeats, "Give me the money!"

"Move," I say, trying to get to the back of the mattress, trying to think quickly. I want to prevent Wayne from seeing all the money and just give him forty dollars. "Wayne, please go get a warm bath started for me. I'm getting the money for you, okay?" As soon as he turns, my hand slides into the mattress so quickly, I amaze myself. I know that warm water would only quicken the contractions, so I throw him the money and say, "Now! I can't wait! Don't have time. Let's go!"

I can't go to Hennepin County Medical Center. They would arrest me there, so I tell R.J. to head west toward Buffalo.

"Way out there?" Wayne says, "Why? I'm not going all the way out there!" "Oh yes you are! When I deliver this baby, they're going to take it from me, and you need to get her."

"What?"

"Yeah, they're going to take the baby. You've never been in trouble with these child protection people. You think they're going to let us keep her?"

I am beginning a last dance with insanity, running into the pain of my heart and merciless personal chastisement: "Sheila, you stupid lowlife! How can you think that you deserve the right to cry over this baby? This life you have created, this mess you have made?! And now all you can do is whine, cry, and moan! Too bad for you!"

Behind closed eyes, I begin repeating over and over, "God, please forgive me. God, forgive me," as the ride begins to feel like forever. I am losing my mind. I have experienced childbirth before, and, having finally reached the emergency room, I know something is wrong, know it in my heart.

"Oh God, whatever happens to me, however horrific things become, I accept the fact that I deserve it" is all I can think as I see R.J. go into the

hospital. A nurse pushing a wheelchair is hurrying out the doors. Wayne has come around the car and is at my door, grabbing my arm. He lifts me and literally throws me into the waiting wheelchair. "Come on, man," I hear Wayne say to R.J., "let's get out of here!"

"Where is he going?" I think. "To park the car? Park? Wayne's going to park the car? Where are you going to park the car, Wayne? Park. The car. Wayne?" He's not parking the car; he's rolling down low just as he's always done, leaving me just as he always did. When the man cuts and runs, he sure don't kiss you good-bye.

Once inside the hospital, the nurse calls for the doctors and says some kind of code. I know that is a bad sign, as they are ripping off my clothes, cutting them from my body.

"Here," a doctor says, "put your legs up here. We have to see what is happening. How far along are you?"

"Six and a half months."

"Okay, she's fully dilated. I don't feel its head. It's a foot."

"Oh God, what does that mean?" I ask.

"Your baby is breech. Listen to me. You have to calm down. We are going to get you prepared for surgery—now. You have to do your best to calm down and be still."

It is so hard to resist pushing, but they have told me if I were to push, I might choke her on the umbilical cord. "God, please don't take her from me. I know I have done nothing right. Please give this baby a chance. Don't punish her for my sins. I promise I will change. This life is killing me—I am going to change. Please help me."

"Okay, honey, start counting backward from one hundred," a masked nurse tells me.

"100 . . . 99 . . . 98 . . . 97 . . ." I am slipping into unconsciousness, or, perhaps, I am already there, and I hear the voice: "Sheila. Sheila. I love you. You are my child."

I am still very groggy from the anesthesia. Everything seems like a dream, though I know it isn't. The conversation with the doctor that is about to unfold hangs in the air like a dark curtain.

"I'm sure you know that we have found cocaine in your baby's system," the doctor says from the side of my bed behind his white coat and clipboard. "We are going to need some information from you, and it is important to the health of your daughter that you be completely honest now. Also, you

need to know that we are going to have to contact Wright County so we can get their assistance on your case."

Oh my. Here we go. *"Okay, what do you need to know?"*

"First, let's start with your full name."

"Sandra Betts." I don't plan it. I am still half-conscious, exhausted, and frightened, and my mother's name just slips out. I almost correct myself, but instead continue giving my mother's address and information.

"What is the name of the child's father?"

"Wayne Sorrell." That too comes out without thinking. I wish for the chance to take it back.

"Now, who were the two men who brought you in last night? The admitting nurse said they seemed quite intoxicated and rather suspicious. Was one of them your baby's father, Wayne?"

"Oh no," I reply. "They were just two guys who were staying at the hotel where I was and helped me out. Wayne doesn't even drink. He's going to be really upset at me for even being in this situation. I don't know what to do."

"Do you have a number for him?"

"Just the hotel number. I don't know if he's back yet from his construction job in Brainerd. We were at the Red Roof Inn. Room 300."

I know he won't be there. Neither one of them had any cash, so they'll be out looking to find a good "lick" hustle.

"Just so you know, we are going to forward this information to the appropriate agency, and then we will get this whole thing figured out," the doctor states.

"Okay. Yes, sir," I say.

"Now, let's go get that beautiful little girl. She is so little, just three and a half pounds. But she is so perfect, and what a tough little girl she is."

Oh God, thank you. Thank you, Jesus! My God truly loves me. Maybe no one else does, but He surely does!

When they tell me my daughter will survive and is doing just fine, all I can do is shout my thanks to God, and I don't care who hears me. I am so grateful, and she is so beautiful and absolutely perfect. Although the next few hours will prove to be the last that I will ever see her, ever get to hold her in my arms, it will be a moment I will never forget, an image that will never fade, a blessing that will guide me for years to come. A thought occurs to me at this ground zero of my life: when your eyes open to the ignorance that has blinded you, there is no return to the shadow it has cast; there is no going back as you move ahead, though you may have no idea how. Seeing the truth within you offers nothing but freedom, nothing but forgiveness, nothing but light.

* * *

The chains were hard to ignore, becoming uncomfortable and heavy. Though they would be but ten pounds on the scale, their true weight could only be measured in the wait. Coldly inanimate, they were oppressively cunning. Even the cleverest of thieves had been unable to steal the sense of freedom the road had given me. I had been running on it all my life, and I had been running my life by it for as long as I could remember. I could not even cross my legs now as I turned to the window, only to stare at the car pulling past the van. *OH NO! THAT'S MY CAR! NO! SURE AS I'M CHAINED TO THIS SEAT, THAT'S WAYNE, SPUD, MY MAN DRIVING MY CAR!* And riding next to him, my best friend, Julie Moot. What in the world were they doing driving my car? It was my car. It was my man. It was my best friend. My mind reeled.

Co-conspirators, they had informed the feds of my whereabouts after a warrant had been issued for my arrest for a probation violation, an experience that had resulted in my first stay in federal prison. Several years before Spud dumped me at the hospital emergency room in labor, I had been given fair warning about my future with him. But I learned nothing from such a past; I had returned to Spud after my release and now was returning to federal prison once again. As unbelievable as it seemed and beyond anything that could be orchestrated, he and Julie were flanking this federal parade in my car. Even if the feds would have conspired with my father in a most sadistic and perverse plot involving Julie and Wayne driving past us on such-and-such freeway at such-and-such time in order to teach me a lesson in whom not to trust, it could have never happened. Both Wayne and Julie would be late for their own funerals even if the reward for being on time were resurrection. My father would not invest his money or influence in a production that was a guaranteed failure. What if I were sleeping when they drove past or just didn't look out the window during that brief moment they were visible? My behavior was too unpredictable in the equation and, by that time, I was the last thing on my father's mind. As for the feds, they would have told anyone foolish enough to approach them with such insanity to forget it. It was ludicrous to think anyone had intentionally caused this event. To dismiss it as mere chance and coincidence was equally ridiculous. Even with a gun to his head, the mob's best handicapper for the races would have had to say there were no odds to be made: this could never have happened.

The variables on both sides of the equation were infinite. But for a thirty-second difference at a red or green light, a decision to stop and get some fries or put some gas in the tank, running back into the house as they were pulling away because Julie had her bag of crack but forgot her pipe, Spud having to take a leak or deciding to hold it—but for any of one of a countless string of possibilities, I would not have seen them. And it would not be just the events of this day. I hadn't seen or talked to them for months. *Chance?* I asked myself. *I think not. A staged production? Even if the script were written, no one would pay to have it produced.* Whatever cause or force had set this stage, it was inconceivable that it was happening and absolutely merciless.

I suspect there is a moment, or a series of them, in everyone's life when you snap, when it all gets to be too much to bear. For me, this was that moment.

I broke, screaming, "IT'S TRUE! NO! How could they do that to me?"

If there had been anything at all left in my life—for I had sacrificed every relationship not directly involved with crack—there was, in that instant, absolutely nothing of it left. Everything went black for an instant. My heart continued to pound lifelessly, but I could not breathe, and my eyes rolled back in my head. For the first time outside a drug-induced coma, I understood "temporary insanity" as the putrid depth of a crack addict's truth was splayed wide open. My mind became a kaleidoscope of past events, whirling crazily, memories exploding one after the other.

*   *   *

I am in a hotel room, naked with Wayne. There is a knock on the door.
"Who is it?" I ask, slipping on Wayne's shirt. He is out like a light.
"It's the manager. I'm just coming up for that $13.58 left on your bill—
you said you'd take care of it once you got back the day after Thanksgiving."
"Yeah, okay. Hold on," I say, walking over to the door. I grab $15 off
the table and unbolt the door but leave the security chain still secure. I am
about to hand the money out through the crack and avoid the necessity of
getting fully dressed.
BAM! The door flies open, ripping the security chain from the doorframe.
Three federal officers, guns drawn, break into the room and throw me to the
floor. They handcuff me immediately, half-naked. Wayne wakes to the
commotion and halfway sits up. "Are they looking at your bare butt?"
The federal officers seem to ignore Wayne entirely.
"Where's the dope?" one of them asks me, "and don't tell me you don't
have any here."
"NO! We don't. We smoked it all," I find myself saying. "Then you
wouldn't mind if we search the room?"
"No. Go right ahead. There's nothing here." They begin to search,
tearing through everything.
"What's with all this stuff in here?"
"This might not mean anything to you," I say, "but I was planning to
turn myself in on Christmas. These are Christmas presents for my children
and other members of my family." It is the truth—as is the fact that it is
about $25,000 worth of stolen merchandise.
"What do we have here?" one of the officers asks, pulling a prescription
bottle out from a pile of my clothes.
"WHAT?" I respond.
"Looks like about an ounce of crack to me."
Truly, I had no idea it was there; otherwise, I would have been smoking
it. Wayne had told me he had none. "It's mine," I blurt out.
"We know this isn't yours. Why are you protecting him? He and his
girlfriend were the ones who turned you in!"
"Girlfriend! No way! Wayne, what are they talking about?"
"Oh baby, I wouldn't do that. Julie must have just got scared when you
threatened her and freaked out last week."
"Yeah, whatever you say," one of the officers replies sarcastically. "Wayne,
don't you know Miss Moot? Are you going to let your girlfriend go down like
this? Gonna let her take the rap for everything—what kind of man are you?"

Julie had sold me out for the dope. She had been my best friend. Julie Moot. I had shown her a love she had never known, and she had told me so. We had shared our hearts with each other.

Wayne? He had lost himself in the drug long ago. Now, without crack, there was no way for me to protect myself from the lies and falsehoods I'd been telling myself. My hideaway life eroded by a flash flood of truth, exposing a raw and vibrant pain within. My mind reeled again—then . . .

I am on the phone talking to Wayne's sister:

"Patrice, I'm in jail. I don't know if you talked to Wayne yet, but I'm wondering if you could get the stuff out of the hotel room that I got for my kids and family and see that they get it for Christmas. Have you heard from him?"

"Yeah, they let Wayne go, returned his money, charged him with nothing." We continue the conversation for a moment, but I will not be satisfied until I reach Wayne, speak to him directly. Julie, who had taken my calls before, now refuses charges. Finally, Wayne answers the phone.

"Yeah, what's up?"

"What do you mean 'What's up?' "

There is some noise and a muffled "Give me that phone."

"Sheila." It's Julie. "Why do you keep callin' here? Obviously, he doesn't want to talk to you! Quit calling!"

She slams the phone down on the receiver, violently, so Wayne thinks the line is disconnected, but she has intentionally left the line open.

"She's out of her mind! I thought it was over with you and her! That's what you told me."

I can hear Wayne laughing, enjoying this, thinking it is funny that Julie is jealous. "Now, how can you be worried about some girl in jail who's about to go away for a long time?"

Now it is my turn to slam the phone down, but I make sure the line disconnects.

Abruptly, the scene shifted in my mind:

Wayne and I are handcuffed in the back of the van taking us from the hotel room to Hennepin County Jail. He is crying crocodile tears. This moves me, for in the ten years I have known him, Wayne has never shown this kind of emotion. "I will be there for you, baby. I'll be waiting for you. I got your back. Make sure you call my mom's house. Just remember, I'm here for you."

I tell him how much I love him, that I know now he really does love me. I reassure him I am glad I took the rap and protected him while, between his tears, he keeps telling me, "Just remember, I got your back."

I tell him I am sorry for doubting his love for me in the past, for getting suspicious of his relationships with other women and not believing him when he told me I was crazy and just imagining all these things because the crack was making me paranoid.

* * *

Even while reliving this, I knew better, as I did then. Others had told me about him getting together with two, three, four women at a time for sex. He would give crack to any girl who would do whatever he wanted to satisfy his twisted sexual desires. I no longer doubted the stuff I heard about the girls and the dogs. He got off on that sense of command and power, and so did those who would subvert themselves to such control for reasons I knew all too well. The drug itself makes you believe you are nothing but an animal. It was true, and it made me want to die in my own self-loathing for failing to break contact with those who had abandoned themselves for such ungodliness, who were bound to and found enjoyment in seeing evil, listening to evil, tasting evil, smelling evil, touching evil, thinking, willing, feeling, speaking, remembering, and doing evil. My heart screamed to Heaven, GOD! FORGIVE ME—FORGIVE US ALL!

I regained a grip on myself just long enough to look once again out the window and see Wayne and Julie pull away from us in my car, laughing as if I never existed. Right then I realized the past ten years with Wayne and crack had been much less than life. Then, without warning or any time to prepare, it began again—relentless and without mercy, a river of past agony and memories of being both abuser and abused. I began gasping for breath; my body began jerking; the chains that bound me rattled. I convulsed in the effort to breathe, as if someone were literally holding a pillow over my face.

"What is going on back there?" a marshal demanded.

"None of us knows," responded one of the cons.

"Hey, man, her lips are turning blue. I don't think she's breathing," the inmate behind me called out. "You guys gotta stop or something. She's having a heart attack or seizure or something."

"Radio the other cars what we got happening here. I'll get in touch with the hospital or paramedics." Both the convicts and the feds were just elevated five levels on the anxiety scale. Everyone felt the building stress. Naturally, the marshals would react to the scenario as a diversion behind a breakout attempt.

The caravan came to a halt along the shoulder of the freeway: three cars and the van, eight marshals outside scrutinizing and directing any cars approaching from both directions. Of course, the traffic slowed to a crawl to take it all in.

"Help her out of the van," the driver said to the other officer. As he stepped outside, I heard him continue to the other officers, "Make sure the darn traffic keeps moving. Keep your eyes open until we get an idea of what this is about!"

It was a circus; everyone loves the ringside seats, so the traffic slowdown was unavoidable. This was great material for the daily office chat: "Yeah, they had a convict in bright orange, all chained up and lying down on the side of the road, gasping for breath. I'm pretty sure it was a female, and there was a slew of officers with guns acting all paranoid. The ambulance was coming, and they made me get moving before I saw what it was all about."

It didn't matter how hard I tried to avoid it; it seemed as if I were always on stage and frequently not getting paid but rather was paying the price for my mistakes while trying to run from the pain of my heart. Drama? Shoot, that was the name of one of my boyfriends.

The ambulance arrived. I lay on my back, still struggling to breathe. "My God," said one of the EMTs, "get her out of those chains—uncuff her!"

The marshals freed my hands by unlocking one of the cuffs. "Here, breathe into this," the EMT said, placing a paper bag over my mouth. "You're hyperventilating. Try to relax. We're going to give you a shot to help you with that."

Whatever it was they injected did the trick. I breathed freely again and was grateful. Once the EMTs determined my respiration had returned to normal, I was recuffed and assisted back into the vehicle.

Everyone in the van felt a sense of relief when we were back on the road. I withdrew, went deep into myself, to a place familiar among the prisoners, a state of consciousness that was impenetrable—almost a nonexistence of self. Though everyone within the caravan wanted to ask me about what had just occurred, what horror I had just experienced within the privacy of my past, there was an understanding among us. They would have to be content with inference and speculation, recognizing my inability to talk about it as complete and absolute. Even if I had been willing to, there was too much to reveal. Things like that just don't happen, and no one would have believed it. I couldn't.

My silent withdrawal was respected. No one said anything directly to me, and, beyond a short immediate discussion, nothing further was said. Everybody had his own cross to bear, both the marshal and the con, for there is connective tissue between such opposing pairings. They all knew I was wrestling with the past. Living in the thrill of the "now" that crack creates, the ghosts and demons of the past cannot exist, and you are free from the pain that resides within, ever-present to resume the rendering of your heart, to eat you alive from the inside out. Keeping such monsters at bay is priority one. It is all about survival. In my experience, there is no drug that creates an artificial "now" more powerful, more immediate, more attention-consuming than crack cocaine—of that, there can be no doubt. That escape was the sole reason why I was here, my soul's reason why I was in chains. I had escaped all the way to prison.

To counter the betrayal and the subsequent feeling that I was the biggest fool on the planet, I did what everyone does who crosses the threshold into the House of Pain: I searched for a thread of dignity and recalled the arresting officers' demeanor after learning the informant was my best friend. I had explained to them how I had been staying in that room for the past two months and had befriended the employees. The officers had allowed me to leave the hotel without handcuffs and were apologetic for their initial aggressiveness. They learned that they were arresting me for a dirty U/A and for failing to report to my probation officer. I was addicted to crack, and they were aware of the strength of its call. They saw my hurt and were gentle with me. I held on to that. It calmed me.

I could not prevent myself from thinking about him. Of all the men I ever dated, Wayne was the most physically unattractive. He had short black hair, a mustache, a pudgy face, and deeply sunken, squinty eyes. Mom said that meant he was a liar; as usual, she turned out to be right. Big but not fat, he was a Golden Gloves champion and a strong favorite for the U.S. Olympic boxing team. His cousin had started him on crack, had seen him as an easy mark. Wayne had had a job that was bringing home better than a grand a week. Mama, wherever you are now, that's one thing I want you to know—I never gave anybody his first hit. Never. Wayne? That was a different matter.

One could not have a conversation with Wayne that did not involve crack cocaine or some kind of game or con. But there was something about him. He carried himself in a manner that demanded respect, very self-assured and generous. He was always dressed in new clothing, hip-hop style: baseball cap, Nike shoes, and jeans. Wherever he went, he was surrounded by people, and beautiful women were all over him. He was the most generous crack user one could ever meet. The main reason I was even here was that he got me thinking he and crack were God—and my mother thought Ray Charles was.

Stuff happens? I think not.

You can't screw with me no more, Mr. Ray Charles! If God is happiest when his children are at play, then surely You are not Your happiest with me, are You, God? 'Cause You know darn well I am not playing ever again. Do You think I belong here? Wouldn't surprise me if You did; everyone else does. Well then, maybe I do.

Exhausted, I went numb and fell asleep.

CHAPTER 2

FLYING BLIND

Amazing Grace
How sweet the sound
That saved a wretch like me
I once was lost
But now I'm found—wait a minute

I AWOKE as we were but a moment from reaching our destination, an abandoned military airport in what appeared to be the capital city of Middle of Nowhere. "How long have I been sleeping?"

"A little over an hour. You feeling okay?" someone responded.

"Yeah, I'm fine, thank you. But God knows I have to take a leak." I looked out the window into a colorless world. The sky was gray, the buildings were gray, the landing strip gray—the cars, suits, and sunglasses black—only a splash of white on some of the buildings and faces. I was looking out into a black-and-white photograph, an ironic drizzle of federal orange upon its surface. Our caravan pulled up to a couple of empty buildings. Off to the side of the strip stood a portable boarding stairway with steps leading to invisible realities. I saw no plane anywhere.

Then, from behind a marshal's mirrored sunglasses, "The plane is going to be late. We are going to wait in the van until it arrives."

This was insane. No one could tell my body all systems must be put on hold. In addition to my need to urinate, I was on my period—heavy—and there was no way to keep that information private. Thankfully, someone brought the subject forward.

"Well, sirs—I got to take a poop. So if we are all going to sit in here much longer, I got news for you: we're all going to find out how bad my poop stinks."

No one doubted the veracity of his claim. I was relieved; either way it went, he was doing me a favor.

The driver grabbed the radio. "We're going have a bona fide mess here in a few minutes, and that's the last thing I need. This day has already been a ballbuster. Find my people a toilet now!" He put the radio down and turned to the inmate. "You best hold it, pinhead."

I saw a couple of marshals get out and enter the one building that still had a few unbroken windows. A few minutes later, we heard the announcement that a usable bathroom had been located.

"Okay, who's gotta go? One goes, we all go. It's potty time, butt wipes, so let's get this party started—everybody up!" said a marshal.

It was filthy. "I know who's going to go first, so get yourself in there," ordered the marshal. From behind the bathroom door, I heard, "Man, there ain't no toilet paper in here."

"Don't let that stop you. It wasn't going to stop you in the van." No toilet paper and no apology. Another marshal located some napkins from another room, and I began contemplating how any of this was going to work with menstruation.

My turn. On the toilet tank was a pile of table napkins that looked like they came from a roadhouse hamburger joint. There was a guard at the door. I had my privacy in the dressing room, but there was no dress rehearsal for this performance. I could not imagine how my life had led me to this dump or how it was going to take place with handcuffs, shackles, and chains. You can only go for it. It's like jazz in Dodge City: improvisation meets the Wild West Show.

After the whole ensemble was done taking their solos and blowing their riffs, we were escorted back to the van—no curtain call, no encore. I heard the plane making its landing, and I thought, *Thank God. Anyplace we go has got to be better than this.*

After about ten minutes, we were directed to the plane. Rounding the corner, I got my first glimpse of the huge military cargo plane, stationary on the runway and surrounded by fifty marshals with M16s, or whatever the government-issue weapon happened to be. It was spooky. With each shuffling step toward the massive flying prison, fear sank through me to my bowels.

It was nonsense you see in a movie—it just didn't seem like I had done anything that even closely warranted this situation. Like watching 9/11, it was surreal yet happening right before my eyes. There were inmates being escorted off the plane and several other caravans similar to ours at other locations on the airstrip. Convicts were preparing to board, federal inmates being shuffled around, male and female. What were these people holding the guns getting paid? Who were they thinking about shooting? I could not imagine some band of mercenaries appearing from out of nowhere and charging the plane, if it was the plane they were protecting. This was theater on a grand scale, but why was there no audience? I mean, we were all part of the show. What do these guys tell their wives after a day of work?

I needed my mother, but she had died several years ago. My heart cried out for her so loudly that I thought others could hear it. Then someone approached our group. It certainly was not Ray Charles or any one of his emissaries coming to save the day. My last attorney was a public defender. My father would no longer extend himself in my direction. Some would call that tough love. I knew it for what it was. Fatherhood, in my dad's case, was just the unintentional result of an ever-present need he had. Had I been living my life to understand his or mine, or was I trying to escape the pain of both? Was there anyone in this world who cared at all about the things happening to me? This was not a time for answers.

We were lined up in front of the mobile boarding stairs that were now accompanied by a massive plane. *Try getting up those steps with shackles and bars around your ankles while carrying baggage no one else knows about or cares to see,* I thought. *Step right up for your thrill ride to Hogs' Heaven, Oklahoma City.*

On board, I was seated in the gutted plane's cargo hold, refitted with seats and no amenities.

"That's it. Everybody is on board. What's the count, captain?"

"Four-hundred and eighty-eight, and let's make sure we get it right this time. No recounts on this herd."

The captain and two other marshals began from the front of the plane, methodically counting heads, carefully checking their lists. There were almost five hundred inmates, mostly men, and the collective consciousness was as heavy as lead. Ironic to be on a plane where almost everyone had lost the will to fly and thought of him- or herself only as cargo. Nine hours on that plane gave me some time to think.

Blind? My father was blind most of his life, but his true blindness was not the lack of eyesight. He sure was blind to whatever I needed from him, and I refused to see he was incapable or unwilling to answer such need. If I were blind, there was my blindness as clear as day. I had been flying blind all my life. I suspected such a thing was true for everyone on board; more than likely, true for everyone I had ever met.

"Flying blind!" I blurted out and started laughing. "We're all flying blind."

"What did you say, you crazy broad?" the girl chained next to me demanded.

"What?" I returned. I did not know the current longitude and latitude of our flight path, but our altitude was unquestionably the lowest place on earth. "Oh nothing," I replied softly.

"Then shut up!"

This was the last place on or off the earth to suggest that you had just solved a major life dilemma. I readjusted my position to one of solo flight and went back to that place within me where I was not quite so alone. Like an egg that had been granted a momentary peek at the whole carton, I pulled my head back in like all the other eggs and embraced my shell of anger and confusion.

In the case of my father, it was his loss of sight that caused his other senses to be heightened. He was quick to point that out. But I knew more about him than he would have cared to admit. He had zero tolerance for anybody else's faults. Compassionless, he seemed to have no insight to his own. Before all this stuff went down, before I was MIA and a warrant issued for my arrest, my mom had called my dad: "Sheila is missing."

It was during that time I, too, had called my dad and asked, "Please, you have got to help me understand. Tell me what it was in you that helped you get past this drug addiction. I need help. I need you to be my dad and explain it to me."

"Well, I-I . . . I, sweetheart, I-I had a little problem with it a-a-and I-I-I just . . . "

He would not give it up to me—that thing—his personal solution, whatever he had caught on to. For me, for many, it wasn't treatment.

I'd been spun drier than July in the Mojave. But he refused to give me any direction. He was still trying to pretend he never had any serious attachment to heroin. *A little problem with it!* He might have said good-bye to the heroin but remained an alcoholic—never could say good-bye to that. He developed liver disease because he drank a whole fifth of Bols gin every day—Bols gin and coffee. He flew it in by the case from Germany. *A little problem?* How little do you think I know? Busted with a stash of heroin to supply the habit of the most sincere junky—on a darn plane with it. Little?

I knew he felt guilty for his brother's death. As a small child, somewhere deep down inside, it was easy for him to think he had been nothing but a problem for his mother—a problem for letting his brother die, causing more problems because he was going blind, his mother trying to find a way to take care of him while poorer than dirt. Any child would think the hell his family was living in was his fault.

My heart went out to my dad: as a child, having to go through that while his mom was kicking his ass, saying he was going to do this for himself, hiding behind the idea she was making him strong so the world wouldn't take advantage of him.

"Don't let anybody tell you that you're a cripple." Dad had often quoted his mother's advice.

Perhaps his blindness hadn't crippled him, but he had believed he was the reason for his brother's death, and he had believed he was the source of his mother's problems when he was a child. That he believed, and that crippled him more than not having a pair of eyes to see with.

I was right; we are all flying blind. Believe you can fly? Believe you can touch the sky? Maybe at the very beginning you have to believe. But all right, R. Kelly, let's see you go for it. Jump off this plane! Let's see how much believing-you-can-fly you got in you!

It was a TV relationship with my dad. I don't care what any of my siblings say; it crippled us all. My father told me he would do everything he could to help in my musical career, and then I didn't hear from him for a whole year! I called him every day after he recorded me. "I'm going to take this around to everyone I know. I'm going to do this and do that," he had said, and I couldn't get a return call from him for a year and a half.

Don't let the world call you a cripple? As far as I was concerned, he needed a lot more than a wheelchair. He was blind to how that would make me feel. Forget being a singer; I mean just being his daughter. He used to say, "Why don't any of my kids just call me and say, 'Hi, Dad. How are you doing?'" Well, I did that every day for a year while he was working my project and could not get a call back telling me what or what not to do.

He removed himself from how his actions affected his children. Maybe it was just me; maybe he didn't want to share the stage with me. I would wonder if he regretted my existence, embarrassed by my presence in the world. But I just couldn't accept that. Part of me felt it was Joe Adams. In my opinion, Joe Adams didn't want to share Ray with any of us kids. Nothing. Joe would say *he* was Ray's family. Well, Joe, if you are Ray's family, who are we—who am I?

As far as I was concerned, after Dad was eight years old, he lost that deep sense of family. Gone. Family? It was business—and never FAMILY BUSINESS. When I was with my father, I accepted the fact that this was no *Father Knows Best* program. It was his loss of connection with family. He was the "do-drop-in" father to all of us. I know that! This is how it was for me. I would go into this role thing, which I knew was not true but had to accept because it was my survival at hand. Mom had raised me to understand this about Dad: "Don't take it personally. It's not that he doesn't love you, but his focus is with the women—being with the woman—period." So every time I would walk into the room, Dad would say, "Oh baby, I love you," and tell me and Mom, "I'm there if I'm lying, and I am truly with my real family now!" And then, once again, I wouldn't hear from him for a whole year.

So I had to hold onto that stuff. Every moment when I had that special time, had those fleeting moments with my father, I held onto them and prayed that the next time would be that same special moment so I could hold onto it until the next time. I knew very well in my heart it was pitiful. Kibbles and bits.

I was tired of living undercover, tired of living like a dog! I was so fed up with all the crap! No more of this. No more dog. I cried silently within while on the outside not a tear.

It was time to land. The line to be processed there at Oklahoma City was startling. It reminded me of the movie *Soylent Green*. It wasn't just the inmates on our plane—there were many such planes delivering inmates to this one central location for transfer to other prisons. I estimated over a thousand stood in lines to be processed.

Intake. *Taking in* was my thought, taken into a building so we could eat and go poo poo like lab rats in some bizarre, twisted psychological experiment. This federal transfer station reminded me of a gigantic human slaughterhouse managed with the emotional detachment of a Nazi Germany medical team. Where was Doctor Mengele?

Hogs' Heaven was more than appropriate terminology: stockyards for human beings. Up an eighth . . . down a quarter . . . where's the ticker symbol for this trade on the commodities board? At what point did we all become animals? Some would say with complete conviction we were nothing more. Some would argue the day we decided not to give a hoot about society and its laws. Others would argue we were merely byproducts of a materialistic delusion, chafe from the psychic machinery of a world that crushes almost everyone attempting to rise within it. Aldous Huxley and the survival of the fittest? Not at all. If the degree of civilization within a society can be judged by observing its prisoners, then I was granted the opportunity for another firsthand peekaboo not only into myself but also into the society into which I was born. This experience was becoming a spiritual journey. This was out-and-out genocide of Spirit, the absolute devaluing of human life, evidence of the failure of the American Dream—the lie exposed.

The band around my wrist was beginning to irritate my skin. I looked at it, numbered and bar-coded. *They are getting more sophisticated with internment,* I thought. *They learned something from the Holocaust: tattooing just raised too many questions when they threw you back to the street.*

I was standing in a line with men who had been locked down for thirty years, decades of being treated like animals. Most had no reservations acting and speaking like one; it was, after all, what everyone expected.

"Look at all this fresh meat just waiting for me to get up inside."

"How 'bout a pizza, wench—pizza what?" I did not find it offensive. There was too much distance between what I was hearing and where I was. How can you take anything personally if you don't exist?

The line moved more quickly than I thought it would, and soon I found myself inside a gutted cafeteria that had once served this Air Force installation. I could see another doorway on the opposite side of the room through which convicts exited. Like everyone else, I made my way in that direction, like the buffalo being driven off the cliff or the lemmings heading out to sea—the group consciousness of the herd. Approaching this exit, I heard the sound of chains rattling, iron meeting iron, muffling the voices of guards directing the activity. I saw everyone ahead of me stepping onto a conveyor belt flanked by fifteen marshals on either side, unshackling prisoners. Behind the marshals, like tinsel on the Christmas tree, hung hundreds of chains, cuffs and shackles from bars running parallel to the entire operation. It was an assembly line that would have made Henry Ford proud. I stood on the slow-moving track like a misused suitcase, limp and lifeless, as I proceeded through the gauntlet, wondering what hogs or cattle thought on their way into the slaughterhouse.

I approached ten guards busy with their duties. One told me to step down. The shackles and chains were removed from me to be used once again to restrain another. I reached out unconsciously to touch them again, holding them in my hands for a moment. Before I could question what I was doing, I felt a connection with the person who would wear them next, and my heart held the thought, *God bless you.* That deep emotion flowed from my heart to my hands and into the chains. I dropped them immediately.

"What?" the guard said.

I had startled us both, but, unlike him, I was unable to respond.

"What?" he said again, this time more forcefully. His anger jerked me back.

"What?" I said, looking at him blankly with the question still written on my face.

"Get moving! You want these back on? You got something wrong with you?"

I was escorted forward, oblivious to what was going on around me, consumed by the experience. As the sensation began to fade, I became conscious of the pain shooting up my arms from the indention in my skin where the handcuffs had been. It had taken me about an hour to ignore the pain after they had put them on; now, I was dealing with the pain of their absence. The only consistent element through the past twelve hours had been the constant lack of compassion. I was brought to a holding cell for female inmates.

Twenty of us were taken into a locker room. "After you are hosed down, get yourself dressed, and you'll be a heading down to get your bedding, clowns."

We entered the locker room. Four guards stood waiting for us. "You five girls are mine." She was female in name only, pointing to a wall behind us. "That's our wall. Take off your clothes and line up over there, your back to the wall."

Everyone's life is like a book filled with stories, some happy and some sad.

"Lift your boobs, if you got any—stick out your tongues and say 'ah,' and shake out your nasty hair."

Some days are so uneventful. They appear as less than punctuation on a page and disappear as but the rearrangement of a collection of words from the previous day.

"All right. Face the wall and assume the position. Hands on the wall and spread 'em. Your fingers and toes. Let's go!"

Then there are other days that seem to unfold and reveal chapters of your life, flooded with new experience or the vision of an almost endless chain of past events that led to the exact place where you find yourself.

"Stand up and back away from the wall. Spread and bend over, ladies. Now cough. Good—now squat way low. You see this mirror on the end of this stick. Don't piss me off and make this take any longer than it needs to be. You are all about the smelliest dogs I've ever seen. OH WOW! It's you, wench," the guard said to a fellow inmate two bodies down. "Now, you all might be praying to Heaven to get this over quick, but I'm God right here and now, and I say it's this one stinking to high Heaven that's out of here first. What is that?"

Sometimes such occasions open up the Heavens, and your heart soars to the sky; at other times, a river of heart's blood is revealed stretching back for years, and we see how our lives change with every breath we take.

"Stand up again. Time to see if you gals got anything under your skin or anyplace else," she said as she pulled a metal detector from her side. "And you'd better hope this detector don't start beeping! I've had enough of this mess for one day!"

And then there are those Twilight Zone days when Rod Sterling's imagination jumps off the screen and manifests itself before your eyes. You don't know if you're an extra on the set or if you've been given the leading role.

"Over to the shower room." She grabbed the nozzle of a large, black industrial hose off a holder on the wall. "Sanitizing time, and I'll make sure those bugs fly. Face me and slowly spin around."

The pressure knocked the girl next to me onto the shower floor. "Put your head down, now. This is the last favor you losers are getting out of me. You got five minutes to take a shower."

My mother said there is always something to be thankful for every day we live, a silver lining found in even the darkest cloud.

"Grab a towel and dry off. Get your clothes over there by the lockers."

There comes a time when we realize we must let go of what is gone, keep the memory of all that is good, and trust that all will end in love, for love—that love—is all there is worth living for.

There were two piles of clothing on a bench by my locker. One pile included a white T-shirt and orange shirt and pants; the other, a pile of socks, underwear, and a sanitary napkin. Strange to think I would be grateful for something so commonplace. It is one thing to realize life's lessons in the midst of daily battles, enjoying minor victories that see you standing at the end of the day, only to be confronted the following day with the next fight. It is another thing entirely to have nothing left to fight for, becoming the very thing you sought to destroy. I was being broken down to a level I would have found unimaginable, but who would do the rebuilding?

Once dressed, we were directed to another holding room where we would report to the medical staff. I told them about my allergies and the plate in my head from my automobile accident. We were then marched to the main building where we would wait for our personal supplies.

"Sheila Robinson: 03318-041."

I knew the routine from my last visit. That's right; I was the next contestant on *The Price is Right*. Come on down! A YEAR'S SUPPLY OF BOB BARKER SOAP, TOOTHPASTE, SHAVING CREAM, AND SHAMPOO, and let's not forget that complimentary comb and rule book. But we're not through yet, so don't pack your bags. You won't need them because we are throwing in an extra set of clothing and your choice of wool or polyester bedding and blanket because we'll be flying you to Prison Paradise where you'll be staying for God knows how long in beautiful HOGS' HEAVEN!

"I need the cotton bedroll."

"Take your admission paper with you, and don't lose it. Your phone-calling code is on there; you have to use it before placing any call whatsoever. The rest of the instructions about phone use are in your pamphlet on prison rules. Make sure you abide by them."

There were phone privileges there with special restrictions. Every call was monitored. Under no circumstances could you give any information as to your scheduled arrival date at the prison of your destination or the general flight scheduling of planes to a given facility.

"Get your ass over there. You're on your way in."

I was placed in the final holding tank to wait for my cell assignment, looking at my Bob Barker toiletries and thinking, *Hollywood—no matter where you go, there ain't no escaping it.* "I tell ya, Sheila," I heard the voice of my mother say, "If Holly could, Holly would." *You sure never lied about that, Mama.*

It was nine o'clock when twenty of us were escorted into the cellblock, and, at last, I was shown my cell, an open-door cell. One of my cellmates was there as I walked in and dropped my bundles.

"You just getting in here? Make sure you go down and sign up for duties. See if you can get on right away. You can get an extra plate, stay up late, and watch an extra half hour of TV. It's their idea of the cookie jar. It might sound dumb, but trust me, you'll want to get your hand in it. You can walk around the courtyard until 10:30. It's just about 9:00—meds time. You can find out from the guard at the station what prison you are being transferred to. They don't have to tell you, so be extra nice."

I made my way to the guard station with the hope I could eliminate some uncertainty and learn where I was heading. Approaching the guard, I asked in my sweetest voice, "Please, can you tell me where I am being transferred to?" I hoped it would be Chicago.

"Robinson. Robinson. FPC Bryan." "What?" I asked.

"Texas. Bryan, Texas."

TEXAS! Anywhere but Bryan FPC! I had already served a year at the facility. To return in less than a year guaranteed a reentry wrapped with the label of failure. My heart started pounding. I was panicking in the same way I did when I first learned of my current sentence. Judge Rosenbaum had seen me two times before this last appearance. Dan Scott was my public defender. There was no anticipation of any prison time. I simply was not complying with my parole. I kept using. The original charge was larceny, receiving of U.S. government property. Stolen mail. I received a sentence of ninety days in a federal halfway house and was released on probation. I reported to my probation officer, and it was discovered I was using cocaine. I was caught and brought up on new charges. The sentencing guidelines were as low as you can get: class C for probation violation—a year and a day. What is that "a day" about? I served that time at Bryan and was released once again on probation, only to return to the drug again and back in front of the same judge. My life was the definition of insanity, expecting different results from the same actions.

The judge said, "Sheila, I've had a gentleman who has been in my courts for twenty years. I will not let what has happened to him happen to you. Instead of sentencing you to prison, I could just add another two years to your probation. However, you would then be in the system for the rest of your life because you do not follow orders. Your personality is so beautiful. The problem is I like you. If I didn't, I would keep you in the system, and you would spend the rest of your life on probation. I know you have a good heart. But it is clear you will not follow the orders of the court. So I am sentencing you to do the time left on your probation—fifteen months—with the hope you will end up in the RDAT program for drug treatment, though I've heard the waiting list is long for prisons with such programs."

My attorney gasped, and I thought I was going to die as the floor dropped from under my feet. My attorney had anticipated the court placing me into some local in-house treatment program. I mean, the charge was merely a dirty U/A. I was handcuffed and taken back to jail to wait for transfer. For four months, I waited in the federal holding facility.

It was hard enough for me to talk to my family. They didn't even come out to the county jail to see me, a thirty-minute drive from their house. Texas? I knew very well none of them would accept collect calls from me every other day—not from Texas. I'd get everybody's phone disconnected. Right then I knew I was alone, isolated in every sense. There were inmates awaiting me in Bryan I had to face again. I moved off to the side of the line and just stood there and cried, motionless.

"You look like you've been through hell." It was the girl who was standing in line behind me. "It's not as bad as you might think. Bryan looks almost like a college campus. Oh, my name's Chris. I've been here a couple of days, and I'm on my way out of here. You don't look like too bad a sister. Wait here. I got to get my meds. I'll be right back."

"God, it's been a long day. My name is Sheila. Thank you." This was a blessing. She was someone whom I knew I could talk to. I decided not to reveal my prior experience at Bryan. She did not need to know and was back quicker than I could think.

"How long do you got, Sheila?"

"Fifteen months."

"That's going to fly by so fast, you won't even know it." Of course, in my mind, I thought, *Please—a year is an eternity!*

"You'll see. It's really quite beautiful there. They have dances, and as long as you do what you're supposed to do, you'll get past it."

She was right, but I knew from experience that federal prison, even minimum security, is still prison. I was relieved just to have someone to talk to, someone without a hidden agenda. I mean, half the time when someone talked to you, she was on the prowl for a "girlfriend." The first thing you learn to say to someone new is "What are you talking to me for?"

"What tier do they got you on?"

"Third tier."

"No matter what you do, don't let them catch you on some other level. I mean, just so you know. I don't think there is one person in here who reads the stupid handbook."

"I hear that. I ain't going to depend on that to educate me to what is going on up inside here," I responded.

"Good. That's it. Most of these freaks can't read, anyhow. Come on, I'll show you around."

"These four rooms are the TV rooms. That one over there is where the Spanish chicks hang out." The rooms were probably twelve by twelve with maybe about fifteen chairs. "Here's the 411 on this crap. If you got a show you really want to watch, it's first come, first served, and these people are serious. We got some that get up in here first thing in the morning and don't move—I mean, they will skip meals just to plant their flag. Of all the places in this joint, this is where you'll see some fights."

Back in my cell, I had time and space to collect my thoughts. The stress of the transfer treatment took so much of my attention that I was glad I had time to contemplate events of the recent past. Clearly, there were forces at work that were bigger than me. The thing with Wayne and Julie in my car—there was no way that was chance or coincidence! The odds of such an occurrence were incalculable. It was something meant for me to witness and endure, orchestrated by something greater than I. No longer did I look at it with fear or dread; it was evidence of things unseen, evidence of God's hand. There was no other way to explain it. Then there was the thing that happened when they took off the chains. It began to fill me with joy, an appreciation for the mystery of it all.

Bob Dylan would say an artist must be in a constant state of becoming. My father told me in the studio once he didn't believe the words I was singing. "Sing the lyric so it is believable," he had said. I guessed I was becoming an artist who was believably blue, for my heart had become the blues it was singing. Believe that! I knew my father would. Ray Charles was blind but surely not deaf. Finally, I was beginning to hear what he was listening for, beginning to see how he did: one with the song. I was hearing what I was seeing. Change is pain.

CHAPTER 3

HOGS' HEAVEN

Once I was alive apart from the Law
But when the commandment came
Sin sprang to Life and I died

ROMANS 7:9, NIV

I AWOKE SLOWLY the next morning, half in this world, half in a dream state. Before I had time to open my eyes, I began planning my day: I would wake up with a long shower, head down to my kitchen, fix something to eat, head back to my bedroom, plop in a movie, and fall back to sleep. I figured I deserved a lazy day all to myself.

"Sheila."

"Hey." I lifted my head and opened my eyes, not recognizing the voice. Oh shoot! What the heck? My plans for the day instantly evaporated, destroyed by the vision of my cell: two double bunks, a toilet and washbasin, and three strangers for cellmates. Last time I had a morning like this was four months ago back in Sherburne where it had taken me a week to awaken with the memory that I was behind bars. There's one thing worse than waking up from a nightmare—waking up into one.

"You look dog-tired. Going for breakfast?"

"Ah, yeah, I guess," I said. I had no desire to get to know them. They were of like mind and out the cell door before I had my legs beneath me. Had I been not so hungry, I would have slept through breakfast. It was optional. Prison rules only required I be up with my bunk made by 7:00 a.m. After a few moments, I shuffled out the door.

Standing on the walkway, I surveyed my surroundings. My perch overlooked the courtyard, watched by a solitary guard at a desk and chair; three floors of identical accommodations, birdcages stacked three high. The second and third stories each supported a walk of iron grill bordered by gray metal rails. Cement block painted off-white formed the walls of the cells, one hundred cells per floor, four inmates per cell, twelve hundred inmates. The place was booked as far into the future as one dared look.

It's time to see what breakfast looks like in Hell's kitchen, I thought, merging into an audible stream of early-morning profanity: "B's this . . . b's that . . . and every other foul thing for breakfast that I wouldn't feed my dog . . . can't eat this crap": confirmation I was heading in the direction of breakfast. The pamphlet provided at orientation was a waste of trees. When everyone is doing the same thing at the same time, there is no need for directions or road maps. I made myself into a line thirty deep with several hundred inmates eating God knew what, embracing the thought I would not be sharing my breakfast with anyone. Join me for breakfast? Right!

A container of milk, a box of generic cereal that served as its own bowl, a small container of juice, and a plastic spoon. Had there been a butter knife, I could have used it to carve a path through the atmosphere of anger, anxiety, uncertainty, distrust, and fear that clogged the air like the festooning vines and tangles of a jungle. Any memories of peace and harmony within me were as weak as a windblown echo. I found it impossible to foster a desire for such recollections. To do so would be inappropriate—an insult to the collective prison consciousness—and I was not strong enough to stand and fight that battle.

After breakfast, I made an effort to relax, making my way to the exercise room. This was as close to outside air one could get in this place. Five feet off the floor, a steel-plate vent let in outside air through quarter-inch-diameter holes, the minimum requirements to ensure the inmates were receiving fresh air. Not surprisingly, this was also the smoking room. Centuries of research, trial and error, application and observation had perfected the method of tormenting the mind of the incarcerated.

I made my way to the shower I had considered earlier. Yesterday, when I was ordered to strip during the intake process, the awkwardness of my nakedness was masked by my personal exhaustion, anxiety, and the group resentment directed toward the guard. Now, when I was removing my clothes in the presence of the other inmates, it was a voluntary act, and I was not comfortable with it. I could sense those who were eyeing me sexually; those thoughts need not be spoken. I looked over at the two who found me interesting—an overweight black sister and a thin Mexican girl half her age. They were talking between each other while eyeing me up. I wondered if I was being viewed as a potential candidate for a threesome because I resisted flipping the bird and just held to my inner meditative mantra: *be strong, be strong, be strong, be strong . . .*

I avoided any eye contact, grabbed my Bob Barker gear, and headed to an open shower stall where a curtain provided a hint of privacy. *This is so completely not me. If those girls decide to roll up on me in here, I'll gouge their eyes out. That's the only thing everyone understands in here.* I understood it. From years in the street, I knew how to go to that place inside me where I didn't feel anything, where my only thought was survival—at least that is the rationale behind it. I was beginning to feel the scared, angry girl wasn't me. I did not want to go there anymore. *Keep your lesbian ideas to yourself. I don't care what gets you off; just don't put it on me.* I had no compassion and sought no understanding. I felt I didn't belong here, felt I was better than this, better than them, and I didn't like that about myself. I needed Mom. I remember asking her how she learned to love others unconditionally. She had turned around and said, "That's not the question. The question is, how did you learn not to?" *I don't know, Mama, but I'm sure going to try to figure that out. Hear me?!*

It was safe to cry in the shower. I lifted my head and pressed my face to the water stream and just stood there releasing whatever tears would come. But the anger remained. Turning it against myself, I scrubbed my hands and body as though I were some disciple of Howard Hughes. I couldn't get clean, feel clean. I rinsed off, satisfied I had done all I could for the moment. Emerging back into the locker room, I discovered my admirers had departed. Relieved, I began drying off and getting dirty all over again: "F-ing this, b-'s that"—the vocabulary was enough to infect a saint. I had no one.

Several days later at breakfast call: "Robinson, you still want the cleaning duty? You can have the showers on this floor."

I recalled my first cellmate's words: *You're going to want my job. It's yours if you want to take it. Trust me. You get to stay up an extra half hour at night to watch TV. It's scrubbing out the showers twice a day at ten in the morning and eleven at night.*

"Yeah." There was no great enthusiasm in my response. "Report to the shower room at 10:30 this morning."

I arrived with the willingness to change, to remake myself into a better person, carrying the anticipation of watching some television later that evening with only a few other inmates. Entering the bathroom, I was assaulted by a foul odor. The guard accompanying me said, "Smells like one of your buddies got a little angry. Happens once in a while. Have fun."

The feces smeared across the walls of the toilet area, as well as blood from an absorbent pad, served to affirm society's impression of what was housed inside these walls. I agreed there was a definite need for some of these people to be locked up, just not with me. My senses so exposed, I dropped the bucket of cleaning supplies, fell to my hands and knees, and discharged my breakfast onto the ceramic tile.

After cleaning up my vomit, I took the job of scrubbing the walls personally, as though it were the walls of my heart I was cleaning. Some inmates were anger personified. Most knew relationships that were self-serving and manipulative. The ability to take advantage of other people was their entire MO. They knew nothing beyond that. Placing no value upon the life of another was seen as strength; that is what the street teaches. They would make jokes, rude and crass comments directed at those who yet held hope of something more. What value resides in an impenetrable heart incapable of holding the idea to place another before oneself? Unconditional love? Forgiveness? Most inmates regarded such principles as impractical, weak, and pitiful. The hardest of the inmates saw such motivation as unreal and false. They truly were a product of the system, and I was determined not to be. I resented the ignorance I represented.

Church services were offered on Wednesdays and Sundays. I made up my mind to go. I did not know if I would find any peace there, but I had attended services at Sherburne and Wright and found it helped me. Plus, knowing most inmates loathed the church services appealed to me. I held the hope I could have a conversation with someone without all the four-letter expletives. It is said everyone turns to God at some point in prison, and there is truth to be found in such a statement. It is unfortunate, but when things are going according to plan—whatever that plan may be—one finds the situation is in control, manageable. It is only when the stuff hits the fan that one turns to God. In suffering, many seek the Divine.

My mother had brought us up in the church. My Uncle Jerry had his own ministry and was a gospel singer. But the chapel within this facility was unlike what most know as "church." It is one thing to stand in front of one's own congregation—people who come willingly to enjoy a sermon or to participate in the production through music, ushering, or sharing in some governing council. There are preestablished ideas on how to behave, how to dress—what God expects of us and what we can expect from Him. There is a general level of respect and authority granted to the minister by the congregation to discuss such things, to deliver wisdom regarding scriptures. Even if an attendee does not apply such principles in her personal life, one recognizes merit in such self-governing structures. Those who attempt to live in accordance with a particular religious doctrine are seen as possessing spiritual strength. They are viewed as virtuous, honorable, compassionate, kind, and merciful. It is an acknowledgment of a higher power within man.

For those educated by the street and raised in the ghetto, the hypocrisy of the church is as clear as water: professing to be a child of God while being consumed by the authority of money. The church claims there is never "no hope" and extols the virtues of family life to those who have neither. Children in the hood join gangs to acquire a sense of family while Jesus spoke of one family. Church members claim they are following Jesus, but many provide meager lip service to their faith, lacking the courage to truly walk the path of Christ. Materialistic and spiritual values cannot be reconciled. In the absolute sense, the two ideals are diametrically opposed. Man cannot serve two masters. So, too, it is not difficult to see which force has the most authority within our society. The church passes the collection plate while talking about Jesus who threw the moneychangers out into the street.

I attended the Sunday morning service. Chapel was held in the big TV room. That alone was enough to piss off a lot of people. Those who delivered the ministry in such a harsh environment bore a love sincere and rare, and I held on to it afterward as if my life depended upon it. It was real. After the sermon, I approached one of the ministers, having decided to reach out to her.

"Do you think I could talk with you for a minute?"

"Certainly, dear."

"I'm so happy for that. Thank you for coming. I can't tell you how much it means to me. I've been feeling so alone and afraid. There is no one to talk to in here."

"Once, I was afraid of everything. Myself mostly. Now there is more love than fear inside me. God leads my feet and quiets my fears. He leads us all."

I was uncomfortable with the minister's words. *How do you KNOW that? How do you PROVE that?* I thought.

"How can you say that? Most of the people here think they're animals and nothing more. I don't blame them—their lives have been terrible. They all have some horrific story to tell from their past. They couldn't care less about anything you have to say."

"I realize that," she said. "It doesn't bother me."

"I remember as a kid sitting in church. I never got much out of it but a good laugh. My cousin and I were always getting into trouble laughing at the old grannies up there singing. It was hilarious to us, and once we got started, there was no way to stop. But there were times when something within me would rise up. I couldn't talk about it. No one else did. I didn't know how to describe it—something deep inside me would be stirring. I remember that and think maybe I'm not so, well, not as hard as many who are here. I'm glad just to have someone to talk to."

"Then you are the reason I am here."

"This isn't like showing up to your own church on Sunday morning with a congregation behind you. I appreciate you going the extra mile."

An inmate passed by, overhearing the conversation. "Extra mile?" she interrupted. "Let me tell you about the extra mile, sister. There is no such thing. You dumb twit! Who drives the car a mile off the pier? There is no extra mile. You think by working overtime you're going to find the pot of gold at the end of the rainbow a mile off the pier?" We both chose to ignore her, and, mumbling under her breath, she left the room.

"Have you been in touch with your family? Have you called your mother?"

"My mother died—while—during my incarceration. But they did let me attend her funeral. She took care of us the best she could. I remember asking my mother how it was that she learned to love unconditionally, and her response to me was, 'How did you learn not to?'"

"Your father, then?"

"That's what I'm talking about. To love him, it must be unconditional. He gave up on me before I was born. He was born in the Deep South, Florida, and was raised by his mother, too. He had a very difficult childhood, went blind at an early age. He should have more of a heart. He knows what it was like growing up without a father. Up until I was fourteen, I had never seen him except as an infant. I have no recollection of that, of course—just talked to him on the phone. You see, my mother believed in Santa Claus until she was eighteen, and she sure believed my father was going to marry her when he told her so. He even called Mom's mother and told her the same, but he broke her heart. She did what she could to make sure we could connect, but it never was what I needed. He has helped me out when I would get in trouble with money and stuff, but he will have nothing to do with me now. Yet to this day, I would be excited to see him." I began crying. "And my stepfather—there were good reasons my mother divorced him."

"Certainly you have someone."

"I called my brother. But I've abandoned him. I left everyone for crack. I've got five children! The thing I hurt the most about is that I wasn't there for my children. Try living with that. I'm guilty of the same wrong, and I definitely should have known better."

"How is it you came to be here?"

"Now, that's the sixty-four-thousand-dollar question, isn't it? I've been asking myself that question so much in the past few days. Drugs. Crack. I've used drugs since I was a teenager to escape. It brought me here, and I feel there is no escape now. All my life I was treated like I was not good enough."

"God tells us we are all good enough."

"I only wish to find peace for my mistakes and remove the anger from my heart."

"Have you admitted you are a sinner and accepted Christ as your personal savior?"

Another inmate swooped down and laughed. "Sin? The greatest sin you could commit would be to regard yourself as a sinner. Don't let anyone talk to you about God. They're only trying to sell you their untruths."

"What?"

"Nobody knows you better than yourself, sister. You know what I mean?" She was just another inmate incapable of resisting the opportunity to exercise her mouth, looking like any one of hundreds I had seen before. Prophets of the street. Too much loss, too many contradictions, too many drugs. I didn't have any desire to acknowledge her, but the pause was deliberate and demanding. I looked the vampire in the eye so she could feed on my attention, careful not to give her too much.

"It's time you came face to face with yourself," she continued. "Feel me? I'm trying to tell you something worth hearing! Nobody can read your mind, no matter what they say. You've got to have some pride and some private time. Hear me? A or B! I mean, whatever, one or two, A or B?"

With that, she was gone.

"Street prophets," I said. "If you don't listen to what they're actually saying, you might think they have something worth listening to! It's wrong. It's just all wrong. This place and every other. That's all I know. God knows I've done everything wrong with my life, but why am I in here with these crazies when there are so many others out there I know have done much worse things than I ever did? I just don't know!"

"We all make mistakes," the minister said.

"Mistakes? My life is a comedy of errors! How can you not help making mistakes when everyone and everything around your life is nothing but a mistake?"

"There's hope. There's always hope. God has a plan for you."

"I don't know if I'd agree with that. Hope? Best I can hope for right now is getting out of here without a clue what is coming next. I got to go."

"Don't close your heart to God."

"I don't know what God has to do with it, but I'll try to stay open."

"Miracles do happen, you know."

"Then pray for a miracle to happen for me, okay?"

The minister smiled in a way that let me know she would. I had no doubt I would be in her prayers that night, and, for whatever it was worth, I found some comfort. I had to move around a bit, try to find something to look forward to. I remembered it was almost time to clean the showers, but afterward I'd get a little TV time.

By the time I had arrived for that extra half hour of television, the program had already been selected: *Judge Hatchett!* Jesus, what were these idiots watching this crap for? Was this the only thing on? The episode airing involved an intervention on Hatchett's part with a young girl who sought emancipation from her mother, a single parent attempting to raise a sixteen-year-old daughter with a serious communication gap. The daughter believed her life would somehow be better with a foster parent. Judge Hatchet had a friend who was a daytime soap star who had grown up in foster care for eighteen years. It had been a negative experience for the actress, and the judge thought she could exert some influence upon the adolescent to reconsider her position.

Upon meeting the actress on the studio set where the soap was shot, the young girl began crying uncontrollably, enthralled by the attention and opportunity extended to her. She saw the actress's life as much more valuable than her own, so much more valuable than her mother's. Without knowing the actress, the girl decided to heed her advice and stay with her mother. With tears and applause, the show treated this resolution like a genuine victory for the justice system, daytime television, and humanity alike. Sitting in front of the TV with about a half-dozen other inmates fortunate enough to witness such nonsense, I thought, *With the media feeding us this crap, maybe everyone is in a prison. Ain't nobody truly free!* It made me want to puke. It was like watching Ray Charles throwing me thirty minutes of his time. Just because you are a Hollywood player, your opinion has more merit? If push comes to shove, I'd have to say it makes it less valuable. I hated Hollywood. I went to bed mad.

"Robinson, 03318-041. Get your things together. You are outta here today!" the guard shouted into my cell. It was 6:00 a.m.

I had been here for twelve days, but it felt like eternity. I couldn't take much more of this. Most of the inmates surrounding me were unreachable and firmly molded. There was no possibility of bonding if you refused to accept your fate.

The second boarding of Con Air was not as bad. I knew what to expect and could relax a bit more on the flight. Though my heart was trying desperately to reestablish hope, the darkness of my past reappeared and obliterated any ray of hope within it. It was as though everything here was meant to remind me of the worst things I had done in life. With that iron fist in my face, hope seemed pointless. On weakened knees, I cowered undressed. One thought, one question demanded answering: *At what point was the joy of my own life stripped from me?*

We began our final descent into a huge cornfield. Within its center was a paved landing strip, like something from *The X-Files*. Isolated from any signs of civilization, it stuck out like a factory in the wilderness. I was in a federal plane, surrounded by federal marshals, wearing federal clothing, my whereabouts known only to the feds, and it finally struck me: I was federal property! I started to feel nauseous. I knew if our government wanted someone to disappear, it would be no problem. I was willing to do anything not to be in this situation, and that is a frightening place to be.

For half an hour, we sat in uninterrupted silence.

"Okay, ladies. Bryan, Texas, here you come." The names and numbers were called out.

I was escorted down the steps to the tarmac. Nothing was visible but six-foot-high cornstalks and six-foot-tall marshals surrounding the plane. Same routine, same guns, same attitude. Seventy of us got off the plane and waited. Nobody was talking, and nobody expected any farmers. I saw dust rising on the horizon from a gravel road, accompanied by a low roar, like a swarm of bees approaching the field. A few minutes later, the tops of two yellow buses became visible over the corn. Someone got the nerve to speak. "Are those buses for us?"

"No, they're here to pick up all those bushels of corn! What do you think?"

"Well, you don't have to be rude!"

"Shut up! No more talking!"

We were lined up for boarding. Ahead of me, there came a groan and then an inmate boarding—another groan, and an inmate boarding. The first step into the bus was a greater distance than the spread between the ankle jewelry and would inflict excruciating pain to the ankles. I was determined not to give them the satisfaction of hearing my pain but found it unavoidable. After hobbling down the aisle and being placed in our seats, a guard came around to give us the rules.

"All right, ladies, listen up. I can see right now that some of you have extensions in your hair. You need to find someone to help you take those braids out now. You've got two hours to get it done 'cause once we're at Bryan, we'll be sitting on the bus till y'all get them out, you understand? I don't want to hear no talking 'bout sex, no cussing, and no fornication. If you have any kind of gang-related tattoos, they must always remain covered. If you think you may have any enemies at Bryan, now would be the time to share those names. We don't want any fatalities at Bryan."

Oh God, I thought, *fatalities? Enemies? God help me.* This prayer seemed to be constantly on the tip of my tongue. It wasn't that much different from the first time heading for Bryan. The anxiety I now felt had to do with meeting others I knew from my previous stay. My mind was reeling and girls were scurrying around, trying to get braids out as hair flew everywhere.

It had been a two-hour drive. Exiting off the main road, we took a course that led to a familiar environment, familiar to most on the bus. The smell of poverty, the run-down properties, people sitting on porches drinking forty-ounce cans of malt liquor and smoking cigarettes, stereos cranked and the boom of bass in cars. The hood. Crack zone. Bum City, USA! Even those who were first-timers at Bryan could sense we were close. There is a fragrance to confinement. It was growing stronger with every breath.

For a moment, we were of one accord, looking at each other sadly, knowing we all had one thing in common: we wouldn't be getting high or drinking or listening to anyone's car stereo. We were all looking at each other's lives, and it didn't matter who we were or where we came from. When we realized we all looked petrified, we turned our heads quickly to cover any suggestion of personal weakness. Ironic, wasn't it? If any one of us possessed inner strength, she wouldn't have been there.

As we turned the corner on Bryan Boulevard, there it was. The facility greatly contrasted its surroundings with landscaping out of *Home & Garden*. The building was a beautiful light rose color with dark trim, immaculate, with manicured shrubs all around, grounds groomed to perfection. Bryan Federal Prison Camp. Chris was right; it did look like a college campus. It was as I remembered it. There was no fence or gate visible, and that was something my eye could live with. But nothing is what it appears to be—and I was determined to be mindful of such a thing from that point forward. I did not let my guard down and refused to form any expectation. I was tired of being let down, tired of letting myself down. No more treading water; I needed to find bottom.

"03318-041!" *That's me*, I thought as I was being called out.

"At least there ain't no fences here," I said as I was being unshackled outside the bus.

"Oh, there's fences, sure enough. They're around back; just can't see them from here. But they weren't put up to keep you gals in. They were put up to keep the locals from coming in for free meals. Now what does that tell you?"

"It feels good to have the chains off."

We were escorted into a waiting area in the administrative building for processing around 2:00 p.m. I was in a state of disbelief. Federal prison round two! *Is this me? Is this real, in this body, in these cuffs, back once again at Bryan? Someone slap me!*

"I'm the captain of the guard here at Bryan. To my right are the lieutenant and sergeant. This facility houses 3,500 females: 1,900 for girls' boot camp and 1,600 inmates sentenced to minimum security prison. You will be assigned one of four housing units we call quads: Brazos I, Brazos II, Madison I, or Madison II. Listen for your name and number as one of us three calls them out. You will be checking in your personal property at this time and filling out your initial paperwork."

It was the captain who called out my name and number. After removing my handcuffs, he ordered me to counter number two. "Miss Robinson, fill out these papers, and do not leave any questions unanswered, whether it applies to you or not. Every question must be filled out and completed. Any questions?" He looked at me in a way to ensure I understood the question was rhetorical and continued, "Good!"

The Department of Redundancy Department, to quote the Firesign Theatre—I had lost count of how many times I had already filled out these same forms. What do they do with them? The insanity of it was torturous. The desire to revolt against it was as natural to me as breathing. I had to be careful not to be undone.

Forty-five minutes later, finished with the intentionally oppressive paperwork, it was time for a picture, a photo to be used on an ID I was required to have in my possession at all times. Being caught without it could result in solitary confinement.

Immediately after the picture was taken, the captain of the guard approached me, put his hand on my shoulder, and whispered, "I highly advise you not to let anyone in here know who your father is. Best to keep that to yourself."

"I came to that conclusion years ago," I responded as he led me to a waiting area for the rest of intake.

It would be the same routine: strip search, the spray down, shower, new clothes, medical check-in. How could anyone tolerate this job? I imagined showing up on the first day, being handed a hose with minimal instruction, and immediately saying, "You've got to be kidding me!"

I was standing on ground zero with no option left but to rebuild. But from what source and image does one reconstruct one's life? The shadow of oneself cannot be seen if she is walking into the light, while turning one's back to that light gives the clearest vision of one's shadow. To walk without shadow is to walk the path of light. Did I have the courage to stand within the light of truth long enough to see what such a stance revealed, or would I reconstruct my life with the faded images of shadow held by others and myself?

The twenty of us were escorted into a large cell with benches along the three walls without bars. In the middle of the floor—dead center of the room, rising up from the concrete as though it were statuary on display—sat a stainless-steel toilet. Its presence and position spoke volumes to me. Who would be the first to sit on it and claim the throne, place oneself on display before the subjects of this tiny kingdom? I wondered if anyone else felt the need as I did. If there were any question as to the icon one would have chosen to represent this institution, the image to be embroidered on the flag to fly above its rooftops, all of us had just been made aware of the answer.

Have you ever watched a dog defecate? There exists a self-conscious wariness and humility in its eyes, as if pleading with you not to watch. Predator and prey alike are aware of the surrendering that occurs during the process. One must let the guard down, relax, and let nature have her way. It is the condition of vulnerability that is the issue. There is a good reason public restrooms are equipped with stalls. There are exhibitionists of all kinds—entertainers, politicians, flashers, strippers, porn stars—but I have never heard of anyone desiring an audience for defecation. For me, at that moment, there could be nothing more humiliating.

It was a most difficult challenge. I strongly resisted my natural need to bend and be reduced by such an act. I was back again trying to avoid the unavoidable as I battled against becoming that dog on the leash. At some point the line is crossed, and it is inarguable. I arose, prepared to suffer the indignation and humiliation by nature herself. As I pulled down my pants, I bowed, and closed my eyes. I went to the altar of my heart and imagined I was alone. I silently asked all others to turn their heads and eyes away from me. But I prayed to God to direct his vision directly upon me and see me for what I was.

If this is the throne that I deserve for my past actions, one earned through the course of my life, then let it be so. I accept it. But I will fall no further. Let this be the bottom from which I rise.

CHAPTER 4

CELLMATES

Guilty?
I'd agree—but for different reasons
God says, "If your heart condemns you
I am greater than your heart
For My grace is sufficient."

WE WERE DIRECTED to carry our newly issued prison clothing and bedding on a two-mile hike to our assigned residence. While walking, I felt a whisper of peace come over me. I was hopeful I really had found rock bottom. That alone would be a miracle.

Escorted through the prison grounds, we marched down a wide sidewalk. The campus midway, as I had learned from the past, was the only path upon which the herd would be driven to any event— church, chow, choir practice.

NO TRESPASSING signs were regularly posted on the lawns. Inmates were to be kept in contact with man-made materials, surfaces approved by the prison board: concrete and asphalt, iron and brick. A group of inmates passed in the opposite direction. I ventured a tentative glance into faces from which a clear, collective message spoke: "We don't give a crap about any of you, about the miserable lives that brought you here."

The mask of self-loathing was well known to me and not difficult to recognize staring back through the eyes of another. We were all of the clipped wing, none for all and all for none. With this thought, a suffocating reminder of the darkness into which I walked was uttered by a passing face, snuffing out the whispered peace. "You all a pack of female dogs."

What seemed an eternal walk finally revealed the glass doors of Brazos II. Inside, the first thing I noticed was a sign emblazoned on a door to my left: *Dorm Captain's Office, Ms. Keller.* Continuing down that hall, we passed another door labeled *Utilities* and then entered an enormous room in the center of the quad where about twenty-five tables were bolted to the floor, each surrounded by four steel stools likewise set into concrete. Female inmates roamed freely in the open pen, revealing the separation of races: blacks at the far end, Hispanics in the middle, whites on the upper end of the commons closest to the guard's table. Taking this all in, I ran right into the person in front of me.

She swore as she turned. "Girl, watch where you going!"

Before I could respond, I heard, "Robinson." The guard stopped before a stairwell. "You go up these stairs with Sergeant Holmes." Turning to the sergeant, she said, "She's in sixteen with Miss Lee and Miss Mary."

"Oh boy, I can't wait for this," my escort replied.

"What?" I asked.

"Oh," the sergeant explained, "they're longtimers and, I guess you could say, set in their ways. They've had this corner cell to themselves for the last five or six years, and these here corner rooms are the best in the house—people wait years for a corner. You got nobody on either side of you, a bit more private. Your roomies' been in here a long time, about ten years or so. They've got what you would call prison seniority, and they like to think they know how to use it."

What type of person serves that length of sentence? What did they do? I thought. *That's all I need, two old-timers riding me when I've had a monkey on my back for years.*

With a heavy heart, I ascended the stairs and was escorted through a framed entrance lacking a door into a room with walls of concrete block painted light gray and a lacquered cement floor of the same color. There were two sets of metal-frame bunk beds against the long wall, two sets of corresponding lockers, one desk bolted to both floor and wall, a small chair, and a solitary light fixture suspended from the center of the ceiling.

Holmes stepped aside by way of introduction. "This is Sheila. She'll be your new cellie."

"What the heck!" The succinct greeting from Miss Mary was punctuated by a look from Miss Lee that expressed the same sentiment. Ms. Lee, an older Asian lady, approached the sergeant.

"Look, I know you ladies are used to having things your own way, but you know darn well we're overcrowded, and you were one of the last to get a cellmate—be glad we didn't assign two to your little party."

"You're right, you're right. It's just . . . it don't matter," said Miss Mary.

Holmes stepped out of the room, and I was left to make the best of it. "Hello. I promise not to disrupt your space. I just want to do my time and go home."

Without consent, tears streamed down my face. I turned away quickly to avoid discovery, but Miss Lee caught me in the act. "Oh, it's okay. I like you. You be all right here, okay?"

With that, they both opened their lockers and began giving me things. Soap. Real soap. *Caress!* They pulled out shampoo, slippers, pens, paper—even a couple of candy bars! And it kept coming: Christmas in Texas. A bag of popcorn, a real hairbrush, a cup, spoon, and fork. My heart filled with gratitude that I had finally caught a break, that my new "cellies" were actually cool.

"This is what we expect," said Miss Mary. "We are immaculate. We want your bed made up tight. There's inspections every day, and we're assigned points for that." She continued, "We each will have two days for cleaning. On Sunday, we try to kick back and relax."

"Sounds good to me," I replied. "I just really need to lie down now. I'm exhausted."

"That's fine, girl. Take the bunk above me," said Miss Mary.

Emotionally drained, I lay on the top bunk above Miss Mary, listening to prison gossip in a half whisper between these two women and finding comfort in just having something resembling a room in which to sleep, to be finally settled in. Though austere, the room offered freedom from some of the uncertainty. I vowed to face the months ahead of me with a positive attitude. *Maybe this won't be too bad. I've got a good room, and I'm with some older gals who might watch out for me if I just pull my own weight,* I thought. I wanted to get outside and check out the prison yard, but the burden of the journey to this two-inch mattress was too much, and I couldn't move. Finally, my need for sleep broke the connection to the conversation I had been following below. I drifted into a well of rest, comatose to anything around me.

"I don't believe this! I've been up all night. She snored the whole night long."

"Yeah, and tossed and turned, too!" It was 7:00 a.m.—paradise lost.

"I was shaking all night. Felt like an earthquake."

"In all my life, I never heard a person snore that loud. This is horrible."

With that, I jumped from the bed to the floor, not hitting one step of the ladder. "You know what? You two got life all jacked up! You think for one minute that if I could stop myself from snoring I wouldn't? It's been days since I've really slept, I've lost my children, my mother died since I've been thrown in this hole, and my boyfriend . . . well, the heck with him. I'm sorry if my snoring upset the prison's finest citizens, but you've got to be kidding me—because of a little snoring, your whole pitiful life is coming unglued? Well, excuse the mess out of me, but my life *is* unglued, and I don't need this crap from you. One darn night ruined. You two are pathetic!"

I was screaming these last comments when I recognized a guard was now standing next to me. "Robinson! What's the problem?"

One thing I knew, a commitment carved by my past experience, I would not be the one whining to the guards, ratting on my cellmates. They would have to be the ones to complain about my uncontrollable, vicious snoring and my ground-shaking tossing and turning.

"Nothing," I said.

"Well, what's all that yelling 'bout?"

"It's cool. We've just been discussing room stuff, working things out," Miss Mary said. I had been here for less than twenty-four hours, and I could already read the writing on the wall.

"Robinson. Make your bed and get dressed," said the guard. "You can come down with me and help sweep around the commons area."

It was my first day, and I had yet to be assigned any duties. Before an inmate could get her work assignment, she had to be cleared by the doctor with a complete physical. I was given a grunge job every morning by the guard within the quad. The conflict within my cell was escalating, and Miss Lee and Miss Mary were not relenting from their position—they wanted me gone. My current cell assignment was not going to work out. The guards knew it along with everyone else.

The following morning: "Robinson. Trash detail."

I was to gather all the trash from the main area and the bathrooms, tie and bag it, put the full bags on a large cart, and, with the help of another new inmate, push it down to the warehouse side of the prison to the reeking dumpsters and toss them one bag at a time. Meanwhile, the only resolution to the cell conflict was to write a request to change cells. The old gals just wanted their cell back to themselves and would not tolerate any newcomer. It wasn't long after the request that I was moved.

My second roommates were much better, C.C. and Karen. They were white girls who thought they were black, the type who enthusiastically and unnaturally talk the "black ghetto talk." I wasn't offended by it; I just didn't understand the need behind it. But they snored and had dreams, and for that I was grateful. Unfortunately, they would be leaving soon, and God only knew what cellmates would be coming my way next.

I had been in prison long enough to know certain routines. Every week, the heads of the compound would conduct an inspection. The cleanest quad would go to dinner first and—considering this meant the freshest, hottest food and any of the good leftovers from the dinner before—everyone made an effort to be first at mealtime. With sixteen hundred women, food disappeared fast.

The menu would change weekly. Breakfast was usually pretty good. Mondays would be assorted cereals, toast or waffles, bacon or sausage on the grill. The Hispanic cook would make chorizo and salsa every day so the system could claim respect for cultural diversity. Lunch could be anything from chicken nuggets to pizza, but Thursday was always hamburger day with fries or chips, lettuce, tomato, and onion, without exception.

On my fourth day, I heard my name over the speakers: "Robinson #03318-041, you are to report to medical immediately." The announcement was repeated. I went to the guard to ask what to do, where to go. She instructed me to follow the midway down to the medical building connected to the captain's office. I had fifteen minutes to get there or face escape charges.

As I walked into the medical building, I recognized girls from Oklahoma who had endured intake with me.

"Hey, what's up?"

It was Sue, a young black girl from North Carolina. She seemed genuine in her question.

"Not much. What's up with you?" I said, taking a seat next to her.

She began telling me about her crazy cellmates. They were Hispanic girls who had decided to be "gay for the stay." They claimed they had never been with women before but decided to pair up to help pass the time.

Sue's bluntness was refreshing. I was on the floor in laughter, and I could feel mountains of stress leaving my body. Everyone was laughing just because of how hard I was laughing. While talking without regard for the time, we watched several inmates go in for examination and come out again as the two of us began to wonder if we would ever get called.

Sue was summoned before me, and I became sad in her absence, as if my happiness had just walked out the door.

Okay, get a grip! It was one conversation, one moment of laughter. That doesn't make you her friend! I said to myself, taking a deep breath, though my heart was not in the same place as my head.

After about twenty minutes, I was called for my exam. To my surprise, Sue was sitting in a chair outside a door that read, *Dr. Robertson, Gynecologist.* The nurse ordered me to step up on the scale, and I looked over at Sue. In an effort not to disturb the nurse as she was recording my weight and height, I silently mouthed, "What's up?"

Sue responded with unabashed boldness, expressing no hint of discretion in respect to the procedure she was about to endure. Though she was just short of hollering the most graphic references in the idiom of the southern ghetto, her complete lack of self-consciousness carried an unexpected and refreshing air of honesty, and I erupted in laughter. Sue's raw candor brought a medicine of spirit no hospital or clinic could deliver.

Such a breakdown of established procedures was disconcerting to the nurse. "Hold still. I don't want to be here all day, and I know you don't want a bad report your first week here!"

Her retort snapped me back to the circumstances, but the joy and laughter yet remained with me, continuing its dance in my heart. I was grateful for Sue. Somehow, she had released some of my fear. I turned with the desire to thank her and was met with an empty chair.

Most of the nurses maintained a strict distance with patients. The coldness of such a conscious effort to disconnect was readily apparent, as though I were a member of an Amish community being shunned.

I was anxious to meet Dr. Robertson and was somewhat relieved as I opened the door to discover she was both female and black. In the past, I had always opted for a female doctor of this specialty, and the fact that she was black also seemed comforting.

"Come in and sit down. I'll be with you shortly," she said with her back to me.

I always wanted to believe there was some common bond, some sort of sisterhood shared within the black culture. But in here, there was little evidence to support such an idea. It was true that a natural racial segregation occurred. I had already witnessed the blacks, Hispanics, and whites congregate separately, but that was as far as it went. This sisterhood was as superficial as the color of one's skin. I felt no greater bonding occur among me and the other blacks than I did with any other race. I was hoping to find it in Dr. Robertson.

She turned around, wearing a very pleasant smile. Love appeared to reside behind those dark brown eyes of hers as I relaxed a little more.

"Okay, honey, we have to fill out some forms. This information is strictly confidential, unless of course you have something contagious that could put the other inmates at risk."

She began asking personal questions pertaining to my sexual behavior and experiences, whether consensual or forced. I had yet to come to grips with the sexual abuse I had experienced. Her line of questioning was making me uncomfortable.

"Why do you need to know that? It certainly can't be good dinner conversation. Besides, you're a gynecologist—not a psychiatrist!"

Sensing the panic and responding to my sarcasm, she said, "Now, come on, Miss Robinson, you are in a controlled environment. We need to assess health risks, both to you and the other inmates for any type of sexually transmitted disease: hepatitis, AIDS, syphilis. You would be surprised at how many women come in here unaware they are infected."

I began to feel a mixture of paranoia and repugnance. I had heard about inmates who would cut themselves and bleed into the food or beverages. *Welcome to the world of AIDS, Sheila. Heaven help me.*

Dr. Robertson said, "We also need to know because we can't have anyone infected in the kitchen or clinic—any job where sharp objects are required."

That came as a slight relief, but the questioning ahead of me chilled my previous mood. Merely brushing against the surface of the dark memories of my past made my stomach tighten and my throat constrict. Divulging as little as possible, I stuttered through the awkward interrogation. The pressure of a full waiting room hurried my exam to an end.

Having been cleared as one who presented no immediate health risk, I could work. No kitchen detail or landscaping, but office or guard work would be acceptable until my AIDS test came back the following week. As I opened the door, I could hear Sue talking.

What was she still doing here? She could be in quite a bit of trouble were she caught just hanging around.

"Hey, girl!" she said. "I waited because I didn't get your phone number or your address; thought I'd pick you up and go clubbing tonight."

I laughed.

"No, really. Do you want to go to chow together today?"

"Sure," I said. "I'm in Brazos II."

Dinner tonight would be especially good. There was a new warden, and we would be enjoying BBQ beef ribs. All of the best African-American cooks were called to work the dinner, rounded up, and sent straight to the chow hall. The new warden felt it prudent to make a good impression on the inmates. Most of the old-timers were not impressed, saying the new warden, like the others before her, would come in like a lamb but end up roaring around the compound like some kind of wild beast. Nonetheless, I was looking forward to a good meal and the company of a friend.

I reported back to the quad, signed in, and took a shower. I dressed and decided to go down to the commons and look at the job listings on the wall across from the TV rooms. After four days, I was finally settling into the place. Looking over the open positions, I signed up for a job at the warehouse. I had done clerical work in the past, and this job description involved checking inventory. As I was heading back to my room, I remembered mail call was this afternoon—4:30 to 5:30. Those who expected mail would report to the commons area. The guard at the desk would call out each piece of mail that had already been opened, inspected, and read by prison security. Outgoing mail was examined in the same manner.

There were about 480 girls in my quad. Today, the commons area would see four hundred of us standing around, anxious to hear our name called for mail. I was sitting at one of the tables when Lisa, a girl I had just partnered with the night before in a game of cards, approached me.

"So is it true? Is your dad really Ray Charles?"

"Who told you that?"

I instantly knew who had leaked the information. It was fresh in my mind. While playing cards, Lisa told me she was a friend of a black female guard who worked intake. The guards would rotate from the quads to administration every two weeks, and an intake officer would be the only person capable of knowing and leaking personal information.

"Who told me doesn't matter! Is it true?"

"Well, yeah, he is my father—so what?"

"What are you doing in here? How come you're not—ah—um— at home? How come he didn't pay to get you out of here—to get you out of whatever you're in for?"

"Who's to say he didn't pay?! You don't know anything about my life. You don't know how much he has or hasn't been involved in it. You don't know what trouble I've been in before or anything. I'm only doing a year when my sentence should be seven to twenty-five. I'm grateful for that!"

Actually, my first sentence was originally three months in a halfway house. It cost my father a quarter million; I got off easy. Dad paid for the best lawyer, Ron Meshbesher, the best of the best of the best. After that, Dad was through with me. I couldn't stop using, but that wasn't any business of Lisa's. I knew it was the guard, the black female guard she claimed was her friend.

"Oh! Really—hmm. That still don't make no sense to me! Well, I just heard that, and I just wanted to hear it from you—see if it was true."

Great! The cat is out of the bag now! I thought as the guard started to call out names for mail.

"Sheila Robinson, 03318-041."

I could find out later who her friend was. I anxiously approached the guard desk and was handed a large manila envelope sent from my brother, Kevin, and a letter from my eldest daughter, Jeanna. Two pieces of mail! I found an open seat and opened Jeanna's letter first.

Jeanna, my eldest daughter, wrote faithfully while I was at Sherburne. She still desired a relationship with me, while Matt, her legal guardian, discouraged it. While I was in the Sherburne County facility, Matt called and told the authorities I was in violation of a restraining order he had in place restricting any communication with Jeanna whatsoever—including through the mail. I was not aware of any such order, but no one in authority would believe me. I was a lying crackhead. Besides, I would refuse to comply with such a demand. Matt claimed that after Jeanna and I communicated, she would act out and become irrational. Someone in authority agreed with him and had an order put in place. It made no sense, and, to this day, I will stand on that conviction—even though it cost me three days in the hole at Sherburne where they threw me fifteen minutes after Matt had called. He had known a larger embrace from my mother but had yet to be capable of one himself.

Matt, a runaway from a broken home, had come to our home with my brother Kevin. He had been living with his father in an apartment complex not too far from Mom's apartment in Minneapolis. Matt was a great basketball player, and that formed the glue in the relationship with Kevin. At the age of fifteen, he was living with Mom on a permanent basis, and his runaway status led me to believe there was something in his family life that wasn't right. It was no surprise to observe his need for a loving and nurturing environment, answered by my mother's unconditional love. Mom was eventually granted legal guardianship of Matt, and their relationship remained close through the years. So, too, our relationship became one of brother and sister—Matt was my biggest fan.

When my mother's health began to fade and she could no longer look after my children, Matt approached me and offered to watch over them. I agreed. We would talk repeatedly about our reunion when I became more responsible and functional as a mother. I knew a strong bond of love existed between Matt and my children. I trusted that relationship would not be threatened when I reentered their lives. To avoid confusion with child protection during my incarceration, my attorney advised me to voluntarily grant Matt custody of my children.

When he initially denied Jeanna contact with me, she ran away from Matt's home. Jeanna had other problems with Matt that ultimately resulted in her being placed in a foster home. Her foster parents held a different point of view and saw no harm in our communication; in fact, they found Jeanna's behavior was better because of it. I saved every one of her letters.

Jeanna would tell me she missed me and hoped I did good this time. She asked me to take this opportunity to really think about my life and the love I had for my children—for her and her siblings. She told me she believed in me, that she wanted to believe in me and would be there for me when I got out. It was unbelievable for me to read her words; they flooded me with hope. I would spend my whole day wondering why she was in my corner. I realized the greatest gift Mom had given me was showing my own children how to love and for me to know the continuation of her love through them. I had given them every reason not to love me, yet they did. The full emotional impact of that knowledge would sometimes take days for me to get through.

I opened Kevin's package and pulled out a letter. "Sheila, Glenn gave me a copy of Mom's manuscript while going through some boxes of their work. I thought this might be something you could look through. Thinking of you always. Love, Kevin."

I didn't bother to pull it out. Though I was thrilled to have it, I knew what Mom's book was about, and I just wasn't ready to go there. I was always made to believe that I was the salvation of the family, my mother's family, in achieving true success, in being a continuance of something great. On the one hand, I did my best to live up to that expectation, but to follow in my father's footsteps when I had so little interaction with him—well, realistically, who could fill those shoes? On the other hand, judging by my current situation, it would be fair to say I had made the very worst of the opportunities in my life. No one in my family really understood the pressure they put on me to establish a career in music; when I could not deliver, for whatever reason, everyone was upset, including me. It destroyed my whole family, and that was insane to me, unfair. I felt that I wasn't anything special at all. My father certainly treated me as if I weren't special, and there was so much my mother desired me to be. Maybe she saw herself in me—my desire, verve, and aspirations. But I never doubted it was truly my father she saw in me, and right now at Bryan Federal Prison Camp, to read her manuscript and memoirs was asking too much of myself. She passed away while I was in prison serving my initial time.

I made it back to my room and put Jeanna's letter and my brother's package underneath my mattress. "BRAZOS I," I heard over the loudspeaker. Then, minutes later, "BRAZOS II." As I walked out, I could see Sue walking in circles at the intersection of the two main sidewalks we called the four-way. It was the only area where one could get away with dragging her feet a bit if there was someone from another building you wanted to hook up with for a meal or activity.

Dinner was great. Sue and I exchanged stories from the street life we had so recently lived. We were just about finished eating when someone came up to Sue from behind and leaned over next to her ear.

"You're sitting with her," she whispered loudly enough for me to hear, "the one we were just talking about."

"Heck no!" Sue responded as the mystery girl slipped away. "What was that about?" I said.

"There's some talk going around that some chick in Brazos II is running around saying Ray Charles is her father. Stupid freak thought it was you."

"Oh really?!" I said in a manner that revealed something to her.

"It's not you—is it?"

"Well, I'm certainly not running around saying Ray Charles is my father, if that's what you mean. If I was the one saying that stuff, well, you would already know—wouldn't you?"

"She's a troublemaker, Sheila. Let's go outside to the track." We continued talking as we made our way outside.

"So you're in Brazos II. Home of Dorm Captain Ms. Keller, or should I say Mr. Keller?"

"What's up with that, Sue?"

"Mr. Keller? Well, she's got it bad for the athletic director. Now, on the outside, I woulda figured the gym teacher would be butch, but in here—well, I guess it's the dorm captain who's got the bigger balls."

We walked the quarter-mile running track that circled the outside exercise area. We had until 9:15 p.m. to be back in the quads. At 10:00, there was a head count conducted and, afterward, the final smoke release until 11:00 p.m. On Friday and Saturday nights, however, we could stay out until 2:00 a.m.

Inside, the track was an open-air, roofed structure under which were found twenty stationary bikes, free weights, aerobic steps, and two TVs for workout videos. There was a small building where inmates could check out various games: Sorry, checkers, cards, dominoes, Monopoly, and the like. Picnic benches surrounded the inner perimeter of the track where just about everyone congregated after dinner. There was good music playing due to the aerobic classes, and everyone seemed to feel a little freedom being outside and so open. I was happy to be able to walk around outside. We walked what seemed hundreds of laps around the track while Sue talked continually. I heard little of the conversation. My mind was on the fresh air and the movements of people on the other side of the chain-link fence.

Inmates were not allowed to stop on the track. Outsiders would occasionally throw stuff over the fence for girls on the inside—everything from drugs to money to letters. Being able to see freedom and yet remain imprisoned made it psychologically difficult, to say the least.

I spent the weekend walking and talking with Sue. Sunday saw us together on the way to the library after dinner. I heard the choir singing at church service. The singing sounded outstanding, the church services energetic and Spirit-filled. The desire to sing swelled within me, but I just couldn't bring myself to get involved at this time. I was involved in the church and choir here the first time around. I would certainly know some of the inmates at the church, and my conviction would be known as weak. I felt I had betrayed God, my children, myself, and other inmates I knew from that past. I felt it only appropriate for me to suffer for a while, a long while.

Sunday night, I was waiting intensely for the work sheet to hit! I came in from recreation. It was 9:00 p.m., and all inmates had to be in by then. I went to shower, still not really knowing anyone but Sue. I just picked someone and asked, "What time does the work sheet come out?"

"Any darn time they feel like bringing it. Sometimes, if an inmate pisses a guard off, you may not see it until the morning, which creates mayhem because there are continual job changes and zero tolerance for tardiness on the job! You can get privileges taken, put in cell arrest, pay cuts. How much lower than twelve cents an hour can you go?" Her response was typical of what I had come to expect.

I decided to hang out and watch some television. There were four TV rooms, two on the same side of the quad's administration office and a third on the other end of the common area where we could sit and play cards and games and socialize in the middle of the commons; the fourth one was on the second tier. There was a noticeable segregation within these spaces—whites, blacks and Hispanic, and gay—these pairings were often fiery and, at times, could get downright ugly. I was waiting in a line to see the job assignment postings, and, as I approached the sheet, I found my hopes had been answered:

Sheila J Robinson, #03318-041:
Assigned to Bryan FPC Warehouse
shipping and receiving Class D entry-level position
Start Time 7:00 AM—Check-In Time 6:45 AM

Now that I had a job, which was thrilling to me, I would have to be up and out the door at 6:00 a.m. if I wanted breakfast served between 6:00 and 6:30. I quickly ran up to my room to share my good fortune with my roommates and find out what I could about this placement. I was happy. I was finally going to be able to move around. As I explained my news, they were not as impressed as I was and began to give me their take on my warehouse job.

"Girl, now you really got to be cool. You'll be watched at every corner. The guards are such a pain in the neck. You'll wish you were back here doing dog duty."

"Sergeant Brady, he's the worst. We all think that he is on meth or some sort of high-tech speed. He can get from one end of the compound to the other in twelve minutes flat—and everyone knows that is a twenty-minute walk at normal speed."

"He'll hide behind the pillars and jump out at you at night or hide under the bleachers. He is mean as can be—scares the mess out of me!"

"I don't care," I replied. "I just need to be doing something to occupy my time."

I left to go down to the laundry room to iron my clothes. While on campus, inmates were required to wear ironed clothes, creased and crisp. Were one found to be wearing disheveled clothing, she could be treated to a write-up and classified as disobeying a direct order. I quickly learned to make my pants stand up and do a salute, determined to not let anything so trivial make my life harder.

With my pants creased and everything ready to go for the morning, I heard the call for the last recreation move at 10:30 p.m. All the smokers from the four quads made their way to the outdoor smoking area, an asphalt patch like a nicotine launchpad for the last cigarette of the evening.

I decided to go see if Sue was out and tell her about my job. It was quite dark, and I couldn't see much of anything, nor could anyone else. I would not have to respond to, "Was it easy? I mean, it must have been nice being the daughter of Ray Charles." Over the past few days, I had been the talk of the prison. Since the day Lisa approached me, everybody in the whole quad was asking me if Ray Charles was really my father. There were as many different opinions on the matter as there were inmates. I was under the microscope, and I told the truth. No one believed me. It soon became, "She's a liar. She ain't got no money on her books. She has to use Barker shampoo and conditioner—ain't buying nothing from the commissary."

I quit responding and would simply look away, having spent a lifetime of making excuses why I was lacking. Yeah, he is really my dad; yeah, I am probably kicking his butt right now; yeah, I was on the cover of the *National Enquirer*; and, yeah, my pitiful story graced the pages of the *Minneapolis Star Tribune* and was whispered within entertainment sections in papers across the country. He was my father; few believed it, and that hurt. Those who did thought they were in here with someone famous—because he was famous, I was famous. Yeah, I'd walk on the red carpet with Dad, and the next day I'd be getting evicted out of an apartment with Mom and my kids. One time, I was flying out to L.A. for Dad's birthday, and I had no present. I asked a dear friend if I could have something of his, a ceramic beer stein from Germany with a pewter top to present as a gift. That's the reality nobody understood, the struggle I had when it came to my father.

None of these upstanding citizens believe Ray Charles is my father. Shoot, everybody in here is somebody: the baddest drug dealers, the most infamous pimps, the most exclusive whores—you can be anyone you want to be in prison—except Ray Charles's daughter.

CHAPTER 5

BLIND MEN ARE HOLY?

"So, mama, what's your number?"
Call me a fool, but I gave it to him.
Blind men don't lie, they don't cheat—
they get you by surprise.

—SANDRA BETTS

I WAS GRATEFUL for the limited light of evening—no one was bothering me. I could not find Sue and quickly called it a night. While I was heading back in the direction of my quad, I heard someone call out to me. It was a voice I knew but could not connect with a face.

"Sheila?"

"Oh my God!" I exclaimed. It was Roberta Davis, my very good friend from my first stay at Bryan. Sitting next to her was a very beautiful girl with long blonde hair that flowed to her waist and the blackest eyes I had ever seen.

"Sheila! Girl, what are you doing back here?"

Embarrassed by her question, I acknowledged my personal failure by simply lowering my head. "What do you think? What do most people come back for?"

As if I were the choir director soliciting a call from the congregation, all three of us responded together, "PROBATION VIOLATION!"

It broke the ice with laughter.

"This is Sharon Fischer," Roberta said.

We talked and caught up with each other as old friends do. I was very pleased to learn Roberta and I would be coworkers at the warehouse, and her reaction to my reincarceration was not condemning but compassionate.

"It's cool as can be, Sheila," Roberta said, "working for Mother Crenshaw—she's the guard over at the warehouse. Look for me at breakfast, and we can walk to work together. I'll show you the ropes."

"Now, I like hearing that, Roberta!" My enthusiasm was authentic and rang through the Texas air. With time for a hurried good-bye, we parted for bed check. The hard reality of federal prison softened, if for but a moment, by something we all need—someone familiar.

That following morning, I was early to rise and the first out the door to the cafeteria. When I arrived, Sharon and Roberta were halfway through their breakfast. I sat down across from them as we continued the conversation from the previous night. Laughter accompanied my stories of Spud and dirty U/As. Throughout the conversation, I could not help but notice the intent and intensity of Sharon's gaze. Her eyes held both an offering and a question, and, before I had the opportunity to question my response, I was drawn to reciprocate. It frightened the dickens out of me. As we said our good-byes, I felt a curious and unexpected reaction to our parting.

By the time Roberta and I reached the warehouse, the other girls were waiting outside, and I managed to gain some distance from the question Sharon had so recently delivered. I stayed close to Roberta, and, shortly after our arrival, I noticed a very large, round, blue uniform approaching from afar, inching her way to the warehouse.

"Girls! Sorry I'm late. I had a very long night," Officer Crenshaw said. "AND YOU MUST BE MISS ROBINSON!"

"Yes, ma'am."

"Oh, she's polite! I like her already," Crenshaw said. "Roberta, when you get a chance, come see me in my office."

Roberta escorted me to my assigned area. I was to inventory all the commissary goods: potato chips, cookies, hair products, makeup, etc. Here was job security if it was ever to be known. This particular task was hated and avoided by all. At the end of the day, your numbers had to match the officers' numbers, and that could be very challenging. It was common knowledge and practice that items were taken from the warehouse; discrepancy was commonplace. After I began the mundane chore, Roberta proceeded into Mrs. Crenshaw's office.

I decided immediately to create a system to circumvent the necessity of counting each and every piece of merchandise. I took the order forms for each product requested, subtracted the delivery amounts, added the returns, and subtracted the irregulars, and that was that. No more counting. Even employing my method of noncounting, it became more than an all-day job—not to mention the incompetence of those doing the ordering. By midmorning, I was finding so many mistakes that people were going crazy. I decided to bring it to Roberta's attention during lunch and see what she had to say about it.

When lunch break arrived, we met Sharon at the four corners, setting a precedent for the following months. When I began to tell Roberta of my findings, she became very concerned. She told me Mrs. Crenshaw always believed that her administrative assistants were incapable of making mistakes; she had trained them.

"You'd better handle this gently. These things have a way of backfiring on you."

"Why did Mrs. Crenshaw call you into her office?"

"You can't tell anyone this. Swear to me you will keep this to yourself."

"I swear."

"She was telling me of her sexual exploits with a younger cowboy that she met at a neighborhood bar. She was asking me for advice."

No wonder things are going to the dogs at the warehouse, I thought. *Crenshaw's out at night with someone other than her husband! Talk about hitting close to home.* I had experienced the emotional uproar created by a "love gone wrong" my entire life. Before we arrived back at the warehouse, I had resolved to leave well enough alone without giving it another thought.

I was glad to reach the end of the day. It had been 101 degrees outside, and there was no air conditioning in the warehouse. Mrs. Crenshaw had an air conditioner in her office window—the perks of management, a common element to the hell inside and outside prison. I could not wait to get back and take a cool shower.

As we were walking from the commissary back to the quads, Sharon caught up with us. We talked and laughed.

"I'll be right back," Roberta said, noticing an inmate she had some business with. "I got to take care of something."

"Roberta has told me about you," said Sharon. "You seem very interesting. I mean, the music and stuff. I know how it is with the drugs."

"So how did you end up in here?"

"I was married to an older Mexican guy. He was in the mafia, the Mexican mafia. The feds had been trying to get him for years. He left the country, and I took the rap for him. I was nineteen when I came in—they gave me eight years because I wouldn't tell them where he was. I don't know. The feds didn't believe me. They busted me with everything that was his. I figure he didn't tell me so I couldn't tell. At first he was taking care of me, sending money, and then all of a sudden, it stopped. He could have been killed or busted or whatever. I just don't know."

"That's horrible," I said with compassion.

"No worse than many of the others in here. So what do you like to do, Sheila?" Sharon asked.

"Not be in prison," I responded. "I mean, who does?"

"Well, what kind of activities do you like to do?"

"In the past, it had been crack. And more crack and sellin' crack. It was my life for the last ten years. I'm ready for a change. You got any suggestions?"

"We can talk about it at chow tonight," Sharon said. "I am definitely ready for a change!"

Yeah. Okay. Whatever, I thought as I said, "Tell Roberta I'll see you guys at supper. I have got to take a shower!"

As I entered the quad, I nearly forgot to stop and make the required sign-in. I had to constantly remind myself of that—were I to forget, it was a write-up—and one too many of those, well, hell would be paid.

I went quickly to my room, removed my clothes, and was off to the shower. Inside the cool water, I began to think of Sharon. "I am ready for a change," she had told me. I knew the look she gave me. How she sought to keep such an advance toward me from Roberta made me aware of a great many things. I had encountered it many times before from men. To explore the offer that was being made would end the friendship the three of us shared. That was a price I refused to pay, no matter how great the desire for intimacy might be. I questioned the sincerity of my convictions and did not know where my answer lay. It was what attracted me to the thought. Curiosity.

My cellmates were out quickly, and I had the cell to myself. I got dressed for dinner and decided to look over my mother's manuscript. I sat down at the little wooden table and opened up the pages of her book. "Chapter One—Blind Men Are Holy." The title alone brought a smile to my face and distance from my circumstances.

*   *   *

I was nineteen when I first met Ray. It was 1960, and he was still climbing the charts, not yet at the height of his career. I wasn't particularly fond of his music. I was not a Ray Charles fan.

I went to college in Cleveland. In the summer, I would go to Dayton to stay with my father's sister, Aunt Catherine, and work for her. She was constantly involved in something, developing new businesses.

I had just arrived for the summer when she told me she wanted to take me to see Ray Charles perform. She said, "I'm going to get us tickets. We won't have to pay; my friend is promoting Ray. Ray Charles. What do you think of that?"

Ray Charles. Oh no, I thought. I didn't want to go, but I also didn't want to hurt her feelings. So I said, "Yeah, okay."

"All right!" she nearly shrieked. "We'll get ourselves a couple of new outfits, too." And we did—long, tight-fitting skirts, and little Bolero jackets with big buttons down the front and white blouses underneath. Aunt Catherine's outfit was black—she always wore black—and mine was red corduroy, with little red pumps to match.

Ray was performing at a ballroom in the black, "let's get busy" area of Dayton. When we walked in, it was wall-to-wall people. Aunt Catherine said, "Grab my hand and just hold on."

It was so crowded that I couldn't see Ray on stage at first, but that was okay. I was more interested in watching the crowd look at him than I was in him or his music. When I finally did get to see the stage, the person who caught my attention wasn't Ray at all but a man standing way off to the right side. He was waving us over to him. I assumed he knew my aunt.

Ray was screaming and hollering as he sang, and the people around us were shouting, too. I was somewhat taken aback with the wildness. I was raised small-town-country, where the pace was slow and deliberate. These people were dancing like there was no tomorrow, giving it all up to the moment, and Ray was giving it all up to them. His spirit burned bright and became the bellows that fanned the fire in their souls. Aunt Catherine turned around and said something to me that I couldn't hear, and I hollered at her, "Your friend keeps calling us." She looked up at the stage and saw him motioning us over. She headed right toward him, dragging me behind. As we got closer, I began sensing that this was not someone Aunt Catherine knew. He sort of reminded me of Louis Armstrong. He was wearing an infectious smile and appeared as harmless as a dove.

When we got up to him on the edge of the stage, he said, "Hi, I'm Duke Wade. How would you girls like to meet the man?"

I didn't really know who "the man" was, but Aunt Catherine said, "We'd love to!"

Duke said, "Stay right here with me. He's getting ready to take a break. You see, I work for Ray. I'm his right-hand man."

I stopped reading and put the manuscript down for a moment. *It was a simpler time then*, I thought, *several years before my birth.* Duke Wade—my father's pimp. My mother was as innocent and naive as one could be.

Soon, Ray did take his break. Duke led Ray to a place on the wing of the stage. I watched Ray just stand there, searching his pockets for something. Knowing he was a blind man created a lot of curiosity in me. I waited, content to watch and observe him. I had never been in the presence of a blind man before. I made up my mind to treat him like I would treat any other person. Duke appeared and took us to Ray.

Duke said, "Catherine, I'd like you to meet Ray Charles."

Ray held out his hand and said, "I'm very pleased to meet you."

Always in command of the situation, Aunt Catherine returned a strong and confident handshake. She responded, "You're knockin' 'em dead, Ray. We're having a great time. We are really enjoying you."

"Well, I appreciate that, Catherine." Duke continued, "This is Sandy, her niece."

Ray extended his hand toward me. While shaking his hand, I placed my other hand on top of his. He responded by gently placing his other hand on top of mine. I said softly, "Hi, Ray."

In an entirely different voice than the one he used with Aunt Catherine, Ray said, "Well, all right, mama! How are you?"

"I'm fantastic!"

"All right, all right. Duke, will you please get my cigarettes?"

Duke left for Ray's cigarettes. I said excitedly, "I smoke," thrilled at the prospect of being able to offer him something. "Would you like one of mine?"

"You don't smoke the kind of cigarettes I smoke. I'm sure of that."

That intrigued me. "Well, what kind of cigarettes do you smoke?"

"I smoke, ah, Kools."

I said excitedly, "So do I!"

"Well, all right, mama, that's so nice. Let me try one of yours."

I gave him a cigarette, and he took it and broke the filter off. "You know, I do smoke Kools," he said, "but I don't like those filters on them." He lit it up and took a puff. "They tell me I'm in Dayton. Is this where you are from?"

"Oh no, no. I'm from a little tiny town in Ohio. I'm sure you've never heard of it. It's called Cambridge." I laughed and said, "Whenever anyone asks me that, I always immediately say Cambridge, and they just naturally assume Cambridge, Massachusetts. I don't bother to correct them anymore. I go to college in Cleveland, but my aunt—I'm sort of her protégé—brought me here for the summer. She's teaching me some of the new businesses she's in. She's always looked out for me. You see, Ray, I'm not just from a little tiny town; I'm from the country—I mean the <u>country</u>!"

"Well, that's mighty fine, mama, 'cause I'm a country boy myself."

We laughed together. I felt as though I were meeting a new friend.

"Ray, when I first left home to go to college, my newfound city friends worked really hard to help me change the way I talked. They'd say, 'Do you have to sound so country?' They were actually embarrassed for me. I didn't have any idea that when you got on the bus, you didn't say to the person next to you, 'Hi, where you-ens goin'?'"

Ray started laughing.

"I felt it strange that people were offended by 'Hi, where you-ens goin'?' I decided to change my greeting. And so I said, 'Good morning,' or 'Good afternoon,' but they still got mad. Finally, my college buddies informed me the only thing I needed to do was pay my bus fare and sit down."

Duke came back with a pack of cigarettes. Ray struck a match and lit one without any apparent indecision as to where the fire was. That amazed me. We continued to talk as if we were old friends. I loved the way he responded to my conversation. He thought it was so funny. He would laugh and slap the side of his leg, rear back and holler, so animated it inspired me to be funnier. I was extremely flattered that he found me so interesting and amusing. We stayed right there on the wing of the stage and talked the entire length of his break.

Duke approached us and said, "Ready, Mr. Charles?"

"Well, all right, all right! I sure have had a good time. I sure like talkin' to you. Could I ask you something? Would you mind giving me a ride to the airport after the show?"

I said, "Oh, I'm not driving—my aunt is. But I can ask her." I looked over to Aunt Catherine, who had been busily talking to Duke. "Aunt Catherine! Ray wants to know if we could take him to the airport after the show."

She looked at me and smiled, "We sure can!"

Ray nodded. "Well, thank you. One thing, though—I-I-I have to stop by my hotel room first to pick up my things. Do you think that will be all right?"

"I know my aunt won't mind that at all."

As he was about to leave, he said, "If you don't mind, I will be ready to get out of here just as soon as I'm done." Ray went back onstage.

Duke introduced us to Ray's manager, Joe Adams, and his pilot, Tom McGaritty. We stayed backstage, and I listened to Aunt Catherine talk to Tom about flying. Time passed by quickly. I became aware that the music had stopped, the curtain was once again drawn, and people were leaving. Soon I heard Ray in a slow-moaning, bluesy-type voice at the piano, without the band. I heard his voice doing a little moan, and he started singing in that old southern gospel sound, "Give Me That Old-Time Religion." Just as if they had been called to the piano, the Raylettes encircled him and began to join in harmonizing. They were just screaming and hollering and having such a good time. I was so impressed. It did not take a musical genius to hear that it was spontaneous and heartfelt. When they concluded, I saw a different type of energy in Ray and knew that I was one of the few who got to hear the real deal.

The band and the Raylettes began piling into the bus to travel to their next performance. The six of us jammed into my aunt's car—Aunt Catherine, Joe, and Tom in the front seat; Ray, Duke, and I in the backseat, with me in the middle. We were off to the Biltmore Hotel.

Aunt Catherine, Joe, and Tom were talking frantically. Ray was shaking, all fidgety. His whole body appeared to be involuntarily in motion. It confused me. I thought, "Is this what blind people do, or is he just nervous?" Just as natural as soothing a baby, I took his hand. Very softly, I moved my hands lightly over his. He just let out a sigh and became silent and so still, I felt I should listen to hear if he was breathing. Ray and I did not speak until we reached the hotel.

When we got to the Biltmore, he said, "Are you going to go have coffee with them, or would you mind coming with me and talking while I pack?" No one seemed upset over that suggestion, so Joe, Duke, Tom, and Aunt Catherine headed for the coffee shop. Ray told me his room number, and he and I went up alone. All the way up, he just held my arm and let me guide him. When we reached his room, he used his key to unlock the door and open it, allowing me to enter first.

Once we got inside, it felt completely different from at the dance. I was in Ray's room. I was a little nervous. It was the BED. It wasn't that I had any concerns about Ray's intentions; he was a perfect gentlemen. Besides, I thought all blind men were holy. I was raised in a fashion that would not permit me to enter any man's bedroom. It just wasn't done. Ray was putting his clothes in his little suitcase and doing the things he did to pack up. My first instinct was just to do what I always do when I'm nervous, talk.

"Ray, if you are from the country, then you must know how hard it is to get used to city folks. I had this great part-time job as a receptionist/employment counselor at an employment agency in Cleveland. I typed résumés and interviewed people. I was proud of my position. My boss, finding out that I lived right on his way to work, informed me that he could pick me up in the morning. Great, I wouldn't have to take the bus. You know what kind of trouble I was having on the bus.

"Well, it turns out two days after I quit that job and left Cleveland, my boss was machine-gunned down on the same morning route we took to work. Ray, it was several days later when I talked to my Uncle Bill in Cleveland that he explained I would have been pumped full of bullets right along with him. My aunt didn't even call, just sent me the newspaper clippings that revealed this man was really a mobster. The employment agency I was working for was really a front for the racketeering operation. I would have never guessed it on this earth! I was just the receptionist."

Ray stopped packing, sat down on the edge of the bed, and again I was thrilled with his interest in my life. Ray said, "Well, I'm sure glad you left Cleveland."

"Like my aunt always said, 'Thank God for Dickens' prayers.'"

"Okay, now, who is Dickens?"

"She raised me as a child. My parents had a one-room house, and they already had my brother, Bobby. And so when they had me, they went to Dickens. Dickens had advertised a basement for rent in her home. It had two bedrooms, and they were thrilled to get it. It was right by their parents' house, you know, my dad's parents' house. So we moved in with Dickens before my mom came home from the hospital with me. And my parents tell me when they walked home from the hospital with me, Dickens says, 'Give me that little angel.' And from that moment on, they couldn't get me back. She never had a child in her life.

"And I can see as clearly as I can see today—I can remember as a child three or four years old—I can still see Dickens. Me laying in that daybed in the dining room—and Dickens just praying. All she ever did was pray. That's all she did. She used to pray all though the night for me. Through the day, through the night, she just prayed for me. She would go to my mom and dad—she would beat my brother with a broom to keep him away from me. She just thought I was the most precious thing in the world."

"I can sure relate to that story. It reminds me of my own childhood."

I could only continue. "Guess what, Ray?! I saw you in Cleveland about six months ago with one of my best friends from college, Diane. She was engaged to Jim 'Mudcat' Grant, pitcher for the Cleveland Indians. The three of us did a lot of things together, and on this one occasion, Mudcat had invited Walter Bond, a rookie with the Indians, to meet us at a dance that you were performing at. Mudcat just loves you, Ray. Both of them were playing matchmaker and thought Walter and I had possibilities.

"Shortly after we got there, you started doing that song, 'Tell Me What'd I Say.' Now, Walter was Mr. Suave, you know, one of those really smooth guys, really laid back, and I was singing, 'Tell me what'd I say'— you know, I was singing, 'See the girl with the red dress on . . .' Nobody stands still to the rhythm of that song, and I certainly was not. Walter said, 'You aren't going to stand here with me and not act like a lady.' I said, 'Everybody's doing that!' He said, 'Uh uh! Not the girl with me!' I said, 'Ooooooohh, well, that's about the only song he sings that I like. I love the *beat of that song.' He said, 'Well, you're embarrassing me. I don't go out with a girl who is going to dance like that.' I immediately quit dancing. I thought he was nuttier than a fruitcake for telling me that, Ray!"*

"Now, I'm not trying to be mean or cruel, but ah, I'm sorry, mama, but I kinda have to agree with the man. I'd feel the same way if I was with a young lady. And there's a difference, you know! I said lady, you hear? I said lady! You see, Sandy, you know, I-I-I'm going to give up these kind of gigs. In a way, it's for similar reasons. If I was takin' a young lady to a dance, I would want her to be concentrating strictly on me. What I'm tryin' to do is strictly concerts; there's a little more dignity doin' that. You ain't gonna dance when I sing. No more. You see, mama, you reach a point when you give everything you got—you don't want to have to get past the hollerin', screamin', people fighting over this and that—'cause believe it or not, there really are people out there that pay their money and want to hear me without all that confusion."

"Well, wow, Ray. That's really something," I said. "When do you think you will be doing that?"

"Well, mama," Ray said, "if the good Lord is willin' and the creek don't rise, it will be very soon. It will be shortly."

I had never heard that expression before, and it made me laugh from the very depth of my being. So I just had to say it. "If the good Lord is willin' and the creek don't rise."

If I had a preconception that show business people were different or somehow beyond the common man, spending time with Ray Charles certainly would have dispelled that illusion. He sounded so gentle and sooooo country. He gave me a warm and familiar feeling of the folks back home. I felt comfortable. He sat there on the edge of the bed, and I sat on the chair. During our conversation, I would get up and walk around, and he would sit in the chair. Then, after a few more minutes, we'd switch places again.

"Cambridge is very tiny, very prejudiced. You know, you weren't allowed to be articulate in school because you were colored. I presented a book report for English literature, and I remember when I turned it in—oh, I'll never forget her, Mrs. Bell; she'd spit on you every time she talked. Oh, I couldn't stand her. And when I wrote my book report, when I turned in my book report, she refused to accept it. She said, 'No one your age could have possibly written this, and I refuse to accept it!' I'll never forget that!

"Of course, I went home and told my parents. They always believed the teachers. No matter what you did, you did not defy the teachers. They said, 'Well, the teacher wouldn't say that if there wasn't something crooked going on.' That's the way my dad felt. Discussion closed.

"You know what Dad used to say when I watched those shows like Father Knows Best—*that would make you feel like you could talk to your own father like that? I had just watched Princess ask her dad if she could discuss something with him. He answered, 'Of course, Princess.' I said, 'Daddy, could I discuss my book report with you?' Daddy said, 'What?! Discuss? Have you lost your mind? We aren't discussin' nothin'. You'd better go somewhere and sit down!' And he walked away saying, 'Well, I never heard the likes of that!' Then he made that ticking sound, sucking the air in through his teeth and slapping his tongue against the roof of his mouth, and you knew he was thoroughly disgusted with you. I said, 'Well, no more* Father Knows Best *for me. It doesn't work.'"*

With that, Ray just cracked up. I've been told that I have a great ability to be funny. To my delight, Ray unexpectedly confirmed that. I've always been one to see the humor in everything, and probably laughter has been an escape for me. However, these were the most painful experiences of my life, and I felt the pain.

Though Ray was laughing, I felt no offense. His laughter was inviting and comforting. And the way he was LISTENING to me! Never in my life, then or now, has anyone listened to me with such intensity. I loved it. It was like taking a swim in the purest of water.

Ray stopped laughing and said, "Keep talkin', mama." He laughed again. "I love it!"

The phone rang. Ray answered. He listened for a moment and then said, "Yeah." He hung up.

"Was Aunt Catherine concerned about me?"

"No. That's Joe. Mother Adams." Ray laughed. "He just wants to get going."

"We have been talking quite a while. Maybe we should get going."

Ray said quietly, "Sandy, Joe works for me. I want to stay here in this hotel and talk to you, and if that's what I want to do, that's what I'm going to do, and it's none of Joe's business."

I sat back down. Thrilled that my stories were having such an effect on him, I racked my brain trying to remember anything that had happened to me. I felt so important. I decided to tell him a story that changed the direction of my life.

"Being colored, you couldn't be pretty, you couldn't be smart, you couldn't be the expression of what you wanted to be. I wanted to be a cheerleader. I never knew how prejudiced my best friends were until I tried to be more than just a colored girl. Now, Ray, you know that you think you are going to win if EVERYBODY in the whole school tells you, 'Betsie, I voted for you!'

"I'm not trying to be egotistical, but I was the best cheerleader out there. But hands down, there wouldn't be a colored cheerleader that year. I wanted to die. From that point on, it took something really exceptional to deny me anything—whatever I attempted to do. Even if I failed, I kept trying. Not to be given a chance is a fate worse than death."

I felt as though I were melting into him, and there was no "boy–girl" in it. The complete and total understanding he projected left me feeling kind of scared. As happy as I was, I didn't know what you did with those kinds of feelings toward anybody. It was much, much deeper than just being attracted to some guy.

Ray said, "Yeah, I know. I know how that must have hurt you. I know you was feeling bad—go on, now."

"I was never one to hold a vendetta. The very person who worked the hardest to keep me from being a cheerleader, I helped her campaign to be homecoming queen. The homecoming dance was coming up. I said to my father, 'Daddy, you know, the homecoming dance is coming up, and I just want to make sure that I get to go.'

"He said, 'You know you never did get to go to none of those things. You'll go to the game with your brother Jerry, and you will be right home here. There isn't nothing for you to do—you'll be right here.'

"I thought he was nuts—I mean, God, there's not a chance I was going to get to do it again. I was a senior!"

The phone rang, and I stopped talking. Ray turned away, trying to avoid answering it. Finally, he picked it up and said, "Yeah." Once again he hung up. I knew it was Joe.

"You know, mama, wouldn't you think that a person would know that in three rings—I know this room is not very big and a person could get to anyplace in this room with three to five good steps—anyplace in this room—so if somebody doesn't answer the phone in at least five rings—Joe knows the size of this room—they obviously don't want to answer it. You don't have to let it ring twenty-five times to know that. I can't figure it out."

I understood how he felt.

"But anyway, mama, what were we talking about?'

"The homecoming dance. So I went to school and told Connie what my father had said, and she said, 'Oh, I'll call him for you.' I said, 'You will?' Ooooh, Heaven has happened here on earth—the homecoming queen! YES—the homecoming queen is going to call my father. I will not fail. I'm going this year. This is my last chance, too, but the queen is calling. I know I'm going!

"She asked, 'What time does your dad get home from work?' "I said, 'Oh, Dad walks in the door at five—by five o'clock.' "Connie said, 'I'll call at five.'

"I sat conveniently right there by the phone, and when it rang, I picked it up and said, 'Betts's residence.'

"She said, 'Sandy, it's Connie. Let me speak to your father.'

"I said, 'Oh, Daddy, telephone.' I mean, I was so proud, I can just relive it like I'm standing there.

"Daddy said, 'Who is it?' He was tired—you know, all us kids.

"I said, 'It's Connie Ankrum, the homecoming queen!' I mean, this was pay dirt at the Betts' house. And so Daddy comes to the phone and says, 'Heeeel-lo.'

"Connie says, 'Mr. Betts, this is Connie Ankrum, the homecoming queen. Sandy worked so hard campaigning. She's been making plans for the homecoming dance. Is there any way you could change your mind? Because we are all looking forward to Sandy being there.'

"I heard my father go, 'Who did you say this is? Who did you say this is? Homecoming queen!' He said, 'Now, let me tell you one thing, queen! I told my daughter that she wasn't going to the dance. If you think that you'd have more influence over my decision than Sandy would have with me, you must be crazy!' Daddy said, 'If I was going to change my mind, she ain't goin' now!'

"BAMMMM! He slammed the phone down. There was nothing you could do with Dad. Nothing! I mean—he was—nothing changed his mind."

Ray hit the floor laughing. *"Now, that's one man I have to meet. I tell you, mama, I had a mother that I am sure would run a close race with your father. You know, my mother would not let my blindness be a weakness. Anything that she thought I could do without my sight, she made me do it. If she thought that I could do it, I had to do it. That is the reason I can do what I can do today. She is the reason I am self-sufficient. One of the things she would make me do was chop wood. One day, the neighbors saw me out choppin' wood and called the authorities on her. They took her to court—you know, children's services, that sort of thing—as an unfit mother. And when they went to court, she said, 'You know, my son might be blind, but he's only lost his sight, not his mind!' That was her defense, and that was the end of that! I'll never forget it. Today, there's nothing I can't do except drive a car. I love my mother for that."*

"I know," I said softly to Ray, "because as much as I remember that strictness, his inability to be moved, as terrible as it was, I love my father for being who he is."

The phone rang again. Here he comes again. Joe Adams. Ray was irritated. I did not feel uncomfortable. Ray was in complete control of himself. As powerful a man as Joe Adams was, Ray was clearly the captain of his ship. I was hoping we could talk forever.

"Ray, when I was in high school, my cousin stole a billfold in the gym locker room. I was in the cubicle next to her changing, and she said, 'Hey, I've got Sandy Smith's billfold, and it's got three dollars in it.' I said, 'Don't tell me about it! Don't tell me about it! I don't want to know about it. I know the wrath of Robert Betts!'

"She got caught. The principal said, 'Sandy Betts and Jazzy Bottom were in the locker room when the billfold was stolen'—well, she was my first cousin; we hung together all the time. Her mom and my mom were sisters. Oh man, they called my parents for a meeting, and I said, 'Jazzy, you got to tell them I didn't have anything to do with that. I didn't even want to know about it!'

"She said, 'If I'm getting into trouble, you're getting into trouble with me.' "And I said, 'Jazzy, we don't have the same kind of parents.'

"You know, her parents drank heavy. They didn't care what she did. She had all the best clothes. She'd steal her parents' paychecks and go shop. They didn't know they lost it; thought they drank it up. She'd go out in the rumble seat cars with the guys and come back and tell you she was fiddling around through the night. We had no way near the same life. She lived on the south side of town; I lived on the north side. Country! She lived where all the rich people lived and the white people. Jazzy knew she wasn't going to see any wrath. That's why she didn't care.

"So, she finally—oh man—my mom and dad had her mom and dad out to our house, and her mom and dad politely let them know that they didn't care, you know, and Jazzy finally said, 'I did it myself.' She had done it herself. My dad put me in the bedroom for one week. I was not allowed to go to school. My meals were in my bedroom. I did not come out of my room for one week. The entire school thought I was guilty. I said, 'Daddy, I know *that you cannot believe that I stole that money.' He said, 'If I thought you stole the money, you wouldn't be here talking to me right now. I'm punishing you for putting yourself in a position to be accused like that. No. I know you didn't steal that wallet, or you'd be dead.' Jazzy never even got a punishment. Her mom and dad just paid the three dollars."*

Once again, I had Ray in stitches. After laughing at a story so painful to me, he said, 'Sandy, I'd be trying to follow after the guys—the cats in the band—where they'd be rehearsing or playing piano, and I'd hear people say, 'You gotta watch those blind boys—they steal.' That really hurt me."

"I hate people like that! You know, Ray, I grew up with two mothers. Remember when I told you just a little bit ago how Dickens was always praying for me? Right to this very day, I have yet to get over her dying. Whenever I had pain—like you must have felt when you heard someone say, 'Blind boys steal'—whenever I was hurt like that, there was no one like Dickens who could soothe the pain. Her soft, warm, big-busted body just felt like a big old cushion. She smelled like vanilla and homemade soap and rock starch."

Ray must have heard the tears in my voice because I knew he couldn't see me crying. I knew beyond a doubt he truly sensed my pain. I went on.

"When my dad's father told him, 'Robert, it's time for you to buy a house,' Grandpa found the house, lent my dad the down payment, and they moved across the field from my grandparents and up the hill from Dickens. All of us were very close together. But to me, if I would have to leave Dickens, I could not have done that. Though I knew my parents loved me as much as Dickens, she was my life.

"Mom and Dad loved Dickens and appreciated the way she loved me, their firstborn daughter. And so they protected me from experiencing her death. Dickens was ninety-six years old. When Dickens told everybody she wanted to die in her sleep, you didn't doubt any prayer that Dickens asked for. They did not want to live with that. But as a nine-year-old child, I resented when they made me sleep in 'their' house. So I'm up in 'our' house, and I'll never forget! Mable Cross saw Dickens's blinds didn't go up. I can hear her now. She's knockin' on the back door. I'm in this room right by the stairway that goes down into the kitchen. I heard her say, 'Mary Dickens, ah, Mary Dickens is dead." My mother said, 'Oh no. How are we going to tell Sandy?' They came up behind me, and I laughed. Strangest thing. Oh, I couldn't stop laughin'. I couldn't quit laughin'. I couldn't quit. I'll never forget that. It's the only way I could deal with her passing. It was like my mother dying."

Ray was leaning his ear toward me intently.

"You know, my mother's death has been the hardest thing I've ever known. The biggest problem was—I couldn't cry. They kept saying, 'Ray, if you could just cry, man.' I got physically ill because I couldn't cry."

Ray became very still. He said, "I was just turning five years old, and, you know, in the South back then, they didn't have swimming pools for black kids. It was a real hot day, and my mother had one of those great big galvanized number six tubs. She'd fill it with water and put it outside.

"I had just about totally lost my eyesight by that time. My younger brother and I were out there playing in the water, and he lost his leverage on the outside of the tub and fell in. Instead of running for my mother, I tried to get him out by myself. He drowned."

We had talked for hours, as if we were old friends—but there was no sexual attraction. At least, I felt none for him. From what I could tell, he wasn't feeling any for me, either. It all seemed so comfortable.

About 5:00 a.m., we heard a key going into the lock of Ray's door. Suddenly, the door burst open, and Joe strolled in, tight, controlled, polite, but angry as hell. I didn't blame Joe for being protective. He didn't know me. I may have been some crazy person who planned to hit Ray over the head and take his money. He didn't have a clue who I was—and we were up there for about five hours.

"Is everything all right in here, Ray?" he asked.

Ray said, "Yes, man, I've been tellin' you, it's just fine." Ray was trying to be nice—to control his anger in front of me as well. It was only later, when we got to know each other better, that Ray let me see how ugly he can sometimes be.

"Well, Ray, it's really time we get going. It's five in the morning!"

"All right. We'll be right down."

I could tell that Joe didn't like leaving Ray alone any longer, but he left, closing the door behind him.

Ray said to me, "Would you mind coming over here for a minute and just sit on my lap? Would you do that for me?"

I thought about it for a few seconds. I wasn't afraid. You don't need to be afraid of a blind man. If he gives you any trouble, you knock him in the head, you clip him in the barrel. Today, I know that Ray Charles is as swift as any man. You'd have to plan a sneak attack to get to him. But at that time, I thought, "Why not?"

He was sitting in the chair. I went over and sat on his lap. He said, "I think that material — don't they call that — I believe that's corduroy, isn't it?"

"Yes it is," I said. "My aunt and I both got new outfits to wear to your show."

"You did that? Well, can I ask you this — what color is it?"

"Red."

"All right, all right. I like that, mama! I like that." He felt the material. "You know, we've talked so long, do you think you could still take me to the airport? We flew my little plane. Would you like to come see it — come and see me off all the way to the airplane?'

I said, "I'd love to!" I meant it.

We came down the stairs and found our four companions sitting there in the lobby looking dragged out. I felt a little guilty — the coffee shop had been closed for hours.

Aunt Catherine said, "So, okay, we're ready to go, are we?" I could tell that Joe was extremely peeved, and quickly we were all in the car on our way to the airport.

Ray's little gold twin engine Cessna was waiting. He said, "Excuse me a minute, mama. I've got to check the gas. Nobody checks the gas but me. That's my job with this plane."

He checked the gas and came back. "I wonder if I could ask you a really big favor," he said.

"Well, what is it?"

"Do you think I could get your phone number? Duke, will you give me a piece of paper and a pencil?"

I didn't know what to do. It had been nice meeting him, but actually, I never wanted to see Ray Charles again. He was only eleven years older than I, but he was an old man at thirty. An old blind man.

"So, mama, what's your number?"

Call me a fool, but I gave it to him. Blind men don't lie; they don't cheat — they get you by surprise. As the sun rose, Aunt Catherine and I talked and laughed all the way home.

That evening, the phone rang at about eleven o'clock. I was already in bed. My uncle came into my room and said, "Sandy, telephone for you."

I got out of the bed and went to the phone. The operator said, "A long distance call for Sandy."

"Yes, this is Sandy."

I heard a voice say, "How you doin', mama?"

"Who is this?" I asked into the receiver.

"This is Ray."

"Uh-oh," I thought. "Oh, Ray," I said. "How are you?"

"Well, I'm just fine. You know, I was just thinking about you. I really enjoyed talking to you last night. I was wondering if you would consider me sending my pilot to pick you up. Maybe you could visit with me again."

"What? Um—oh no," I said. "I have to work."

That didn't slow him down. "Well, could I call you tomorrow?"

I had to think for a minute. "Well, I suppose you could—but, you know, this is kind of late to be calling me."

"Oh—I didn't realize—I'm sorry," he said. "I'll call you tomorrow. Good night." And with that, he hung up.

"Where in the world is he, and what the heck is he calling me for?" I thought.

Friday night, about ten o'clock, the phone rang again. My uncle picked it up and listened for a minute. Then he said to me, "It's probably that blasted Ray Charles calling again, because it's the long distance operator asking for you. Did you tell him we're working-class people and his hours are disturbing?"

I took the phone. "Hello."

"Hello, mama." (Initially, I thought he was calling me "mama" out of affection and found it rather endearing. Later I learned that Ray calls everyone "mama." It isn't anything personal. I've heard him call waiters, stewardesses, the mailman "mama"— it doesn't matter what sex they are.)

"Listen, Ray," I said, "My uncle is kind of upset. It's late here."

"Well, I just wanted to see if it's all right to send my pilot out to pick you up."

The man would not let up. I wanted to say no but didn't know how. "Oh," I finally said, "I'm on my period. I'm on my period." That's what I had always heard girls should tell a guy in order not to have sex. And that was the only thing that I could imagine he had in mind.

He came right back with, "What possible difference could that make? I just want to talk to you. I just want to see you."

There was no denying that the time we shared was of a much higher quality than what I had just reduced it to. I felt ridiculous.

"Oh," I said. "Ah . . . I don't think I could come."

"Well, could I call you back?"

"Well . . . okay." Why was I saying yes again when I wanted to say no?

The next morning, the phone rang again. Aunt Catherine answered it.

"Oh, Sandy?" she said, her hand over the receiver. "Telephone. It must be Ray again. It's long distance."

Oh no, please, God. "Tell him I'm not here."

That got her angry. "I will not! You are not a little girl; you're a woman. You get on that phone and tell him not to call here anymore. Tell him you don't want to see him. Tell him anything you want, but I'm not going to lie for you!"

Filled with dread, I went to the phone. I held the receiver up to my ear and listened. "Hello?" I said.

"How you doin', mama?"

I threw the whole phone down and ran into my room. Aunt Catherine followed me. "What are you doing?"

"Aunt Catherine," I said, "I can't talk to him right now."

She looked at me with a mixture of anger and compassion. "Well, I'm not going to do anything about it. It's your business, not mine."

I stayed in my room for several minutes. Finally, I got up the courage to go back to the phone. I picked it up off the floor and put the receiver to my ear. Silence. Ray had hung up.

I was weak with relief. I knew I wouldn't have to deal with Ray's calls anymore. I didn't want to hurt his feelings, but he had become an annoyance. He upset my aunt and uncle. He was eleven years older than I was. He was hitting on me big time. I just wasn't comfortable with his calling. The thoughts swirled around and around in my head.

I knew that getting rid of him was the only way I could handle the situation, his attention, and still feel good about myself.

The problem was that I didn't feel good about myself. I looked at the phone still in my hand and told myself, "At least it's over."

Surely you got the message there, Mr. Ray Charles!

CHAPTER 6

COMIN' FROM WHERE I COME FROM

Conditional love—
It conflicts with everything I know love to be
Chafes the very core of my heart's experience
Love has no need for words
Love is
Love does not ask
Love does not control and we have no control
over whom we fall in love with
For me
It just happened to be a man named Ray Charles

—SANDRA BETTS

I WAS MISSING MOM so much now—her stories, the way she talked. It was like hearing her again as clearly as if she were in the room with me. It was the most treasured possession I could ever have received. I continued reading her manuscript that had become more of a narrative outline or a collection of memoirs . . .

You Can't Fight Destiny.
    I went back to Cleveland and returned to school. I began dating attorney Clarence Taylor, and I got a job with the Sheraton Hotel chain. My relationship with Clarence was more than encouraged by my parents. When

he proposed, I accepted more for them than I did for myself. My job with the Sheraton organization had blossomed, and I received a promotion requiring travel to Portland, Oregon, for several months. Away from the influence and pressure of my parents, I began to seriously question my decision to marry Clarence. Through a series of conversations with my good friend Willie Mays, I decided to move to Los Angeles, leaving both the Sheraton and Clarence behind.

I moved into the Waverly Hotel where the elderly Ben Ramsey, a veteran bit-part actor, befriended me. I took a job as a receptionist at the Los Angeles College of Optometry, still questioning my decision not to marry Clarence. He could only be considered the ideal husband for any parent's daughter. I was somewhat frightened at this first act of complete obedience to self, as it ran contrary to my parents' desires and wishes for my future. Such were my thoughts as I listened on the phone to my parents. They were telling me how proud they were to have the newspaper clipping announcing my forthcoming marriage to Clarence and how they had remodeled their home. Though it was difficult, I found the strength to tell them I would not be home for Christmas, and I was not going through with the marriage. They were not happy with me!

I was grateful for a friend like Ben—he looked out for me, and I accepted his invitation to attend some holiday festivities. I love Christmas, and other than my friend Mary Anne, I knew no one in L.A. As I walked into the party with Ben, what a surprise to hear, "Oh my God, Ohio! What are you doing here?"

I was puzzled for a few moments. Then the recognition hit me; it was Duke Wade.

Duke continued, "Ohio! Wait until I tell the man!" At least this time I knew who "the man" was.

Duke emphatically said, "Just give me your phone number."

The phone was ringing as I turned the key to my room. It was Ray. We conversed at length. Ray's focus during the conversation was why, where, when, and what I was doing in Los Angeles. I enjoyed answering all his questions. I knew he really wanted the answers. The memory of our first meeting was very clear. I could feel his ear through the phone. I told him about my job at the College of Optometry. I informed Ray that I was moving to the Phillis Wheatley Home, a residence for black businesswomen. I gave Ray the number there. Ray told me that he would be out of town for a few days; he would get in touch with me when he returned. I was very glad I had heard from him—in fact, the word "Ohio" was a blessing.

Touching the Garment of the High Priest

I moved to the Phillis Wheatley Home. Ray called me there daily. We had a series of pleasant conversations. Ray was in the same place he was a couple of years ago, asking if he could send his pilot for me. I was in no way unprepared. Lovers. Friends. Enemies. I knew it was all about to happen. Ray asked me if I would consider coming to hear him in concert at the Shrine. I accepted the invitation.

My friend Barbara and I went to see Ray at the Shrine. We were seated offstage in the wings. During the performance, a man wearing a white robe flew out of the audience, ran across the stage, and embraced Ray. As the white-robed man was rushed from the stage, he passed Barbara and me, proclaiming he had touched the garment of the high priest—the genius—Ray Charles.

We watched from backstage as Ray came out from behind the curtains. He was led to a man and started to converse with him. I heard Ray mention my name. Joe Adams brought Ray over to me. The photographers and the news media followed. They were persistent. They wanted a story. When he could no longer ignore them, Ray told them to leave him alone and talk to Joe. He turned to me and asked me out after the concert. I told him that I couldn't because I had a one o'clock curfew at Phillis Wheatley. I knew that he loved the fact I was living where there was a curfew. I could see it in his smile. He continued to call me daily.

Becoming very close friends, Barbara and I spent a lot of time together. On one occasion, we had an impromptu photo session with Earl Green, a photographer, who thought I would make a great model. I did not see the opportunity in myself but was complimented by the offer. Invited to a champagne lunch at Earl's studio, I asked him if he would take some "cheesecake" pictures of Barbara and me. We went into the bathroom and pulled down our brassiere straps to see how "cheesecake" we looked with a towel wrapped around us. We were having fun and decided we could really look sexy—in a most harmless manner. It was then that Earl took the pictures that were to become far more than a momentary amusement.

I did not feel it strange when Ray brought me to his suite at the Olympic Hotel on our first date. He treated me just as he had on that first night in Dayton, Ohio. The only difference was that he opened up more about himself. Ray talked about having two mothers when he was growing up. He said, "It must have been meant for me to have two mothers 'cause I sure needed everything they both taught me." He continued and revealed the prejudice that existed within the small town of Greenville, Florida, where he was raised. Every story he told related to the way I was brought up. How could I ignore the similarities of our youth?

He told me the physical pain (caused by the severe glaucoma he developed in childhood) was the reason his eyes were removed and that he didn't care much that he couldn't see. He said, "The things I hear about are bad enough. I don't need to see them."

Because of the large chalkboard indicating business transactions between Ray and ABC, I knew Ray spent time here conducting his business. My lack of inquisitiveness left Ray with a complete feeling of ease and allowed our time to be filled with joy and laughter. A closeness beyond words existed between us. I had no need to touch what already embraced me. The lack of that need became the fuel and truth in the phrase "burning desire."

I had no doubt that he was moving away from a marital situation that had nothing to do with me. I felt complete in developing a relationship with Ray. Through telephone conversations and just being together as friends, Ray and I became very comfortable in a routine of being together.

Crawling Inside His Mouth

Ray became a man very easy to fall in love with. I did not know what I was going to do when the question of sex inevitably presented itself. When he would call and ask me out, my excitement came from not knowing what on earth we were going to do. How many times can you just have a conversation? Frankly, I had run out of stories.

Ray Charles is a very shy person, and I have never been aggressive on the feminine side of things. We were truly at a deadlock; something had to give. Finally, the call came that stole my heart. Ray said, "Mama, I've been thinking about you all day. How was your day?"

"I've been wonderful!"

"I really want to see you tonight." His voice was as sensual and as forceful as if he were pulling me by the hand. I knew our time had come.

Later that evening, very gently, Ray took my hand and invited me to sit beside him on the bed as we watched television. I was so intrigued with his interest in television that I almost missed the most romantic night of my life.

Lying next to me in bed, Ray removed his glasses and placed them on the nightstand. It was the first time I saw him with his glasses off. If you can just picture newborn babies, their eyes don't tell you anything—you *love everything about them. Ray didn't move his eyelids. They just stayed shut except when he got excited; then they would flutter a bit.*

Those glasses belonged to Ray Charles the entertainer, the man I saw on stage. When he removed them, it was as if he lifted a hundred pounds off his back. He had removed their burden, and in their place came a man whom you knew was not Ray Charles the entertainer. He was MORE powerful. This WAS Ray Charles.

Lying there, feeling somewhat awkward, my next thought was, "Lights on or lights off?" I was a virgin. My natural inclination was to turn the lights off. That would make me feel most comfortable. I considered Ray's feelings. Would he think that I turned the lights off because I didn't want to look at him? I didn't want him to feel uncomfortable. I thought about it and decided it didn't make any difference to him, and it didn't make any difference to me. Lights on.

The thing that overwhelmed me the most about him, being with him, was his mouth. It always held the fragrance—and his skin—of fresh fruit. The first time that I kissed him, I wished I could crawl in his mouth. It was so fresh. Never smelled like the odor of anything he ate, drank, or smoked— never, just fresh, like a baby, like a newborn baby. We just kind of moved like we were made for each other.

His hands moved across my skin like a whisper, so soft and gentle and yet so loud and strong. Ray and I made love for the first time.

AWOL: Absent Without Leave

Unhappy with the rules at the Phillis Wheatley Home, I moved into an apartment with my friends Faye and Gerri. They didn't know I was dating the Ray Charles. They only knew I was dating a man named Ray and that he called me every day and we went out together every night. Ray's valet or driver always came to the door for me.

Ray would wait in the car—occasionally in his gold Corvette, but usually in that big pink Cadillac.

The two of us became all but inseparable. We spent much of our time together sharing and talking about our future.

Ray became the picture of things I had not seen. He was so amusing. I was in love. Once I got over my amazement with the capableness of Ray as a blind man, blindness was never an issue in our relationship. In many ways, it allowed us to become closer and share things I had not shared with other "sighted" people, as Ray would say. It did, however, change the dynamics of the dating and courting ritual. Visual flirting was out.

So much of the usual boy–girl game revolves around the visual. The flirtatious and coy expressions of the face, the eyes, the lips, the body language used between a man and a woman; the makeup, the color of your lips and nails, your dress, the way you fixed your hair—almost everything involved in "getting ready" for a "normal" date—Ray was incapable of noticing.

Ray exercised his strength and power overcoming blindness. He was not intimidated by his lack of sight, enabling him to interact with sighted people as though he possessed sight. So powerful was his personal victory over his handicap, it was quite often what others found intimidating about him. When Ray would greet me and say, "Mama, you look so beautiful," I had no doubt that he meant it, that he truly saw me that way, and I would see myself as he saw me. It endeared me to him.

I attempted to entertain and be endearing to him with my voice. I made a firm commitment to myself that my voice would always be honest, and I would always mean everything I said to him. Without any discussion, Ray understood that about me. He respected that honesty.

As with all things in life, nothing is perfect. A crossroad appeared. Ray was late every time we were to be together. I found this very disrespectful. In the normal process of dating, that was a knife in your back. I knew that I would not accept that behavior from anyone and told him so. He heard my conviction. He responded by providing every number that existed where he could be reached. Not understanding the entertainment industry, I expected him to keep his word; 7:30 meant 7:30! Ray explained that the type of business he was in and his schedule caused his chronic lateness.

The next evening was the beginning of the weekend. Several boys from the San Diego Marine base were down visiting my roommates. Ray told me he would pick me up at 7:00 p.m., and 7:00 p.m. was fine with me. Joe Adams called to let me know that Ray was going to be late. I hung up. I am not unreasonable, but 11:00 p.m. was not within with my range of reasonability. From 7:00 p.m. to 11:00 p.m. is always a hang-up for me. I put on comfortable clothing and relaxed. I sprawled out on the couch and thought, "What am I about to do with my life?" I was definitely saying good-bye to Ray Charles!

Lying under the table that supported the stereo, I listened to James Moody and "Moody's Mood for Love." I was prepared to move on with my life without Ray Charles.

Knock-knock at the door. Without even rising from my position under the table, I reached for the doorknob and opened the door. Herb Miller, Ray's driver and valet, was standing there. Ray stood beside him, looking like a five-year-old boy. At that moment, I was signed, sealed, and delivered. As they moved into the apartment, the TV was turned off, and someone turned off the stereo. There was complete silence. This Ray was the Ray Charles! You could have heard a pin drop in the apartment.

My heart melted with his posture. "Ray, let me go get dressed. Herb, will you introduce Ray to the people here?" With "get dressed," Ray knocked off his glasses in a very nervous gesture.

My roommates were the all-time party girls for the San Diego Marines. I was with Ray all the time. I worked during the day. I was unaffected by the behavior of my roommates. Ray, however, was very much affected by their behavior. I had to be removed.

He took me to the Olympic Hotel. Then he went to New York.

After Ray went to New York, I called the hotel manager, Pidge, whom I met through one of Ray's drivers. I had previously discussed my marketing abilities with him and my success within the Sheraton Hotel organization. Pidge asked me to join him for dinner with the head of public relations for the L.A. Lakers with the intention of business networking. I gratefully accepted. He then excitedly told me that Ray Charles had left for New York with his "wife" last night after a five-day stay at his hotel.

I was devastated. I hid my reaction from him. My mind was like a kaleidoscope. I knew Ray had been with me for the last five days, yet I also knew he had just left for New York. I could fight it no longer. I confided in Pidge. At the dinner, I could only sit and cry.

I called Big Al Strong, an employee at Ray's, who rushed over and answered any doubt to this woman's identity. I learned she was looking for similar answers of her own from Ray. She wanted to know why Ray wasn't in New York with her, as he had been in the past when he was not touring. Angry, dismayed, and distressed, I ran up a considerable tab at the hotel. I was unable to believe Ray would move me out of my apartment because of his jealousy into a hotel where he was staying with another woman. That was not within my reach of sanity. I flipped. I was miles away from my bus route to work, and frankly, I didn't give a darn. Because Ray was in New York and I couldn't communicate with him, my feelings were intensified. There was no question about it. I knew he was with another woman. My pain was intensified.

Several days later, Pidge, in shock and concerned about the bill, called me to explain the situation was out of control, while I was possessed with the idea of running it higher. Even a corporate bill could not go that high without receiving an immediate payment. I was cut off. In my state of mind, cutting me off of anything was impossible. My account continued to grow. Pidge called Joe Adams, and I was informed the bill was paid. Ray followed shortly with a long list of expenses in Braille. After a lengthy command to sit and listen to every detail, Ray asked me, "Did you do this, or did these suckers put this on my bill because they know I got the money?" I said through my tears, "I did it." Ray responded, "Then come and sit on Daddy's lap."

Ray and Me in the Hood and Miss Understood

Ray informed me that he was going to find me an apartment and pay for my rent—but I wanted an apartment that I could afford with money I'd earn from working. Herbert Miller said there was an apartment available in the building where he lived.

I moved into Herbert's building. Hazel, Herbert's wife, quickly became my best friend. Ray spent most of his time at our apartment—eating, sleeping, talking, and making love with me. As our relationship developed, I began to observe the things that made Ray tick. Ray's idea of a perfect evening was uninterrupted time alone. Experiencing a complete and sudden change in lifestyle, I found a desperate need to interact on a social level. It compelled me to tell Ray, "Take me out."

Ray, not knowing my habitual furniture rearranging, became secure in a month's time knowing exactly where everything in the apartment was. He had not been out of town during that month and was comfortable when he entered the apartment, having learned the position of every piece of furniture. Overcoming his blindness, he exemplified confidence in his stride and posture. It did not work this time. I had just rearranged the furniture. Ray went to where he knew the bed was, took a backward dive, and landed on the floor with such impact and surprise that even before he started laughing, I was in tears with fear and humor. He looked so funny. His glasses were one way and he was another. His sense of humor was larger than his need to recover his dignity. I loved him more. Through his laughter, Ray said, "Mama, you have to remember—you sighted people do things a little differently than I do. So if you'll just leave the furniture in the same place that I last saw it, I'd appreciate it." We lay on the floor together laughing.

Ray told me that I shouldn't associate with Hazel so much. I told Hazel what Ray had said. We both knew why. Hazel was also a very good friend with Ray's wife, Della. We continued doing almost everything together and concealed our relationship from Ray.

I had yet to tell Ray that I had lost my job during the fiasco at the Olympic Hotel, thinking I'd find another soon. Ray learned from Herbert that I was jobless and without money. Herbert came to me as a friend and told me, "Betsy, listen. Hazel and I have plenty to eat and a dollar here and there to get you to a job interview. It's not earthshaking in our life. But honey, your man is Ray Charles! Whether you like it or not, he is not poor." He looked at me and said, "Betsy, I think you're the only woman who loves Ray. They're wearing lynx, and you got on a raincoat trying to figure out how to eat. Tell Ray you are not working."

I was so ashamed of the hotel bill, I wanted to pay my own way. Herbert told me he had to tell Ray. It didn't make sense to him. To confirm Herbert's story, Ray showed up unexpectedly at the apartment during the time I should have been at work. Ray explained to me that he was embarrassed that his woman was without money and allowing someone beside himself to help me. Shortly thereafter, Hazel and I both found jobs at the Community Chest and started working together. Hazel and I borrowed bus fare from each other to get back and forth from work. Grateful for the hamburgers we'd buy ourselves on Friday, Hazel and I had much more in common than she and Della. Hazel's beautiful spirit and integrity were vexed by the two friendships she cherished.

Ray was receiving some award at the Palladium—Gerald and Nancy Wilson were going to be there. Ray wanted me to go with him. I accepted. I ran downstairs to my landlady's and told her that Ray was taking me to an award ceremony that night, and I needed something to wear. Oh, did she get me dressed.

Joe Adams and Ray came to pick me up. Ray and I were in the backseat, and Joe was driving. Ray was feeling my fur that I had been given to wear from my landlady. He said, "Ah, ah, where did you get this fur coat?"

"It's the landlady's. And this is her dress. And these are her shoes."

"Ah, ah, let me tell you something, mama. As soon as you get home, you take that off and give it back. And I'm tellin' you right now, don't you ever borrow anything from somebody that costs that much money."

"Oh, all right, Ray!" He was really mad.

I didn't drink at the time—not at all—but when we arrived, Joe ordered champagne for me. Ray had to do a recording session after the ceremony, and I drank that split of champagne. I was all fired up. Standing behind me, Ray put his hands around me and said, "Ah, ah, okay—I'm going to tell you right now. I hate that I have to go, but this is how I pay the bills. But, girl, I don't want you to ever have anything to drink when you are not with me."

"Oh—what? Why?'

"Now, if you're that friendly after you drink a split of champagne and I've got to leave, what if somebody else comes in here—are you still going to be that friendly?"

"Oh, Ray! This is you and me!" And I'm hugging and kissing him, and he's like, "No way, mama! I can't have it! No more! That's it for you and the drinking!"

Born Out of Love

I began having cramping abdominal pains and feeling nauseous. When I told Ray, his first reaction was, "Mama, you're probably pregnant!" I didn't believe it and thought more likely there was something seriously wrong with me.

Ray told me to see his doctor—and close friend—Robert Foster, who ran some tests on me. Dr. Foster was to tell me nothing. He called Ray and informed him that I was pregnant. Ray called me and said that everything was fine, that he would see me shortly. He arrived, very excited, and told me that we were going to have a baby. I was stunned.

There was one piece of furniture that I desperately wanted to get rid of. Ray was obsessed with the rocking chair. Within moments of coming into our apartment, he was in that rocking chair with me on his lap, pregnant! I felt protective of my body and did not know what to do when he would rock to the edge of the rocker. Teetering in midair, I would scream, "Ray, honey, we are going to fall!" Ray would say, "Don't you believe it, mama, we're fine!" He explained his ability to understand balance. I never questioned it anymore. I just teetered.

We would spend hours just talking about our future together. Ray explained to me that he respected his wife, Della. He was sad about the confusion, fighting, and destructive nature of their relationship and how it affected their children. Before they were divorced, Ray wanted to repay her with the things he thought she deserved.

Our plans were simple. We were in love. Ray would tell me that he wanted to have a small house with a picket fence. He didn't need that much. Because of his brother drowning, he truly did not want a swimming pool near the baby. The baby and I were his focus.

Ray and Herb went out on the road. I missed Ray terribly and told Hazel that I was going to call him. Hazel advised against it, but I didn't listen. She knew about the "action" on the road. I knew better. No one who had made love with me that intensely and was so ecstatic about our child could need anything outside of that. I used all my knowledge to assess the situation. Reason and logic were not my friends. I called him at his hotel. The "other woman" answered the phone.

I broke into tears and called back again. This time, Ray answered. He tried to assure me that he was alone, but I didn't believe him. Feeling completely insecure, I asked Ray to send me airline tickets so I could go see my mother before I started to show. Ray knew how deeply I loved my mama and dad. He knew if they were to know I was pregnant, it would make my life a living nightmare. Our plan, which made sense at the time, was to maintain the secrecy of our child until we were married so as not to upset my family.

The Other Woman

Ray immediately wired me the money for airline tickets. I dialed TWA. I told them that I was Mrs. Ray Charles and I needed a ticket to Dayton, Ohio. I needed to prove something to myself. Ray literally begged me not to go back East. "Don't destroy our life together. Stay in L.A. Stay at work."

I landed in Ohio and saw Aunt Catherine. I felt secure again. I then called my uncle Todi in Kentucky. It was not easy to tell him I was having a child and not yet married to Ray. I had to tell someone. I was hurt and confused, and I wanted to be soothed. Ray was a part of my life. I needed Ray.

Ray was going to be in Louisville, Kentucky. I flew to Louisville to join him. I never followed another man again in my life. While I was en route, Ray had called Aunt Catherine, and she told him that I had checked into the same hotel he was staying in. Ray was not happy about this. He called my room at the hotel.

Aunt Catherine drove down to Louisville and met me. We went to the performance, arriving quite early. Aunt Catherine left with Ray's pilot for dinner. I went backstage, where I talked with Cassius Clay and his brother Rudy and intrusively helped make up the Raelettes.

After the concert, Ray put me on the group's bus, and we drove to the airport. He took me onto the plane with him and told me that he loved me. Aunt Catherine showed up with the pilot, and she and I drove back to Dayton. I went to Cambridge to stay at my parents' house. A few days later, Ray called and told me that I needed to fly to Los Angeles before he left for his European tour.

Uncle Todi and I flew together to Los Angeles. Ray met us at the airport but quickly became angry with me—jealous of the man with me, Uncle Todi. Ray did not believe that he was my uncle. He stormed off to a recording session. Joe said, "I never saw the 'man' meet mama at the airport before 10:00 in the morning."

Uncle Todi and I got a hotel room. Ray showed up sometime after midnight. Kentucky was still affecting both of us. Ray had to feel insecure that my jealousy would allow me to react so strongly. I was matching his feelings with my refusal to be the other woman. Ray expressed his concern about the sheriff sitting in front of my door. I explained there was a group of jurors staying in the room across from ours. I saw a strange concern in him that went beyond the answer. I told Ray what I had done—had vacated my apartment and quit my job. He was shocked. He emphatically attempted to help me understand that no matter what he or anyone did, our relationship could not or should not be affected. I knew Ray would handle the situation. When he told me he would, it was not news to me.

Our being together took over; nothing else mattered. Sharing verbally and physically the love we had for each other, we became grounded in the knowledge of its permanence.

I'm Going to Drown in My Own Tears

Ray tried to keep me from experiencing any problems and asked me only one question: "What area do you want to live in?" I always wanted to live in the old neighborhood. Ray immediately put Joe on the case. Joe knew there was nothing he could do to manipulate, overpower, or control Ray's relationship with me. He found a new apartment for me across the street from my old one. I moved in. Unaware that in a few months all hell would break loose, I settled down, wondering what I would do next.

So far, Ray and I had kept my pregnancy secret from everyone in my family except for Uncle Todi, Aunt Catherine, and my brother (who was about to become our next problem).

Happy as larks, Ray and I were at home. Laying his ear on my stomach to hear our child and seeing the love on his face took away the struggle during the time he was on the road. I was content, fat, and happy.

Surprisingly, I was confused by Ray's objection to my brother and his wife moving to Los Angeles and living with me. Ray was concerned that they would take advantage of me. Though he used financial exploitation as the reason, Ray wanted nobody around to disturb the privacy he and I shared. I had recently awakened in the middle of the night to a man trying to enter my bedroom window. After that, I was not getting any sleep. My brother and his wife brought me a much-needed companionship, as Ray was on the road so frequently. I began hiding them in a hotel when he came to town. I avoided the issue.

My friendship, my sisterhood with Hazel, also created a problem. Every day, Hazel shared with me the compassion that women have with each other during pregnancy. Every day, it intensified. Ray was trying to get Hazel out of my life, and Hazel was trying to keep me peacefully in hers.

Hazel's husband, Herb, went on the European tour with Ray. During their first stop in London, Herb was unfaithful to Hazel and had an affair that resulted in pregnancy. Apparently, Herb provided the "other woman" in his life with his address, for she wrote a letter that arrived a few days before his return. Opening the letter, Hazel was heartbroken to discover her husband's infidelity and the woman's claims to be pregnant with Herb's child. Hazel confided everything in me.

On the day Ray and Herb were on their way back to Los Angeles, Hazel called me and asked me to come over. When I arrived, Hazel showed me a picture of Ray and a Swedish girl in Jet *magazine.*

I ran back home to discover Ray and Joe at my door. I controlled myself until Joe left and Ray and I were alone. Then I began a tirade that even surprised me. The jealous rage over the picture Hazel had just shown me was my greatest performance to date. I knew Ray appreciated my refusal to curse and how I carried myself like a lady, but I used every four-letter expletive I could recall, then made up some of my own. Ashtrays flew, glasses crashed against the wall, and furniture was knocked over. Exhausted, pregnant, and tired, I gave up. I told Ray to call anyone he wanted to. I was through. Ray called Joe, who came over and spent a couple hours with Ray, trying to convince me that all I needed to know was that Ray loved me. Ray and Joe left.

I began to feel insecure, asking myself if I would love anybody who acted the way I had just behaved. Ray was gone, the baby was kicking, and my only thought was, "Maybe this time I went just a little bit too far."

Somebody Lied

I found the list of numbers Ray had given me. It was the first time I had a need to use them. Calling every number on the list, I was unable to locate Ray. I looked at the number to be used only in an emergency and dialed. Della, Ray's wife, answered the phone, but later I was able to speak with Ray. By this time, through conversations with his employees, I could tell when he was high on heroin. He definitely was, and he responded in an unfamiliar way to me. Not making a great deal of sense, Ray told me that he was going to call my mother and inform her that I was pregnant. I was uncertain how to react—and even more uncertain about whether he would really call my mother. He knew that would hurt me more than anything in the world.

Ray did indeed call my mother. He told her that I was pregnant, that he loved her daughter, and that he intended to get out of his marriage honorably and then marry me. He also told my mother that I called his house and that he went into his marriage respectfully and he was going out respectfully.

But Ray's wife, Della, was listening on another extension and overheard the entire conversation. She heard Ray tell my mother that he truly loved me and that our child was truly conceived out of love.

Soon after these conversations, my phone rang. It was Della. Mrs. Ray Charles. She asked if Ray was there. I was surprised that Della knew of my existence, let alone my phone number. I told Della that he was not. Della then explained that she had put Ray out of the house because of his conversation with my mother. Della explained he should leave her house like a man or she'd be throwing all his belongings out for the neighbors to see. She continued, telling me that I was not the only one. There were many women in Ray's life. She had learned to live with them. She had put Ray out because Ray had said, "Mrs. Betts, I truly love your daughter."

Ray called, trying to wash his hands with my heart. He moved into a hotel. The game had become too deep even for him. He then departed for New York. Della continued to call me, her emotions vacillating wildly during the time Ray was away. She convinced me that she and Ray had no plans for divorce. I believed her and decided to take action. I told Della I believed

Ray was getting a divorce. Della then asked me if I remembered the twenty-five hundred dollars I received from Ray in New York. She told me that Ray had told her to send it to me for an abortion.

Somebody lied!

I Betts You're My Attorney

I informed Della that I would not be seeing her husband again. I also let Della know that it was my intention to have a legal paternity established for our child. I called the law offices of Betts and Loomis and made an appointment—a choice I made solely on the basis of the last name of Betts. The attorneys wanted some evidence of my relationship with Ray because there had been many false paternity claims against prominent Hollywood entertainers.

Attorney Peter Kaplanis went on a stakeout. He sat in front of my apartment building for several hours and eventually observed Ray enter.

Inside the apartment, Ray laid his head on my stomach and let me know he could hear and feel the baby. I wondered how I could possibly say good-bye to the man I loved and who was the father of my firstborn child. Yet I was driven by the words of Mrs. Ray Charles—that Ray had chosen to abort, to destroy what was living inside of me. I made the decision to move forward with mixed emotions.

I met with the attorneys again, and they agreed to take my case. They drafted papers for Ray to sign stating that he was the father of my child. Ray refused to sign them. Shocked by my decision, he became an angry contender in the battle that was about to begin.

I filed a paternity suit with the court. Ray was served a subpoena. I was penniless and without Ray's financial support through the remainder of my pregnancy. Knowing within myself that he would not want our child to suffer, I called. He was colder than ice. I refused to accept that from him.

With two friends, I drove to Ray's house. I knocked on the door. Della answered and told me that Ray would not see me. I waited in the car with my friends until Ray came out with Joe Adams about four hours later. I confronted Ray, and he agreed to give me some money. Joe Adams delivered the money to my apartment later that evening.

The Biggest Scandal in Showbiz

Uncle Todi had accepted a job with the Los Angeles Board of Education and moved his family to California. For support through this difficult time, I moved into a spare bedroom in their home.

I learned from some of Ray's friends that he was angry with me for not trusting him and not doing things his way. Ray had tremendous resources at his disposal with which to fight this suit. He hired a team of detectives to investigate my background in an attempt to find something incriminating.

My pregnancy became increasingly difficult. I became ill and would not eat or leave the house. Confused and distraught, I went into my bedroom and dialed Ray's number just to hear his voice. He was still not accepting any of my calls.

Physically ill and emotionally drained, I locked myself in the bathroom. Pregnancy had given me long, beautiful fingernails. Scraping the walls with my fingernails, I watched as they broke, replacing an unbearable pain for another I could deal with. Was it really over?

A pretrial was scheduled for August of 1963. Ray and his wife, Della, appeared in court together—I was too overwrought to attend. At the pretrial hearing, I was denied any financial support from Ray, but I was granted quick-date on the court docket. The paternity suit was slated for January of 1964, and the publicity surrounding what was termed by Sepia *magazine as "the biggest scandal in show business history" began.*

I Can't Have My Cheesecake and Eat It, Too

Ray's team of detectives began a relentless investigation—questioning anyone and everyone having any association with me. I had very limited resources. My attorney, Peter Kaplanis, informed me that I needed to do as much "legwork" as possible on my own. This meant I needed to acquire statements from my friends and associates and provide the attorneys with a list of people willing to testify to the relationship I had with Ray. I was surprised to discover the reluctance some of my friends and others presented, afraid of Ray Charles and his power. Most offered very little assistance, unwilling to testify against Ray unless they were under subpoena.

Peter was anxious to question Ray and was granted a court order to do so. Informed by Ray's attorneys that Ray was busy with an engagement on the East Coast and could not come to Los Angeles for a deposition, Peter flew to New York to take Ray's deposition in a very plush New York City hotel suite. My attorney observed that we were quite a pair. The sadness was profound in both of us. I felt good that he was as miserable as I was. Ray was then required to take a blood test. I only wanted the blood test to prove that Ray was the father. Even in my determination to counteract

Ray's stubbornness, I almost decided at that point it wasn't worth it. I only wanted to go on about my life with a child who did not have to ask who her father was.

Sheila was born on September 29.

The cheesecake photos that Barbara and I had taken now surfaced. The editors of Sepia magazine informed Peter that they had purchased the pictures but were willing to turn them over to us if I would agree to grant them an interview. I gave them an interview—the only one I ever granted. Once Ray's attorneys were contacted about my interview, the game was on. Ray came back with an interview of his own. Peter and I then learned that Earl had sold the photographs to any and all interested buyers. This was of great concern to my uncle Todi. He was putting his position on the line as a highly acclaimed educator. He did not want scandal in his life.

Of course, the attorneys wanted to play up my naïveté and innocence. It was no secret that in 1963, having an illegitimate child by anyone was disturbing, let alone a blind man who was married and a living legend. Once the news media had a story, it became necessary to isolate myself within the cocoon of my family. Roommates, best friends, and acquaintances (those who could reach me) wanted to convince me Ray Charles would not be named the father of my child through the court system. Who did I think I was?

I became increasingly depressed. I would sit in my room for hours, rocking Sheila, thinking about Ray, and wondering how all this could have happened. For my own welfare as well as Sheila's, Doctor Foster—not relinquishing his friendship and professional care from me—conferred with Uncle Todi and Aunt Ann.

Ringling Brothers Take Second Place in the Circus—No Women Allowed in the Center Ring

The paternity suit began on January 13, 1964. When I arrived at the Los Angeles County Courthouse, I was mobbed by reporters. With the help of Uncle Todi and my attorneys, I was able to make it indoors, only to be mobbed by more reporters. The suit had become a media circus. I refused to make a statement.

A predominantly male jury was selected.

A senior partner of the Betts and Loomis law firm assisted Peter in presenting my case. Ray's attorneys presented the cheesecake photographs into evidence, trying to portray me as the "playgirl" of the sports world.

Overwhelmed because Ray had asked for a jury trial and discovering Ray's defense had paid witnesses to testify, Peter insisted on my parents taking the stand. My mother, the only one with a testimony, was afraid to fly. My father said that he would be there if he had to walk. They both came. Daddy was detrimental. His emotions were out of control. During recess he screamed, "I'll shoot him just like I do those squirrels and rabbits back in Cambridge!" The circus was in full force.

Witness after witness was called, but nothing damaging about me was revealed. Mrs. Herman, the housemother from the Phillis Wheatley Home, testified that she kept a record of all the girls' menstrual cycles. When she was unable to produce her "record," she was laughed out of court—even Ray found her amusing.

Ben Ramsey testified but refused to say anything bad about me. He later revealed to me that he was paid to testify against me but couldn't. He told me, "I don't care what Ray's people do to me."

My mother testified about Ray's telephone conversation with her. She told the courtroom that Ray informed her of my pregnancy, that he had said, "I truly love your daughter. I wish to get out of my marriage honorably and then marry her." Ray denied everything when he took the stand.

I was called to testify and was questioned for many hours. I had become very ill. I was unable to eat. Dr. Foster took me to the courthouse cafeteria, telling my parents that I was his for a moment. Once in the cafeteria, he explained, "Even if it's Jell-O, put something in your stomach." Dr. Foster handed me a tuna fish sandwich and tried to force me to eat it. "What do you think this is about? I am Ray's friend, but believe me, he is here to win!"

I couldn't comprehend that word "win." I placed the sandwich in my pocket and told him I would eat it later. I felt I was the loser no matter what!

Mama's Baby—Daddy's Maybe

Ray and I were ordered to come before the jury and bring our daughter so that they could determine the resemblance between her and Ray. The jury was giving me the sign of victory from every direction. Holding Sheila, I broke into tears. Handing her to Ray, I knew that this was not the right way for her to have her first experience with her father. The word "win" became more of a joke than ever. I ran from the courtroom, leaving them in each other's arms.

On January 20, 1964, eight days after the trial had begun, the jury determined Ray Charles was Sheila's father. On that day, Ray's absence from the courtroom was noticeable to everyone.

Upon hearing the verdict, Judge Scott looked at me and said, "I find it hard to believe that anyone can be as naive as you claim to be. If it had been my decision to make, I don't think this would have been the outcome!"

Peter ran to the telephone to call his wife—a young man sharing his victory with his partner. Having forgotten about the tuna fish sandwich I had put in my pocket the previous day, the one Dr. Foster had tried to force me to eat, my clothes smelled horribly. In the phone booth with Peter, that smell was the only comment I had to make about the victory.

The foreman of the jury then came over to my father and me and said, "Miss Betts, we deliberated for fifteen minutes, and fourteen of those was trying to figure out who the foreman was going to be!"

Shortly thereafter, a reporter for The New York Times approached me and said, "I would just like to compliment you on the dignity and class you have shown throughout this situation. Miss Betts, it was obvious that you were totally honest and truthful. You gave me the impression that you were incapable of even telling the smallest lie. If I had been sitting up there and you had said that I was the father of your child, I would have to question any claim that it wasn't true!"

The day after the decision was reached, Ray and I, with our attorneys, met in court with Judge Scott to decide the amount of child support. Judge Scott, being very much in Ray's favor, instructed Ray and his attorney to step outside and decide what they felt the settlement should be.

A monthly amount of four hundred dollars was agreed upon for Sheila's child support. The judge stipulated that all the monies had to be administrated by a trust established with the Bank of America. Ray was granted visitation rights with the stipulation that he inform me with a written notice three days in advance. Unknown to me, Peter Kaplanis also agreed to a clause stating that I could not leave the state of California with Sheila until Sheila reached the age of twenty-one. I signed the agreement. When I learned of the travel restrictions that had been imposed on me, I was livid. Peter had sold me out!

I left the courtroom and was instantly surrounded by the press in the hallway. I overheard Ray tell reporters, "As far as I'm concerned, this child will be just like a foreign child I support." Emotions are no guarantee for truth. Shortly thereafter, Ray told me he received a call from his only living *relative, his aunt, and she asked him, "That lady in the* Jet *magazine holding that little baby . . . do you think that baby is yours?" Ray told her, "Yes, ma'am, I do." His aunt responded by saying, "Well, good! I'm glad you do, 'cause if it ain't yours, it's your father's, and he is dead! She looks exactly like you— like you just spit her out!"*

Sheila and I moved out of Uncle Todi's house into an efficiency apartment. Upon moving in, we were immediately asked to move by the management. Unlike me, rarely perceived as black, the little bundle inside the blanket was dark-complexioned. A young Jewish couple had befriended baby Sheila and me and then informed management after seeing Sheila. They were shocked at discovering she was black and intended to use every measure to evict us.

Discovering who I was, the management used the publicity from the paternity suit as an excuse to conceal their policy of no black residents. They informed me that my character was unacceptable. I was not strong enough nor did I have the desire to stay where anyone did not want me, especially after what I had just been through—the demeaning of my character.

Ray and his attorney, Henry Reese, refused to comply with the court order's visitation rights. Della, Mrs. Ray Charles, recalling Ray's conversation with my mother, remained angry and threatened. After all, Ray had said, "Miss Betts, I truly love your daughter," and the court had just sanctioned the legality of Ray's child with me. Della had told me on numerous occasions about Ray's other women. I could not understand why she held such animosity toward me. After all, I had become a willing part of her reform.

Together at Last: Della, the Swede, and Me

Even though the Wilshire area provided a feeling of safety and comfort, I realized it was time to go back to the neighborhood where I had been living with Ray. As painful as it was, it beat the hell out of living in racism and fear. I decided that anytime someone hated a child because of her color, there was nothing to do but leave.

After moving back to the neighborhood, Ray was as regular as clockwork visiting Sheila. Soon he was coming with intentions other than seeing his daughter. Ray wanted to resume his relationship with me. Ray began to visit us at his own convenience. On one occasion, I explained that the baby was asleep. Ray said, "No need to wake her. I would just like to sit here and talk to you."

During following visitations, Ray began to embrace me affectionately. Though I was not over the pain, I could not deny that I was still in love with this man. I could not afford to weaken. Only a fool would want to experience that pain again. Ray became so upset with me that he screamed and hollered at each visitation.

I was humiliated in front of my neighbors. They began to treat Ray's visitations as if it were a three-ring circus. They were the audience and Ray was the show.

On one occasion, Ray insisted on going into Sheila's bedroom and, touching everything in the room, Ray said, "I want to see what you are spending my money on."

At the end of another visit, Ray hollered from his car, "I ain't takin' care of no woman I ain't sleepin' with and givin' her my money."

Doing just a tad better at the conclusion of his next visit, Ray hollered, once again from the car, "I hope you fall in a river and drown!"

Ray's attorney, who was driving, shook his head and drove off.

I invited my minister to help keep everything smooth and insisted that Ray keep his three-day notice before coming over.

After the paternity suit, I was terrified living in L.A. Once, people threw their clothes at me in the Laundromat. I couldn't even get in a cab where they weren't talking about the Ray Charles paternity suit. I was taking Sheila to a checkup after she had been sick. We got in the cab and the driver said, "Hey, remember that Sandra Betts–Ray Charles paternity suit?"

I said, "Oh, I might have read something about that."

"You know, I drove her to court. When she called Yellow Cab, she told them, 'I don't want nobody taking me to court but that one driver.' That was me! I had her and that baby."

"You did?" I said. "Whatever happened?'

"Well, Ray Charles has to get up off that money—that's what happened."

Inside Dr. Foster's waiting room, I found myself with Della, little Bobby, and Rita the Swede. Had this situation occurred prior to the paternity suit, I would have been very uncomfortable, but I had removed myself completely from that little triangle. The attitudes that Della and Rita may have had at the moment were only an amusement to me and certainly did not compare to the pain and profound loss the court experience had left me with. I was truly beyond that pettiness. Dr. Foster was more affected by the situation than I was. When I finally saw him, he said, "Now you know my receptionist knows better than that. When I looked out and saw all three of you sitting there, I couldn't believe it! My receptionist also makes my appointments, and she has got to do better than that!"

"If you think that's bad, you aren't going to believe what happened to me!" I said as I proceeded to tell him the story about the cab driver.

He said, "I hope you told that man who you were! People ought to quit. I'm sorry, but I think I can do you one better about how dumb I can be. I was on my way home from the office the other day, and I stopped at Ray's house. When I walked through the door into the living room, Ray was sitting at his piano with two or three other guys standing around. I heard them mention Sarah Vaughan. So I just butted in and said, 'Speaking of Sarah Vaughan, who dresses her? She looks awful!'

"Ray struck a chord on the piano and said, 'Could you repeat that one more time, Doc? I didn't hear you.'

"I said, 'She's the worst dressed woman I've ever seen! She looks bad! She's the worst dresser—she just looks awful!'

"Ray says, 'Just so I'm sure who you're talkin' about, Doc, could you repeat that one more time?'

"Now, I'm not crazy, Sandy. I'm figuring around about this time something isn't making sense. I could feel my face getting hot.

"Ray starts laughing. 'Well, Doc, why don't you ask her husband here? He's standing right behind me!' I thought I would fall through the floor. Why can't people just learn to keep their mouth shut! I wanted to find a hole in the floor to fall through! And then Sarah's husband asked me if I could give him a ride downtown! The last thing in the world I wanted to do was to ride downtown with him in my car. Of course, I told him that it would be no problem. Sandy, I'm telling you, you should have said something to that cab driver. I guess you never know who you are talking to!"

We both laughed and laughed and laughed.

Busted! Confusion Is My Bed Partner

My mother was involved in an automobile accident in Ohio. My nerves were shattered. I went to Doctor Foster. "Dr. Foster. I need to go home and see my mother. Ray will not let me go. The court order he has states that I cannot leave the state of California until Sheila is twenty-one. Now, that is very hard for me to accept. Dr. Foster, I might as well be in prison. The only difference is that my prison is the whole state of California. Dr. Foster, I know Ray loves me. But this is possession—not love! I will not be governed by money. The Bank of America has told me that if I leave, I will not be able to receive the check from the trust." Not revealing what I was going to do, I asked him, "Do you really think I would get in trouble if I left?"

"Not only do I think, I know! Sandy, Ray Charles is a very stubborn man. You have to do what the court has ordered you to do!"

I once again asked Ray to permit me to leave.

Ray said, "No deal! You wanted the court to control our life. Well, I have a court order, in case you don't know. All I have to say is, 'Ask the court.' You like the court. Ask the court."

I explained to Ray that it would be so wonderful for our daughter to be around her grandparents, her many aunts and uncles, hundreds of cousins, and would he please give the okay for us to go?"

Ray said, "Our daughter don't need nothing but me and you. It only took me and you to bring her in here. She don't need nothin' else."

Turning away from Ray, I knew I was leaving.

I booked a champagne flight to Las Vegas connecting into Ohio, but as fate would have it, I was busted! Dr. Foster. The chances he'd be on that plane were frightening!

As I moved down the aisle heading for my seat, Dr. Foster was staring right into my face! "Sandy Betts!" he almost shouted, "What are you doing? I thought we talked about this!"

I said, "Please, Dr. Foster, don't say anything. I'm going home!"

After we had conversed during the flight, Dr. Foster's final words were, "Sandy, you are real special—but awful dumb."

Sheila and I returned to Cambridge. I got a job working nights in a factory in order to support Sheila and myself. I resumed an old friendship with Cecil Smith, who quickly fell in love with me. I did not respond to Cecil—he was an older bachelor who bragged about his women. There was nothing about that life that attracted me. I was not in love with Cecil. I tried to keep him at a distance.

Eight months had elapsed since my flight from Los Angeles. On New Year's Eve, I spent the night with Cecil, and we made love. The following Friday, I received a call from Peter Kaplanis stating Ray knew where I was and had obtained a court order for Sheila to be returned to Los Angeles. A court-appointed custodian would be flying to Ohio on Monday for that purpose.

I became frantic. My mind was in complete confusion. I had made good my promise to Della, that I would not see her husband again. I'd read the article where Ray said his concern was money. I gave them both what they wanted. I stayed away from Ray and certainly was receiving nothing from *him in support of our daughter. I had no recourse but to return to Los Angeles with Sheila. I was working the graveyard shift, and after paying my babysitter, I did not have enough money for an unplanned plane fare to Los Angeles. Cecil gave me the necessary money, and Sheila and I were on a flight to Los Angeles Saturday morning. I did it their way, and it wasn't enough. They were calling me. Confusion was my bed partner.*

*   *   *

Mom! Dad! Why? I rested my elbows on the table, placed my hands on my head, and leaned over, trying to control the uncontrollable. I cried silently.

"What's your problem?" It was an inmate passing my cell, seeing my tears.

I just looked at her. *What can I say to that—comin' from where I come from?* I thought, and I started laughing. I couldn't stop. There was no way, comin' from where I come from.

CHAPTER 7

BLAST FROM MY PAST

*. . . But God came along
and told me just to leave my past behind. Now!*

—*KEVIN L,*
SOULED OUT

I WENT TO DINNER unaccompanied by anyone from my quad, wondering what my life would have been like if Mom and Dad had married each other. I stared at a plate of spaghetti in front of me as though I were studying tea leaves at the bottom of a cup, capable of finding answers to that which haunted me through divination of pasta noodles on a plate. I wanted to talk to someone from my family. *Spaghetti*, I thought. *No one made spaghetti like Mom.* Had she been alive, I would have ditched the spaghetti and called her right then and there. She would have accepted a collect call from me without hesitation. I desperately wanted to talk with my father, but another collect call to him was something I was not willing to attempt. I did not want to risk further rejection. Now that I was working, I knew in a couple weeks I could purchase a phone card. I would call him on my own dime. Oddly, that thought encouraged my appetite.

I picked up my fork, lifting my head to a sea of khaki uniforms. Within a giant mess hall filled with hundreds of inmates, I knew fewer than the fingers on one hand. That is all I had to count on. As I twirled noodles with my fork, the oral grunting sounds of the girl sitting across from me grabbed my attention. She was shoveling the spaghetti into her mouth as if she hadn't eaten in weeks.

"Witch," the inmate sitting next to me said to her, "what are you doin'?"

Immediately her feeding frenzy was arrested. Within a frozen face and open mouth, a fistful of noodles and sauce dangled over her lower lip and chin. She looked comical, like a George Lucas *Star Wars* creature hailing from another planet. I was about to laugh.

"Who taught you how to eat? You're jackin' up with my dinner!" Glaring back, Spaghetti Face responded in a pasta-induced muffle, "Go to where the sun don't shine!" The noodles began swaying to the rhythm of her words. "Don't mess with me!"

She kept eye contact with her challenger as she sucked in the protruding noodles like an insect retracting its feeding tube. The remnants of spaghetti left on her plate insignificant for her to trifle with, she got up almost instantly. Turning to the inmate who had criticized her, this time with a foodless mouth, "I've kicked the mess out of men for less than that. You watch your mouth and your back, witch! When I get back—'cause I'm coming back, right back to this here spot—you better be gone."

If that were not enough to ruin the thought of food, her absence across the table revealed Lisa, the virus spreading the Ray Charles crap, one table away. She was pointing her finger at me in a discussion with a couple of her friends. Showing no concern, her eyes locked with mine, she continued with her self-appointed mission of disseminating the gossip over my questionable ancestry. I lost all desire to eat and threw the towel in on dinner. *It wouldn't have been as good as my mother's anyhow,* I thought. *And no, Lisa, you did not win this little battle!* I decided to go to the exercise area and get some air.

Without one bite of dinner, I stood abruptly. My dinner companion could not resist a parting comment. "What in the world is wrong with you? Am I the only normal one in this hole?"

I left without a word, thinking how easy the *good-bye* is when there is no *hello*—the brightest thought within my day. Just last weekend, I was running around the track with optimism; now, avoiding confrontation was the best I could do. Tread water. Stay afloat. Mom was dead. Matt and Becky had closed my communication with my children, and I had closed the door on anything good in my life. Unable to lift my spirit, I paced about and decided to head back to my room, write my father, and get a grip.

After I took a shower, I grabbed pencil and paper and followed through with that letter. I told my father how sad it was to see others who actually had a better life inside prison than they did on the outside—"three hots and a cot." There was more than one inmate who thought this was a great life. Understand that. Prison was a good life for a great many of these women. That's how bad their lives were on the outside. Clean clothes. Three meals. They were sad when they had to go back to life on the outside, back to the same crap. I told him I needed to understand why I had abandoned everything to come to this, realizing I had to find a way to quit and make it stick.

With the rumor that Ray Charles's genes were roaming about the prison, the next few weeks rolled by with little change in my disposition. I became accustomed to the routine at the warehouse and learned not to rock the boat. The main warehouse unit had a thirty-foot ceiling, perhaps higher. The top shelving stored the good stuff, twenty-five feet off the floor—the stuff you had to spend most of your paycheck on: cosmetics, work boots, hair products—the stuff that would be easy to steal and sell inside the quad. No stairways or ladders; they were too dangerous. It was forklifts and a cherry picker like the telephone and power companies use, a small crane with a semi-enclosed area in which you stood. By the third or fourth day, I had the cherry picker down. I actually looked forward to the little rides. Like at those small county fairs, the carnival so dear to my heart, I became both rider and carny. *I could work the midway,* I thought. An imaginary fellow carny appeared in my mind, inquiring of my training and the very first show I had worked. *Cherry picker, federal prison, Bryan, Texas.* It was all right with me—a Ferris wheel or Tilt-a-Whirl along with some fresh-spun cotton candy could never be removed from my heart.

I came to expect some form of drama. There was always some nonsense going on with an abundance of inmates willing to fight over a trifle and with little provocation. Roberta was always talking to Crenshaw about her infidelities. She was serving five years, and it was a way for her to pass the time and connect with something outside the walls. Prison could easily become a lifestyle if one were not careful. Roberta was heavy metal and a big-time meth dealer prior to getting busted. I recalled the conversations we had about the gay thing and her attitude back then. "I'll kill anyone coming up on me with that bull!" And now she had flipped that entire script on me. She tried to hide it from me, but when we were hanging out as much as we were, such things naturally reveal themselves. In the past, I had told Roberta this was the first and last time for me. My conviction was equally as hollow as hers. As for me, I could not keep a glass pipe out of my mouth. Hurt and pain were everywhere as far as I could see.

Even on a cloudless day, I saw no sun. I knew no shine. It had been several weeks since I had received mail, continuing to write to my father every day without response. I was frightened by the thoughts within my depression, asking myself what would really happen if I took off and ran. After my first fifteen-dollar paycheck, I bought a phone card and called Yolanda, Dad's secretary. I asked her if my letters were reaching him. She said, "Yes, Sheila. I have read every single letter you have sent him."

Well, what's up with no response? In a true hour of need, there is nothing more depressing than learning the lesson of calling "wolf" too often, discovering you had burnt all your bridges or they had been swept away by the flood. I was writing Dad about my feelings, what I was hoping to gain from this experience, and how I was resolved this was it for me: the last time I would be incarcerated, the last time I would fight with my addiction. Crack had taken complete control of my life. Up to this point, it had been just a game—"if you play, you pay"— the big-time hard stuff. This time, however, it was big-time hardship; within my letters, I was trying to reach out to him to make that clear.

Fear and the sense of being utterly lost were taking a toll on me. No letter from Dad, and every night I cried myself to sleep. *How many more times do I have to ask him to forgive me?*

I hated myself because of my drug addiction. Once so addicted, the drug called me. I needed to love me more than I loved crack, and when you are using the drug, that's impossible. That's the trick. As long as I was high, I didn't care if anyone knew my truth, especially me. Now within sobriety, I felt I had created such a mess with my life that any love others held for me must surely be gone. Looking for love from someone, from anyone, I became convinced it no longer existed. How do you get over that? I had to deal with all of it—my complete failure.

There were a few people who shared something of their lives with me, coming to my door and caring about me in a superficial way.

"What's up, Sheila? How you doing?"

"Why you being so weird? What's up with that?"

"Can't talk or walk with nobody? Can't show up to play cards and games no more?"

I was in such a blue funk, I didn't want to talk about anything. The issue of whether or not I was Ray Charles's daughter had died down, and for that I was grateful. I had become completely fed up with everybody's bullcrap, including my own!

"I'm feeling depressed about everything, having succumbed to the adversity of my life."

"You see. Sho nuff, that heffa thinks she's betta than us—one of those propa niggas—'having succumbed to adversity'!"

"It ain't like that. It was how I was raised. I can't help that. Can you?"

It was my one and only attempt to respond. I should have known better. My best friend back in Cambridge, Marcia, took it upon herself to teach me how to talk "black." It angered me. My grandfather, Grandpa Betts, was very strict, and every member of his family was required to speak proper English. It was drilled and beaten into us to speak properly and address others with respect. Then there was Aunt Evette and her mother's finishing school. "School! Oh, she needs finishing school if anyone ever did, Sandra. I'll call my mother, and we will take care of this immediately! My mother will teach her how to be a proper young lady."

I could have protested, but it would have been to no avail. Proper table manners, how to walk with correct posture while balancing a book on my head, proper pronunciation and enunciation, correct telephone etiquette—the entire nine yards. Of course, being a Betts and Ray Charles's daughter, I had private lessons. The other black families were not to know I needed the services of finishing school. Both blacks and whites had it in for us Bettses. Grandpa Betts and his three brothers owned the entire hill, Betts's Hill. It sat above Black Bottom, the black ghetto of Cambridge where all the other black families lived.

Conversely, the families I would be introduced to through friendships with white girls would lead me to hear a frequent response to the question, "Who's the nigger?"

"She's all right. She's just like a white girl."

I would hear that and want to die. I got it from both sides, a characteristic of society that rang true inside and outside of prison: on one side, acting as if you were better than other blacks; on the other, not good enough to be around whites. Either way, both sides saw you as a *nigger*. There could be no win in the game except for the one to be found within me—so much for those who came by to cheer me up. They only added to my depression.

It was Friday. At the end of every week, we had to fill the orders from the commissary to ensure it was fully stocked for the weekend. Riding the cherry picker up twenty feet, I was anticipating mail from someone. My birthday was a few days off, and I was counting on someone remembering. When the afternoon shift ended, I was the first out the door. Marching toward the quad like a POW awaiting news from home, I realized I had set myself up for a big letdown if no mail were to come. I waited with bated breath, sitting in the commons during mail call, hoping for news about Jeanna. I distanced myself from my surroundings, consumed with my own agenda and wanted nothing from anyone around me.

"Sheila Robinson, 03318-041."

Hooray! I got mail! Great! I was thrilled walking up to the guard's desk, even more so when I saw a huge manila envelope bulging from its contents. I looked at the return address: Bev Paulson, a friend of my mother. Though I was hoping it would be someone from my family, my happiness didn't dissipate. I did use the minor disappointment to conceal my joy, unwilling to be perceived as someone who would gloat over such a thing. When you got mail, you were someone important in the eyes of the other inmates.

Like a child on Christmas morning, I returned to the table excited, ripping the package open before sitting down. The girl next to me was someone I knew informally. We had played a game of cards together just the other night, watched some TV to pass the time. She was familiar with the rumor I was Ray's daughter. I dumped the package's contents and saw my past displayed in pictures upon the table—my father and me, my children, and friends. There was a copy of the *National Enquirer*, the one in which I had hit the front page, published somewhere between the issue of Jimmy Carter fathering alien-human hybrids and Nostradamus predicting the end of the world. There it was, proof in the pudding.

"Ray Charles really *is* your father!"

I paid no attention to her. How stupid was that?! With computers today, you could splice ten different people together or turn an anorexic into that fattest person in the world. A picture could not prove a darn thing. It sure wouldn't to me. Photographic evidence? On the table, as clear as day, lay a large photograph of Dad and me, close together with smiles and shine. I stared at it in front of me, wondering who we were!

I opened the *Enquirer* that revealed my dirty laundry to the world. I reasoned she had sent me a copy as a reminder of why I was here. *It wasn't necessary, Bev,* I thought, as I began to reread the article in spite of myself. Whoever provided the information to the *Enquirer* had been paid. We looked into it. Twenty-five hundred dollars. I felt they could have held out for more and preferred the informant remain a mystery.

According to the *Enquirer*, I went around stealing mail as a part of the world's greatest mail theft ring. Though I was close to the people involved in the operation, I wasn't in on it! I had no clue what they were about. I had people at my house who were friends of friends. The feds found stolen mail in my apartment, mail stolen by others. I didn't know what was occurring within my residence, and for that I was guilty, guilty through association. The federal agents knew more than I did. Most of the details I knew about that operation, both then and now, I learned from the feds. My guilt, what I could not forgive myself for, was my crack addiction.

"Ray Charles' Greatest Heartbreak"—hearsay from someone claiming to have heard Dad make such a pronouncement. The *Enquirer* never interviewed my father directly about the matter. Of course, these allegations broke his heart. The article revealed my crack cocaine habit— she's a junkie—she's homeless now—blah, blah, blah! The moment it appeared, people were asking me, "How can you do this to your father?" while I was thinking, "Forget that! How could I do it to myself?"

There were pictures of my father and me at the Mall of America. It was a private party, a celebration of the grand opening. Dad had sung "America." Mom took the pictures backstage while I tried to fake myself through all of it. Afterward, she informed me Dad didn't want to hang out with me. "Ray is not signing any autographs or pictures, not anything with the public. He wants to go back to the hotel and relax with me."

"That really sucks, Mom."

That's the night my mom gave me the speech about not taking it personally. "Your dad has never been much for his children. With him, it's all about the women."

Well, thanks, Mom, like that would soothe my heart. I felt as if I had been raped. There were people walking around who felt a right to be there more than I did, his daughter! Bigwigs at the private party, those who would receive the privilege of greeting him, able to make the claim, tell others how they shook his hand or told Ray Charles how much they loved him.

Mom took my children with her to Ray's hotel room, and Lee, a friend of the family, took pictures there. I was not invited to go. Dad had done his thing with me. He didn't feel well and was taking a red-eye flight back to L.A. that evening. He wanted to get going. We hugged each other, and it was, "See ya later." I felt hurt. This was no family picnic; this was no family.

Whenever at a public function involving my father, Joe Adams, my father's domineering business manager, created the impression that he held a passionate love for Ray's children—for all of us. That was a transparent front to everyone but the general public. In my opinion, Joe's ego was bigger than my father's, and, for me, that is saying something. Joe always wanted to be the star, the one out front, not the one behind the shades.

I went on a binge for three days after the mall episode. I was always a Daddy's little girl. I would save things: a napkin and fork from one of the times at a hotel with Dad. Mom would crack up laughing at me. She would say, "You are saving a plate? You *are* him. Are you nuts?" Mom was rough like that. She kicked my tail but really wanted to kick my dad's. She wouldn't. When she was in his presence, she did the same thing I did—go into that little girl voice. "Well, hi, Ray!" When he would call, her entire persona would change. I looked at the pictures of Dad with my two kids. I wasn't present. I wasn't invited to the party. Talk about touching a nerve. I couldn't take it anymore. Once again, I was forced to deal with my environment.

"You are really Ray's daughter! Let me see the pictures."

The crowd had gathered, and I really didn't want to deal with it. Just moments ago, I had been the insane idiot claiming Ray Charles for a father; now, I was something bigger than life. Instantly, a crowd formed around me. I had to play like everything was cool. I departed the area as soon as I could, headed back to my room to deal with my past privately. I wanted to understand Mom's point of view. I was ready for it, and it was waiting for me back in my cell within the pages of her story.

*   *   *

It was always so much easier being Sheila. Trying to explain my relationship with Ray just complicated matters.

Ray was going to be the featured artist at the grand opening of the Mall of America. Naturally, all of us wanted to be there. Under the pretense of being Sheila, I called the mall office and said, "Hi, this is Sheila Raye, Ray Charles's daughter. My father will be performing at the grand opening event, singing 'America.' I wanted to make sure I could get tickets. I know that promotional tickets are usually available for people associated with the performers."

Actually, I wasn't sure of this at all, and I wasn't concerned about a ticket for myself—I rarely went to Ray's performances. I did know that Ray was going to be the featured artist at the opening and that I wanted his daughter and granddaughter to be part of it. I also knew that the mall people would be thrilled to get a picture of Ray's granddaughter at Camp Snoopy, the mall's indoor amusement park.

The woman said, "I didn't know Ray Charles's daughter was in town."

"Yes, I'm here working on my music."

"Would you be willing to perform at the mall?"

"Oh my. I'd certainly need more than two or three weeks' advance notice to go on any stage with my father. I'd want to be extraordinarily well prepared for something like that. I'll have to think about that one. But what I really want to know right now is if I'll be able to obtain some tickets."

"Well, let me get back to you. If I may have your number, I'll get back to you in a half hour."

I gave her my number, thanked her, and hung up.

The phone rang but a few minutes later. "This is Sherry Simon. Let me speak to Sheila Raye."

"Sherry Simon," I thought. "Hadn't the Simon brothers built the mall?"

I said, "This is Sheila Raye."

"Now, let me just ask you something. If you're the daughter of Ray Charles, why don't you get your own tickets?"

I had to use all my self-control to stay calm. When you deal with power people, you can't be yourself. I hated having to do things this way, but the fact was that Ray hadn't called yet. I said, "My—to whom am I speaking? Is there someone else I could speak with? Because I don't know why you would talk to me like that."

"I own the mall."

"Then why do you think I would call and lie, being that my father is going to be performing? Why would I represent myself as his daughter if I weren't? What sense would that make?"

"And who do you think you are that you can call up here two weeks before the opening and ask to perform?"

"I don't want to perform! I never even thought of performing there! When I called for tickets and explained what I was doing in the city, your assistant asked me if I'd perform."

"That isn't the story I heard!"

"Well, somebody there is advising you wrong."

"Nobody here is aware that Ray Charles has a daughter in town. It doesn't make sense to me. If you were his daughter, you wouldn't need anybody to give you any tickets."

"Well, my father doesn't operate like that. When it comes to money and the things it can buy, like tickets, he feels that you should get your own. That's the way he is."

"Let me tell you, I've had more trouble dealing with Ray Charles than any entertainer I've ever had to work with. I've gone through hell!"

"Oh, who'd you deal with, Joe Adams?"

"Yes!"

"He's certainly been a thorn in my flesh in my association with my dad, but I'll tell you this: he's probably been the best thing that ever happened to my father. He truly cares about him."

That broke the ice a bit. We talked for several minutes in civil tones, and finally Sherry said, "Okay, I'll send you the tickets. Maybe I can hire you to perform here one day in your own name and to heck with your father."

"Now, I'd like that. Thank you, Sherry."

I hung up, enormously relieved that everyone was going to be able to go. But an hour later, the phone rang again.

"Hello."

"Is this Sheila Raye?" The woman's voice was unfamiliar.

"Yes."

"Sherry Simon asked me to call you back and tell you that if you want tickets to the mall opening, you'll have to contact Joe Adams at Ray Charles Enterprises in Los Angeles. I'll give you that number."

I said, "How about I give you the number? 737-8000. Look, all I want is some tickets."

"I'm sorry," the voice said flatly. "Good-bye."

"Well," I thought, hanging up the telephone, "no tickets!" I still hadn't heard from Ray. I went through the motions and called Joe Adams's secretary, but I knew he wouldn't return my call.

I was angry with Ray. He should have called by now. The mega mall opening was no minor league event. It was being broadcast over satellite, and everybody who was anybody was going to be there. Not that it meant anything to me, but his daughter and granddaughter deserved to share in the celebration.

Why couldn't he care enough to call and arrange for tickets for us? It was no secret to him—we couldn't afford to pay seventy-five dollars per ticket to go to the opening of some glorified shopping center. As close as we were to him, we did not have his money.

* * *

Things were becoming clear to me. I could not be angry with Mom. It wasn't more than six months ago that I had found myself in the hospital pretending to be her. And now, here I was in federal prison and she was gone. I loved her in spite of the collective insanity, perhaps more because of it. I began rummaging through some of the other photographs. There were quite a few from my trip to Las Vegas—Pat, Ray Junior, Ray, and me. It was my 32nd birthday and I was going to spend it with Dad while he was performing at Caesars Palace. There he was, in front of thousands of people saying, "Here's a birthday song for my little girl!" That was the best birthday present ever! I was in seventh heaven, and all my heart could say was "Dad, I love you! Forgive me for ever thinking anything but."

I was flipping cartwheels. Afterward, Pat and I went around Las Vegas with my brother, Ray Jr., and some members of the Ray Charles Orchestra. We were all hanging out, and I was floating on clouds. We got VIP everywhere we went. It was more than a great moment. I had gone out there to bring him some music I was working on. Dad said, once again, that he would help me. That is why Pat and I were there.

I had met Pat in 1991, about two years after we moved to Minneapolis to record at Paisley Park. Money was getting tight waiting around to hear about a record deal. I answered a newspaper ad for a receptionist on the north side at Rob Lord & Associates, a mailing company. Pat was helping to manage there, and she hired me. I was impressed with how she dealt with the employees and how she handled the business. She also had a company of her own called Vision Holders, which would require her to fly all over the United Sates consulting on personnel selection and management. As a consultant, she would interview people and rearrange positions. After her work, those companies would call back and ask her to help with other projects. That impressed me. She knew what was needed to make things work. After Mom and I began having personal issues, it made sense to ask Pat to take over my professional career. Besides, Mom was drinking heavily. You can't go into a business meeting intoxicated. At that point, Mom just didn't care, and no one dared to bring it to her face.

It is also true my mother's spirituality just seemed to go out the window whenever money or alcohol was involved. Money has never been my motivator, but it was like a drug to me and the rest of my family. I was more concerned with love and acceptance. You can go off the deep end with that need, especially when you are seeking it from the wrong people. And that is when I began getting into the stupid stuff, the drugs. Nothing seemed to be working out. I had to fire my mom—I was through. She would no longer have anything to do with my career.

The way Pat handled everything was so completely different from my mother. Mom was forceful; she always felt she had to overpower the situation. There was no unified work relationship. With Pat, however, it was simple. If it works for you and it works for me, then it should work together. Mom lived in uproar; she liked and functioned with it. Pat's approach was very peaceful. Needless to say, Mom and Pat didn't jell at all. I don't know why no one ever really liked Pat. It's not as if she did anything wrong. Pat was really trying to help me—she had invested twenty-five thousand dollars of her own money into my career.

It was Pat who paid for the trip to Las Vegas. We were there for four days. When I came back, Mom was in bad shape—down to ninety pounds and telling everyone she had the flu. I had gone over to pick up Jeanna and Jamie. Matt wasn't around at that time, having entered the service. That's when I put Mom into detox. Then the whole family wouldn't talk to me. Of course, that made it easier for me to do my thing. I didn't care anymore. And, of course, that was all Pat's fault, too. I had consulted with Pat. Mom wouldn't go willingly, so I called the police. I was scared. She was puking everywhere, a near-empty half gallon of vodka beside her! Pat arrived before the police, and she drove Mom to the county detox.

There were some pictures of Mom, Dad, and me when Dad came to town by himself to perform with the Minnesota Orchestra. He loved that orchestra. And then there was a letter that my mom had written. I was not yet ready to handle looking at myself through the eyes of anyone close to me, especially her. I went back to the preface of her book to see my father through her eyes. I was safe with that. I needed only to love her, and I missed her beyond words. I was not ready to handle the hurt I had caused her. I just needed her love.

*   *   *

The greatest distraction I've had in life is what man has deemed love to be. Many inner battles I've waged attempting to conform and adhere to the preconceptions and conditions I've placed on love. Conditional love conflicts with everything I know love to be and chafes the very core of my heart's experience and understanding. Love has no need for words. Love is. Love does not ask. Love does not control, and we have no control over whom we fall in love with. For me, it just happened to be a man named Ray Charles.

It wasn't until our relationship had become firmly established that I realized Ray was not going to meet my expectations of love. Through his music and career, Ray has given his life to the world. His professional life always comes first. I've learned that if you need to be number one, you can only lose with Ray. You'd be a loser before you even started. I don't care to play second fiddle to the world, and I could never be a shadow. Never.

Ray is a man of wants and needs—the king baby. "I want what I want when I want it." I came to know and accept that about him. My head told me loving Ray was a no-win situation while my heart cried out that Ray was the one, that I belonged with him. The choice was clear. I have never been able to deny my heart.

I was brought up believing that everyone was good and could be trusted— in an idealistic cocoon. For some strange reason, I was never able to remove myself from the Betts girl consciousness. Feelings of love and usefulness substantiate life. My parents instilled that in me, and Ray affirmed it.

As my self-understanding evolved, I realized that my personal development would be incomplete if I remained attached to Ray. Nothing was removed by loving him. Nothing was removed by living my life independent of him. It was my decision to play or not play in the world he lived in. I am not a victim.

My heart never separated itself from Ray. He respected me for holding true to my own personal knowledge. I am grateful for every moment of my life, every experience. Lacking one of them, I would not be who I am. I am not a victim.

Ray has always been there for me—even in the darkest hours. He has always connected, almost involuntarily, to the spirit of my life. He was the first person I called when I received word that my mother was dying of cancer. He was my first call again when my family was trying to reach a decision regarding my mother's surgery. When I received word of my mother's death, Ray and I were in the studio together, recording with our daughter.

No matter what our difficulties and conflicts, no matter how hard we tried to separate and distance ourselves from one another, we could not. Through it all, we have remained together.

* * *

I held on to my mother's words.

"BRAZOS II" came blaring out of the prison loudspeakers. It was time for dinner, and I was ready for that.

It hit me before I made it to the chow hall. Everyone was coming to me with the Ray Charles stuff. It was stupid. There was no escaping it. What was it about my dad? After dinner, I decided to head to the quad and the distraction of television.

As I entered the rec room, I heard, "Girl, you ain't gonna believe it. Your dad's on TV!"

It was an episode of *The Nanny* in which my father had appeared, an episode more than familiar to me along with the rest of the world. Everyone I met, high and low, knew that episode. It always creeped me out when I saw him on TV, in interviews, performances, commercials. I did not want to see him in the media or as an entertainer; I wanted him in person as my father. Even his voice on the radio was enough to make me cry. Whenever I was out in the street, even if I was in someone else's car, I would insist they turn the radio off or change the channel when one of his songs came on the air. No one seemed to understand that, within me, it was bittersweet to connect with my dad in that manner, through his voice. It was simultaneously soothing comfort and excruciating pain. Raw.

"Oh yeah! I've seen it," I said as I glanced at the TV. "Geez, I forgot something in my room. I'll see you guys later."

Upon returning to my cell, I had to share the pictures with my cellmates. "There's my mother, Sandy, and that's my eldest daughter, Jeanna, and her sister, Jamie. And that's my dad and me in Las Vegas."

After a moment, I told them I was tired and just wanted to read. They were understanding and left me to myself, giving me more latitude now that I was some sort of celebrity. I melted into my mother's story.

* * *

I was lying in bed on a cool, beautiful June morning, listening to a light rainfall outside. Our granddaughter, Jeanna, lay there next to me. For some reason, the warmest feeling came over me. As naturally as it was to breathe, I reached out and drew her to me, just as I would Sheila when she was a young child. Jeanna is dear to me—another part of Ray and myself.

Ray calls me the Universal Mother. He tells me, "You can't be a mother to everyone!"

When I see a need I am able to answer, I heed the call. It is not a matter of contemplation. It's not a matter of disciplined behavior. It is obedience to myself.

Holding Jeanna tenderly, I made a silent promise that I would always be there whenever she needed me.

The phone rang. I picked up the receiver and said, "Good morning."

"Yes, ma'am," came over the line.

"Oh my God. Ray, where are you?"

He said, "Don't worry about that, mama. Don't worry about that right now."

"Where are you?" I had to laugh to myself because a few months earlier, I had given him a hard time. I had told him that, after thirty years, I realized that he was definitely not flowers and candy, but he could certainly afford a phone call a few days in advance of his visits.

"Now I know the game," Ray said. "Before I get the wrath of Sandy, let's just hang up, and I'll call you right back."

I hung up. He sounded excited, and I didn't blame him. He was at a tremendous point in his career with the Pepsi commercials and his constant touring. I was so happy for him.

A minute later, the phone rang again. Picking it up, I said, "Good morning. Where are you, and what are you doing?"

He said, "I don't want to upset you. I know I should have called earlier. I just got in town on a corporate call for Pepsi. I'm out at the Airport Hilton, and I want to see you so bad. I don't want to make you mad. This thing just came up. I have to fly out tonight, so we won't have a great deal of time together. Now, I don't want you to be angry with me, but are you able to come out to the hotel?"

I thought, "Oh my God. I've got Jeanna. Who's going to watch her, and how am I going to get to the airport?" I didn't have a car or even money for a cab. I knew getting to see Ray was going to be next to impossible.

"Of course I can come to the hotel," I said. "Give me an hour."

"I'm glad, mama. Room 819. Hurry. I want to see you!"

I said good-bye and hung up. I thought for a minute and then called Sheila. "Good morning, honey. Guess what? Your dad is here. Can you come and get Jeanna so I can meet him at the hotel?"

There were a few seconds of silence on the other end of the line. Then Sheila said in her hard voice, "No, I can't. I won't. He didn't call me."

"Oh, Sheila, please don't do this to me. You know how your dad is. I can't make him be different. You're grown—you're not a baby. Don't put me between a rock and a hard place. He's coming right back to town in a few weeks, anyway. If he doesn't see you every time he visits, at least he calls you!"

"Well, he hasn't called me yet—and he probably won't once you two get together. I'll talk to you later, Mom," she said and hung up on me.

I had to stop at that point. This was not easy and was more than merciless, in prison revisiting the past through words of my mother's experience. I wanted to throw the manuscript down but was compelled to continue.

It took me several calls, but I was able to find a neighbor girl who was willing to stay with Jeanna while I went to visit Ray at his hotel. Now I had to figure out how I was going to get over to see him. After several more calls and another half hour on the phone, during which the babysitter arrived and amused herself by watching me become steadily more frantic, I finally reached Robert, a good friend of my son Kevin. Robert said he'd be happy to give me a ride and that he'd be right over. I hurriedly got dressed, gave the sitter some instructions, and impatiently waited for Robert to arrive.

An hour and fifteen minutes later, I was standing outside in the rain, still waiting. Rob had not shown up. (Quite a few people I know are like that. Their intentions are pure, but their follow-through is somewhat questionable.)

I had no money. The minutes were ticking away. I wanted to be with Ray. He was only six miles away—yet seemingly unreachable. Tears began to flow. Wondering what I was going to do, I started walking down the street.

A moment later, I heard a voice. "Hey, Mom, what's wrong?" It was Kevin, returning to the apartment.

"Kevin!" I said, "Ray's here, out at the airport, just until tonight. You were out and I couldn't find anyone to drive me, and I don't have any money for a cab."

Kevin sighed and shook his head. "You certainly have your problems hooking up with Ray. Come on. Get in the car; you're getting drenched."

Ray opened the door and let me into his hotel room. "You won't believe what I went through to get here," I began, then stopped what I was about to divulge. One look at him swept everything from my mind. I was back to love.

"I become so desperate when you're in town," I said. "My life becomes so crazy. I wouldn't miss an opportunity to see you."

"Well, mama," he said, "let me tell you, people would surely think I was crazy after all the battles we've been through if they knew I was seeing you. I still can't stray away from you." And, as if to himself, he said, "Silly boy. Such a silly boy."

"Ray? How much do you really want to see me?"

He smiled. "I can't believe you asked that question. You'd better ask yourself that one. You couldn't even get to me if I didn't want to see you. That's the way my life is." Then laughing, he said, "One thing I do appreciate—you always make it possible for me to get to you."

With that, he walked over to the bedside table and picked up the little telephone directory he carried with him. "You think I don't care where you are? Obviously, you can't read this. It's Braille." He leafed through the directory. "But you see this page and this page and this page? These are all your numbers. You change your phone number more than any person I know except for Aretha Franklin. She's the only one who can beat you!"

I had to laugh. Certainly, I've moved around a lot—had to move around a lot. But I've always landed on my feet spiritually, and I've always let Ray know how and where to contact me.

Still laughing, he said, "I just can't figure it out."

I couldn't respond to that. I didn't want him to figure it out. I couldn't afford a babysitter today. I was standing in the street in the rain, crying, and feeling like an idiot. I couldn't afford to take a cab to the hotel. (I have never felt poor—even while being evicted. I've never felt poor. Even when I am poor, I don't feel poor. I don't project that. I've never brought him that.)

Ray must have picked up on my feelings, and he said, "You know, mama, one thing that's real important about this life—know who you are. One thing about being in this business that I'm real comfortable with is that I don't allow them to take me up, and I don't allow them to take me down. I know who I am. I may not be on top of the charts, but I'm always there. I sail straight out. I don't waver. I'm always there. That's what I like about who I am. *They may tell me I'm a genius—I don't care. They may tell me I'm a dog—I don't care about that neither. I'm standing right where I am. Knowing who I am."*

I sat down in a chair. How many hotel rooms had we been in together, having a conversation just like this one? I was half-delighted, half-frightened. I said, "Ray, no matter how much time goes by, when we're together, it's always the same."

"Mama, when the love is pure, the love is pure. You can't corrode it. You can't cover it up. When it's pure, love comes to the top. I don't question it any longer."

I looked at him and had to shake my head. I felt like a schoolgirl—wide open and totally free. I felt completely obedient to where I was at the moment. I think that's what youth is all about.

"Ray," I said, "I'm fifty-one years old, but I feel like I'm eighteen."

"Is that something to complain about?" he said. He walked toward the bed. "I feel like I'm twenty-five when I'm with you." He was sixty-three.

I said, "Ray, you know it really hurts Sheila when you and I are together. She suffers because she loves you so much. She needs a dad, and you're her daddy. So what do I do?"

He lay down on the bed. I watched him try to relax. "Let me tell you one thing. This stuff between you and Sheila has to stop—NOW! It makes me crazy." He took a long, deep breath. "This may sound crazy to you, but I don't have much control over my schedule—it's so hectic. Half the time, Joe has to tell me what city I'm in. I just go where and when they tell me to go. Sometimes when I'm here, I have so little time, I just want to spend it with you. Sheila has to try to understand that."

I went over and lay down next to him. All I could do was reach out to him, try to make him understand me. I was ready to tell him things that I hadn't been able to in thirty-two years. I gently took his hand in mine and just held it. He became very quiet and still, just like always.

After a few minutes, his face fixed on the ceiling, he said, "Why? Why are you doing this? Why are you in Minnesota? You say you love me. I live in Los Angeles. I live in Los Angeles, and you're not there."

The answer was in my mind immediately. *You may live in Los Angeles, but you don't control me. I love you, but it's not enough for me to be only 10 percent in your life. It's just not enough.*

But I didn't answer in words. Instead, silently I moved to him. He responded, and we made love. Gently.

When it was over, we lay in each other's arms, contented for a long while. Finally he said, "I'm sorry, but I have to get going. Please don't be upset. I have this corporate stuff I have to deal with."

He got out of bed, cleaned up, dressed, and got his things together. I heard him call his valet and tell him he was ready to go.

Walking back over to the bed, he said, "Listen, I'll be back in Minneapolis in August. I have to do the opening of that mall. They want me to sing 'America.' One song, 'America.' Pretty short gig, huh? I'll get tickets for you and the kids, and I'll see you then if not before. I'll call you, okay?"

There was a knock at the door. "Yeah, sure, Ray," I said. "I love you."

"You, too," he said as he went to the door. I heard it open. "Good-bye, mama."

"Good-bye, Ray." And the door closed.

Everyone thinks that I'm so strong. I'm not really that strong. My heart hurts all the time. Sometimes I hurt so bad, I can't stand it.

"Mom," I thought to myself, "I love you, and I don't care. You will always be the rock of Spirit, strong and unbreakable." With that, I cried myself to sleep in her arms.

CHAPTER 8

WHO'S YOUR DADDY? RAY'S UP AND DOWN

Choose my instruction instead of silver
Knowledge rather than choice gold
For wisdom is more precious than rubies
And nothing you desire can compare with her

PROVERBS 8: 10, 11

A TIDAL WAVE of unwanted celebrity hit full force as everyone learned Ray was my father.

"What was it like growing up being the daughter of Ray Charles, being the daughter of somebody so famous?"

"How did he become blind?"

"Were he and your mom married?"

"How many brothers and sisters do you have?"

I never knew there were twelve of us. I only knew Ray Junior, Bobby, David, and Evelyn, so I would respond, "I have three brothers and a sister."

"How old was your mom when she passed away?" "Did your dad come to the funeral?"

"Does he know that you're here?" "Is he mad at you?"

"Is he going to come and see you?" "If he comes here, can I meet him?"

Everybody wanted to be my friend, to hang out, seeking answers to a world I knew nothing about. They didn't understand, unable to imagine my life had been similar to their own, running and hiding from pain and poverty. Drugs. Dope. I could tell stories about seeing Dad for a couple days, or a day, or a couple of hours. A splash and a flash were all I knew of him, and that was it. What did I have to tell them? Why can't I just be me?

Leave me alone if I have to be something for you. Once it was clear that Ray really was my father, inmates, especially the ones who had talked about me like a dog, hounded me like paparazzi.

"First of all," I said to one who felt an apology was necessary, "if it was up to me, you still wouldn't know. I didn't go around announcing anything—someone else did! I hate it! I never did like anyone knowing who my father was, never in my life. Why would I start once I got in prison? But thanks for your admission of disbelief. Now what do you want me to do?"

Nobody understood the source of my anger over the relentless questions or considered my feelings when the next round of speculation came.

"I bet your dad is really disappointed in you." "I bet it was on the news."

I was already down and out. I didn't want to talk about how I made the rest of my family feel. I made it back to my room and walled myself off. If trying to escape the pain of my past led me to prison, then even prison offered no freedom from the root of my pain. Were I a psychologist in the research field, I would, like Freud, use myself as a subject to explore a heretofore undisclosed psychological malady that I would term *the Ray Charles Syndrome*. It's deeper than one might imagine—relationships predicated on the celebrity of Ray Charles. In my case, he was my father; in my mother's case, a man she loved. Inside the privacy of myself, I retrieved my mother's manuscript from underneath my mattress. I found them there, both staring me right in the face.

"Ray, I've been writing a book about my life with and without you. I've been thinking about including some of the stories you have related to me and events that I remember firsthand. For the sake of accuracy, I want to go

over a few things with you, things I think the world would like to know
about you. I told you one day I would like to do that."

"I-I-I might remember you—you saying that, mama, but the world
isn't interested in my life. They just want to hear my music."

No way, Dad! Were that true, then what were you thinking when
you wrote the book *Brother Ray*? You are just saying that—pretending
to be someone who does not understand the pretense of your life!
What? Pretending you are worth all the money you have because
you are not something special. Wasn't it you who called it what it is?
THE BIG LIE! You said, "The best musicians I know, most people
have never heard of!" And Mom, it makes me sick! Who's zooming
who in this farce?

"That's not true, Ray. I just want you to sit back and get ready for the
easiest interview you've ever had. I got the questions AND the answers. I
wrote this from memory—things I've heard you say throughout the years.
Let me get my pad so I can make any corrections."

"All right."

The pad. Nice touch, Mom. Please.

"Okay, Ray, this first one—this first thing that I've written down
reminds me of a great man in the Bible who did not require evidence to
confirm acts of authority because he himself was a man of power and
authority. There was a wealthy man whose servant was ill. He went to
Jesus, telling Him he knew that He had the power and authority to heal his
servant by simply speaking the words. Jesus offered to go to the servant.
'No,' the wealthy man said, 'I too am a man of authority. I know that if You
speak the words, it is done.'

Puke. Vomit! What is this tripe? Who is Dad, Jesus or the other guy?
A man of power and authority! In Dad's case, it is just celebrity and
money. We are not talking about curing someone from a critical illness
long distance. Power and authority? Who do you think Ray Charles is?
Anger erupted in me as I saw this exchange in my mind's eye. Knowing
them both, I knew this unquestionably as a conversation verbatim.

"You were in France at a restaurant your promoter owned. You had
promised him that you would come to dinner at his restaurant. Throwing
on a sweater and dress pants, you reluctantly went. As you're sitting down,
a man walks over to you, speaking with a heavy French accent, saying,
'Monsieur, Monsieur. You cannot be here without a suit and tie.' At the

same time, another waiter with the same heavy French accent is rushing over, saying, 'Wait a minute, wait a minute. That's Mr. Charles. We're so sorry, Mr. Charles. He did not know it was you. Please sit down and enjoy your dinner.'

"You said, 'Oh no. Oh no. Isn't that your rule—that you have to have *on a suit and tie? I have a business, and I have rules myself. If you were to come to my business, I would want you to obey my rules. I'll be right back in a suit and tie.'"*

Ray laughed and said, *"Two things, mama. First, the sweater I had on cost about two or three hundred dollars. I wasn't lookin' like a tramp or nothin'. And second, the only thing wrong with what you just told me is the restaurant is a French restaurant in New York. And yes, it is owned by my promoter. Very good! All right!"*

It was all about your rules, Dad. You went through all that dumb stuff because you were about to pull the sweater over your promoter's eyes and have the upper hand by being able to say to him, "I played by your rules; now you play by mine!"

"Remember the response you gave when you sang for Ronald Reagan at the Republican convention and all the black people were so upset with you? I asked you, 'Why DID you perform for Reagan?'

"You said to me, 'I'm going to answer the questions for you. But I do *not explain myself to anyone. Here's exactly where my head is. This is what I do for a living. The Democrats called me and asked if I would sing "America" for their convention. I asked, "What does it pay?" They said, "Well, Ray, we thought that you would just do that for us." I said, "I wasn't aware that the Democratic Party was a charitable organization. Like I said, what does it pay?" After that, they said they would get back to me.*

"'In the meantime, here come the Republicans dangling the president in front of me at the Republican convention. I asked them the same thing that I asked the Democrats. The only president I want dangling in front of me is them dead ones on that piece of paper. So I asked them, "What does it pay?" They said, "Ooooh, the Democrats called. What do you want, Mr. Charles?"

"'You see, Sandy, I do not sing when I am working for a cause. Those people, no matter what they believe in, are paying me to work for them. I just concentrate on my work. So, if you see me doing a charity, then I believe in that charity. Otherwise, I'm working. Matter a fact, I'm a Democrat.'"

Now there is the truth, Dad! Greed. The first honest words I can find in this little exchange. It's all about the money—you do not get more antispiritual than that! At the same time, I know you gave millions to charities. Which man is the real Ray Charles? Or maybe there was some tax advantage to the charitable charade.

"You once said, 'If there are two words in this world that you truly need to learn the meaning of—I mean truly understand what they mean—those words are yes and no. If you really understand what they mean, you will have conquered the majority of your problems.' Would that be correct?"

"Yes, ma'am."

"Do you remember when your friend, one of your longtime partners, was in the VA hospital far away from his family?"

"Yes, I do."

"And he had a very short time to live. He was somewhere in the Midwest, and his family was on the West Coast. No matter how hard they tried, they couldn't get him transferred. You said, 'Now, I make it a practice not to use my influence, but I had to make an exception this time. What I am trying to tell you about pity is that it is wasted energy. It doesn't help you, and it doesn't help the person who is receiving it. When I lost my sight, I knew the thing I hated most was pity. If I can't help change or better a situation, I sure am not helping it with pity. In this particular situation, I could do something. I picked up the phone and called the governor of California. I thought if I had a favor coming from him, it would be best spent on my friend. I knew sooner or later they would be askin' ol' Ray for a favor. I was glad he was moved and able to spend his last days with his family. I went to see him after he was transferred. He called me and was scared about dying— which is normal. When I sat there with him, trying to comfort him like we do in those situations, it was hard to say something. I told him that "there is one difference between you and me, my friend. That is that you know approximately when you are going to die, and I don't know yet." 'Cause that is one thing that is truly fair—we are all going to die.'"

Ray said, "You know, mama, that's exactly right. And that is very true about me. I hate pity, and the Lord knows that's the truth. I do not throw my weight around."

I smiled, remembering how he wouldn't complain when the hotel sent him the wrong food or messed up an order for him.

Please! What do you call holding out for the big bucks? Not throwing your weight around?! Ego! My father's was huge! You threw your "weight" around on the most defenseless—the women who were or are in love with you, the children you neglected, the ones you expected to tolerate your behavior because you were Ray Charles. And that's supposed to make it all better. PLEASE! How blind do you think the world is? You have no idea of how your "weight" messed with my brother Kevin's life!

"You truly know a man is your man when he gives you his time and his money. Now if he gives you his time—that's half your man. If he gives you his money and no time, that's half your man. But I'm tellin' ya—if you got a man's time and his money—that's your man.
"I know that's right!"

* * *

Mom, were you deaf and blind? Why was there no respect for me? Dad knew exactly who he was. If he called the governor for a favor to help a friend, I know he could have called a record company and hooked me up. I was, at the very least, talented enough to be positioned in a development stage for a major label. The only compassion he showed me occurred when everything hit the fan. I was in an auto accident and just about dead. He paid for a portion of my recovery, but he never came to see me. I was in the hospital for six months! That was not compassion, and his money was no favor. I was sixteen years old. It was his responsibility! When my life had become a complete shambles and I got into legal trouble, he said, "This is the one and only time you will receive any help from me."

I was gaining an understanding why Mom's relationship with him was such a struggle for her. It was the simple fact he was her heart. She had no choice in the matter. For most of my life, I resented my father for that.

He understood what he was doing to her, not to mention the effect it had on my brother and me. There is no way I could be made to believe he was ignorant of the impact such a thing was having on all of us. There was some self-glorification, some giant ego thing existing inside Ray Charles that could never be justified by any rationale, at least not to me. Never! You do not play with the human heart in such a manner and claim you are clueless about it. It was easy for Dad to remain in my mother's life—he was her king. He knew it. Reading these stories drew a double-edged sword through me, love–hate.

My mother would reach a point where she would have a good man in her corner. We were living in Columbus, Ohio, when I was thirteen. She was dating Elson Craig, an instructor of ophthalmology at Ohio State. He proposed to her, and Mom said, "Give me a little time. I have to think about it."

She came to Kevin and me to ask our opinions on the matter. We responded in sync, "Are you kidding? We love him!" He had a huge house, indoor and outdoor swimming pools, lots of cars. "Are you kidding?! We want a stepdad like that. Do it!"

Dad could smell it when Mom was having a meaningful relationship. I swear, if it happened once, it happened countless times. Elson was over when the phone rang. It was Dad. He wanted two days with Mom. She could not hide her face when she answered the phone, and Elson was standing right there. It was as if the sun itself had put a glow on her. We all saw it and heard it in her voice. That's how my father played it! How he did it is as mysterious as life itself. Kevin and I knew it would dissipate in a week, but right then and there, she couldn't conceal her heart from Elson.

It was an inevitable conclusion to the relationship Mom developed with any man. At some point, the "Ray Charles" flower would bloom in her heart. Every man would come back with the same thing: "Who can compete with Ray Charles?" Which brings back the million-dollar question, "What is it about Ray Charles?" It wasn't just the current manifestation I was contending with, the inmates thinking I was something special. My life's history was replete with it.

Mom's connection with Ray was no secret. Even the perverted sexual interest directed toward us often had its roots in our connection with him. It was sick.

"This is Sandy. She had a daughter with Ray Charles." "This is Ray Charles's daughter, Sheila."

It was never, "This is Sheila."

I had no clue who I was! All I heard was, "Blah, blah, blah—the daughter of Ray Charles." My mother raised me that way. She would say, "Are you nuts? All you need to know is Ray Charles is your father." Well, what does that mean? I could not find *me*. In spite of it all, my heart embraced those stories about my father, while all my life I had tried to hide that fact.

I kept thinking of escaping, just walking off the grounds one day and disappearing. I had been running all my life, but it was clear now— there was no place to escape. The crux of the disillusionment revolved around the relationship, or lack thereof, with my father who, ironically, was the only family member I saw while incarcerated; as impersonal as ever—on the prison's television. The circumstances of my life were unavoidable.

I knew the only way I was going to survive another day was to admit to myself I had suffered enough and it was time to surrender. It was time to move beyond the thoughts I had formed of myself, to return to a place within me, a place I knew as a child, a place that was good. I knew a dream yet lived in me. I needed to connect with whatever force was truly responsible for my existence. It was the time of truth for me, the time to release myself from the madness.

I decided to go to church, where the choir was awesome. The singing was home to me. I love to sing. I could no longer deny such a great part of myself. I had been avoiding it from the first moment I heard the choir practicing. No one could deny me that, not even myself. This was a positive decision for me, having identified something of myself that was true, something I could embrace that made me feel good. And if I got it from Dad, then I could embrace him as well, if for no other reason. I could handle that; what else could I do but heed the song of my heart?

I was by myself on the day I decided to walk into church. After breakfast, five Sundays into my second stay at Bryan, I returned to my room to freshen up. I went into my locker and withdrew my Bible, one of the few possessions I had. It was black, the cover made of a thick paper impressed with a texture that gave it the appearance of leather. It looked brand new, and rarely had I opened it. I held it in my hands and stared at it. *The Holy Bible, King James Version* was imprinted into the front cover in gold letters. I wondered who King James was and why he had his own version. The exposed edges of the pages were flocked with gold paint as well—all in all, as fine and fitting a Bible as I could imagine. It was a gift from Adeline, an elder woman somewhere in her seventies. It made both her and the Bible special to me. She came to Sherburne once a week to witness, and no one messed with her. I recalled her saying, "Now, Sheila, I want you to have this." That memory answered any question about whether to bring it with me. I flicked the pages with my thumb rapidly from front to back, like a cartoonist checking the animation within a sequence of frames. I liked the sound it made. I headed outside, tucking my Bible underneath my arm with a smile. Somehow, I felt Adeline right there with me. It was remarkable, an unforgettable feeling, inexplicable and undeniably real. The power of that experience manifested a decision to start dealing with the things the Bible claims we are: light, salt of the earth, eternal beings, God's children!

I felt something lift from my shoulders and eagerly anticipated the opportunity to sing as I opened the quad doors and headed in the direction of the chapel. The feeling insulated me from the prison's environment, but unlike the shell I had used previously for protection, it felt more like a bubble of joy. Not only that, every part of the landscape seemed to change.

God, I thought, *this is wonderful. Why had I taken so long to get to this place?* I became aware of the sun's warmth on my face and stopped in the middle of the walk. Closing my eyes and lifting my head, I allowed the sun's rays to wash over my face. "Thank you!" I said out loud. "You were right, Adeline, it is a blessing to be alive, a miraculous gift! God IS merciful!"

With renewed conviction, I headed toward the chapel doors. Entering the service, I saw a small platform in the front where the choir stood behind a small podium for the preacher. It lacked the ornaments of churches I had been in before. There were no pews but rather folding chairs where the congregation could sit. I took my seat just as a choir of about fifty girls began singing a song called "Mercy." The first words of the song were, "Lord, today I thank you; I thank you for your blessings—not because I've been good; it's only because of your mercy."

I just about fainted. I felt the moment was meant just for me! Why that song, at that precise moment in time? Why would these be the very first words I would hear inside the prison chapel? I dropped straight to my knees and cried. And the choir kept singing, sounding like something from Heaven. I kept crying. I never heard a choir sound that powerful. The sincerity within every voice created a vibrant, moving force in the church so real and apparent to me, I was reeled in—hook, line, and sinker.

I found myself at the lowest point in my life, recalling the memory of spirit and innocence, and I surrendered myself completely to it. Intuitively, I understood the same experience occurred with members of the choir. It was evident in their voices, an understanding given through Spirit. Enthralled and undone—the song's lyric empowering, affirmation of my heart, I was filled with a simple joy. In spite of what my life had been, I was free of disease, unmarred in anyway, and love was inside me. The Bible tells us, "God will meet you where you are." How could it be any other way? Were there a ladder to climb up to Heaven, I suspect there would be a lot of people making the ascent, but as far as I know, no such thing exists in the world. If I was going to meet God, He would have to come to me, or at least show me the way to meet him. The way to God, at least for the path I was on, was to allow Him to meet me in Bryan Federal Prison. There was nowhere else I could go.

Miss Sharon, the director of the choir, was serving a twenty-year sentence. She had two more to go when I met her. Eighteen years in prison, she was one of the few inmates who could leave the compound, a hospice nurse who worked out in the community. She and fifteen other girls were so privileged and wore a uniform easily distinguished from the khaki everyone else was sporting. They would leave in the morning and return in the afternoon. I never have heard a voice like hers—could she sing! She approached me after the service, not saying a word, just held me in her arms. Just held me for the longest time. After I calmed down, she let me know this was where I could come to feel the love. I told her that I really wanted to join the choir, and she invited me to the practice Wednesday night. I said thank you and left.

I was excited about the singing. It was in my blood, but I was still unsure of the church/salvation equation. In the past, it was something that was fleeting for me. I was never able to stay rooted to the joy of such experience, and I did not want to slip and fall this time. After all, I was in jail, and, were I to fall further, I had no idea where that would put me, fearful it would be somewhere from which there was no return.

I headed toward the exercise area, thinking, *Upon which rock do I stand? The Rock of Christ or the rock of crack?* I observed Roberta and Sharon on a bench smoking cigarettes and approached them.

"Hi, guys," I said with a bright smile on my face.

"You're one of them now?" Sharon pointed to several other church-goers as they were walking past, purposefully speaking above the crowd, remarking how bad the smell of cigarettes was in the clean, fresh air.

"Come on, Sharon! That isn't fair. It certainly isn't going to change our friendship. At least, it doesn't have to."

"Good," said Sharon. "Come sit down next to us, then."

As soon as I did, she cozied up to me, and I was aware of her intentions. I felt uncomfortable with her closeness, not because I was offended but rather because it called to me. "I had a pretty good time tonight at the service. The choir director asked me to join. I'm going to the rehearsal on Wednesday night."

"So that's what you are doing there," Roberta said. "You just got to sing. Too bad you can't sing something else besides the Holy Roller stuff they sing in there."

"Yeah," I said. Now I was uncomfortable with Roberta and my response to her assertion. "Well, look. I'm really tired and want to hit the sack early tonight. I haven't been feeling the best lately. I think I'm coming down with a cold or something." I got up quickly and said a fast "see you later" as I headed toward the quad.

I was trying to resolve all sorts of issues dislodged from below the surface of my skin, dark truths I had told no one. I decided to do something about the pain, depression, anxiety, frustration, panic, and terror that stretched all the way back to my childhood. It had been ruling my life for years; I just didn't know how to get rid of it. I lay down to sleep that night and became aware of an overpowering anger within me—anger that had stripped my spirit countless times. I didn't even feel right feeling good, to know hope and have no one to share it with. My sexual drive presented itself, a desire my mind found impossible to resist, a longing to be touched, to be soothed. My thoughts turned toward Sharon and what she offered: acceptance, companionship, compassion, and intimacy. It was something that caused me to question my convictions. Thoughts stirred inside me that commanded my attention. I resisted, but it was a futile effort as my past came to the surface, and guilt took its seat in the jury box. There she was, Sandy, my babysitter, when I was six years old.

It was a memory I had smoked my way through in the past. In here, there was no such anesthetic, and my mind thought of it as something wrong, forbidden, sinful. Sandy was our neighbor in Columbus, Ohio. She was sweet, and Mom just loved her. When Mom asked her to babysit, Sandy was eighteen years old. Kevin was already asleep before she arrived, and, almost immediately after Mom left, she turned to me with a strange look on her face and asked, "Do you want to feel something good?"

"Yes," I said, thinking she was a little nuts for asking the question.

"Let's go up to your room."

"Okay," I said.

As she began removing her clothes, I thought, *Oh good, we are going to play dress-up in Mommy's old clothes.* Taking off her bra, she told me to come over to her and stand at her side. I was surprised at how big her breasts were. Mine did not look like that.

She told me to lie back on the bed and continued with, "Now just relax. This isn't going to hurt a bit."

I felt an unknown sensation arise within me . . . as she continued with me from there . . .

A day later, that same arousal and sensation arose while I was riding my little toy pony hobbyhorse. I thought it was all right to allow myself the experience and further my exploration of what I had been so recently introduced to. But something about it was evident to my mother, for she yelled, "Sheila! What are you doing?" I dismounted instantly and never rode that toy pony again. I decided to say nothing of the experience with the babysitter. Learning it was a bad thing to experience something of that nature—I felt dirty at the age of six. Guilty.

I pulled away from the memory and got up from bed nauseous, moving quickly to the toilet. I vomited. It was as though I were physically trying to remove the experience from my life.

"Sheila," one of my cellmates called out, "what the heck! You okay?"

"I'm all right. It must have been something I ate." I got up from my knees and began washing myself. Getting back in bed, sweating profusely, I wondered where the peace, joy, and hope had vanished to while knowing the origin of the memory of shame. I thought to begin a journal and found a piece of paper and pen.

JOURNAL ENTRY ONE

With this prayer, these thoughts, may I begin this journal dedicated to a greater and yet greater understanding of Truth, Love, and Light within me, to guide me toward that which is more than I am and absolutely what I AM so I am freed from my past.

I do not know how it is I survived in darkness for so long. I desire to be free from this "Flashback Reality." I don't want to live my life with those mirrored images, Lord. I pray you will remove them immediately. I need no window to my life of ignorance and sin! God, please keep me in Your Light, for when the Darkness attempts to invade my mind with its will, it will not be able to exist within the illumination of the Divine Flame within me. Praise God—All begins and ends in Your Love; you are the Alpha and the Omega!

I found peace in that; it quieted my mind, and I went to sleep.

I awoke in the morning with a lightness of being, feeling renewed, overjoyed, and consumed with a presence I recalled long ago as a child. I was filled with wonder and love. I consciously made an effort to remove the smile from my face as I sat up to begin my day. I could not. The paper and pencil remained on the bed next to me, and I picked it up, partly with the idea that the effort of writing down this most unexpected start to my day would diminish the glow upon my face. Such a dramatic shift in my outlook would surely be noticed, and I really was not prepared to account for it when the inevitable questioning occurred.

JOURNAL ENTRY TWO

Last evening I recalled an experience from my childhood; Sandy, the babysitter. I can never forget her. I did not feel comfortable with that memory! I thought I was past it decades ago. Having so recently relived it, I can't help wonder why she chose to approach me in such a manner. Why me? What made her think I was a safe target? The memory of it made me feel dirty, and the memory of God within me feels pure.

In my past, I can recall precious moments of a Divine nature, but none more spectacular than this moment. My Spirit is filled with great Joy. I have a soundness and clarity of mind never before experienced. To know God's Love, Grace, Mercy, and Presence in my life is a reality. It has been made evident to me, my faith in The Heavenly Father restored. I pray my Faith be as long, as wide, and as deep as the sea and then—more! Thank you for this day, Father.

I did not quite know what to do about my current condition or what to make of it. It just felt good, throwing everything that's normal out the window. It was no surprise to me that I was greeted with the fresh morning air gently warmed by an early morning Texas sun, the birds singing in the maples and oaks. For the first time in my life, I truly felt free—God's property! It was somewhat frightening to me, such a radical shift of perspective. It would be hard to conceal from Roberta and Sharon. Impossible. The gloom and doom was gone from my countenance, replaced with an inexplicable joy and a sense of lightness. I am not a small, petite girl by any measure, but I was walking with the thought that were I to step on a scale, I doubted my weight would register anything over a pound.

"Hi, Roberta!" I said, having made it to the four-way.

"What happened to you?" She smiled, and her voice changed. "Girl, you got laid, didn't you?"

"I ain't no Mrs. Crenshaw, now, Roberta. Just keep a walkin', 'cause I ain't a talkin'!"

With quiet determination, I promised to claim God alone as my Father.

CHAPTER 9

SOMEWHERE UNDER THE RAINBOW

I travel down a dark, lonely road
On a path meant for no one but me
To a place I alone must go
No one else need follow me

—*GLENN SWANSON,*
SHOES ON THE TABLE

OVER THE NEXT SEVERAL DAYS, I clung to the hope Wednesday night choir practice might deliver the same feeling I had encountered during Sunday service.

I was the first in the door, the chapel auditorium split in half by a folding curtain. A short, rotund, robust black woman stood by the piano, poring through some music. She wore small oval spectacles that gave her the appearance of a professor, an attitude that was all business. Possessing a beautiful spirit that shined through her, Ms. Sharon owned a voice that required no microphone. The discipline evident within the choir eliminated the need to speak of her competence. More important, there was a genuine love and connection she had with God I recognized as authentic. I trusted her faith.

Anxious to know her embrace, I advanced unnoticed toward her and the piano. Bumping into a chair on my way to greet her, she raised her head and looked at me. Before I could say hello, she smiled and said, "You're here early. I'm glad to see you. Aren't you the one who's supposed to be Ray's daughter?"

"Yeah. You got it—the right one, baby."

She said, "Girl! Honey, what you doing here in this place?"

"That's a question I've been asking myself quite a lot these days," I said with a smile.

"Now, I know you can sing!"

"I've been looking forward to it beyond anything you can imagine. It's been some time since I sang, and I hope I don't disappoint you. I have been running from all the important stuff in my life for quite some time. I intend to put an end to that."

"Now, don't you worry about that 'cause God always shows up in His house."

I started laughing, and that broke the ice. I sat and waited until the other girls showed up. They started to straggle in, a few familiar faces from around the quad and a couple I had seen sneaking a cig or two on the smoke pad—about thirty girls in all that night.

"Ladies," Ms. Sharon said, "we have a new member to the choir, Sheila Robinson. Let's give her a big welcome."

They clapped and smiled. It made me feel good.

Ms. Sharon continued, "Everyone turn to your right and give your neighbor a hug."

After the embrace, everyone moved together into a circle for prayer. Ms. Sharon said, "Lord, we thank You today for Your blessings, the gifts You give us freely. Thank You for unity and peace on the compound. In Jesus's name we pray. Amen."

The choir began to assemble as Ms. Sharon asked, "Sheila, what part do you normally sing in the choir?"

"Second soprano or alto."

"All right, then—second soprano it will be."

"Total Praise" was the first song I would learn that night—the quickest hour that ever passed inside federal prison. After the rehearsal, I felt renewed and energized. It was 8:00 p.m. What do I do now? In the past, after a rehearsal or gig, I would hang out with the band or friends, do something to unwind from the lift. I wanted to go eat, party, or get high—it was an entrenched habit. Everyone left with a "see you on Sunday." I thought about looking for Roberta and Sharon, but instead walked the track, unwinding from the experience. The choir was incredible, and I was thrilled to be able to sing, though my voice wasn't in condition and my throat was sore. Back in the quad, I was left to contend with reality, reduced by an environment designed to remind one of failure. Reconnecting with the church and music lifted me, but I still felt unworthy of love. I was trying to understand how it had come to this. It's more than just becoming clean— it's understanding why you went there in the first place. Drug addiction is a symptom, an effort to prove one is worthless. Defeated by fear and insecurity—by thought, word, and action—I no longer resisted the memory of events and experiences that delivered so much pain. This was my test of faith.

*   *   *

I lay in bed, drifting back to somewhere around the time of my seventh birthday. With crystal clarity, a distant yesterday appeared inside walls of memory. Four apparitions began to coalesce and solidify into human form—my mother and two others close to my family—May Bea and Mr. Shirley. The fourth person within the vision, the first to take complete form, a young girl standing no more than three and a half feet tall, wearing a flannel nightgown, the right side of her body concealed behind doors that led from the den to the living room, her left arm hanging limp, her hand clutching the arm of a teddy bear dangling downward at an angle, equally limp and devoid of life. She was motionless and appeared to be in a state of shock, her eyes unnaturally wide open, her lips partially separated, her face frozen in disbelief. She made no attempt to conceal herself— caught in a game of hide-and-seek. Fear had left nowhere to hide.

I moved toward her with the desire to help, reverse her rigor mortis. Melting into her, I looked out through her eyes and recognized the scenery. It belonged to my past, the living room of my childhood home. Standing mesmerized at events transpiring but a few yards away, I felt the grip of fear and confusion strangling what I knew to be holy, merciful, and good.

My mother lay naked and alone on the floor. A dozen or so candles surrounded her and were lit as if she were the sacrificial offering, the lamb whose blood would purify an unholy altar. I did not know what was being worshipped before me through the high priest and his follower, but I knew it was not of God or love. In a most real sense, I loved her as any child loves her mother—with love that IS of God. Pure. What was worshipped before me was of man. It was not holy, it was not pure, nor was it good.

Two bodies, one male and one female, were intertwined with each other like a human pretzel. What were they doing, dancing? What was wrong with my mom? Why wasn't she stopping them? I recognized them. A natural instinct presented itself, the recognition of wrong. It could never be right, and they had no business being like that—what was this about?

My heart began to fill with pain and fear. It went on forever— their hands, their mouths, their bodies.

I was afraid. I knew that man, and I was very afraid. I had trusted him. I had believed he loved us. But this wasn't love. No way was this love! It continued for an unbearable length of time. While paralyzed in shock, wave after wave of fear swept over me, through me. The man let out a loud grunt; the woman was laughing and twirling around merrily. Capitulating, she dropped on top of my mother, as if Mom were a mattress, her mattress, and she were lying down for the night.

"Ooooh!" My mother finally made a sound.

"Look, baby! She likes it!"

It wasn't a sound I related with goodness or expression of pleasure! My mother appeared lost and disoriented. It was a sound of pain and nonrecognition, and it was too much for me.

"MA!"

Their eyes turned on me. Turning my back on my mother and the two of them, I ran. I looked back to see them rolling Mom up in a blanket or rug, removing the evidence of whatever had been done. Jumping into bed and quickly pulling the covers up over me, I prayed, *God, please don't let them know it was me.* I shivered in fear. *How could they not know it was me? Clearly, they had seen me! Oh, please! Maybe they will think it was Kevin.* I wondered if he had ever seen such a thing. *Should I ask him? Was I in trouble? Oh, I don't want a spanking. Oh God! I won't say a word! Not one word, I promise!*

My heart was beating at an uncontrollable rate, and I just squeezed my pillow as tight as I could with the thought, *Just go to sleep, go to sleep, go to sleep!*

Somehow, by the grace of God, I did fall asleep. In the morning, Kevin and I were up and heading for the kitchen. Though I had no stomach for it, I made every effort for breakfast to be normal—more than willing to pretend everything was as it should be. They were there as we entered the kitchen.

"Good morning," she said in a voice very close to the sound of my mother's.

Mom, where is Mom? I thought. "Mom, where is Mom?" I asked in a voice that was more revealing than I wanted.

"Oh baby. She's still sleeping."

There we go with that "oh baby" stuff, I thought. *Sleeping? Yeah, okay!*

"Froot Loops! How does that sound?"

"Sounds good," Kevin said.

I was still trying to assess the situation, wondering if I was in some kind of trouble, but neither one was addressing anything of the previous night, and it appeared on the surface to be just another day. May Bea and Mr. Shirley? They didn't seem to know each other in the manner I witnessed last night. Was I dreaming?

"Sheila, come here, honey, and give Mommy a kiss," Mom said.

Finally, she's up! I thought. Immediately abandoning the television and Fred Flintstone, I ran to her and held her as tight as I could. Mom reciprocated my hug, and I felt secure.

The day passed without a word and no indication of any abnormal occurrence the night before. That evening, however, I overheard my mother on the phone. Mr. Shirley was out of the house at work, and May Bea had returned to whatever hole she had crawled from.

"Nancy," my Mom said. "Nancy, I've got to get out of here with my children! Something terrible happened here last night. May Bea and Mr. Shirley were here, and all I can remember is a glass of wine. The next thing I know, I woke up half naked, bruised, and battered. My head is killing me! I think they gave me a Mickey or something! They did! I'm sure of it!"

What is a Mickey? I didn't know and didn't want to know. I sure didn't want them to Mickey me. I continued to listen to the conversation as Mom told Nancy it was terrible, it was bad, it was wrong. I knew right then and there the feeling I had the previous night was right—what had occurred indeed *was* wrong. This was evil. *I should have protected Mom,* I thought. *She would become so mad and angry with me. I won't say a word, not one word!*

The day would end with my mother's drinking—more and more. Her relationship with Mr. Shirley over the passing days worsened. He was becoming physically abusive to Mom, and other people started to get involved—family members came in for the rescue. For love and family, there was an effort made to work things out.

Over the following weeks, I began to think things might be all right. There was no violence, no anger. A general air of respect had returned to the environment. But civility was no more than an illusion. The knock on the door was heard all too soon; reality, once again, turned to nightmare. Mother, letting alcohol work its way in her life, had passed out before I had gone to sleep. From the security of my bedroom, I realized "Bonnie and Clyde" were out in the living room, laughing and talking.

They stole every ounce of love and security a child would know. I resolved in my heart I would not let them do terrible things to Mom again—unaware they had totally different plans for this evening.

"Hey, baby! Let's get you ready for bed," May Bea said.

I knew something was up. In the bathroom, there were candles lit everywhere.

"Isn't it just beautiful?"

It wasn't unusual for May Bea to get me ready for bed, but the candles sure were.

"Where is Kevin?" I asked.

"Oh, he's already in bed. He's only five. He doesn't get to stay up like you. You're a big girl!"

As the bathing began, it was as normal as anything until I observed Mr. Shirley looking down into the bubbles—watching intently. Watching what? I looked down into the bubbles. *It's just me,* I thought. *I'm just imagining things—I'm being weird.*

Mr. Shirley whispered something to May Bea, who then turned and said, "Open yourself up down there. You know, down where you go pee. Little girls have to stay clean down there, fresh and clean."

I didn't have any idea I was dirty. How would dirt get in there, anyway? I obliged. As my audience watched, their eyes seemed to pierce me.

What's coming out from his body and the unusual nature of his vocal sounds? It's outside his robe now. I knew what that was used for—I started to cry.

"What's wrong, baby? It's okay. Let's get you to bed."

"I'll get some lotion and a nightgown, and you will be set," said Mr. Shirley.

"I want my mommy."

"She's sleeping, baby," said May Bea.

"She sleeps all the time now," I said and began to sob.

"Hurry up," came from the doorway. Mr. Shirley said, "Lotion, get me the blasted lotion."

I was lying naked on the bed. Let the lotion begin. I was feeling sick in my stomach and a weird gurgle in my tummy as I continued to observe his unnatural behavior. I was afraid.

"I don't want any more lotion. I want to go to sleep."

"Oh, baby. Here, put your nightgown on," said May Bea.

"I need my undies."

"You will get them in the morning. They are in the wash."

She tucked me in, and I was relieved they were gone. I could still hear them laughing. In the far room, my mother lay unconscious, snoring loudly. I couldn't get to sleep. *Squeak, squeak, squeak* went bedsprings on the other side of my wall. They stopped. Shortly, footsteps approached my door, and it slowly opened. They were naked.

"Sheila, Sheila, Sheila?" he spoke in a creepy whisper.

I pretended to sleep, my heart pounding. He moved my nightgown over my hips. I turned over to avoid him, but his hands were unwilling to grant me a reprieve from the will of an ancient force awake within him.

"It's okay," he said.

I was frozen in fear. My mind went numb, but my body did not . . . as it continued, something shattered within me—deep.

Somehow, I found a way to sleep that night, a rest that would be disturbed many more times in the future. *Bonnie and Clyde*—thieves of innocence and joy ushered in many subsequent demons with different faces that all seemed to know each other inside of me—the fracturing of self. Experiences that led to a life of lies, tears, and a fifteen-year crack cocaine addiction—eventually delivering me to federal prison. Broken. For years and years, I believed all men and women harbored such demons. This is what I was working with. This is what life had taught me.

* * *

As I pulled away from that memory, I felt that little girl's heart, still alive, waiting for me to rescue her, return to her, not for a visit but to reunite and never leave, to never abandon her again. For the first time in my life, I felt it was possible—almost within my grasp. Now, through the grace of God, I sensed the ever-pure state of Spirit.

I lay there with but one question on my mind. *How DO I fix myself?* In my khaki prison garb, I found myself shuffling my way to breakfast, name tag in pocket, with hundreds of other girls all going the same direction. Is there no one who gets this? I am in Hell. I want to get out, and it doesn't matter where you put me. I felt dead. Why would God allow such things to happen to me when I was so young? *At least the roots of the dysfunction were exposed,* I thought.

"What's the matter with you?" Roberta asked.

I looked at her as though she did not exist, consumed by a past from which there seemed no escape. I wanted to know something good, remember life pure. And now it seemed obvious why I had resorted to drugs; they repressed memories that did not belong in any child's past. *How many in this prison share such a past with me? How many in this world?* I wondered if the easier answer might have been in the question, *How many do not?*

I sat down at breakfast and tried to force down something into my stomach. The need to expel the bite of eggs overtook me, and they began to rise in my throat. I gripped the edge of the table with my hands and forced the bile back down; sweat appeared on my forehead. Why could I not let go? I felt I had been robbed of a great part of life. Where is the toilet to flush that?

The urge to vomit was not surprising. After all, I was in the process of expelling the mental garbage of caustic memories. Shame and guilt flooded me. The awareness of truth has always been a double-edged sword.

Why did I not cry out, tell them to stop? Fear. They would not have listened to me. Why did I not say anything about it afterward to my mother? Fear. Perhaps I could have protected Kevin, protected them both, and survived for my children. I felt responsible for so much wrong, miraculously touching hope and filled with contradiction.

I recalled a quotation my mother gave a reporter that was published in *Sepia* magazine:

"I intend to tell my daughter who her real father is when she is old enough to understand this reality. It will be my job to condition her mind for this type of understanding. My own childhood was very, very sheltered. I have found my earlier training was inadequate to allow me, as an adult, to cope with situations outside my own little sphere. I was brought up believing everyone was good and trustworthy. This kind of thinking led me to my present plight. My daughter will know the realities of life because I will teach her."

I understood the statement Mom was trying to make and, all too well, the mistakes she had made. Certainly, she had not intended this plight for me. These words were spoken with the hope I would avoid such experience—the epitome of irony. *Mom, I love you so.* She had trusted Ray with her heart, and he was not deserving of that trust. Did that mean she would trust no one? She apparently trusted Mr. Shirley. Why? She was blind and deaf to a large part of this world, unable to lift the cloud of her own naïveté. Equally amazing was the realization that, despite the chaos surrounding my life, the love I held for my mother ran deep. It was easy for me to forgive her shortcomings. On the other hand, the chaos and mess I had made of my life knew no forgiveness within me. If that was not enough to fuel self-loathing and disillusionment, the best was yet to come—the heinous realization of the chain of abandonment I delivered into the lives of my children. If there was one who clearly knew better, it should have been me.

JOURNAL ENTRY THREE

Lord, some things just don't seem to go away. How can they when they are such a great part of your past? It's not that I expect You to rewind my life, transport me back in time and have things turn out differently. I am not asking that of You. What I am asking for is wisdom, a place to stand where I can see the past without the hurt and self-loathing, a place of understanding so I can say a final good-bye and know a future free of darkness. That alone would be some kind of miracle, one of which I feel undeserving.

Powerful experiences of God in my life had been present before, but after their occurrence, I was unable to stay in touch with them. I had to go to court regarding the placement of my children during my incarceration. The county had it in for me—my history of drug abuse was a matter of public record. While pregnant, I was using cocaine. My youngest son and daughter were both born into this world crack positive. The county was through with me. *I'm going down,* I thought. *Big time. I am never going to see my kids. I could make a very good argument that I do not deserve to know them. But I still want to—to somehow rise above it all—after I find myself.*

There was a court hearing regarding Jonnica, my last baby, dumped at the hospital by Spud—when I told the hospital admissions personnel I was Sandra Betts. A female sheriff, Nadine, was assigned to watch me at the hospital while I was shackled to the bed. At that time, they didn't know I had a federal warrant out for my arrest. They thought I was trying to avoid paying the hospital bill, providing false information regarding my identity. That and the fact that my baby and I were cocaine positive were the reasons for their investigation. I grew close to Nadine. I had no one else to talk to and finally broke down crying.

"Look, I got to tell you something."

"What, honey? I want you to know that you can talk to me about anything."

"I got dumped at the hospital by the guy I loved, and he is the worst! I am strung out on crack, and he resents my addiction, even though he helped me become addicted. I can't blame anyone but myself, although he sure wasn't willing to snatch the pipe away from me at any given time and not give me the dope. He literally dropped me here and took off."

"That is just awful. I am so sorry to hear that."

"Well, you guys got it all wrong. My name is Sheila Robinson. I'm not trying to avoid paying my bill. I have medical assistance. There is a federal warrant out for my arrest." I just melted into the realization that the truth was going to set me free. What was the point to continue the charade? I was shackled to my bed, and the situation was hopeless.

"Sheila, you need to get that lowlife sucker!" she responded.

It wasn't much later that I was being escorted to the Sherburne County federal holding facility to await both an appearance before a federal judge and the county court to determine the fate of my children. I was in the courthouse holding cell, walking in a circle, praying, *God, I know I am not worthy, I know I don't deserve any favors from You, but please don't let them take this baby from me, never to be a part of her life. To never see her again would be unbearable. You said You would never give more than I could bear. I could not bear this.*

I already knew I was going back to prison. That was unavoidable. What was I doing? What was I trying to prove? Everything I was not, I had become. How did that happen? It was almost impossible to breathe. Where had the memory gone of anything good? I was completely in my mind—or out of it. Everything was of the darkest thought.

Something came over me, as though I had taken the strongest sleeping pill known to man. I had to go to sleep, and in that dream state, God told me to not worry. For the time being, my children were where they needed to be, but I saw visions of my children all around me in the future.

I awoke as the guard came to bring me lunch. Afterward, that same feeling came over me. Entering that dream state once again, God let me know the judge would be merciful on me and not to worry. I awoke. This was unbelievable. I thought I might be going crazy or I was already certifiable. I had written the judge a letter, asking for the opportunity to remain in my children's lives. I held hope to come out of this victorious. Jamie, Jeanna, and Alicia were already in the custody of Matt, and baby Jonnica was with Matt at this point. Child protection representatives had gone down to Matt's several days earlier and checked it out; they thought I was lying about the whole thing. I told them my history was horrific and not to be surprised. I wasn't trying to lie about anything. They acted as though I had not been forthright about my past, as though I was trying to conceal something. I said, "I did not walk into your office and try to lie. I knew you would find out every single thing. For

God's sake, Jonnica was dirty. Why would I try to lie about it? It is a matter of record!"

In the courtroom: the judge, my public defender, the CHIPS petitioner, and the county attorney.

"This woman has been a detriment to all of her children. She's been on crack for the last ten years. She is a danger to herself and her children. She is a threat to them. We want her to have zero contact with her children and request parental rights be removed."

The judge said, "Wait a minute. Hold up. I have a letter here from Sheila. She is by no means demanding the baby be placed in her arms while she is in federal prison, spending a length of time yet to be determined. She is not asking for that. What she is asking for is an opportunity to be a part of her children's lives. Being the maternal parent, this court cannot find any reason why this should not be permitted. That door will be left open for a time in the future when she has shown she is ready for that responsibility."

"But your Honor! Your Honor!"

"No! I will not be moved from this position. I will not allow you to force me to strip a woman's maternal right from her when she is going to be given the opportunity to grow. They are going to give her treatment. They are going to help her when she gets into the system. Why even demand she undergo treatment when everything she would be working for has already been taken away?"

The representatives from child protection and the prosecutor were irritated at the judge's decision. My eyes were full of tears, and I had an uncontrollable smile on my face. I was not supposed to have any hope. I was to be drowning in my tears. I began to praise God with my hands up in the air without caring who was looking at me. You can't tell me God isn't real when everything He said would happen happened exactly the way He said it would. The joy of the Lord is undeniable. David danced right out of his clothes. I love that story.

JOURNAL ENTRY FOUR

Dear Children,

If anyone in this world comes against you because of what I have done, what other members of our family may have done, or what you yourself did or may do to cloud the thought of who you really are, hear this one simple thought. Greater is that which lives in you than all that is of this world. The Heart of God lives within you, loves within you.

The tallest tree comes from but a single seed and was always within the seed, but to become the tree, the shell of the seed must be broken as it begins the process of growth, reaching for the light. And when your shell breaks, be not afraid of the bigger you that awaits, for that shell must be discarded as you grow into the light and become stronger in the awareness of who you truly are.

JOURNAL ENTRY FIVE

I woke up this morning feeling as though I had begun a new life. Indeed I had. Scriptures say we must die daily, crucify the old and take on the new. As of now, I am a new creation. How awesome our Creator is. I think of Jesus and how wonderful He must have felt, walking completely in the Will of God, without sin, shame, anger, or resentment. When I wake in the morning and I pray, may it be but to remember all that is good and pure so I may see myself in the Light without the faintest shadow—the darkness forever passed. Amen.

CHAPTER 10

FINAL DAYS WITH MOM

I walk my own path
In your footsteps I follow
The strength of your yesterday
Becomes the strength of my tomorrow

—*GLENN SWANSON,*
SHOES OF THE SOLE MAN

IT IS EASIER TO KEEP GOING as things are even if you know a greater joy, a brighter path. For that reason, little seems to change in this world. Relationships change when you change. It is a reality. Change.

Sunday morning came, and I found myself in church, early once again. The choir was the core of the church, as it is in any congregation. We were the first to arrive, assembling in the front around Ms. Sharon to warm up our voices. Ms. Sharon would not tolerate an attitude or a personal issue brought to the choir during rehearsal or service, unless it was to bring it to the group and work it out, share it to find resolution. Consequently, everyone was upbeat and filled with a genuine sense of sisterhood. It was a great change for me mentally within that first week. I felt a part of something bigger than my personal problems.

The prison had a chaplain full time who conducted the Sunday morning service. Chaplain Mike. He was a tall, large-framed, balding man with a soft, sweet voice, especially for someone his size. He wore a purple robe with a white collar and black ornamental scarf that had doves woven on its surface with gold tassels on the bottom. He was the king of dry, a Lutheran kind of dry, conducting a nondenominational prison chapel worship service. I was familiar with the fire and brimstone preaching of the black southern Baptist ministers from my hometown, but I found his love sincere. I was drawn to his words and spirit.

After the invocation, Pastor Mike would have the choir sing several numbers, sometimes as many as five. At the close of the service, the choir would sing a final song. It seemed as if all the songs we sang contained lyrics meaningful to my current circumstance. I felt renewed in a manner that could not be concealed. Music is very healing.

Before we left, Ms. Sharon said, "All right, ladies, when you get back to the quad, tell those girls who didn't show up this morning to make sure they are here tonight for Pastor Chris's service!"

Pastor Chris was black, with his own congregation in town, complete with a radio broadcast. He came to the prison with an agenda of personal ministry apart from the prison system. He spoke with a fire of Spirit I responded to. From time to time, he brought outside speakers with him—people who had a story inmates could relate to. He held greater appeal to the black inmates because he was from the hood, reformed from a past that was similar to our own. Whenever a speaker was coming— someone who had been there before—the chapel would be filled to capacity, while other times, the choir was bigger than the congregation. That first night with Pastor Chris, even more so than the morning service, I was not conscious of singing for anyone present. I felt as though I was singing directly to God. A deep fervor and passion ignited within me, immediately noticeable to everyone.

I was now watched from an entirely different point of view. It was no longer, "There's the daughter of Ray Charles"; it became, "There's Sheila; she's going to church now."

"Oh, I'm smoking a cigarette. Does that bother you?"

"Oh my! I just said a curse word. I know you are going to church now. I'm sorry."

I did not desire or ask to be looked upon differently now that I was attending church. But some of the choir members had all the rules and verses memorized and had put a great deal of effort into it.

My approach, on the other hand, was effortless and simple: remember God in all things. It made me happy, and people would gravitate toward me because I was happy. It was manifesting on its own. You cannot beat somebody up, especially yourself, and then tell someone you are doing it in the name of God. Wars are fought in the name of God, both sides claiming He is on their side. Where is the love in that?

There were activities such as bingo, cards, and Scrabble tournaments that the Rollers would not participate in because they might hear "bad words." It didn't bother me, and I kept going to those activities when I felt like it. In the midst of playing cards on one such occasion, another inmate in the game said, "F_ you!" as a couple from the choir passed by. "Oh, such language! It's such a vexation to my spirit."

I turned and said, "Your spirit is not hurting. It ain't got nothing to do with it. Love is what you should be concentrating on, not judging others. What brought you here in the first place—your perfection?"

I was hanging out with Roberta and others while they were smoking and talking their stuff. Someone passing by from the congregation said, "You know, people put themselves in a position to backslide"—rolling her eyes—"when they hang out with people who ain't going to help them grow spiritually."

Sharon said, "If that is what it means to have God in you, to act like them, then no thank you!"

"They got it wrong. It's all about the love thing. There are others who are genuine. Don't look for the truth of God anywhere but within yourself," I said and just kept pushing forward, working on myself.

It was Jeanna's absence of writing, her runaway status that was driving me nuts. I held myself completely responsible. I had never been the mother I wanted to be for her. Mom was there for her, and consequently, Jeanna and Mom became inseparable. In the past, I removed myself completely from their lives. When Mom became seriously ill and was hospitalized, Jeanna was scared to death with what was transpiring.

Prior to sentencing, I was out on bail and able to visit Mom at the hospital. She told me, "Sheila, you have got to get it together. Your daughter just asked me, 'Mom-mom, what will I ever do if something happens to you?' Be there for Jeanna, Sheila." Well, if that didn't kill me. And Mom, I just knew her to be made of rock, and rock never dies, and now, now I knew something different.

I was in a federal halfway house. My original sentence was for ninety days. My aunts—Aunt Terry, Aunt Marsha, Aunt Tony— were flying in and out of Minneapolis to see Mom, now known to be critically ill. Lung cancer had spread to her brain. The cancer inoperable, there was nothing a doctor could do. After I entered the halfway house to serve my sentence, Mom wanted to be moved from the hospital, and the doctors agreed. "Let her smoke if she wants to. The main thing right now is just loving her through this and enjoying whatever moments you may have left with her." Aunt Cathy and her husband, Jim, took her in with them.

Dad was very aware of Mom's cancer. He bought the hospital bed out at Cathy's and then told Mom, "I'll buy you this bed, but, you know, I, I, ah, can't really afford to do this. Don't ask for nothing more." I resented the heck out of him for saying that. I could not understand his heart. Never. This is how he treats his TRUE FAMILY? Mom's end was near. She was getting worse and worse. Mom had begun to speak audibly with my grandparents and others who had passed away years ago. The nurse said, "Usually this is a sign that they are very near to that final day. You'd better get the children here. Get them involved. Now!"

The nurse and all my family were calling the halfway house. I had been working, I had parenting classes, and I of course had the drug treatment program. Karen, my counselor, was the one who was assigned to oversee my sentencing stipulations. She was a good woman. She called me into her office one day and said, "I've got some news for you." Before she got any further, I went psycho. "Your mom is not doing well. They want you to come and see her. I've granted you a pass for four hours."

It was an hour drive to my Aunt Cathy's, so by the time I got there, I had only two hours to visit. When Mom saw me, she could not speak, but her eyes said everything. I will never forget that look on her face. It was a look of absolute peace. She was satisfied now that she was able to see me, only hours from the end. I sat and read the Bible to her and sang. I sang and sang and just held her hand, and she held mine. Two hours went so fast. She held on so tight as I was about to leave. I had to go back to prison and—and she would not let go. It was the hardest thing I had to do in life—to pry my hand out of hers. I was in a river of tears, but I knew she forgave me, and that was what I needed. I needed her forgiveness. That was a big part of my healing.

I knew my mother's love but could not reach her surrender or understanding. The way my mother ran stuff was so incredible sometimes. I would never claim to be as wise as Mom. She could be as philosophical as Aristotle when she needed to be and have the whole world mesmerized by stories when she needed something provided! She counted on me to be strong enough to deal with it. If you were weak of mind, she would lead you around by your nose.

Dressed in rags, walking down the street like a homeless person, she would command the respect of everyone. You would have to stop in your tracks and say to yourself, "Who *is* that?" It is something no one could take from her. At times, living in abject poverty, she would present herself in front of Ray and his people as though she lived a life of excess. Were you to tell someone she was penniless and about to be evicted, you would be looked at as though you were crazy. No one would believe someone living in such circumstances could carry herself in such a manner. Absolutely above it all. That's what I miss about my mom, the thing that is every part of my being—that's why this world is a different place now that she is not physically here.

Under her wing, no matter what was dumped on her, you were safe and knew she could handle it. The word out in the world is Ray Charles was something special, someone bigger than life, who overcame his handicap to live a life known but to royalty. That may all be true, but I can barely attest to that reality. I was not so privileged. What I can stand witness to is my mother's life, one of adversity. She took care of countless people along the way. She made things happen out of thin air when there was nothing but a thread of hope. So indestructible. I sometimes think I made a mess of things just to see what it would take to make her fall.

I witnessed my mother and father together but not as much as I wished, perhaps not as much as either of them wished. And I can say this: next to my mother, Ray Charles was the baby, and it was her love that intimidated him. He loved her. But she surpassed him. Sandra Betts overwhelmed my father. He could not resist her. If you question the veracity of such a claim, ask yourself, "What was Ray

Charles, after countless years of fighting, still doing in her life, still returning to her for her embrace?" I don't give a darn what I did; when the world was kickin' my butt, I called Sandy Betts, and, on her own, she was my Seventh Fleet. My mother *was* royalty. She did not need the world to tell her so.

The very next day, they let me out for another four hours. When I got to Aunt Cathy's, Jim was saying the Lord's Prayer with her, and she was literally taking her last breath. At that moment, I realized that every sense of security I had ever known was gone. Lost. Irreplaceable. There's something about Mom always getting the last word. My 36th birthday was but a few hours away. During my birth, she claimed she was in hard labor for so long, she began hallucinating, and it was a fight from the very beginning. Now I was fighting to let her go. God is my sufficiency, but it doesn't replace the woman who brought me into this world. I grew up knowing her love, and, for me, no mother's love could be greater.

I had to immediately return to the halfway house. When I walked in, no words were necessary, nor were words possible. They immediately started to make arrangements for me to attend the funeral. It was unusual, highly irregular. Never in their history had an inmate been allowed to leave for seven days across state lines without a marshal escort. I was to keep that information private. The inmates could not handle that—most people there were hardcore. Other counselors and people of the system had problems with the decision as well. "If we do it for her, then we have to do it for everybody else." Those words were on everyone's lips, but God handled it. There was no getting around it; things like that just don't happen within the federal penal system! My counselor herself said, "I don't know why I am doing this; I just feel compelled to." It was her choice, and she stood on it above anyone's understanding, including her own.

Matt drove me (along with Jeanna, Jamie, and Becky) to the funeral in Cambridge, Ohio, straight through for sixteen hours. Kevin rode with our cousin Jeremy. The girls and I stayed at Alicia's, a very good friend of mine, and, over the next day, I saw almost everybody I had gone to school with.

As for everyone in our family who had passed before, the funeral was held at Scott's Funeral Home. Chuck Simpson, a minister and

Mom's first cousin, spoke at the service. They were the best of friends. It was as Mom would have wanted it, lots of laughter, lots of funny stories about her. Chuck said, "Sandy is up there and is saying, 'It's the bomb up here!'" My Uncle Jerry spoke and sang, and, of course, my brother Kevin, one of the few who was truly glad I was there, did his thing.

Kevin had been drinking heavily in order to make it through all of this. His love for her was unsurpassable. When he got up to speak, I was concerned for him. There was not a soul present who was not aware he was drunk. Kevin always had the ability to show out beyond anything *imaginable*. I love and understand him like no other. If something was not right by him, he would tear the house down. Literally. There was a great amount of tension within me observing him in his condition. I did not want anyone speaking ill of my brother. I would show out in his defense, and then it would become a free-for-all. He is my brother like no other and the true son of my mother. When he began to speak, I was filled with awe, and any concern for his condition vanished from me. Mom and I were so proud of him. If there was ever a small miracle that clearly gave evidence of the spirit being stronger than the flesh, it was that moment he began to speak with an eloquence and verve known only to the Greatest Orator. He had surrendered to something far greater than himself, and everyone in that little funeral chapel knew it and stood witness to it. God, through him, showed up in a manner no amount of alcohol could lay claim to and outdid any performance a drunken stupor could precipitate— the Holy Spirit was present within him.

And so the service continued, and not only had disaster been averted, but the entire service had also been elevated to an entirely different level. There was talk about God's word and the impact of Mom's giving, how much she loved others, her love for God, and how she imparted that in other people. To this day, people talk about Mom's greatness in their lives, how she brought about a hundred-and-eighty-degree turn for them.

They wanted me to sing, and I had planned on it. I couldn't. The only thing I was capable of doing was to read a poem I had constructed out of the letters of her name. I could hardly make it through that. Instead of singing, I played a song from Soul Food called "Mama," the words of which were the exact picture of my mother. I could barely breathe. I had to deal with all the looks from my family. As far as most everyone was concerned, I delivered most of my mom's pain—they all knew it; I knew it—and she died of cancer, and cancer is pain eating you from the inside out. Aunt Cathy could not even look at me.

You've got to blame somebody. Mom was only fifty-seven. She was still a baby when she died. I embraced the idea I was the cause of my mother's death, but God would not let me go all the way with it. If I had, I would have killed myself before reaching bottom. It was an abyss of pain and guilt, a personal hell the depth of which none should know—there is no round-trip fare in that journey. I was considering taking my own life; that's how intense the guilt had become. My Uncle Jerry said to me, "Sheila, you know God loves you. We hope that you make it through this. You need to do it for your mother now." But I was hearing him say, "You are so screwed up. You screwed up! That is the last memory your mom had of you. Screwed up." If looks could kill, Aunt Cathy would have dropped me on the spot.

Mr. Shirley was there, and so was May Bea. Now that *will* mess you up. May Bea approached me outside before the service began and said, "Oh, baby. They really have put it together nicely. Wait 'til you see her! They have got her looking so nice." I was looking at her as if she were absolutely out of her mind. They went out of their way to be as friendly and charming as anyone could be. It made me want to puke! May Bea is nuttier than a fruitcake, to say nothing of her partner, Mr. Shirley. I can't look at him, and he can't look at me. I was thinking, *That's okay. Don't look at me. If it wasn't for you, I probably wouldn't be a crackhead and in prison! And you don't have a thing to say!*

When Mom was writing her story, it was no secret to May Bea. She told Mom directly, "You'd better leave me out of that story, or I will sue you!" Please! I had all I could do to hold my tongue. No wonder Kevin was drunk! And I was thinking, *You'd better know that were it not for Sandy Betts raising me in love and introducing me to a yet Higher Love, my people would be here, and that would be the end of you!*

Into silence we now stared. Looking at them—looking back at me—looking at them—knowing they knew the memory lived on— that I remembered—that I knew—sure as they did. Especially Mr. Shirley. Several years earlier, I brought the past to him, the raped to the rapist. He had the nerve to tell me he didn't know what I was talking about! Most everyone present felt I was responsible for my mother's death to some degree. Facing oppressive personal guilt, it is a wonder I kept my mouth shut.

It was a short drive to the cemetery, just a couple of miles. Withdrawn, looking out the car window, I wondered how much more of this life I could take. The hardest part was watching them roll her casket down into the ground knowing Mom was not there—already flying free! She was telling me within my heart, "What are you doing with that body? Are you people nuts?! I could care about it! Why should you?" She would not want anybody to feel sad about her passing. I know that for a fact. Mom would say, "Cry at a birth and laugh at a death!"

In the cemetery, the Betts family has a plot, and Mom was buried next to her mom and dad. On the other side of her was Santa Claus—the man who played Santa Claus when we were kids. I found it a fitting place and all as it should be as the leaves fell from the trees on the neatly kept, late September grass.

Though there were travel advisories, I complied with the deal made with Karen, and in a blizzard drove back to somewhere I could not call home—at times, well in excess of the speed limit. We arrived two hours late, and I was in trouble. I had to do a U/A. Gratefully, I jumped through the hoops.

I pulled back from that recollection again to Bryan FPC. Great. How am I supposed to go to sleep now? I went to my mother's book again and found an entry at the end somewhere. It was five or six pages written in her hand: a letter to my father, written at the time when I was at the height of my insanity and drug addiction. Again, I asked God what this was all about behind the shades and the walls of federal prison—part of the answer to reclaim my life? All I could think to do was read this letter. And I did.

Dear Ray,

The conditions and circumstances that surround our daughter and grandchildren have given me the courage to write you. I need to know I have left no stone unturned in assisting them toward their productivity as vital human beings. This is deeper than the dollar, Ray, and I ask you to look at this situation with openness and concern.

The media is filled with stories these days of the abuse and neglect that children are currently suffering. It is ever-present within my own family, and I decided to sit down and reflect on the pain and suffering we have brought to our daughter and grandchildren.

There was a child in the news recently, caught up in a whirlwind with your friend Bill Cosby. As I took a look at what your daughter and grandchildren have gone through, my heart identified completely with this child. This Cosby child, because of money and fame and a need to create more money and fame under the pretense of some false image, she had to pretend that she was not a part of the greatest love a little girl could ever have—the pride of being her father's heart.

Most fathers have room in their heart for all their daughters. My dad had room for six, and each was the apple of his eye. I want to, both in spirit and words, express a deep gratitude for the circumstances this child has brought to my soul as a deep and moving "wake-up call." One that just might save our daughter's life and stop another generation of suffering in our bloodline. To feel unworthy of being a part of a man you were told was your father, to be hidden away as if you have done something wrong before you even get out of your mother's womb has to be devastating. I wish these young people were past the needs of the flesh and could know they have a Father who will never hurt them—Our Heavenly Father. However, that is not the case, and like myself, we need an earthly daddy. Yes, this little girl in Bill Cosby's situation is responsible for my wake-up call. Thank you, little girl; whether your father is Bill Cosby or not, you have paid the price. Famous people are just like us. They too must meet their maker as responsible human beings to what they have brought forth on this earth. I am very clear on this issue!

Over the years, the sadness of our daughter's drug addiction caused me to go into a shell that would not allow me to face any truths. I couldn't afford to because I would then have to look at myself and discover that maybe, just maybe, I wasn't the mother I could have been. Well, my dear, no one is. Hindsight is a beautiful thing. Standing behind our daughter with hope and prayers, I have experienced many things. I have had threats on my life on issues that had nothing to do with me. I have gone months without knowing where she is. I have had to look into the eyes of our grandchildren and reassure them that God would take care of their mommy. With integrity, I held on to my faith in God and refused to give up on the vision of a healthy, productive family. In coming face to face with myself and finding no hiding place in the truth, I must proceed to exhaust every avenue available to me to see our daughter and grandchildren have a chance of living life productively.

In your recent documentary, you share with the world you have four children. None of those four shown include our daughter, Sheila Raye. I want to know what mental closet I was hiding in when I would watch that rejection and not see her pain and fear. Watching our daughter not being a part of the pride of your life. After all, she is your legal daughter. Sheila certainly is not a secret. I listened to Pastor Joyce Meyer define rejection: "to be cast aside, to be seen as having no value." Yes, from the pain on her face, that is what Sheila felt every time she watched your life story. I am the one who was blind!

With a cringe, I think back to when she met her brother, your youngest son, Bobby, at a nightclub in Los Angeles. This is when the reality of the rejection hit! Bobby was just thinking that he was meeting an attractive girl he could get to know! Sheila, seeing a guy who looked like her other brother she had met on the road with you, asked, "Is your last name Robinson?"

"Yes," Bobby responded.

"Well, I think I'm your sister!" Sheila announced.

The two became elated by this truth, and Bobby took Sheila soon after the meeting to the house that you provided your ex-wife and children. I had raised Sheila not to see you as a financial giant but as a father, a man who loved her. I had raised her on the four hundred dollars a month you had given us for sixteen years of her life. To the best of my abilities, Sheila lived healthy and well with me. Her wealth was a loving family of grandparents and relatives along with myself.

I can personally attest to that, Mama. I remember as I was growing up how Mom was always so full of love. She was always telling my brother and me how much she loved us and that we were her all! It was not necessary; we were aware of the exceptional love within her—not just for us, but also for God and all His children. How do I know this? Because she WAS my mother. And always will be. Within my brother and me, my mother's love lives. If there was a reason for silence over events of my childhood above any other single thing, it would be that those dark secrets would have destroyed her. In spite of her love for Ray Charles, what it did to her, what he allowed to happen to us, and the profound confusion that resulted within all of us because of it, her spirit remained ingenuous and her love remained pure. I speak for my brother, all her grandchildren, and all those who called her MOM, collectively as one child, when I say, "Let the world know, no child more proud, Dear Mother Mine!"

I was not prepared when she returned from Bobby's house. In a quick moment, all I had tried to do was rejected. It had no value anymore for Sheila.

"Mom," she said, "how could you do this to me? Is this the way the children of Ray Charles live?"

With my head still buried in the sand, I could not deal with her feelings and became defensive. I had given her a good life.

"But Mom, you never told me my dad was rich!" she protested.

Our daughter was now on a new path. Loving her mom and really being more mature than me, she saw my defeat and said, "That's all right, Mom. I'll make my own money."

I was still hiding, so how could I see her pain? Just before this incident, our daughter had asked you to help save her car from being repossessed. You said you couldn't afford to help her. Not having a reference for your income, she believed you. She herself put it best: "Is this the way of Ray Charles?" Note that she said "Ray Charles"; she did not refer to you as Dad! It was hurting her. She had been hoodwinked, bamboozled, run amuck by the both of us.

I do not blame you, Ray, but maybe you can join me on this wake-up call to give a chance for our children to be drug free and feeling good about themselves with the recognition that Daddy, Grandpa, the Living Legend somehow fits them into his value system. When child protection called you to tell you your grandchild was in need due to problems and they needed to contact all relatives, I know you did not think it was a joke. Why? You called me and said that you would help. I needed to get into a larger place that would accommodate and meet the specifications of social services. I informed you that our grandson had to have open-heart surgery and that he would need all the love and support that he could get. I still had my head in the sand. Ray, I told you: trying alone to deal with our daughter's drug addiction, trying to support and care for the two grandchildren we already have is too much. I am having a difficult time. What would you think of buying a small house that would meet the requirements of the state? I told you I didn't need to own it. Add it to your empire. Just let me get away from our daughter's eviction every other month and create some stability for the grandchildren. We would pay you rent when we could. You said, "I'll have to think about that." That was about a year ago. Are you still thinking?

Your daughter made an appointment to speak with you—just as any other common person who wants to speak to the great Ray Charles must do. Her friend flew her to Las Vegas to meet you. When she arrived, she was frustrated. Even with an appointment, Sheila had to beg to see you, her OWN FATHER! At least Ray Jr. was nice since it was her birthday and took his sister out for the evening. I thought that I had heard it all until she came back just as much in the dark about you as while I raised her. With a genuine sense of accomplishment, she said, "Mom, Dad agreed to do a song with me. He usually charges $150,000 a song, but, because I'm his daughter, he is only going to charge me $50,000. He said as soon as I can find an investor, I should let him know. Dad told me, 'Now, Sheila, don't have me going to get a release from my record company for nothing.'"

I thought I would vomit. Your daughter is on welfare, trying to recover from a drug addiction just like you did. The only difference between you and your daughter is money. She is truly blind. So that's it. You put the three of us together, and you have the three blind mice.

Not being able to raise the money, the favorite word—REJECTION—is once again in full play. She was completely set up for rejection. Ray, with the talent you say Sheila has, why would you have not reached out to her like a father and given her a chance? You have admitted not only that she can sing but that she has exceptional writing ability. Oh, I forgot. One time you did record all her music in your studio in Los Angeles, owning it yourself and paying her like a pauper. Music she wrote! There she was again not really seeing you! "Oh, Dad. This is the first time I've ever been paid. Thank you!" She had no clue that a $180.00 union wage you gave her meant that you would own the work that she was doing with you or that you would ever find the time to do anything with it but own it. I pray, Ray, Sheila will not be like Natalie Cole, singing to a video. You said this is your only child who has talent in the music world. That is your world. It seems only natural I would finally figure out who is your REAL family: the world! That is where you give yourself. Your bloodline is not even in the running. One time I was watching a television interview with you. There you were, saying that if you have one fault, it would be that you were stingy. Well, that never mattered to me because I do not look to you as a supplier of my needs. However, I cannot pretend another thirty-five years when your child and grandchildren's lives are on the line, while you run and hide from any form of support. I know Sheila is a grown woman, and you have no legal obligation to your grandchildren. What about the moral *and spiritual obligation? The last time I spent time with you, you were doing a benefit for handicapped children. We talked about invisible handicaps and the need for that awareness. I now talk about the "charity that begins at home." Being that you cannot help our daughter and grandchildren get started with a new life, perhaps you could do a charity benefit for them.*

As I've told you many times, I want nothing from you but to continue my life. I do not have to be with you. I don't have to see you or touch you to love you. Love is inside of me and has nothing to do with what is going on outside.

God bless you, Ray. I pray God will soften your heart and lead you to a more caring relationship toward your children. They deserve to know that the man who the world loves is loving them as well as he loves the world.

When we spoke, you asked about the new granddaughter, and you said, "How many babies can our daughter bring you?"

I answered, "No more!"

You repeated over and over, "I do not believe you."

I finally responded, "This is our bloodline—Ray, as many as God sends!"

"I wish I had the magic words to spare you from our daughter."

I have no doubt you meant that I should turn my back on the problem as you have. Well, I wish I had the magic words to make you see she is worthy of nothing being spared. The vision God has shown me of her is my constant focus, and it is beautiful. Why can't you be a part of this vision for our daughter, Ray?

Ray, I say this to you in closing. I am not that little girl who ran from reporters in 1963, who did not want the world to know her name. Who (after our highly public litigation) fled from a lousy Laundromat in tears because a woman recognized me and threw dirty clothes on Sheila, our baby, and me with the words, "There's that lady who took advantage of a blind man."

Oh no! I am a mother, a grandmother! Do you hear me? A proud black woman who will leave all sense of false pride behind to do what it takes to save the life of her children.

Free after thirty-five years.

Love, Sandy

PS: Remember when you told me, "I will tell you one thing, mama, about love. You can't corrode it with anything. You can pile anything up on it, and, if it is true, it still remains true love." I am counting on that!

I will say it again, this time just for me, just to you. To all those whom I may meet, I will let them know: no child more proud, Dear Mother Mine.

CHAPTER 11

LIKE FATHER, LIKE DAUGHTER

It's a scary place when you awake inside this dream
to realize how unconscious you have been
witness to the great extent of your coma
when you look around with shocking awareness
most everyone is fast asleep

—*GLENN SWANSON,*
SHOES ON THE TABLE

AT THE FOLLOWING Wednesday night rehearsal, after the customary hug and prayer, Miss Sharon said, "Sheila, I'm going to give you something to work toward—your first solo. I think it should be 'One More Day.' I have been praying about it, and God put it on my heart. It seems to fit where you are right now spiritually."

She handed me the words, and I took a moment to read them. *Time after time, I start out my day with a made-up mind. I say in my heart, that this is the day I would make a new start. But when the end of the day had come, nothing for Him that I had done, and I'd begin to pray for one more day. So I thank God for one more day.* Initially, I felt challenged by these words, as though Miss Sharon viewed my progress as minimal. I shrugged off my need for recognition, considered the matter more carefully, and discovered I had to agree. The strides I thought I had been making toward God were nothing more than putting to rest ghosts of the past. My mind was still engaged in activity that was all about me. Not to say it was a bad thing—it was necessary to get past the past—but my life had yet to be about discipline. These words were right on target with the way I was thinking and acting. I needed tomorrow—one more day.

I said with a newfound respect, "Oh, Miss Sharon! This is perfect. You most certainly received the gift of discernment because—these words—I can relate to them perfectly."

"Good. Come to the next rehearsal a half hour early, and we will go over it. I expect we will be performing it one week from this coming Sunday."

Marcia became a friend from the first moment I joined choir. There were two new girls who came to audition that night. Miss Sharon had them sing before rehearsal began. They were, to put it kindly, not ready to enter the choir, and, despite our efforts to the contrary, Marcia and I started laughing. I don't know what it is, but when you are in church or listening to someone's audition, the idea that you can't laugh only increases the desire to do so. At some point, the threshold is crossed, and it's all over. We were laughing tears, and Miss Sharon wasn't having it.

"Marcia! Sheila! What do you find so funny?" She was grinning ear to ear, equally amused by the auditioning talent. She wasn't as angry as her voice indicated, but I felt a little ashamed over my response. I knew it was unnerving to audition, and someone laughing at you can hurt. Silently, I asked forgiveness as Miss Sharon politely excused the two girls who auditioned.

Miss Sharon pulled me aside as the choir was released. "Everyone wants her moment to shine, and some of the girls have been waiting for months to be the featured singer. I bumped you up ahead of some of the other girls. I just wanted you to know you might catch an attitude from one or two of them."

Why did she say that to me? I started to look for that in the other girls. It was the last thing that I wanted to see happen. I just wanted to feel the support of the other members, feel a part of the group.

"Okay."

The Sunday of my solo arrived. I was nervous about it. It had been so long since I had sung solo in front of people. Was I going to be as good as they were expecting, especially now that everyone knew I was Ray's daughter?

It was the featured song, the second song of the service. I walked up to the microphone. I could see my hand shaking and wondered if anyone noticed. I said a little prayer: "It's all yours, God. You will have to take control." As soon as I opened my mouth to sing the first note, I was carried away. Like the previous two Sundays, I was not conscious of singing for anyone present. I felt as though I was singing directly to God and He was responding to me as a deep longing once again ignited within. The choir was supporting me not only with their voices but also with heart and soul. I could feel that. When the song was over and I returned to being conscious of my position inside the prison chapel, I looked into the congregation and discovered a great many inmates with tears in their eyes. Humbled, I thanked God.

After the service, Miss Sharon said, "Sheila, that was wonderful. Your calling is to sing God's music."

I turned to her and asked, "What is it—about singing, I mean— my love-hate thing with it? There is no doubt I was born to sing, for when I am singing, I am the happiest I can be. When I was out in the street doing my thing with crack, I couldn't even listen to music. It made me aware that I was not at all happy with anything."

"For me, Sheila," Miss Sharon said, "music is the most healing thing for the spirit—God made it so. When I first came here, off the street from the life I had known, it was the one thing in here that saved me."

"It has always been such a confusing issue with me. People would say, 'Sheila, you sing your ass off!', and others would say, 'How can you be any good? If you were even half a singer, with Ray Charles as your father, you should be on top of the world.' I would think about that and have to agree! Whenever something was close to happening with my musical career, it fell apart or I did."

"Trust me, girl, you can sing, and you need to!"

Now I was on a high, and I didn't feel like being alone. "Marcia, how about you and I go for a walk?" So we did. Her thing was crack, too, and we talked about it and her ex-boyfriend. He had drugs stashed on her property, and they busted her. It seemed as if everyone was in here because of dope, enveloped in its culture of lawlessness in one way or another. Horror stories of abuse were as commonplace as the khaki uniform.

Growing up out of childhood, there comes a time when we realize this is not a perfect world. The timetable of such awareness differs for each of us, depending on the circumstances of life. Perhaps it is through the loss of a loved one or through the loss you see in another. Perhaps there are some who are gradually overtaken by such understanding, the true depth of such realization coming but moments from the end of life. Others have the darkest human ignorance thrust upon them during the earliest of ages for reasons known but to God—so traumatic and incomprehensible to the ingenuousness of the child, that a fracturing occurs within the inner core of one's being, profound and complete, the memory of such experience buried and walled off inside by a mechanism of human consciousness, forced to proceed through life in a manner dead to a great part of self. The compromise made, of course, is that we are allowed to live free of such conscious memory, for such experience brings the entire production within the theater of our world to a complete halt. We must continue to act within the drama, get up and eat breakfast, continue with our lives as we write our life's script. That is the reality.

I came to realize the process of reliving buried memory had begun years ago. The dawning of such an awakening came shortly after the birth of my second child, Jaymi. Through her birth, the labor pains of my own rebirth would begin and continued yet into these initial stages of the quickening. I had distanced myself from that which was so critically important to me—the love and embrace of my family—something I desperately sought without knowing how to claim it. The awareness of blocked experiences of rape, sexual abuse, and physical violence inflicted upon my mother and me were about to return with a vengeance, both in the physical and subsequently onto the screen of memory.

I was self-absorbed within a mindless approach to establishing a musical career that I personally sabotaged through self-destruction. If it wasn't the drug use derailing me, it was my ill-founded faith in Ray's, my mother's, or somebody's misguided insanity, such as traveling to France for the Midem Festival on a nickel and a dime without any musical product to speak of. I had spent most of my life completely unaware of the true nature of my dysfunction, clueless that I was clueless. Yet the clues were all there.

The day I returned from France, Lovey, my cousin, had agreed to keep my daughters, Jeanna and Jaymi, for an extra night so Drama and I could be alone. Drama, the two girls, and I were all living together in a rented house. The night of my return, while he was out with his brother, I went to the store and bought some wine and appetizers— cheese, crackers, and such. I started the fireplace and lit some candles and incense, creating an atmosphere I thought to be romantic, eerily familiar to a setting within a memory from childhood. After a bath, I slipped into some red lingerie I purchased in France. I was ready and waiting for my man. The evening started out wonderfully with laughing and talking, and the wine had me feeling good. For whatever reason, I was freer sexually than I had been in the past, and soon, we were in the bedroom. Intimate.

"Do you want a glass of wine?" I asked Drama. As I stood and turned around, he hit me so hard that I went from the bedroom to the living room in one instant. I picked myself up off the floor, dazed, and he started to beat me with a closed fist, up one side and down the other. I dropped again to the floor, and he began kicking me like a dog.

"What are you doing?" I screamed.

"Who did you buy that lingerie for? You must have been sleeping with someone in France. You never acted like that before, wild like that. Who taught you that?"

Clearly, he was out of his mind and the one messing around. Shortly thereafter, his ex-girlfriend arrived, and Drama left while I was left alone with the drama. I had never seen that side of him. He had always treated me with civility. In a state of shock, sobbing, choked from the inside out, and with a new life but two months old who looked just like him, I thought, *Who is this guy?* There was no way for me to see this coming, and with that awareness came an important revelation. I had never been physically struck like that before, the catalyst to precipitate a distant memory. With a blood-soaked sheet wrapped about her, inside intense emotional energy, Mom had forcefully grabbed and held me with her eyes as she said with conviction, "Don't ever let a man beat you, Sheila, or hit you or in any way abuse you!" I saw Mom's face and heard her voice as clear as the day she spoke those words as I lay on the floor. Beaten.

Paul Cooper was a black belt in karate. For me, it was wonderful to have a stepdad. He had a million-dollar house with a beautiful swimming pool in the back. He was a genius, the head engineer for NCR, a computer wizard. He had met my mother through a mutual friend in Cambridge, and they fell in love. She was the happiest I had known her. I was ten at the time and thought, *This is it!* This was going to be my family. Security. Stability. Someone we could trust. We moved to Columbia, South Carolina. Lived there for about a year, and then, well, he just flipped out, thought he was the Messiah. He started to do kung fu on Mom. Blood was everywhere. Mom had a large gash on her head and was naked. She had emerged from the shower and went into the bedroom and got kung fu-ed—out of nowhere, blindsided with a vengeance. For no reason, he just snapped and, to my knowledge, remains in an asylum to this day. "I am the Messiah! I am the living Christ!" he shouted, walking around the house with a shotgun. Kevin was in his bedroom when Mom and I ran outside. Mom was still naked when the police and the ambulance came—the neighbors had called. The paramedics brought Mom a sheet from their ambulance. Impervious to her own circumstance and injury, her concern was for her son. "He's trapped in the house with a crazy man who's got a gun. A shotgun!"

The police, through a megaphone, talked him into releasing Kevin. Out the front door he came crying, scared, running into Mom's arms. Paul was brilliant, but in the blink of eye, he lost it completely. All we had known as security vanished! What was that all about? Ray and Mom? Mom did not give Paul a second thought. After the police had taken Paul away, Mom told us to gather a handful of things quickly from the house. When we hit the Greyhound bus stop to head back to Cambridge, Kevin and I left with nothing to hold onto but a paper bag of clothes. Mom, she kept her sheet. She left him, that house, and everything in it without looking back.

It was on the bus back to Cambridge when she told me he had hit her the night she allowed me to go to a concert—Donald Byrd and the Blackbirds, The Brothers Johnson, EWF, and Chaka Khan. For my twelfth birthday, I was allowed to go to the concert with the next-door neighbor, my best friend in Columbia. She was thirteen; her sister, who was nineteen, served as the chaperone for the two of us. I didn't know it was against his wishes, although they were arguing when I left out the front door. That's when Mom said, "Sheila, don't you ever let a man hit you."

Mr. Shirley beat Mom, jealous of her and the attention she received from everyone. Some would have observed that Mom needed to feel loved by all, others would have said she just saw a need for love and tried to answer it, but I always thought it was her inner need to understand her love for Ray Charles and get everyone else she knew involved with it. I sat there on the bus, heading back to Cambridge, wondering what it was about my mom that caused her to get into all these abusive relationships. I resented her for that. I would get built up inside and then get knocked right back down: Ray Charles, Mr. Shirley, Paul Cooper. I did not have any compassion for Mom; I felt she should have been able to see it coming— the crazy in Paul, the crazy in Mr. Shirley, the crazy behind the shades. Now I was on the floor, beaten by Drama, and I understood. You can never see the crazy coming. It's buried beneath the surface of most everyone. I never held it against Mom after that—after experiencing my blindness to it.

Nancy, a dear friend of my mother's, told me how Mom would go over to her house to call my father. This was after Mr. Shirley would take the phone with him whenever he left the house—his way to stop Mom from calling Dad. Of course, at Nancy's, she would call Ray and bill the calls back to their number. Mom didn't understand that her love for Ray went beyond all things, nor what it did to the minds of other men in her life. The unfortunate consequence of her misunderstanding was physical and emotional abuse directed toward her, my brother, and me.

With this one beating from Drama, the truth hit the fan, and everything surfaced, all the darkness and abuse. It is so outside any story or nightmare I had ever heard. It was not reality; no one was aware of this but the guilty. Why me? Why us? I mean, clearly, these experiences were not commonplace—if they were, the world would have fallen apart years ago. I came to a fully conscious perception that Mr. Shirley was one of the principal roots of the fracturing of my self, the distance I maintained from Spirit, the joy I surrendered. He was the first and violated a trust I felt unbreakable. After such an occurrence, I lost faith in my inner understanding—the world was not consistent with how I knew it should be.

It was amazing to me how complete my denial of such memories had been. It made me angry and confrontational. I had related to those experiences as though they had never happened, as but fragments of a nightmare that had never occurred. I continued to find myself interacting with Mr. Shirley throughout the remainder of my life—though, at times, such interaction would span many years. In retrospect, it is beyond my comprehension how complete and solid the wall surrounding those memories had been. This capacity of consciousness would be completely unbelievable to me were I not the one who underwent such experience and subsequent reawakening to the nightmare.

For reasons of my personal freedom, I revisited the initiation to my drug addiction. I had to keep grinding away at it now that I had some support inside of myself—to understand how it began—to look in the mirror and let go—to use the time in federal prison to discover freedom.

My first experience smoking cocaine was free-basing—I still don't know how it ended up being called crack—because even back then Mr. Shirley was doing it with the ether. It was called freebasing because it was being freed from the base, removing all the impurities, all the noncocaine elements added when it would change hands; people would hit it with something, and dealers would step on it. Back in the seventies, it was more pure than by today's standards. It was pink Peruvian flake and my eighteenth birthday.

Three of us girls were contemplating my birthday celebration. What is it about the birthday excuse in the drug user or the alcoholic? At some point in life, the harmless birthday party for a child turns into an excuse for full-blown irresponsibility as though there were an unwritten law that this was a "free day" when it came to such things. Not only do you get to use your birthday as an excuse, but everyone else gets to as well. If that is where you want to go, any reason will do.

The acceptance of experimenting with drugs was just a part of my culture. It was always around me, and few knew how much it surrounded my childhood. Mom didn't. Earlier that same summer, I had snorted coke with a girl named Blue, the one who had given us

LSD in liquid form. We dropped it in our eyes. I could have gone blind! The acid made me shave off all my eyebrows and go through a crying jag. I had smoked herb, snorted THC powder, and eaten mushrooms. We all smoked reefer and had fun telling stories about when we were little kids. Where were the stories about Mr. Shirley raping me at the age of seven?

Cambridge to Columbus was an eighty-mile trip. My birthday plan—visit Mr. Shirley's, and go out in the city and party. It made sense to everyone because he had the stuff. Marian Warren, once again, came up with the idea of hitchhiking, and my friend Dorothy and I went along with it, even though I had a Datsun 260Z sports car at that time. When we got there, we made up some story that we had taken the bus. We didn't dare tell Mr. Shirley we had hitchhiked. Go figure!

Mr. Shirley, he was the MAN. All the professional athletes, the football players from Ohio State, all the musicians who were the who's who (Nancy Wilson was a friend of his), all the professional people from Columbus—he was their dealer. The world supported him—just as they supported Ray Charles, my father! I knew that; I lived it! Why fight a war against the world when there was no win in it? There was no one who would take my side or believe what I had to say. Mr. Shirley was the MAN. Ray Charles was GOD. Abuse and neglect were what I knew of the world, though my heart always knew something different.

To remain beneath the radar screen of the authorities, Mr. Shirley worked a decent job all those years, very clever and careful in the manner in which he conducted business. He never lived above the means of his daytime occupation. Except for customers and suppliers, he was able to completely conceal that part of his life from friends and family. Kevin and I got his keys one day and opened a locked basement door. We found garbage bags full of money. I must have been eight or nine years old, and we instantly became the sole family members aware of that side of his life.

When I was fourteen and Kevin was twelve, we went to visit Mr. Shirley. I stole about a half ounce of coke, a whole bunch of soapers, and a sheet of acid—stuff we had found. I was in high school, and by that time, I knew what the deal was. I tried to steal some coke and spilled an entire ounce on the floor. I sucked it up with a vacuum cleaner and blamed it on Kevin, and he got a real bad spanking. I'd take piles of pot and hide it in the lining of my suitcase. He found it one time. I told him that I brought it with me. I imagine he didn't put up an argument because he was afraid of what I would say or do. He left the matter with, "You know, Sheila, you can get into a lot of trouble with that stuff."

So Mr. Shirley was the party guy, and I was eighteen! Marian was nineteen, and Dorothy was twenty-one. Mr. Shirley was doing his thing and came out with wine and stuff. I felt like I was grown. The three of us thought that we were "hot stuff." He cooked up some coke. It was a long pipe with a big bubble in the middle. He had a propane torch so it wouldn't leave carbon on the glass and all kinds of paraphernalia. I thought it was very glamorous.

It was a gorgeous day in September, Indian summer. I'll never forget the first hit I took. It was probably around four o'clock, and the sun went "bling" into this beautiful, warm, and intense thing. The color of the fall leaves took upon a vibrancy I had not previously known. Every sense was heightened, and I was filled with a euphoric high. It was the best feeling I had ever experienced in my life. There was no chase in it. We took a hit, and then we would talk and laugh without the uncomfortable feeling of needing another hit.

For whatever reason, Mr. Shirley thought it would be okay to show me all these pictures of my girlfriends who were now attending Ohio State. I can only imagine that he thought. *What in the world?! We're all high.* I had introduced them to Mr. Shirley so they would know someone in Columbus, someone who could show them around town. Now he was revealing to me, in pictures, those same friends drinking wine, doing drugs. They were naked. My God! He was saying, "Remember this girl? Remember this girl? How about this girl?" No! Up to that point, I was having a good time. I was already starting to get weird behind the drug, but that was the definite "I have to go now" signal, and we left. We hitchhiked back to Cambridge. That was my eighteenth birthday.

I had yet to deal with quite a few things—experience of trauma and fear that remained buried from childhood, experiences of rape and Mr. Shirley. I had blocked them out, and I thought no one cared. I wanted to vomit. Now I was thinking about the girls I had sent to Mr. Shirley, the girls in those pictures. What was I thinking? There was more than one father in this world, fathers who would have killed Mr. Shirley for what he had done, and they too would not be thinking— just reacting—just furthering the web of pain and ignorance I somehow could not remove myself from. How was I to get beyond the guilt of my unconscious behavior? Better yet, how was I to get free of my unconscious thoughts and behavior in the future? I kept revisiting my past.

The memory of feeling good through drugs was what I sought when I began going through my ups and downs within the music business. My addiction really took full effect after the birth of my first daughter, Jeanna. I lost my mind with some freaky chemical imbalance. I left the hospital in Columbus, just walked right out of there like a zombie two or three days after her birth. To this day, I can offer no explanation to it except that I had some postpartum syndrome, depressed beyond words. I didn't say anything to anyone. Mom was able to get Jeanna out of the hospital. My mother, brother, and daughter and the rest of the entourage moved to Minneapolis. Though I was to record at Paisley Park, Mom was to meet a writer interested in her story before I was scheduled to record. They all left me MIA. I was out in the streets and ran into an old friend all cracked out. I went on a three-day binge with her. I had sixty-five hundred dollars, my portion of a loan that we had received from a longtime friend of Mom's—money for my project. Mom had hers, and I made sure I had mine. I ended up spending seventeen hundred of it.

I could not believe what I was exposed to in that crack house. Literally, in the same room I was in, girls were having sex for crack, begging for the stuff, giving someone oral sex for a hit of crack. I was sitting at a table with someone who was nine months pregnant, and whoosh, her water just gushed all over the floor, and she would not stop smoking. If you haven't witnessed it, when your water breaks, there's a lot of water.

People were screaming, "Oh my God! My God!"

I heard someone say, "If that baby comes now and dies, we are throwing you in the alley—somewhere!"

I was mesmerized by the strength of her addiction. They had to hold her down, get the pipe from her, and call an ambulance before she would leave; otherwise, she would have still been sitting there with that baby coming out of her! Everyone had to vacate the house—it was an abandoned house or one they had taken over. When the ambulance did come, even if she said people were up there smoking crack, there was no one left. It would be obvious to the medics. She was looking crazy, her hair was sticking up everywhere, her lips looking purple, her skin looking gray—when somebody has been up for days, you'd have to be blind not to know something is wrong.

I was still bleeding, hadn't changed clothes for three days. That moment of time was evil. After that, I was through. It doesn't make sense how I got caught back up in it like I did after seeing that. I was thinking, *If this is what the stuff does to you, oh no!* But at that point, I was still new to it. I had not yet become sprung. There were periods when I wouldn't smoke for hours; I was just sitting around waiting for Doreen and talking to people. Mom and my child were on their way to Minneapolis. My binge was solely because . . .

There I go again. What am I thinking? I had just had a baby, and I was at the party. Party? What the heck? The water broke, and that is what ended the smoking. Everyone had to leave; the ambulance was coming! I called one of my mom's friends and said, "Look, come and get me. I'm sorry; I've been with my friend." He picked me up at the gas station and brought me to his house. I took a shower, got cleaned up, and made flight arrangements to Minneapolis. I lied to everyone and thought that they didn't know any better. I didn't have any history of being cracked out like that, not for three days running. That entire scene freaked me out. My heart was killing me—at least the people there had had enough compassion to make her stop and call an ambulance—she had a pocketful of money. They probably just grabbed her money. I don't know.

I never looked at drugs or getting high that seriously. Not like that. To see someone so addicted scared me. This was a peekaboo into my forthcoming problem and yet not enough to prevent me from going down that road. I also had a girlfriend who did PCP and put her three-month-old baby in the oven and was going to bake it because she thought it was a turkey. What more did I need to see? Drugs take you completely inside of your own delusional hell. But the crack high was not something I needed at that point and felt I could remain above its power. I was ignorant and mindlessly arrogant. Blind.

On my bed, in my cell, I considered these things. I asked myself how I could sit inside that crack house for three days under those circumstances, so far removed from anything that would indicate the faintest shade of sanity. I had just given birth to my first child—the one whom I desperately longed to hear from! How pitiful my take on life had been. For the first time, I understood that I never understood. That's a big pill to swallow. I choked on it—there—in my cell. I made it to the bathroom and puked. Choked on it again, then puked some more.

This is how it works. Karma. Momentum. The first week I was in Minneapolis, we called around to see where we could go and get our hair done. Having been advised to connect with a black hair salon on Lake Street, I found myself sitting in the hairdresser's chair. The hairdresser, Hollywood, leaned over to my ear and said, "Hey, do you need some of that good stuff?"

"Some of what good stuff? Some hair care products?" There was my genetic link to Sandra Betts and perhaps evidence of a naïveté gene.

He recognized me. I was on the front page of the "Variety" section of the *Star Tribune*: "Ray Charles' daughter moves to Minneapolis—Recording at Paisley Park." I was not trying to cop nor hide my father's identity at the time.

"Some of thaaaat good stuff." He continued to press the point.

"I don't know what you are talking about. I just want a hairdo. I don't mess with thaaaaat stuff." I said, though I certainly did know what he was talking about.

It did, however, plant a seed. I knew where it was if I ever did want it. I had no intention of ever going to a crack house again after what I had recently witnessed. It scared the heck out of me. I was letting that part of my life go. And I did leave it alone. I was in the studio every day. I was feeling really good about what we were recording. It had kind of a rock-funk feel, and I was into that. I wanted to be the black Janis Joplin. I was hyped when it was finished and mixed; I thought it was the bomb. We sent it to the record companies, and they came back with, "Big fat NO! You can't come in through the back door. This is Ray Charles's daughter. You got to come through the front door with R&B, jazz, and funk! You are not going to rock us out, Miss Raye!" And that's when I was too done with it.

What happened to "You are my daughter; of course I will help you!"? Several years and more tears earlier, I had recorded with my dad. That stuff was still on the shelf. What happened to making sure that the doors were open? Even if I sucked, with an insider like Dad, I mean, if you have a gimmick, and I had a gimmick—I was the daughter of Ray Charles, the only child of his that sang. And I was young; someone could have molded me, a well-known producer, someone like Quincy or Baby Face or whoever could have made a hit by using me. That's when I began to think my father or Joe Adams or both of them were not blessing my place in the industry because there was just one Ray Charles. And so I said, "Forget you, and forget that!" That's all I could say about it: "Forget it. I can't go up against my father."

Things were getting hard. Of course, everybody was waiting for my wings to spread; that is how everyone would take flight. It was getting harder and harder to carry that load. At the job I was working, I met an intern named Roy Taylor. He was a parolee, just out of prison, and he fell in love with me. My mom would talk to him on the phone! He had one of those deep, wonderful voices, and he knew those words that were as long as a page. He was an older black man and educated. Mom liked him. He ended up being the biggest drug dealer on the north side where he had a really nice house—his safe house—where all the dope was. He had his workers on the street, but when I wanted anything, I went to the safe house on the down low. Nobody messed with me. I would have to see him when he got his furlough so he could go up there.

I would get my paycheck on Friday and buy a gram, drive around in my car and smoke it, get halfway home, turn around, buy a gram, drive around and smoke it, get halfway home and turn around, and keep doing it until my paycheck was gone. That's when I first started saying, "Okay, what am I doing?" Then I would have to go home and say, "I didn't get paid this Friday—it's next Friday!" though I got paid every week. I was able to manipulate things that way—at least at the beginning. It was crazy, but that is what I did.

"What are you doing?" Roy asked. "If you were going to spend six hundred dollars, why didn't you just buy a quarter ounce, spend half the money, and get more dope on top of it?"

That's how I learned about that—the beginning of the cycle. Somehow, I was still maintaining. It would be just a thing on Friday or the weekend. I was cool through the week, probably because I was broke— holding onto a couple bucks to get back and forth to work and stuff, but basically, my whole paycheck would be gone. I was still able to work, and I knew that I could get through the week still under everyone's radar

So it would continue until it led to the birth of Jaymi and my first beating when everything from my past dislodged and memory returned. No longer held at bay, those ghosts and apparitions began haunting me, hunting me in the halls of my mind. At that point, I saw no fix except another fix. Another hit. Crack. Please!

No child grows up with the life aspiration to become a crackhead, a drug addict, or an alcoholic. Period. No mother sees her child in such a light. No father pushes his child out the door and says, "Now go out there and smoke some dope—show 'em how it's done. Make your daddy proud!" But it happens.

For me, the pain and contradiction were too great. I was tired of being the object of my mother's insanity, her need to stay connected with Ray Charles, her inability to let go, her obsession with seeing me follow in his footsteps. I was sick of my father's empty promises and his vacancy in my life. I was through with everyone within my mother's camp holding her vision of me emerging into superstardom. And I was completely through with having to witness this theater of mind, the memories of physical, emotional, and sexual abuse. It was overwhelming. I refused to believe what was happening to my life and chose to go forth with the addiction as though this were what my life was meant to be. I no longer gave a care, and I knew few who actually did. The very things I held precious and dear, desperately sought from my parents, I denied my children. Try living with that! I tell you, it cannot be done. That is why I chose death—the death found inside rock and pipe. And now, behind concrete and bars, I fought for life.

Part of my answer was found in developing forgiveness for myself, and part of my answer, what I thought I needed at that moment, was found in Sharon. We spent hours together, sometimes day after day, laughing and sharing stories of our past.

CHAPTER 12

CALIFORNIA DREAMIN'

My father who art in Hollywood
Ray Charles be thy name
To Thy kingdom I come
My mother's will — be done

MY MOTHER WAS NOT into school activities; she was never a PTA mom. Once I got out of grade school, she never came to school functions. I was always in the choir, and Mom rarely, if ever, came to hear me sing. During ninth grade, however, the school was having a talent show on Friday night—a show my mother would attend. It was a big thing in town, and they were billing it as a *gong show*. Fashioned from the TV program, they intended to "gong" the bad performers off the stage.

I was a contestant and was going to perform "Feelings," a song that was on top of the charts at the time. The entire school was there, some with the sole intention to throw stuff at the bad performers. Others, the goody two-shoes, were there to support the cheerleaders performing their routine. Grant Hafly, the DJ for the local radio station, was the MC for the show and had been hyping the event for weeks on the radio. It was to be a live radio broadcast. It was a big thing.

From behind the curtain, I saw the auditorium packed, filled beyond capacity. I was out of my mind with nerves. I was singing acapella; there were no supporting members to my ensemble. When

Grant Hafly announced, "And let's hear a round of applause for our next performer, Sheila Robinson!," I froze solid.

I walked out onto the stage, took the mic, and looked out into the audience. Stage fright? I wanted to die. I opened my mouth as fear and nerves took an audible expression inside two unaccompanied syllables— a soft quivering at the very bottom of my range—the lowest sound my voice could produce. "Feel—ings . . . " I sounded like a dying cow. I threw the mic down and ran off. Had I been billed as a comedian, the performance would have been top notch. I was on stage for such a short duration that there was no time for anyone to throw anything or for the gong to be struck. The only thing the audience had an opportunity to do was laugh.

My cousin David Hollins came running backstage and found me. He said, "Sheila, you are by far the most talented person performing here. You can do this. Don't worry about a thing. Just let God take you in his arms, and forget there is anyone else in this auditorium but you and Him!" He gave me a big hug, and my fear just fled from me. David went out and calmed down the audience's laughter and uproar and asked if they wanted me to come back out. The crowd responded by clapping and was willing to give me another shot— the comeback kid.

I walked out on stage with a newfound confidence. My reappearance must have been some spectacle because my mother told the story with such enthusiasm. "My little girl whipped that mic behind her like that," as she would gesture dramatically with her arm, "and walked out there like she owned the stage!" I just put the mic in front of me and sang. As soon as I finished, Grant Hafly grabbed the mic and said, "Oh my God. It's Sheila Robinson! The world is going to hear from her. Can anybody believe that talent?!" The crowd was clapping and carrying on. I could hear my mother above the roar of the applause screaming, "THAT'S MY BABY!" I was so proud.

I won the show! My mom found me afterward and gave me such a big hug and held me tight. She said, "My God, Sheila. I never knew you could sing like that!" On the way back in the car, it was Mom's show. "OH MY GOD! Did you hear that? Now no one can tell me that talent does not get passed down through the genes!" And then, when we got home, the first thing she did was get on the phone to call Ray. "Ray," she said, "You will not believe our daughter." That night, I was on such a high. I'll never forget that, the very first time my mom heard me sing.

This became the solution to my mother's concern over my lack of direction in life. I had been getting in trouble, hanging with the wrong crowd, and running away. My mother thought most of my problems came from not having a father figure. I had no memory of meeting Ray Charles. My only contact with my father had been through the telephone. It was no secret to any of my mother's family that I was having problems, though no one knew the true source of my confusion. I had it buried deep, a secret I kept even from me.

My mother thought proximity might be the problem for Ray's lack of any direct involvement in my life. Her newfound awareness of my singing ability gave her the idea to put my father's words to the test. "How do you expect me to have a relationship with Sheila when you do not live in Los Angeles?" he said. My mother and my Uncle Jerry, her youngest brother, who had been living in California for several years, called each other regularly. He was a minister and a gospel singer, and his wife, my Aunt Connie, was one of my mom's best friends. My life had been spent around my Uncle Jerry, and I thought he was a great guy. He was always lighthearted and would make everybody crack up. It was natural the two of them would agree to the idea—I was to move to Los Angeles and live with him.

"Jerry!" Mom said in an excited voice. "So nice that you would call!"

I didn't glean a great deal from the one-sided conversation, but I knew it was about my moving to California when Mom said, "Okay, Jerry, I'll talk to Sheila about it and call you right back."

It was the summer before tenth grade and my fifteenth birthday when I moved out to Los Angeles. Uncle Jerry knew Kenny Traheel, a gospel music director for a huge church in Los Angeles whose choir was doing a gospel album. Jerry had arranged auditions with Knott's Berry Farm and Disneyland for me to be a featured vocalist with the jazz ensemble. I was to audition for a school of the arts, the Maurice Allard Academy. Jerry had all the information and paperwork.

Mom was excited for me to go. Jerry agreed to watch over me as a father figure, and that soothed Mom's concern over the problems we were having. She did not like the fact I was continually on the go, on the run. On the other hand, I had mixed feelings over leaving my friends from Cambridge. If there were any roots to my life, they were to be found within the soil of that little town, my friends and family. On the way to the airport, as Aunt Cathy drove, I knew what I was leaving behind and unsure of what lay ahead.

At the Columbus airport, we walked to the gate and checked in my luggage. I went looking for Kevin to say good-bye. I figured he had gone walking around the airport to check it out, but Aunt Cathy knew differently. She called into the bathroom, and Kevin walked out the doors, his eyes red and puffy. We hugged, but he wouldn't look me in the eye. He was twelve, into sports and boy stuff, but we had a closeness that could not be denied—he had a hard time with my departure.

Before I left, Mom brought up the idea of hanging out with Dad, visiting him and stuff. I could not understand why she would want that. I was confused. How could she still be in love with Dad? Her love for him was mind-boggling. I had grown up over the years hearing painful stories about the paternity suit and all of her struggles with him—someone throwing clothes and spitting on Mom, saying she was a horrible person who had taken advantage of a blind person. As a child, that was a scary thought to me. I knew my mother's heart. She did not take advantage of my father. Mom loved Dad in a way no words are adequate to describe. Why she would be so deeply in love with him was beyond me! I did not want to see him. As far as I was concerned, he behaved as if I did not exist. After a while, I started wondering, *Why pursue a relationship with him? He should be pursuing one with me!* I told Mom I didn't want to see him.

Arriving with great expectations, the first thing I did was to audition for school. I was accepted and enrolled. It was a private school Dad paid for. I was the youngest student ever accepted there and very proud. That is where I began my formal training in music, with Uncle Jerry as my manager. During the summer and fall, the auditions for the jazz ensembles at Knott's Berry Farm and Disneyland produced several contracts, and I performed there.

Though he was making things happen for my singing career early, I began having problems with my Uncle Jerry. He was the spittin' image of my mom's dad, and my mom had raised me to avoid that cocoon-type of child rearing in which she was brought up. She felt it had left her defenseless from the ways of the world. I agreed—she didn't even know what happened to me within her own household during my childhood. I was well beyond fifteen years old and I had to be chaperoned? I couldn't go to any dances, and everywhere I went by myself, I had to take my little cousin, even if it was just to the park. I couldn't deal with Uncle Jerry being so strict, so hard. As far as he was concerned, I couldn't be trusted, and I had to have responsibilities.

I was used to my mom's attitude—"If you want to go out there and run it the way you are going to run it, then you have to get used to the repercussions of it." My mom was the mom every kid in the state of Ohio loved. She would tell my friends, "If you are going to be out there, out in the streets, especially those winding roads, driving the souped-up muscle cars, drinking and driving, that is how kids are getting killed. You can come right here, and I will tell your parents I will not allow you to be out drinking. If they are going to drink, wouldn't you rather have them be chaperoned and puking in my toilet?"

My friends loved my mom. "You've got the best mom; she's the coolest," they would tell me as they were drinking and smoking. It went for every other kid but me—she would knock my head off. That took all the fun away from it. It was the sneaky part of it that made it fun.

After I had been out there for several weeks, I called Mom and told her I had had a change of heart. I wanted to go see my father. She called Ray and got us on a three-way.

"Oh my God!" Ray said. "You sound just like your mom. Just the sweetest voice."

Instantly, I desired to have a relationship with him. It was all I could do just to say hi.

As soon as I heard him say, "Oh baby, I love you so much," I began crying.

I wasn't expecting that emotion and, quite frankly, didn't know where it was coming from. My mother and I shared something in common when it came to Dad; we both needed something from him that our hearts could not deny. I couldn't stop crying once he started crying, and it took some time for us to get on with the conversation.

I was so filled with emotion and just as many unanswered questions. I had to ask him, "Dad, what happened? Why weren't we together?"

"You know, I just got some papers a few days ago that your mom is taking me back to court," Dad said. "Don't you ever think I don't love you. We would have had a closer relationship if your mother had not taken me to court in the first place. I was going to give you kids anything and everything."

I replied, "What did I have to do with that? That didn't have anything to do with me. I needed you then, as I need you now."

"You see, Ray," Mom responded, "our daughter is the one who is truly blind. She thinks that somehow, someday, she can do something that will make you see that!"

"You know, Sheila, your mom doesn't need to take me to court. I will give you anything you ask for anyway."

Mom jumped in and said, "OH NO! The only way we can have anything consistently is if it is ordered by the court!"

"I-I-I . . . now, mama!"

"Ray," Mom said, "Sheila wants to come see you, and I think that is wonderful. So why don't you put that together?"

"Wednesday at two o'clock, Sheila. Can you get here to my office?"

"Yes!"

"Okay, Sheila," Mom said. "Say good-bye to your father, and, Ray, you stay on the line because I have a few things to talk to you about after this."

"Good-bye, Dad. I'll see you Wednesday."

"Well, all right, then. I love you, and I look forward to seeing you then," Dad said.

"Bye, Mom," I said and hung up.

I knew Mom was going to get down and dirty with Dad. She had enough respect to not conjure up any ill feelings on my end because she knew I was in Heaven. I was thinking this was something more than wonderful. I was on cloud nine. *Maybe we'll go to Disneyland. I am living only a few blocks from there. Maybe he'll take me to his house, and we will have dinner.* I got the feeling that he wanted to be Dad to me. Though I didn't know what to expect of him, I just knew that whatever demented experiences from my past with my stepfather— well, it would have to be better than those. To meet my father was going to be really cool! Thus began a pattern of behavior that never changed throughout my life. I called it the "do-drop-in" syndrome.

It was in the black ghetto part of town. The building's first floor housed the NAACP office, and around the entire building were a huge gate and a drive. Uncle Jerry pulled up. After pushing the button on a little speaker box, he announced that we were here.

"Who is it?"

"Jerry Betts driving Sheila, Ray's daughter. She has a two o'clock appointment."

"Okay! Thank you."

The iron gate in front of us retracted, and we drove in. I thought that was pretty neat. We sure didn't have anything like that in Cambridge. It was something you would see on a television show. I had no idea who my father was. It was an environment far removed from the hills of Cambridge, not that we did not always have the best of everything or want or need something. There just wasn't anything like this where I came from. There was a coldness to it, and I was feeling more that this was a business meeting rather than a meeting of family.

We walked through the front door and proceeded up the steps to the second floor. The reception area was a mauve color, and we approached the receptionist's desk.

"Hello," I said, "I am Sheila Robinson. I am here to see my dad."

"It is so very nice to meet you. I'm Yolanda," she said.

"Yolanda!" I said. "It's so nice to get to meet you." I had heard her name in telephone conversations my mother had.

"Well, take a seat, and I'll let your dad know you are here."

Uncle Jerry and I sat down on a bench, and I could hear someone— Carl, Joe Adams's assistant—say into an open door down the hall, "Oh my God, Ray. Wait till you see her. She is beautiful."

I thought, *Wait till he sees me?*

After a few moments, Yolanda said, "Okay, Sheila. Your dad is ready to see you. Follow me, and I'll bring you back to him."

I walked into his office. It was huge, and there were awards all over the place on shelves and walls, black leather furniture, and all kinds of electronic gadgets, including a phone message machine that Dad was checking when I came in. "Hello, Ray, this is Sandy." It was the voice of my mother. He didn't let it go further than that and clicked the machine off. He arose from his chair with a big smile on his face, doing his weaving thing, rocking back and forth.

"Dad," I said. I walked up to him and hugged him, trying to conceal my astonishment at how small he was. In my mind, I had pictured him as a big guy, a big piano-playing guy, bigger than life, a giant. He was little, and I felt I could have carried him around in my arms. I would have embraced him longer had I felt he wanted to. I just didn't know! I wanted to hug him for ten minutes. Out of fear that he wasn't comfortable, I cut it short, abandoning the hug that would have put me into him and him into me—a soul hug.

I sat down, happy and smiling.

"What are you doing out here? I want you to tell me everything."

"Well, I'm living with my Uncle Jerry. Oh, Dad, I just got accepted to Maurice Allard Academy. I am the youngest student to get accepted there."

"Ahhh!" he said, smiling. He hugged himself and started to get excited, rocking. "Now that's what I'm talking about."

I told him about Kenny Traheel and that I was going to be singing at his church that Sunday. I was going to be recording a gospel album, *Heavenly Cruising,* and that was one of the songs on the album and "Light of Love" another song, and I would be doing three songs for the first demo.

"Dad, when we finish with that, would you like to hear it? Could I bring it to you?"

"Well, of course I want to hear it. That would be so wonderful. Make sure you get all the information from Yolanda in case you don't have time to bring it by so you can mail it to me."

"My mother has always raised us to love you even though I didn't see you. So I have always loved you. She would say you could love God and not see Him; you can love your father the same way. Now that I have seen you, I love you even more."

"We can have a relationship separate from your mother, Sheila. We'll stay in contact."

"I am so glad I have you in my life now, Dad."

"It never was any other way, Sheila."

Before I left, he gave me five hundred dollars and told me he would be recording and on tour. We concluded with the promise we would stay in contact with each other. I was thinking that I would be having a relationship with my mother and a separate one with my dad. I was in Heaven.

He walked me out to the receptionist area where we hugged and said good-bye. That was the first time I ever saw Evelyn, my sister. She walked past us in the hall. She was gray, even back then.

I asked Yolanda as Dad went back to his office, "Who is that?" There was something about her that I recognized, something familiar.

"That's your older sister, Sheila. Evelyn."

She just kept walking, and I left with Uncle Jerry, thinking she looked like she could be my dad's mom. She looked so much older than me.

When I got back to Uncle Jerry's, I called Mom. She told me she was so happy for me and, of course, wanted to know if he had said anything about her. I told her we really didn't talk much about her, but I did say I heard her message on the machine. She said that was when she was trying to call him and tell him about me. Mom wanted to make me think that she didn't call him and talk to him about other things, their things. I always knew that they had that thing, that kind of relationship. They loved seeing each other. And Mom got pregnant by him again when she was forty-two and had a miscarriage. No one could resist Mom.

Several days later, Uncle Jerry said, "Sheila, the phone is for you."

"Hello."

"Sheila! It's Evelyn, your older sister. We passed in the hallway at Dad's offices."

"Evelyn, how wonderful. I asked about you, and Yolanda told me you were my sister. But by then you had already vanished somewhere, and my Uncle Jerry had to get going. Where are you?"

"Florida. I asked about you, too. I'm sorry we didn't have a chance to talk."

It gave me a sense of family, of connection to my father and his world. I ended up going to Anaheim High School. I got on the swim team and hung out with some really cool kids. Relationships that were developing at school started to conflict with my uncle's strictness. They would say, "Hey, we'll come pick you up." I couldn't go unless Pershelda could go. Pershelda was eleven. "Well, what's your little cousin's name?" "Pershelda!" That tells you right then and there where I was coming from. That ain't country—that's hillbilly!

I could no longer deal with it. I had already recorded with Kenny Traheel and sang "Because He Lives" at his church. The entire congregation, about twenty-five hundred people, were all crying. I had all these really good things happening, but I couldn't deal with the lack of any personal freedom. I ran away—went over to a friend's house and sat in her basement, and the two of us smoked some reefer. She asked her mom if I could spend the night, but she said, "No! It's a school night!" She called Uncle Jerry, and he came and got me.

"We've been looking all over for you!" They had called Mom.

No one understood my stand on personal freedom, the need to feel in control. Instead of it helping my situation, it just made it worse. Jerry told me I was on punishment. I could not figure out what that was because, as far as I was concerned, I was already on punishment.

I called Mom. "I am not going to be on punishment when I already feel like I am on punishment. How bad is this going to get? It's too much crack the whip. I'm on the swim team, and I can't even stay after school with my teammates and hang out for a minute. He's crazy! I want to go home." After she asked me fifty times if I was sure, she said, "Of course, honey, come on home."

When I got back to Cambridge, I was the bomb! I had just gotten back from the big city, Los Angeles. I had just met my father, Ray Charles. I did elaborate on the story. Huge! Everyone wanted to hear about my experiences with Ray Charles and Los Angeles and Hollywood. I was an instant star. I now knew how my mom got caught up with it.

I got to see Dad, but it was, "Well, make an appointment!" It wasn't what a little girl's dream of seeing her dad was, not like I was going over to my dad's house to spend the night. I never saw where my dad laid his head. There was no teddy bear there, no Disneyland. What was I thinking? I made stuff up. I had to. But he was going to listen to my music. He promised.

My friends had continued to hang with Mom while I was gone. They were so excited to see me, we spent all our time together. I finished the tenth grade. I started to go out to the bars out in the country. That's when things got crazy. I started to take Quaaludes. Mom went out to a bar to get me one night. The drinking age was nineteen, and I had developed my womanhood early. I had been 36-24-36 since I was nine. I looked like a woman, but I don't understand how I got served with my baby face. Mom was very angry. That same night, the husband of one of my best friend's sister tried to stick his hands down my pants. He was drunk and pitiful. He scared me. What did I do to make a man, any man, feel like it was cool to do that with me? I wasn't dressing like I was asking for it or anything. They just seemed to bring it to me for no reason. We did send Dad the tape I did with Kenny Traheel—sent him the demo and never did hear anything about it. I called him several times. No response. Thus began the up and down relationship with my father— mostly down. Now behind bars, I was beginning a relationship with my Heavenly Father, one that was one way—up!

JOURNAL ENTRY SIX

Greet God in the morning and He will be with you all day. This was an awesome morning. I woke with the gift of life not only physically but spiritually, and God's Spirit cried out to the Spirit within. I prayed for guidance and wisdom, and God was faithful to provide an abundance of both. He has saved me from the darkness; he has brought me into the Kingdom of the Son He loves. Because of what Jesus did, all of my sins are forgotten. I am free.

Sharing is so much more joyous than not sharing. I have a sense of accomplishment and peace when putting another before myself. I become so sad observing meaningless patterns of habitual thinking in myself and others. It is something that has always existed within me, though I had not recognized it for how truly pitiable it is. Now that I acknowledge the presence of God in my life, I see God's love in everything. It must have always been there because the essence of His Love is so familiar and no stranger to me. It is I who was but a stranger to my Self. I thank God that Now I See!

I want to be "right," but I want to be right with Him. To admit to being in Love with Him is a very personal thing. He knew me before I was in my mother's womb. He knows my beginning, my middle, and my end. In spite of everything I have done, He loves me. I don't think He loves me any less for saying a curse word in some emotional outburst. Do you think I believe you know the God in you if you love me less for all the mistakes that I make? If your God is like that, I don't know Him. Judging others, as far as I am concerned, is not right. To keep it real with me—to keep it spiritually correct, I must act within my memory of Him.

When that memory comes, I know it is not an imagined thing, no clever invention of my mind. It is Real. It swells inside and lifts me up. When such a feeling comes over me, there are no words. I come to stand within the very living presence of the truth. It vibrates within all things.

This is what is meant when it is said, remember God in all things. I feel if one knows what that means in its totality, that alone will set you free. It means remember your own memory of who you are, a child of God. You were created before anything of this world. REMEMBER! Remember God in all things. And spiritually I know that is the truth. Ignorance does not recognize itself while Truth, when so revealed, is self-evident—you know it's the Truth because you are the Truth.

The love our Father *is*. It is beyond what the natural man thinks, not based on condition. There is no reason for It that we can invent! He said, "You don't think like I do." I for one can think of nothing to be more thankful for.

Dear Father,

Every two weeks, there is a new shipment of inmates. They need something; they come here stripped of everything. It is frightening what it does to your mind—the people overseeing the inmates are at times worse than those they oversee. Everything in here is designed to remind you of the very worst thing you did in life, so how can you grow?

Dear Father,

There are seventy-year-old women in prison for not paying their taxes. Their husbands had been doing it for them all their life, and then they leave them for some thirty-year-old youngster, and now these women are in prison for not paying their taxes. Our government is merciless; those women are truly lost in here. They need something real. They need you. We all do.

My dad, Ray Charles

One of Dad's many great performances

Dad and I, along with Ray Jr.

My mother, Sandra Betts,
with me and Kevin

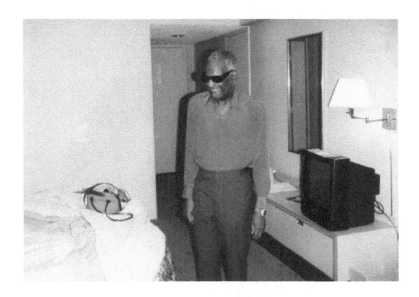

Dad in a hotel room

Dad with one of his granddaughters—Serena
McClellan, Raenee and Kevin's daughter

Dad

One of my own blessed opportunities to sing

Dad and Mom

Raenee and Dad in the studio

Photos © Kevin McClellan

CHAPTER 13

LOCKED DOWN, LOCKED OUT— HOPELESS, HELPLESS, SMOKELESS

I believe that unarmed truth and unconditional love
Will have the final word in reality.
That is why right, temporarily defeated,
Is stronger than evil triumphant.

—MARTIN LUTHER KING JR. ACCEPTING
THE NOBEL PEACE PRIZE, DEC. 10, 1964

I HAD ALWAYS IMAGINED myself to be a people person. Now I began to believe I had merely sought comfort in another's arms, a comfort I could not find within myself. I had lived in the shadow of my mother and father, each who wore a pair of shoes I felt inadequate of filling. Solitude ushered in my unlimited capacity for self-loathing. Ironically, the confinement of prison would not only deliver me to a hell of my own creation, but also bring forth a profound understanding of self.

My greatest fear was returning to the comfort zone of my former life, for I felt I had yet to pay adequate penance for my disappearance from the lives of my children. Though I knew God's comfort and joy as real, I always fell out of such Divine Grace quickly in the past. I knew His forgiveness but had not forgiven myself and did not expect forgiveness to be easily gained from my children. When I was running away using drugs, it was easy to feel as if I was only hurting myself, but it doesn't work that way. I was harming my children, offending God as well as myself.

In addition to these regrets, I felt deep conflict regarding my feelings for Sharon. I was not going to give up a relationship with her just because the church said it was wrong. Were I outside of prison, it would never have been an issue. Certainly God had created sex as a beautiful expression of love, but not as something to be done flippantly or with members of the same sex. Yet here I was with those feelings, drawing me toward an intimate relationship with Sharon. It was like wearing two left shoes; it wasn't supposed to be comfortable. But if you don't have any other shoes, that is what you wear. In prison, there were no other shoes to wear. How are you going to stop the sexual energy or the desire for the loving caress?

After dinner Monday night, I was hanging out with Roberta and Sharon. There was an irresistible sexual attraction between us. I could tell Sharon didn't feel completely comfortable with my involvement with the choir and church; she was not a believer. It was common knowledge prison church attendees often arrogantly professed God's absolute disapproval of gay relationships. I was convinced my desire for a relationship with Sharon was not something outside of God's love.

Roberta was in for a seven-year sentence. She and her husband were sticking together. Roberta had shown me pictures of him. When I had first met her, I had proclaimed I had given my life to God, excited about the "feel good" part of church, unaware of the depth of my attachment to Spud and the lifestyle we led. Holding the thought of a future with him and our daughter, Alicia, I was unaware of the fragility of my conviction, my faith. When I told Roberta several years ago I had changed, she believed it. I was the very last person she thought she would see again behind bars. I now felt anything I had to say about spirituality lacked credibility. Embarrassed because of such a failed stand—my proclamation about having found God and salvation, how I wasn't coming back to prison—I wanted Roberta to know my conviction this time was firm, at least of a more profound depth, and hesitantly decided to come forth with more of my story.

"I've got to tell you guys how I ended back in prison and what happened to me. Prior to going to the Sherburne County federal holding facility, I was in the Wright County Jail. That is where I was taken after the birth of my last child. She was a crack baby, and Spud had just dumped me there at the hospital. I already told you about that. Over a seven-month period within those two facilities, some powerful experiences occurred, and I want you guys to know about some of those things.

"After three months in Wright County Jail, I found myself in Sherburne. My cellmate was in for using meth. There is a demonic force coming from that stuff, even more so than smoking crack. She had seen me reading and singing—just eighteen years old and calling me Mom. I thought it so strange, never being much of a mother to my own children. Maybe she had to feel that closeness to me just to cope with our dehumanizing environment. Taking a dump two feet from where we slept, sitting upon one seamless, stainless steel entity—sink, toilet tank, bowl without seat or lid—washing your face while straddling the blasted thing. It took me three months to get over the idea that the same water between my legs was not in some way associated with the water I was brushing my teeth with. Maybe we both needed to feel a connection of family to cope. I sang for those who would ask, and other inmates respected me for that. Once I sang "The Way We Were" for one of the inmates and her boyfriend. They had not seen each other for six months. We had choir in the middle of the quad there. Singing just always made me feel good.

"For whatever reason, Julie, my cellmate, told me about how she and her boyfriend cooked meth and how it worked out where they lived. Some took a van and converted it into a meth lab while others moved their labs from house to house. Everything in the process is poison. They would pray over the meth and say things like, 'Please, God, let this be the best meth ever made so people will come and buy more and more from us.' They cast spells over it, really putting energy into it. And it worked; they had the best stuff and were getting all the customers. Other meth makers turned Julie and her boyfriend in because of it. I can tell you there were dark spirits around this little couple. I could feel it.

"Julie started going to church with me. At the first few services, she would have fits, get real antsy and have to leave. I knew there was an active force, a presence, trying to keep her from hearing words of love, words of truth, words of acceptance and forgiveness. When we were together, I could see in her eyes when she was present with hope and joy and when the dark presence would overcome her—her eyes got as black as coal, and that look came over her face.

"This particular night, I knew it was going down. God had put it on my heart to try to do something for her. I looked into her eyes and knew it wasn't her. It wasn't the real her. I saw her looking at something that was behind me and knew if I turned around, there was going to be something I could see. I could feel it—the presence of something evil behind me. I said, 'I rebuke you in the name of Jesus. God is my sufficiency.' I went on and on commanding the dark spirit to be gone. Finally, Julie just fell back on the bed exhausted and started to cry.

"'I don't want this anymore. I don't want this anymore. Sheila, I love you. Thank you. I love you. I know God is real. I love my boyfriend, but what am I going to do?'

"As far as I was concerned, he was a child molester! She was only thirteen when she got with him, and he was a grown man—I mean twenty-five at least. At that moment, I wasn't concerned about him! Her mother was a meth addict. That is how she hooked up with this guy. Her mother threw her out of the house when she was twelve years old.

"After Julie had been on the bed for a minute, she got up and said, 'Sheila, this is so amazing! I felt something leave me. I haven't felt like this since I was a little kid! I have to go call Rick and tell him.' She left and came back.

"Julie kept going on, 'My boyfriend is so upset! I talked to him and said I had met a wonderful person, and she is trying to help me. I was telling him about you.'

"You see, guys, she was taking the rap for him, trying to keep him from getting into further trouble. He has a file on him as long as his arm. I mean, he is paranoid about getting put behind bars. Julie and I prayed together, and afterward she asked me to come to the phone.

"While she was talking on the phone with Rick, her entire face drained of color. I was concerned she was falling back under his influence, the spirit or the memory of the drug. I took the phone and listened to him—she put the phone up to my ear. The voice on the other end was something that cannot be described. 'Don't you listen to her.' He sounded satanic, possessed. His voice was the creepiest thing I ever heard. I took the phone away from Julie and said, 'You'd better believe she is listening to me!'

"He said, 'What are you doing with my girlfriend? Why are you screwing with her mind?'

"I said, 'I rebuke you in the name of Jesus. You cannot have this one, Satan. You will not take this child back!'

"The next day, Julie came to me in tears. Rick had just been put in jail, and Julie could no longer communicate with him. I don't know how he got busted. I thought it was a good thing, but her compassion for him made me remember God's love for everyone, so I said a prayer for him. Shortly thereafter, Julie was released to a halfway treatment program.

"Several weeks later, a seminar was conducted about meth. It was so prevalent and such an industry, half the people behind bars at Sherburne were in because of it. Someone who was a meth chemist had written this book, *Meth=Sorcery*. I had already seen the demonic, dark side of that drug with Julie. I knew it was real. It came to me as no surprise when the guy in the seminar described the way God revealed to him the witchcraft of making the drug—how spells were cast over it. Everything they use in making that drug is poison, puts holes in your brain. Red phosphorous, battery acid—there is not one ingredient that does not say, 'Do not ingest into the body.' It seems we are going further and further into a society where either you are dirt poor or filthy rich. Money is seen as God, and drugs are a means to that end."

"Oh my God, Sheila," Roberta said, "I believe it. There *is* evil to that drug. You are always awake through the night. You know, I remember all of us sitting around seeing the same thing, some spirit or apparition. It's how that drug goes down. Could you really feel the evil of that spirit?"

"I am telling you, that is how it was. I do not understand how it works, but that is what happened. If I am lying, I am flying and haven't seen a bird all day!"

"I do not know much about God. I am not ready to say He is real, but evil? I know that is as real as it gets! Do you have a copy of that book?"

"Yeah! I do, as a matter of fact. I'll bring it to work tomorrow for you."

I could tell both Roberta and Sharon were very moved by that story. As I continued, my exuberance amplified. I was thrilled at seeing how God's love could work simply through the acknowledgment of evil.

"In Sherburne, there was a girl who was schizophrenic. This girl had been in since before I arrived. She, too, had been a meth user on the outside, and that just added fuel to her fire. Over the first month or so of being there, I witnessed her getting worse and worse. She was mentally ill and needed psychiatric help. The guards and officials did not have any compassion for her and saw her as nothing more than a part of their business. They simply needed to keep her from killing herself. She needed some sort of medication, and it was taking forever to get her records. Other inmates felt sorry for her. She began talking in a little girl voice, asking for something to write with. Someone sneaked her a piece of paper and a pencil, and she started to stab herself. Without adequate medical facilities to deal with her—no straitjacket or whatever—they had to tie her down with sheets. After trying to bite off the fingers of one of the guards, speaking in different languages or tongues, and acting as if she were possessed, matters escalated. She had been disrupting everyone. It was horrible. Finally, they hauled her out in the *Silence of the Lambs* wheelchair. Something you would see Hannibal Lecter in. It was barbaric, and I had just become familiar with this type of psychological delusion, this 'spirit,' through Julie. In fact, this was all going down at the same time."

I paused for a minute and looked at Roberta and Sharon. I knew the story I was telling more than held their interest. There is something surreal about the extremes of psychological pressure, something of which I wanted both Roberta and Sharon to know.

"I want you to know that when I first went to Wright County after giving birth to a crack baby, I was suicidal. Though I made no outward attempt on my life, I truly wanted to kill myself, and I was scared and frightened by that desire. I turned once again to God through the help of the Network for Life, a group of devout Christians who visited Wright and Sherburne County jail; the two facilities were in close proximity. There was one woman I met there of note, Adeline Vasseur, who was nothing short of a living angel. Through her faith and love, I was strengthened to reattempt communion with God. The fact I no longer felt suicidal was something more than miraculous to me.

"Anyway, while at Sherburne, I met an African lady upon the first day of my arrival. She was short, kind of grandma pudgy, and possessed a tiny sweet voice that spoke in a whisper. She was at a table in the commons area and extended a kindness and concern toward me immediately. I knew she had faith in God. She told me a part of her story; having failed to file taxes several years ago, she was being deported back to Africa. Bush had gone crazy after 9/11, throwing many with a visa from a foreign country into prison. I became friends with her and quickly knew her as a prayer warrior. It was easy to see why she had been given the nickname 'Ma Dukes'—she had the faith of a giant.

"After several weeks of observing the schizophrenic inmate, I knew she had used meth, and Julie had convinced me there was some way to spiritually assist her. Nothing the prison officials were doing was helping, and I think inmates were purposefully giving her pencils to stab herself with just to have something to talk about. Sitting around the table with some of the girls, I brought up the idea of going into her cell and praying for her. I knew I could not handle it by myself. I mean, it was dangerous for me to go in there.

"I said, 'I'm going in there to pray for her.'

"Ma Dukes said, 'Yeah, I'm down for that!' With her at my back, I felt confident to proceed.

"Before we went to speak to the guards about it, we prayed and asked God to open their hearts to the idea. I found the guard and said, 'Please let us go in there and pray for her.' And without a great deal of deliberation or hesitation, they agreed.

"The spirit of the devil was so real in that room. I was trying not to focus on myself and be in the spiritual realm. My hair was standing straight up in the air. It was something not of this world. I felt like *The Exorcist.*

"'Satan! You have no control over this body.'

"She began spewing forth spittle and bile and talking in a voice and manner that could be nothing but evil incarnate. We were praying. 'We stand in the gap where she is not mentally capable of removing this influence of evil. We demand it to be removed in the name of God.'

"She made one loud scream and began speaking in tongues. The evil must have come out her mouth because the room was filled with some kind of dark cloud or presence that was undeniable. Where that energy comes from is anyone's guess, but that it is real cannot be doubted. I believe it comes straight from Satan.

"'Let the evil not come into any of us here. God, let this evil be completely removed from here! Cover this room with the blood of Jesus.'

"We were in there for about an hour, and I began thinking, *Is this the reason for me, my purpose? I ain't no exorcist.* The guards could not believe it. She started talking normally and never again tried stabbing herself—right up until the time I left.

"Now, this is what I really wanted to explain to you. Before Sherburne—the three months in Wright County Jail—I resisted embracing this newfound spiritual feeling. I could not take another failure, another rejection from anyone, including God. Is this just going to be for another week or another month only to once again fall away, evidence of my failure or the weakness of the good of God? A temporary fix? The scary part of surrendering to your true self is how far down you fall the next time you return to the false. I was elated at no longer wanting to kill myself and began thinking there was a possibility I could see my children sometime in the future. What if that never happened? What if I found such a hope was all in vain, such an expectation was too much for society or my children? Would I lose faith and return to drugs to anesthetize the pain and remove that expectation?

"Each time I did so in the past, the fall was greater. How great a fall is this one going to be? If I go back to the world that led me to incarceration, I am not coming out. I'm in prison—how much lower can I go? I am not coming back from this next one. Not only am I in prison, but I came from sleeping on people's floors and having a one-pound crack baby. That is about as low in my mind as you can get. What was I going to do differently? I was praying then, 'God, what are You going to reveal to me? Because I can't do it! I want to die!'

"In Wright County, three girls who occupied cells on the other end of the row were leaving the next week. They had been busted for prostitution and drugs—two sisters and a white girl. Though I never had much interaction with them, I knew their story through overhearing one-sided telephone conversations with their pimp. It was unavoidable; I was never much of an eavesdropper, but the telephone in the quad was located almost directly in the middle of the small common area. Crystal, one of the sisters, belonged to the select group of inmates who felt the need to let everyone know her business, loud and proud of her life outside. I had a cell to myself, the lockdown cell. It had only one bed, and I was assigned there simply because the facility was filled to capacity.

"Of the three of them, Cathy was the youngest, twenty, and she did not want to return to that life. She was white, a blonde with a sizable chest and a cute, angelic baby face. Every time I passed their room, the two sisters were talking to each other while she was either off to herself in the corner or out in the common area on her own. I had talked with her on several occasions, and she seemed to look up to me.

"'Sheila?'

"I looked up from the small desk to the doorway where, as fate would have it, Cathy stood. 'Yes?' I responded.

"'There's something about you that I really like,' she said. 'You got something I can't put my finger on—something most don't have, in or out of prison.'

"'I am no different from you, Cathy,' I said. Trust me, Roberta, I was trying to avoid any conversation about church, Christ, and God, aware she was trying to take me there. I did not feel worthy to offer my answer to someone else. I was yet fulfilling the destiny of emotions attacking my body and leaning heavy on my angel, Adeline, to bring me out of my own thoughts of suicide. 'I carry a lot of painful memories from childhood and beyond. That seems to be everyone's story.'

"'Can I talk to you?'

"'Please, yes,' I said. 'Come on in and sit down.'

"'I don't know what I am going to do. I really want to go back home when we get out next week—Crystal, Jade, and me. Where are you from?'

"'Los Angeles, by way of everywhere: the Midwest, Ohio, Colorado. I was born in Los Angeles and have been living in Minneapolis for some time. How about you?'

"'I grew up in Des Moines, Iowa. That's kind of close to Minneapolis. I see you talking to other girls and stuff. I'm scared.'

"'Scared about what?'

"'I'm afraid they are going to hurt me.'

"'You got to rewind a bit here, sister.'

"'I met them after running away. My mother and father were alcoholics. They would get drunk, especially my dad. He would beat my mother and me. My mom would say, "That's it!" She would leave with us kids for a few days, but then we would all end up back there with him. I couldn't take it anymore.'

"'I know about it—trust me. I know it's a terrible thing. I'm sorry. How did you hook up with those two?' I asked, flipping my head toward the direction of their cell.

"'After I ran away from home, I made it to Chicago and met Crystal out on the street. She introduced me to "Money"—Jay White. He took me in, and it was good for a minute. He got me into smokin' crack, and, before I knew it, I was in over my head.'

"'Oh, Cathy!'

"'You know, for a while, I thought I was really doing something good getting five hundred for a trick. Now it makes me feel like crap!'

"You know, guys," I said, staring Sharon square in the face, "it was textbook as far as I was concerned. I knew the whole story by this time. I could see the two black girls, streetwise and pulling her in, telling her exactly what she wanted to hear, finding some lost little lamb out on the street just looking for someone to love her. Nothing more. Of course, the pimp told her he loved her, while sleeping with all three of them. And then they would end up fighting each other, each one wanting to be the head girl, THE ONE! God, it made me sick knowing the story before I heard it. She finished her story about how they made the money in their little prostitution/drug ring, moving around to various truck stops in different states. I knew what I was going to say to her before she had started telling me her tale.

"'You got to do whatever you have to; just get out of there! Go on a trick and call the police. Do whatever and just go. Get out of there. Go home.'

"'I feel like I'm, like—kidnapped. They got all my family information back home.'

"'Why would you give them that information?'

"'I just didn't know.'

"'You don't need to go there anymore. How about going to church with me tomorrow? You can turn it over to Jesus.'

"'I don't know about that. Who is Jesus, anyhow?'

"I had never in my life encountered someone who had not heard or did not know the story of Jesus Christ. It was unbelievable to me.

"'Haven't you ever heard of Christmas? That's Christ's birthday. Jesus is love and forgiveness. You should talk to the Network for Life people. Maybe they can help you with somewhere to go.'

"'No one ever told me they loved me or they cared without having some other reason for saying it.'

"'What? That's crazy. I love you. I know the salvation of Jesus Christ. I have seen it move so many times within me and other people. God cannot be limited to anything. He isn't even limited to what we think is all things.'

"'You shouldn't talk so loud. My two friends might hear you!'

"'What?! Bring it on. Bring them straight to the front line. I'm not afraid of them!'

"'Please,' Crystal said from the doorway. Neither one of us knew how long she had been standing there. 'Excuse me, loser! Cathy! Don't listen to that weak woman. Go ahead—go there and see what good it does you. As soon as you get out of here, you are going to go back to the same thing. You won't be thinking 'bout no God!'

"'Don't try to start no crap around here, Crystal,' I said. 'I think it's best that you just get on going.'

"'Yeah?' Cathy said. 'What do you know about it, anyway?'

"'All right then, Cathy. If that's the way you want to play it,' Crystal said with an attitude and left.

"'Wow, Sheila! Thanks, girl!'

"'I don't know about that,' I said. 'You just got to stand up for yourself a little bit, and it's going to be all right.'

"Later that evening, I overheard a conversation about how Crystal and Jade told someone it was all Cathy's fault they ended up getting busted. I asked her about it the next day.

"'Apparently, someone from the restaurant at that truck stop became suspicious. Somebody told the police what we were doing there,' Cathy explained. 'Crystal and Jade had warrants out for them from Chicago. I didn't know anything about no warrants. I didn't show up at the side of the truck stop where they were waiting for me—where we were to meet after doing the tricks—so they came looking for me. The police had caught me red-handed in a truck with a trick. I was telling them some story about what I was doing and said to the police, "Look, I'm with those two girls over there." The truck driver rolled on me, and I got busted. It ain't like they didn't know Jade and Crystal were doing the same thing. They ran them through their system and found out they had warrants or whatever, so we all three got busted together right then and there.'

"Over the next few days, we kept talking to one another. I told Cathy the story about Spud and having our baby just like I did to you guys.

"'I was sitting there, suicidal. Though my child was born premature and cocaine positive several hours after her birth, the doctor and nurse brought my daughter to me and told me she was perfect. The second night, they had to airlift my child to another hospital because she had breath apnea. There was nothing anyone or any living thing could do to allow me to love myself through it. I was consumed by guilt. I felt like I deserved death, like I was the lowest form of life on the planet. I could hold that position; no one could take that from me. On top of that, I was away from cocaine and could not, in the light of sobriety, deal with the reality of my past and Spud. I hated him for treating me the way he did. In spite of all the horror and effort to live that lifestyle, the thread around my heart still bound me to that past. I had a sick, warped sense of panic when I wasn't around him, like I was going to die and my world was coming to end. I wanted to bust out of jail just to be with him. I had been trying to reach Spud and talk to him. God had put it on my heart to forgive him and myself for having done all that dumb stuff.

"Spud answered the phone, and I told him about salvation and coming to a spiritual reckoning with God, that He loves you in spite of yourself. I asked him to be saved. The salvation prayer is Romans 9: 9–10. I said it to him, and he said he didn't believe he was saved yet. I told Spud I did. I believe if that is what you want in your heart, that you want God to be at the helm of your ship, God will do that. I asked Spud if he wanted that, and he said yes. We said the prayer together, and I could tell it was emotional for him. At that moment, I was completely released from my tie to him. I no longer had any desire to be in his life in any capacity except to love him as a brother through Christ.

"'Wow, Sheila, do you think that could work for me?'

"'Why not? Of course it will!'

"That Sunday, Cathy went to church with me and shared a joy in spite of what we both had been through. Cathy was excited, never having been to church, and Network for Life really was the bomb. It made a difference I could see in her, and that made me feel wonderful. I came back from the service feeling like God was at the helm of my life and feeling like I could survive this thing. My heart wasn't tormented anymore, at least not every day and to such extremes as in the past.

"Tuesday, they held a surprise inspection. It occurred once a month—a random search. There were three guards. One guard would escort the inmates out into the common area. Two guards wearing rubber gloves would go through the cell—pull the mattress out onto the walkway, go through the locker and everything you had in there. It was no secret drugs were available inside. It's automatic, five years tacked on to your sentence. Nothing could be worth that as far as I was concerned. These girls were eighteen, nineteen years old! What were they thinking?!

"The guard watching me led me back to the cell. I grabbed the mattress and dragged it to the door. The guard exiting the cell spoke into a walkie-talkie clipped to his shoulder. 'Robinson! Yeah, we found something in Robinson's cell.'

"'What?' I said. The guard proceeded to the next cell as though I had not said a word.

"About a half hour later, I heard over the loudspeaker, 'Robinson to the main door.' It was shift change. We all had to be in our locked cells. Hearing the lock release from the cell door, I left immediately, knowing something was up and anxious to understand the nature of whatever it was they thought they had found. I was thinking, *Maybe it was that apple I snuck in the other day.* Unaware of any serious infringement of policy, I proceeded with uncertainty.

"The officer in charge was there and said, 'Sheila. We've got some bad news for you. We found your marijuana.'

"'What? I never smoked marijuana. It isn't mine!'

"'Possession is nine-tenths of the law.'

"He brought out a small plastic bag of marijuana containing but a few crumbs and dust. It was found in a crevice between two cement blocks of a wall inside my cell.

"I told him, 'I have no idea how it got there or how long it has been there.'

"'Well, we are going to have to conduct an investigation. There is going to have to be a meeting about this. Regulations state we have to make a decision after the findings within seventy-two hours. You can report back to your cell now. You'll know what we are going to do soon enough.'

"Wednesday morning, I was brought to Jo Carpenter's office, the jail coordinator. She asked me the same questions. I gave the same responses.

"'What is going to happen to me?'

"'Because you had sole possession of the room, something is going to have to be done. You can get between one to ninety days of solitary confinement. There could even be an extension to your sentence or a new charge. We will let you know.'

"Later that day, they came to my cell. 'We have made a decision and have found you guilty. It was found in your room. You were the only one in there.'

"'That is a crock of crap! What if you found a dead body in the concrete? Would that have been my fault, too?'

"I appealed the thing all the way up to the highest authority in the jail. On the third day, Jo called me into her office for the final report. 'Guilty.'

"'I know this isn't really fair,' she said. 'That stuff could have been in there for a year. It could have been overlooked from a prior inspection. We don't know.'

"'I don't even smoke weed. And why would anybody, especially in here, keep such an insignificant amount like that? It doesn't make any sense!'

"'I could give you thirty days. I have been thinking about this, and it doesn't make any sense to me, either. But I have to do something— I'm giving you fifteen days.'

"My heart dropped. I felt betrayed by God. I was innocent. How could that possibly be right? I cried. I was escorted immediately back to my cell. It WAS the solitary cell.

"'Now, Cathy.' I could hear Jade and Crystal outside the door. 'Look at that. She is locked up for having weed in her room. Ms. Holy Roller. Mrs. Church Do-Gooder! Now, what does that tell you about God?'

"They were trying to negate my stories, my words. It didn't bother me what Jade and Crystal thought. I knew I was innocent, but I couldn't understand why God would let that happen to Cathy.

"'That saving salvation is weak. She's just up in there smoking weed!' Crystal was yelling outside the door.

"'I don't even have a lighter. I have never had a problem with weed.' I yelled, 'Crack was my problem. Let's get it straight!'

"I was as angry as one could get at that point. I had been asking God to soothe my heart from the mental stress of being behind bars and also the childhood memories I had been reliving for the past several weeks. I had just started Bible study and attending drug counseling. I was trying to be open and honest with my circumstances. I was trying to make a positive change, and I felt as though God had turned His head. I had prayed and asked God for His intervention, that any charges would be dismissed. After all, I was innocent. After having made that appeal, I was filled with a sense of peace—as if everything was going to be okay. *Now*, I thought, *what's up with that?* I found myself locked up, wondering where His watchful eye had been. Somehow, I was on a different page from the one God was reading. I felt betrayed once again!"

Roberta said, "Well, that is how it has been for me all my life! Whenever I prayed for a little bit of help, nothing turned out right for me."

I said, "Well, look at this, Roberta. You were the one who willingly made the sacrifice for your husband and children. It all seems to have worked out pretty good on that end. You have your husband, your children are not in child protection, and you guys seem to be committed to staying together. All in all, I can see God's hand behind it. Can't you?"

"I guess if you put it that way," she said, "I can agree."

"Sharon, Roberta, check this out! Do you think there is anything worse than eating, sleeping, and going to the bathroom all in the same place? Wild dogs don't even do that. During my fifteen-day stay in solitary, I could take a shower once a day. When it was required for me to cross the courtyard for any reason, all inmates had to return to their cells so I couldn't see them and they couldn't see me. Everyone was mad because I was ruining their free time.

"I kept asking God, 'Why would You ask me to witness to Cathy and then have me end up in lockdown? I don't think there is anything left in life for me. I am in prison—completely by myself. Solitary. How can I come up from this place?'

"I opened the Bible, and there was the verse: 'Some are here to plant the seed, others to water it and nurture it and still others to harvest it, but it is always Me.'

"God broke it down to me. From within me I heard, *You were there to plant the seed. I will see that it grows within her. Your responsibility was to plant the seed. She connected with what was happening in you. Now I have you to myself so that I can further its growth in you, uninhibited by the outside. I will elevate you from here. You don't have any place to go but up. Watch me now! Let's establish this relationship right now. I am directing this ship.'*

"There was no outside influence, nothing else coming at me. I had to surrender. That excited me!

"That became a process for me. If I had a question I asked of God, I would either just open the Bible, or there would be a voice that said, 'Go to this book, chapter, and verse,' and there the answer would be, in perfect harmony with the question I had put forth. God answers your every wish—that is why He says be mindful of what you ask for. I thought it was really amazing; out of everybody in the universe, He heard me. It makes you feel special. It is so easy to feel insignificant. There is so much coming at you from the outside. Life had taught me I was a victim. God, on the other hand, was saying that was false—I was not a victim, and no man had authority over me.

"This thought came to me in lockdown: *Jesus said if you have the faith as small as a mustard seed, you can move mountains. My mind says I have that much faith. What does that mean? How little faith and wisdom do I have? I mean, I obviously do not have any faith, and yet I know I have that much faith, mustard seed faith. Am I to look at it in a different way? Faith has got to be something that your mind can't even think about, and I have to look at it in a different way. Otherwise, it makes God a liar. I prayed and I worshipped and I sang. Am I completely twisted around about who or what God is? I gave God all the glory before I went back to prison. My mind did not think that God would want me to be in prison, and I got as much time as the judge could give me. I did not know at the time that it was God's love at work. God's faith is not of the mind—it is of the soul. It is something you must experience. The faith in drugs and money is not faith at all; it is something that you can see. What kind of faith is that? There is no higher or lower place for you to go. It is something that you know works, at least in the manner of the world. There is no faith in that. Faith is of the things hoped for and the substance of things not seen.*

"Roberta. Sharon. The street faith is a trick of the mind, but it never fails you. The street life is all about the money faith. That is what makes the world go 'round in that mind-set. You have to have the money to even cope in the streets. I was an addict, a dope fiend. My street faith was very strong; the calling of the drug was very strong. I learned quickly how to juggle drugs, how to supply my habit, how to become a hustler. I saw the fruit of my labor. I saw the turnaround, and I didn't even know what the hell I was doing. When I knew I had to kick in and survive, it was unbelievable how my mind began to work. Learn how to manipulate. I could buy a gram, sell half of it, recover the hundred dollars, and smoke the other half so I could keep going. It's the same thing—the strength of that faith.

"Now I was trying to figure out how to use that same drive, that same verve, in a different way—that same hunger, that same need to stay in the Light. It's so hard to come to that place with God. Why?

"So I tell you again, Roberta, my whole life changed, regardless of my flaws. The person I am today is not the same person I was before. God did something different in me. What is going to happen has not yet blossomed, but I know He planted something.

"I felt the need to cling to anything I thought was mine fade away. In its place, I felt something stirring through me, a joy beginning to rise within. I felt fear recede and strength return—the strength to move and look at things through different windows, the strength God nurtures and sustains so that someday we find the courage to tear the whole house down and stand wide open.

"I had felt it. Hope and faith. Love within. I look for its return, and I will hold it closer next time and remember there is no need to go back to what never was, that I am not as I once was, and I know I am capable of freeing myself from that which never was. I was trying to become aware of that something within me that always said I was more than whatever life had shown me, to study it, to recognize it, to remember it. I was beginning to have hope that I once again might fly.

"So there I was in lockdown. I wasn't allowed to have any communication with anyone. Some of the girls from choir and church would write to me and slip little notes under the door. They would be unsigned, and I would tear them up afterward and flush them down the toilet.

"This is why I know God will take any circumstances or do whatever He wants to do for the betterment of me for Him. Nothing was going to change this. It was ridiculous. Why me? Why did He want me to have that time alone with Him? Within those fifteen days, I spent all of my time with Him. Solitude is the price of freedom. Every minute of the day, from the time I woke up till the time I fell to sleep exhausted, I was reading the Bible and praying. I lay down on the ground, spread my arms out like Christ on the cross. 'I am here at the lowest point, humbly beseeching you, God. Fill my heart with your love. Fill my mind and consciousness with Your wisdom, with Your spirit, with Your grace.' I wrote and wrote inside that cell.

"I began singing at night. The girls would beg me to sing. Some of the guards would tell me to be quiet; others would just come and stand outside the door to listen.

"'We love your voice, but you have to be quiet, Sheila.'

"One day there were two girls fighting, arguing back and forth in a catfight. They were down in the commons.

"'I am going to kick your big fat butt, WITCH!'

"'Bring it on, CRACKHEAD!'

"'Forget you!'

"It was escalating into something really ugly. When they let them out, I knew that they were going to hurt each other. I looked out through a little window on the door of the lockdown cell. I saw them out there about ready to fight and the guard was calling for backup. I prayed for peace and asked God to soothe their hearts, and then I sang. Immediately, everything became quiet. It was like God put socks in their mouths. It was so amazing to me. I was absolutely happy. They didn't know what happened."

"Sheila, are you sure about that? God listens to you?"

"It's not about Him listening to me; it's about me listening to Him. While I was in lockdown, I was given an inspiration, a story, a theatrical production I call *Prodigal Praise*. It's a story about a girl who becomes a crack addict fashioned out of my experience, loneliness, and confusion. In an attempt to fill a void in her life, she hangs out with the others suffering from the same confusion and, in the end, by the grace of God, is brought into a higher understanding and purpose in life."

"Listening to your story is all well and good, but the Christians I have listened to have always turned me off to God. There is so much hypocrisy in them."

"It is not uncommon that when one begins a relationship, a deeper connection with God, it can make you feel as if you have done something, gained something, and all of a sudden, you forget where you were before the experience. It can go to your head, and then, just like me the last time, you fall instantly out of that grace."

"What do you mean? You make a mistake and then God turns his back on you?"

"No, it isn't that at all. It's that you simply return to your old self and not turn to God."

With that, the warning siren went off, indicating that it was time to return to the quads and call it a day. I was more than ready to retire, and they seemed more than prepared to withdraw. "I'll see you guys tomorrow, and thanks for allowing me to get that out. I really wanted you to know I am serious this time about what is happening to me spiritually."

"No problem, Sheila. We love you and are sorry for all the stuff you had to go through. See you at work tomorrow."

This was quite a long story, even in prison where one has nothing to do but tell and listen to stories. I held their attention for that length of time, and, whether they would admit it or not, I could tell by the look in their eyes that love was in their hearts.

CHAPTER 14

PRODIGAL PRAISE

PRODIGAL: giving lavishly or profusely
PRAISE: the act or fact of saying words or songs worshipping God

ACCORDING TO MARCIA, it was a special night when Reverend Green came in for a revival. He came regularly, at least once or twice a month, or so she told me. It was the first time for me as I made my way in the warmth of early evening summer air. Judging by the crowd heading in the direction of the chapel, the church was going to be packed that Saturday night. Filled with anticipation, a calming breeze brushed my face.

"Sheila!" It was Marcia calling from behind me.

I stopped and waited for her. "I guess you weren't lying about this guy. Everybody is coming. I don't think I have seen this many inmates coming to church before."

"He's always on fire," Marcia said. "He was a pimp, drug dealer, and addict at one time. I guess we all can relate in some manner. He gets everyone going. I like him."

That is all well and good, I thought to myself, *but because someone has gone through treatment doesn't mean he will not use again, and because someone claims he has found God doesn't mean he has. I was the perfect example—where was my transformation?* I sat next to Marcia, listening to Reverend Green's opening prayer. Afterward, he asked, "Does anyone have a word she wants to give as part of the service?"

I immediately stood up. It was unexpected—involuntary. Standing in amazement, I chuckled to myself as everyone turned to look at me and I headed toward the front of the congregation, going with the flow of an inner urging. I began talking about using cocaine and crack and how my last child was born with the addiction. I listened to myself publicly reveal experiences as shame and fear fled, grateful for the fact my child was healthy and in a safe place. "God sometimes has to bring us to this place so he can work on us." I talked of my experiences in lockdown and the songs God placed in my heart, the source of my inspiration for the play *Prodigal Praise*, which I wrote during that time.

"I realized right away," I continued, "how blessed I had been in lockdown those days. The imposed discipline of the situation was a blessing I now see. When we find our bottom, God can grab our full attention and bring forth something greater for our lives. God loves us dearly, and every day when I wake up and feel the warmth and joy of His presence, I know just how much His love means to me. If it is okay with Reverend Green, I'd like to sing a song that came from inside solitary." I glanced quickly in his direction, and he nodded his approval. "Glorify Him."

I sang acapella. It was only my second week of being in the choir, and it felt wonderful to sing. I couldn't sing enough.

After the service, I received a warm embrace from a new inmate. She was a big, black, buxom woman with a heart of gold, very earthy looking, wearing no makeup. She appeared to be six feet tall and weigh two hundred fifty pounds. She appeared to me to be about fifty years old, wore wire-rim glasses, and had a very serious but warm, gentle spirit. I was drawn to her immediately.

"Sheila, your testimony and song were just beautiful. My name is Helen."

"Well, thank you, Helen," I said. "You know, you look familiar. I think I saw you the other day. Are you in B-2?"

"Yeah, I just got here. We should hang out sometime—you know, I'm thinking about starting a prayer group every night before bed count."

"Well, I'm down for that!" I said with enthusiasm. I meant it. Her conviction and strength of spirit were undeniable. I could feel it. Helen's spirit possessed a gravity that was irresistible. Spirit and soul can make its presence known. Music is all about soul, and that soul is real.

One week later on Saturday night, Helen and I were sitting on the bench by the football field. It was another warm evening accompanied by a beautiful, refreshing breeze. She spoke slowly and deliberately, with a soft and thoughtful deep southern accent that never became overly excited or out of control. Her presence was comforting, a rare quality to be found in another inmate, and she possessed an authority over herself that allowed her to be present in the moment. Helen informed me she was from Mississippi and had a ministry that was developing a large congregation. Her organization had just started a television evangelism program.

She inquired of my past. I told her about my father and some of what I had been through. Helen inquired of the play I had mentioned the night of Reverend Green and asked if she could read it. I was uneasy with allowing that, always paranoid about how others were going to respond to my creative expression. My past had paved that road, replete with both Dad and the record industry saying my work was not good enough, my efforts fruitless.

"All right," I said against my insecurity. "It's titled *Prodigal Praise*." As I continued to talk with Helen, I felt a glow come over me, a comfortable self-confidence.

A fellow inmate caught our attention as she approached. Her long black hair was blown about her face. She stopped in front of us, brushing her hair aside, revealing a young Mexican girl about as beautiful as anyone could be.

"My name is Liz. I saw you guys going to church the other day. I wonder if I could talk to you." She spoke in clear English.

"Well, certainly," we both said simultaneously. Helen and I parted in sync and made a space for Liz right between us. As soon as she sat down, she broke down and started to cry.

"What is the matter dear?" Helen said softly.

"I can't believe that I am here. I didn't do anything to deserve this. I took the rap for my man."

"I hear that quite a bit around here," I said. "I'm here of my own doing."

"I went to the doctor yesterday," she said, struggling. "He told me I had cancer of the cervix. They checked it twice because I am so young. I'm only nineteen." She broke down and cried some more. It was difficult for her to speak. "They want me to go back in three days to find out what they're planning to do. An operation, some treatment plan, or something."

Helen said immediately, "Do you believe in Christ and ask for forgiveness of your sins? Do you accept Him into your heart? Do you believe that you can be healed?"

"Yes," Liz said.

Helen prayed and then spoke in tongues. She placed one hand on Liz's back and one on her abdomen, and Liz spoke between her tears. "I believe in the healing. I receive the healing." Helen continued speaking in tongues while I watched the events unfold within an undeniable and perceptible "bubble of Spirit," an energy or something.

It was over sooner than one would think. Liz calmed down, wearing a relaxed expression, and she had obviously been comforted. I looked over at Helen in amazement, and she said softly, "Jesus said, 'Whatever I claim in my name, that authority is within me, the very source of all things. If you have enough faith, it will come to fruition.'"

The sun had receded, and the yard lights were on. It was time for us to go in—bed count at 10:00. I was feeling grateful for being part of something beautiful, having stood witness to Helen's faith aglow with Spirit.

"Sheila, I am here not because of what I did on the outside. I don't know how it happened, the books of my ministry getting messed up and money embezzled. I am here because God brought me here for other reasons." Helen continued as we walked to the quad, "You see, Sheila, God wants me to be here. As soon as the judge pronounced my sentence, I knew God was calling me for reasons completely unknown to me. If for no other purpose, I was here just for that prayer right now for Liz and for what God just did."

As we walked into the quad, I overheard, "There's the one who wants to turn the exercise room into a church." I turned with the intention to tell her to get lost as Helen grabbed my arm and turned me into her eyes.

"Good night, Sheila," Helen said with a smile.

"Good night," I said. Capturing her atmosphere, I ascended the stairway. Helen was on the first floor; my cell was on the third tier. I went to the bathroom late and saw the light on in Helen's room. I was very curious about her.

Back in my cell, I prayed. "I really don't understand You, God. Why should I be allowed to be aware of Your presence? Who am I? It just doesn't make sense to me, but I thank You nonetheless."

With the thought of Helen's faith being absolute, I was filled with a sense of peace and wonder and slept like a baby. The next day at lunch break, I told Roberta and Sharon about the events of the previous day. That is how I am; whenever something good happens in my life, I just want to share it. I got to the point where Helen prayed and spoke in tongues, and they started laughing. Sharon said, "Speaking in tongues?"

"Speaking in tongues is a Spirit-filled gift that just happens somehow. There are those who say if you can't speak in tongues, you don't have the Holy Spirit. But why say such a thing? Flip that and you will find many who say if you speak in tongues, you have lost your mind. The first time I heard people speak in tongues was at the Way Ministry—I mean, it freaked me out. Kevin and I were on the floor laughing. Peeing in our pants! One thing I have learned—God is not the author of confusion. All of a sudden, we were standing there in church, and the entire congregation started speaking in tongues. It sounded as crazy as crazy can be. We didn't know it was coming—it sounded like 'blah-blah-blah.' Kevin and I looked at each other, and we were on the floor! Later, I came to know my mother to speak in tongues. Now, there's a difference—the babble in that church was completely different from when I heard someone speak in tongues filled with Spirit. I am not saying that those people weren't, but it seemed more orchestrated, like BAM, 'Now! Speak in tongues!' You can't demand, 'Speak in tongues right now!' One must allow the Holy Spirit to come over you, as it does, and then do it."

"For that matter," Sharon said, "why would you want to fake it?"

"When I heard it later in life, it was different," I said. "Beautiful. There are those who can interpret the speaking in tongues. Sometimes people speak in a completely different language. Perfectly. And those who know that language know exactly what it is they are saying—like French or German. There are other people who just have the gift of discernment of speaking in tongues and claim to know what is being said. It is an awesome phenomenon.

"I have also been slain in the Spirit. I used to laugh at that, too. I thought it was all a bunch of bologna. But I actually had a lady touch me; God moved through her in such a way—knocked me right out. Twice she did it. Not her, God. Gloria Bloomingame. She was a prophet who came to Minneapolis from Texas, of all places. This was before I ever went to prison. I went there with Mom and Bev Paulson. She took us to her church. Of course, Mom told her about everything that I was doing. That was when I was MIA a great deal of the time, and everyone was worried about the hold crack had on me. They wanted Gloria to pray over me. I was fighting it. I was thinking, 'Whatever!' Standing in line about the fourth or fifth person in, watching these other people ahead of me falling to the floor, I thought, *I am too sure! Ain't no way! As soon as this is over, I am going to find Spud, and that is that. At least I did this for Mom and Bev.*

"Gloria said, 'Sheila, God has ordained your life. You are going to have such greatness. You will not be speaking in front of thousands of people but rather in front of millions. Know that God has this in store for you. You will go to places and reach heights that you have never dreamed of.'

"So she prayed over me and asked God to come into my life. Then she asked if she could touch me.

"Well, I felt a warm presence flow through me. I went weak and fell to the floor. I can't imagine what it would be like to be in the complete presence of God. It's overwhelming—a complete surrender to the Holy Spirit. You can't do anything but bow to it."

"Do you go unconscious?" Sharon asked.

"No. Nobody goes unconscious."

"You did not just intentionally drop to your knees?"

"No! I wouldn't be sitting here telling you this if it was like that."

"It caught you completely off guard?" Roberta asked.

"Completely off guard. Like I was looking at the three people prior to me going like, *Yeah, rrriiiiight! You got me twisted. I am not going for it!* Once again limiting God's ability. It isn't them. God was channeling through her, or whatever you want to call it. All I know is that it was and is real."

"What did it feel like?"

"It felt warm and wonderful, and it was a place that I didn't want to leave."

"How long were you on the ground?" Sharon inquired. "I don't know. Probably about five minutes."

"Five minutes!"

"Heavens, yes. That was just praising and thanking God, and the biggest skeptic had turned into the craziest person there. I went back to see Mom and Bev, and they were both crying. My mom was so worried about me. It makes me so sad now knowing all the dumb things I did."

Roberta and Sharon saw the sadness come over me.

"My mom told me of a time my great-grandma held me in her arms and said, 'Sheila Robinson, she is going to be very famous.' I never bought into the nonsense. Famous! I am here in prison right along with all of you!" I started laughing. "Now, how about that for famous?!!"

At that point, in spite of all I had witnessed, I could offer no explanation for 'the Power of God' and faith healing. My enthusiasm for the recent episode with Helen and Liz had tricked me into painting myself into a corner. I left the topic as we walked in the early evening light. The sky was clearing after a day consumed with a heavy rain.

"For whatever it's worth," I said, "I am glad I have you guys." A large grasshopper flew up and almost hit me in the face. I darted out of its way, and the girls started laughing. On occasion, after a rain, the grasshoppers and the crickets went crazy. Everything is huge in Texas. When you would be walking, they would be popping all over the place. It was crazy. And the geckos? The little lizards would be all over the windows.

Three days later, Helen and I were sitting on the bench again. It was already becoming a little ritual with us. We saw Liz come running our way.

"I went back in to get my treatment program today, and there was no more cancer. It was gone. That is what the doctors told me this afternoon!"

"What?!!" I said. "Oh yes! Praise God!" I could not contain myself and started running wildly out onto the field. I began doing cartwheels, and that alone must have looked completely ridiculous. Then we all started to dance around together, praising God, shouting and hollering. We were nuts!

I was filled with wonder. God can be known in a personal way. It is the most magical of all things. The most holy place is found within us, within you and me; the kingdom of Heaven is found within, to move in us, so we can know great things. From direct experience, I was learning not to depend on me. In the past, when I would see a situation where I could gain by manipulating another human being, I would. I realized I actually took pride in it. Such an epiphany provided the biggest belly laugh I had had in quite some time.

Helen told me that the next week, we were going to start a prayer group and had received permission to use the exercise room in the quad, the only space available. We looked for other girls who wanted to participate. As soon as it was discovered a prayer group was going to meet in the exercise room, everybody wanted to start working out. At 10:00, who pumps iron? It was a big joke, and it wasn't funny.

Helen inquired again about *Prodigal Praise,* and I brought a copy to her. I had told her a little more about the story, how it came to me while I was in lockdown. She asked about how Mom and Dad had met, and we talked about my life.

The next day, Helen came running up to me. "Honey! Did you write this? It is really good!" Helen told me she had wept while she read it and thought it was the most beautiful thing. She kept asking if I wrote it, rhetorically, in a manner of praise. "This is about you, isn't it, Sheila?"

"Yes. Some of the things are just things I witnessed but did not participate in. Other things of my past I did not include, but for the most part, it is autobiographical. God just moved me to write it—to be honest about things everyone goes through."

In contrast, Helen didn't reveal much of what had brought her to prison. She was always mindful over what she said to everyone. Very cautious about how she approached others, she always made sure she was interacting in the most positive and constructive way. In such a manner, she was a great teacher and planted a seed within that which had yet to completely bud and flower. I was so grateful to her for that. If Helen didn't think *Prodigal Praise* contained a positive message in alignment with Christian values, she would have said so. I was very glad to hear her approval. She thought I should try to perform it in prison. That gave me the strength to propose it to the chaplain, and I committed myself to doing so.

"There is something that is weighing heavily on my mind, Sheila, and I am led to talk to you about it. I know that you have an inner conflict with the blonde girl you hang out with."

I was caught off guard. "I am wrestling with that."

"I am not the only one who would know this. Don't you think it is a negative to what you desire to represent?"

"I am less concerned about it than others. Why would God have an issue with that more so than all the other things I have done in the past? How did you know that?"

"I can see it; that is all."

Neither Sharon nor I flaunted anything in front of people, and Helen was a new arrival. She had no evidence I was in a lesbian relationship—she just knew it, and I knew how she operated.

"Helen, I prayed about it. The desires of my flesh often work against my spirit, constantly it seems, and it always comes back to that battle going on inside. In human relationships, I know love can exist between the same sex. My experience is such—the love between Sharon and me is far deeper and more right than many affairs I have had with men, relationships that were out and out abusive. I remember Christ said, 'What is of man is of man, and what is of God is of God; man cannot serve two masters.' To me, this means one has little to do with the other. I can make the point that there can be more love in a gay relationship than a straight one, so how can anyone judge? In the Bible, we are asked, 'Are you so foolish? After beginning with the Spirit, are you now trying to attain your goal by human effort?' I left my confusion there—what is of Spirit is of Spirit—and the more I return to that, I guess the rest will just work itself out."

"Well, Sheila, I'll continue to pray for you, and I hope you will pray about it, too."

"Of course I will. When do we hold the first Bible study?"

"This Wednesday. Tell those who are interested."

We parted, and the next day I went to the chaplain with a copy of *Prodigal Praise*. "I'll need to read it and think about it. I don't think we ever did anything like that before, but that doesn't mean it's a bad idea." Chaplain Mike was busy all the time. There were always inmates bringing questions of faith to him. As I left his office, I caught myself once again thinking, *Is it good enough?* I answered myself, *Are you so foolish?* And I smiled.

I knew the play was going to receive the approval of the chaplain; it no longer mattered how I knew. I started to consider people to cast in certain roles. There were several inmates who were a perfect fit for several leading roles, but I knew they were in gay relationships, and including them would create a stir in the church. I briefly considered the opposition and formulated my response. "God created us all, and all should be loved by the church—it can be no other way. Why exclude them? This is an excellent opportunity to bring those in, if you need to look at it that way."

I remember my mom saying, "If your religion is speaking the truth of God and love, then why would I have to join? I am already a member." And I understood that truth. God is all-inclusive. I stood by my connection with such truth, operating with what I felt God truly gave me—divinely—my personal thing with Him. I felt so washed. When you feel dirty for fifteen years, a filth no shower in this world will wash clean, and Spirit enters and you become cleansed from the mistakes and crap of your life— well, that is enough to make you say *forget you* to anybody who is saying you are a piece of crap. Fellow church members actually told me, "God is totally not looking at you right now because you're in a gay relationship."

"Whatever!" I responded. "Don't even try it. I am not going for it. Not after I have come this far." I am telling you, whatever anyone has to say about the cleansing, you cannot accept anyone's criticism about the dirt they see in you. That is not my understanding. If I feel clean, I am seeing you as clean. That is how it works. I mean to say, if you see dirt in me, it's dirt in you that you are feeling. Don't try to take me backward! I know God wants the best for me, to see me in love and peace and joy. He does not want to see me make mistakes, yet I make mistakes, and he loves me through it. That is how we learn.

If there is anything I completely grasp of Christ's message, it is to stand within love. And excluding anyone from that program was not Christ's stand, according to my understanding. I saw this as a challenge, a way for me to interact with the church, when in the past I had a problem with the whole membership program. If I could change that or work around it, I could tolerate the members of the congregation who found it necessary to voice their disapproval. I needed to do things my way, and no one could tell me what to do or whom to love. Certainly, I loved Sharon.

At our first Bible study meeting, everyone was to bring a verse pertinent to her life, whatever she was going through that week. I was very excited to bring my thoughts and brought up the subject that when we pray, God lives in us, so actually He is praying to Himself. When we pray, it is as if God is praying to Himself!

As I spoke, an eighty-year-old lady smiled at me lovingly. She was one of little words from the outside, part of the ministry outreach within Bryan. She appeared to me as the embodiment of wisdom.

Helen said, "When you want to talk about such intricate spirituality in depth, you want to be sure that you can speak of it with conviction and understanding."

I felt like I was being attacked. It was not only Helen who thought gay people were going directly to Hell. The nature of our relationship was the subject of gossip. It was no secret that Sharon and I were always doing something together.

After the meeting, Helen came and talked to me about it again. "Lesbianism is the den of the Devil."

"Did not Saul—killer of Christians—become Paul, beloved by God and Jesus?"

Helen said, "If your sinful nature controls your mind, there is death. But if the Holy Spirit controls your mind, there is life and peace."

I said, "The Holy Spirit is love and fills me with love. If I am going to Hell for loving this person and having a relationship with her, then why is this happening to me in the middle of God growing inside of me? Why am I being confronted with this right now?" I was becoming angry. "Why does it appear to me that everyone in the church thinks God does not want us to be happy? I think he made us that way—to be happy."

"Every time that you go through a temptation, Sheila, and you do not yield, you increase your power. There is the victory in Christ."

"My best friend from Cambridge, Marian Warren, shared a part of my heart as deep as any I have known, a love that was based on friendship, a loyalty that was unbreakable. Such a bond between sisters can never be viewed as anything less than divine. I am not convinced the love I share with Sharon or anyone is outside of God's love."

"We both need to continue to pray about this, Sheila."

Another week passed quickly. No word from the chaplain. It was time for our prayer meeting, and this week I was bringing something completely different to the group. Forgiveness. I needed a deeper sense of it for myself and for everyone. It was almost easier for me to forgive those who had abused me in the past than it was to forgive myself or forgive the members of the congregation who so harshly judged me. I could feel it.

"My verse this week is on forgiveness. Matthew 5:14: 'For if you forgive men when they sin against you, your Heavenly Father will also forgive you.' If we have a loving God who forgives our faults, we should forgive others. By not forgiving those who had wronged me, I hurt not just myself, but I perpetuated that wrong and was consumed by it. When I began to forgive, I was allowing myself to feel joy.

"Those who have forgiven much love much. Forgiving yourself is the most difficult thing—feeling unworthy, shame. By forgiving ourselves, we are renewed and break the chain that binds us to wrong action, thought, and deed. The victory to realize every day is that nothing is too huge to overcome. Paul said, 'It is not I that lives, but it is Christ who lives in me.'"

"Confess, surrender, and walk with faith is my topic for this week," Helen said. "From John: 1. 9: 'But if we confess our sins, He is faithful and just to forgive us and to cleanse us from every wrong.' Don't let anyone lead you astray with empty philosophy and high-sounding nonsense that come from human thinking and from evil powers of this world, and not from Christ. For in Christ, the fullness of God, lives in the human body, and you are complete through your union with Christ. He is the Lord over every ruler and authority in the universe."

"Helen, I can't have any more of this. I am not impressed with your knowledge of the Bible—it is your faith, how effortlessly you respond to the inner direction, that impresses me. I was here at Bryan for a year and a day a couple years back. I went through the same thing with religion then—studying the Bible, learning the verses and rules. It doesn't work for me. I couldn't even follow the conditions placed on me to stay out of prison. My faith has to be transformational. I watch you and marvel at how you are in touch with the inner voice and respond without doubt. I have some experience with Spirit's inner workings, but my faith and obedience to that can't be forced. It is not in my nature, and it is not strengthened by dueling Biblical verses."

The following Sunday, the chaplain came up to me after the service and said, "Sheila, I have read the play and think that it would be a good thing for us to allow you to perform it, but you will have to get approval from the warden."

"Thank you!" I shouted. "Praise God!" This was an affirmation I would keep to myself. It seemed that in spite of the message I was receiving from others regarding my relationship with Sharon, God was still moving forward with his work with me and through me. All of life is significant to Him.

Monday morning ushered in great excitement with the presence of a western diamondback rattler outside the front door of my quad. I was never fond of snakes. In fact, of all the earth's natural creatures, snakes freak me out the most. I won't even watch snakes on TV. This one was at least three feet long and poisonous. It created quite a stir, and I got a pretty good look at it before it slithered off. *The serpent*, I thought. *You can't get to me. God is on my side, and I'm on my way to the warden!*

During dinner, standing in a line, one would find the head of the medical department, head of education, head of administration, warden, head of recreation, and captain of the guard—all the decision makers on the compound were available every night for any inmate to approach. There were so many people waiting to talk to the warden, I almost gave up on the idea.

She was a very attractive older woman and had arrived at the prison a few days after I did. She reminded me of Barbara Walters; at least they both sported the identical hairdo. White, blonde, very by the book, astute and articulate, she always wore a two-piece dress outfit—skirt and jacket. All the professional administration dressed without uniform. Her only visible sign of authority was the badge she wore marking her position.

After a considerable wait, I approached her with a great deal of confidence. "Good afternoon, Warden Winters. I am Sheila Robinson. I have a play I wrote and want to get permission to perform it here. I have already talked to the chaplain, and he gave his approval. He instructed me to bring it to you."

"Let me discuss it with the chaplain and find out what his opinion is. I will get back to you through him. If he said it was okay, then I don't think there will be any problem with it."

I knew it was a done deal. From here on out, it was all about going through the proper channels. You started at whatever level, worked your way up, and then let it filter back down. They wanted you to always be reminded they were in control. *She probably would not even discuss it with the chaplain,* I thought, *just say something like, "One of the inmates came up with some stupid play. If you think this is a good idea, then let her know she can go ahead with it."*

"Thank you, Warden," I said, making an effort to remain calm, though I could hardly contain myself as I returned to the table to finish dinner.

Out in the exercise area, I ran into Sharon, and I couldn't contain my excitement. "I talked to the warden at dinner. I think everything is going to be fine, and I'll get the okay to do the play!"

"Well, isn't that good for you! I guess that means you are going to be spending even more time at the church!'

"You know, you're right," I said in a sarcastic tone. "It will be good for me."

On a human level, Sharon was all I had, and I did love her. It hurt me that she would not embrace the idea of my getting something like that off the ground. It was a girl/girl thing in our physical space. There was no boy in it, and, as far as she was concerned, church was like another lover.

"Don't you think the whole thing is a little hypocritical, Sheila?"

Great, I thought, *it is not enough that I am getting crap about our relationship from all sides in the church; she has to bring it to me, too.* I honestly did not see a contradiction between these two relationships.

"Forget what others say. It is my personal relationship with God that matters to me. I am praying on it and asking for some revelation about what He would see come of us. Until then, can we just be happy? Let's go play some volleyball."

"I am uncomfortable with you going to church. I can't stand it. It makes me feel guilty, and I know what others are saying about us."

"It makes me love you all the more for saying that," I said, and we walked to the recreation area together. "Besides, what do they know about it? Just let me hear someone talk some mess to me."

Sharon was crazy about me, and I felt I needed that. I loved her companionship and laughter, and that part of our relationship no one could argue with, but the supersexual attraction between us was not easily disguised. A female babysitter had assaulted Sharon, as had mine, providing our relationship with roots in a childhood of common ground. Outside of the churchgoers, most of the inmates were cool with us; at least they didn't make a really big deal about it. Homosexuality was rampant in prison.

An inmate at the next prayer group who had not been willing to share much in the first two meetings was the first to speak. "Let Heaven fill your thoughts. Do not think about things down here on earth. For you died when Christ died, and your real life is hidden with Christ in God."

I wanted to challenge her understanding of those words, but I liked her. I wanted her to receive the approval from the others so she might be strengthened. I remained quiet, but within me, I quietly said, *Dear sister, I agree with Heaven filling your thought, but I think by this you mean one should think of Heaven, of your idea of Heaven. It is so much more than that. It is real. In order for your mind to be filled with the thought of Heaven, the thought of God, your mind must not bring any idea to it at all. We did not die when Christ died. We are very much alive, and so is Christ. As to our life, that is far from hidden; it is an open book to all.*

The old lady brought this to the table: "Great men and women speak from inner perception and connection with Soul. Someday we all will. We understand on one level, but they often are speaking deeper truths of which we have yet to become acquainted."

As she paused and smiled at me, I looked at her with amazement and wonder and was filled with the idea that she had heard or read my thoughts.

She continued, "In our own inner journey, our day-to-day experience, we should walk in this world with the unconditional love for all of life. Though we will be defeated countless times by fear, insecurity, and habits, when we fail with the intention of truth and love, we yet have accomplished more, even in our defeat, than if we had not attempted such a life.

"I say that to reveal my simple prayer. With every breath I take, my Father, may I be aware it is by You I breathe. It is You I breathe into me so that I may be filled inside-out with Your presence. May I exhale all that is of this world; let it be no longer desired by me."

"That was beautiful," I said. "I wish to read II Corinthians, chapter thirteen.

"And now I will show you the best way of all.

"Suppose I speak in the languages of human beings and angels. If I don't have love, I am only a loud gong or a noisy cymbal. Suppose I have the gift of prophecy; suppose I can understand all the secret things of God and know everything about Him. And suppose I have enough faith to move mountains. If I don't have love, I am nothing at all. Suppose I give everything I have to poor people, and suppose I give my body to be burned. If I don't have love, I get nothing at all.

"Love is patient. Love is kind. It doesn't want what belongs to others. It does not brag, it is not proud, and it is not rude. It does not look out for its own interests. It does not easily become angry. It does not keep track of others' wrongs.

"Love is not happy with evil, but it is full of joy when the truth is spoken. It always protects, it always trusts, it always hopes, it never gives up. Love never fails, but prophecy will pass away. Speaking in a language that has not been heard before will end, and knowledge will pass away.

"What we know now is not complete. What we profess now is imperfect. But when what is perfect, the things that are not perfect will pass away.

"When I was child, I talked like a child, I thought like a child, I had the understandings a child. When I became a woman (man), I put childish ways behind me.

"Now we see only a dim likeness of things. It is as if we were seeing them in a mirror. But someday we will see clearly. Someday we will see face to face. What I know now is not complete, but someday I will know completely just as God knows me completely.

"The three most important things to have are faith, hope, and love. But the greatest of them is love."

After prayer group, I returned to my cell with the question, *What is faith?* And the answer came: *The confident assurance that what we hope for is going to happen and the evidence of things we cannot yet see.* I was beginning to understand, beginning to enjoy the ride. Love is the Greatest of All Things.

CHAPTER 15

SWEET SIXTEEN

The Holy Spirit gives Life
Those who belong to Christ Jesus are no longer under
God's sentence
I am now controlled by the Law of the Holy Spirit
That Law gives me Life because of what Christ
Jesus has done
It has set me free from the Law of Sin that brings death

ROMANS 8: 1, 2

I WAS WORRIED TO DEATH about Jeanna. There was still no word from her, and I knew all too well about the runaway syndrome and what could happen, how vulnerable she was. I was about the same age as Jeanna when I ran away. I wanted to grow my arms hundreds of miles long and blindly feel around and find her. If this is how God teaches us, it can be a very painful lesson that He imposes. Some call it karma. Some say for every action there is an equal and opposite reaction. In the hood, I knew the principle simply as, "What goes around comes around." I sat down to write her a letter. It was the only thing I could do—the only thing I could think of to keep from going crazy. Truth be told, it was a long prayer to God asking Him to watch over her, a way of saying, "I get it! I learned my lesson. Don't make her have to pay for my mistakes."

* * *

I was back from Los Angeles at the age of fifteen—back in Cambridge, Ohio. Though it was my decision to leave California, I hated being in Cambridge, a small country town with a slow, deliberate pace. I had just returned from life in the fast lane: Los Angeles, Disneyland, glitz, glamour, and Ray Charles. It's not that I didn't love Cambridge; I just didn't want to live there—one bowling alley, seventeen bars, and one sheriff. There was nothing to do. At that time, the population was around 8,000; when my mom grew up, 1,500. That's where she was coming from. I always loved going home for the holidays and special occasions, but to live there, well, it just wasn't my thing. And there were a lot of painful memories—too many.

It was the summer before eleventh grade and a couple months before my sixteenth birthday when I ran away. I was always with older kids, searching for a sense of family and rarely at home. I was not without roots, but from numerous transplanting experiences, a stable taproot was never fully developed. Born in L.A., taken to Cambridge, back to L.A., back to Cambridge, from one house to another, from one man in my mother's life back to Ray Charles, to another man in my mother's life back to Ray Charles, to North Carolina, back to Cambridge, to L.A., back to Cambridge. When I was at school, I was a straight-A student with some of the best grades in my class. But I hated the whole cliquish behavior, the competitiveness, and how cruel kids were. I hung out with the scrubs—the hole-in-the-jean kids with the long hair and dirty T-shirts, the ones who smoked cigarettes outside at the row, as we called the dirt access road that surrounded the school's football field. Mom wanted me to be a cheerleader, the ancient blindness of parenthood. That's what she wanted as a schoolgirl, something she was denied. Quite naturally, that's what she wanted for me. On top of that, I was a Betts.

My mother's family was well respected as far as society went in Cambridge. Silky Betts was the first black freed slave in Ohio. Her freedom papers are in a museum. Both the white and the black community regarded me as the "black sheep" of the family. Maybe I should say the "white sheep" of the family. I was into rock 'n' roll and entered my biker stage and Ozzie Osborne; no one in Cambridge knew who Ozzie was. At that time, I had no idea what was driving me, what I was searching for, what caused me to intentionally stay out of the house. Steeped in confusion, the past was dark and buried. I never spoke about it. Those experiences were walled off—deep. I had no conscious recollection of half the stuff that happened to me as a kid. Within such a caustic soil, it's no surprise my roots were superficial and undeveloped.

The last event that occurred, the principal reason I ran away, was consistent with the darkness of my childhood—sexual in nature. My mom's best friend had a son we called Juice. He was a pudgy, jolly, little black elf. I loved him and don't know of a single soul who didn't. Juice's brother-in-law, his sister's husband, hit on me. He wanted to have sex with me. That just freaked me out. Of all the sexual abuse I had witnessed and endured from early in life to that point, it was the only time I told somebody. I felt safe talking about it because nothing happened. I saw it as a personal victory. It was a real big thing between the families, and it was ugly. Juice's sister ended up getting a divorce. Though I knew that Mom as a "take no nonsense" person and that she had my back, such knowledge didn't relieve the stress on me. I was accused of making baseless allegations.

I was filled with guilt. Maybe I should have just kept quiet. Nothing ever went down between us. I didn't let anything happen. It just freaked me out, and I had had enough of that kind of harassment. He was thirty. Juice's brother-in-law apparently had had episodes with younger girls in the past, and he wasn't supposed to have any contact with minors.

Also, my family already had an underlying, sickening dislike for me—shamed by my mother and the national news coverage of the paternity suit with Ray. Just because she won that battle or that Ray had called my grandmother and announced his intention to marry Mom did not improve the circumstances for either of us. I was born out of wedlock with a married man as my father. That was the prevailing wind, and it was horrible. It was never openly discussed, but it was always present under the surface. And now, an infection festering beneath the surface for years had been opened, and it was stinking to high Heaven. I was the talk of the town—home wrecker, that type of thing. Mom, of course, wasn't having it. But when she was drinking, things came out of her mouth equally hurtful. Talk about soil erosion around your root system; this was a flash flood.

My best friend, Marian Warren, came up with the idea to run away. For whatever reason, I always saw her as being more mature and worldlier than me. It was natural to lean on her and discuss this latest episode. One of our best friends, her aunt, Paula Walker, was like her big sister, and we always hung out with her when we had the opportunity. She was three years older than us and had joined the Marine Corps after high school. Though Paula knew little of my rocky past, she was aware of the abuse Marian had endured from her stepfather. Sympathetic toward both of us, she had already talked to Marian about living with her once she got her own place. Marian approached me with her clandestine departure and invited me along. Our past had already acquainted us with such operations. Her stepfather had forbidden her to hang out with me. I would signal her from the bushes, and she would jump out of the second-story window and sneak out like that. Marion's suggestion was just a natural extension of what had already been set in motion.

So it was three months before my sixteenth birthday that early summer when Paula came back to Cambridge on leave, and I was ready to go.

"I'm stationed at Camp Lejeune." Paula said, "You guys are welcome to come down there with me. I am moving off base. Jacksonville, North Carolina. It's right on the Atlantic Ocean. Beautiful."

Marian and Paula turned to me and said, "Let's go!"

"OH yeah," I said. "That's the program."

I was in it to win it. We hitchhiked all the way down there. When we got out of one truck, there was another waiting for us. The truck driver we were with would call on the CB to get us another ride. "Yeah, we've got three beavers here that I'm dropping off headin' to Camp Lejeune." I didn't know what a "beaver" was, what they were talking about, but there were ten trucks lined up down the freeway to pick us up, and so a convenient and inexpensive road was forged.

Once within the city limits of Jacksonville, we learned Paula could not immediately move to her trailer; it wouldn't be ready for three days. We had no place to stay but in her barracks. We made up names, wore fatigues, went to physical training with her, and, in every way possible, pretended to be part of the corps. Surprisingly, no one was aware of our infiltration. That is how it was. Three days later, during an inspection of the barracks, Marian and I hid under the bottom bunk at the end of the barracks, backs against the wall. Paula was a smooth talker and was able to prevent the sergeant from gaining a clear look at where we were hiding. Having overtaxed luck and grateful for Gomer Pyle, we left the base that morning and moved into Paula's trailer.

Paula had a huge housewarming party that delivered eight men to every girl. On the base, there were thousands of men and far fewer women. It was on that first night I met Rick Bule and his friend Mark Scheffer. Rick was California beautiful. He had a really dark tan—almost as dark as me—jet-black hair, sky-blue eyes, the whitest teeth you could ever see in life, and a smile that would melt any heart. Every girl wanted his arm. I told everyone I was eighteen and somehow ended up with Rick. We started dating regularly within two weeks.

Rick and Mark were both Marine corporals. I was young and foolish—Rick could have been court-martialed for just being with me—fifteen and a runaway, not to mention Marian, who was up to the same thing. And let's not forget Paula, orchestrating and permitting this whole thing. How we were able to do this is beyond me to this very day. It was one constant party.

A dairy farm adjoined the trailer park where we were living. Up against the fence separating the two properties were vast mounds of cow manure. One of Paula's neighbors discovered mushrooms growing from them, mushrooms that provided the hallucinogenic psilocybin. We made some tea, and, sometime thereafter, I called my mother, just to let her know I was okay. I had no intention to return home. Marian and I had already had jobs, and I was quite beside myself having become so established, to say nothing of the effects of the tea.

"Mom, I just thought to call and say hi and let you know I was all right."

"Oh my God! Sheila! Where the ___ are you?"

"Florida."

"Are you crazy? You'd better get home here right now."

"Home? Heck, Mom, I'm married."

"Married! Are you nuts?"

"What do you think of that?"

"Tell me what's wrong because if you're running from it, I need to go with. I got to get away from it, too! If it's that bad, why wouldn't you take me and your brother with you?"

"Why does it always have to be about you or about Ray?"

"Listen, Sheila, you'd better get yourself on a bus back here immediately!"

"And quit my job? No thank you!"

"Sheila!" was the last thing I heard as I hung up the phone. The conversation had gone as far as I wanted. I was high and just wanted her to know I was all right.

It was billed as my nineteenth birthday party. Everyone bought it. We were out for a drive in Mark's truck, all four of us in the cab— Marianne, Rick, Mark, and I. Mark had never touched alcohol before in his life. He had had a few beers and got a buzz and couldn't drive. Rick ended up behind the wheel of Mark's truck. At that time, I was pleased at having such a responsible "man."

It was raining as we drove down the freeway. A sign indicating a fifteen-mile-per-hour hairpin curve had been bent over, no longer visible. The Atlantic Ocean was on one side of the road, and mountains were on the other. When we came upon that curve, Rick applied the brakes, but the water on the road made the effort useless. The truck flipped with all four of us squished in the cab. Seated next to the passenger window, I somehow flew past Marian, Mark, and Rick out the driver's window, a young lover's flight fifty feet through the air. I landed on my head, face-first, and immediately went unconscious.

Later, I would learn all my facial bones, my nose, and my sinuses were crushed. Teeth were protruding from my cheeks and lips, pieces of them embedded in my flesh. My bones were sticking out of my legs, my head was crooked, and my right eye was pushed and sunken down into my cheekbone. I had suffered a broken arm, a cracked pelvis, and lacerations everywhere, even between my fingers and toes. I was taken to Onslow Memorial Hospital in Jacksonville, the only nonmilitary hospital for forty miles in any direction of Camp Lejeune. By the time I arrived at the emergency room, my head was swollen almost twice its normal size. I was in a coma.

Inexplicably, Rick had only one tiny scratch on his stomach. The truck had gone over the edge of the cliff and ended upside down at the edge of the Atlantic Ocean. Had it been deep water, the three of them would have drowned. Mark had a broken back and had to be cut out from the truck's cab. A helicopter came for him and flew him to a military hospital. Marian had deep lacerations all over her legs and a broken pelvic bone. Determined not to go back home, she provided the hospital our fictitious identities. Hardened by her stepfather's intolerable abuse, Marian was in total control of the situation, prepared to bite her tongue until it bled.

Five days later, I woke up in the hospital, high on morphine with Marian next to me. Disoriented, I looked over at her and asked, "What happened?"

"Sheila, I love you! You won't believe it. The truck rolled over and down into the ocean. You flew out the window somehow." She started crying. "You look a sight."

"What do you mean?"

Marian started smiling at that point. I observed the pronounced lisp I was speaking with but could feel no pain. I became aware I had suffered injury. Marian then began crying, and I became very concerned for her. She pulled herself together and told me Rick had come in several times while I was unconscious. "I didn't tell them who we are, Sheila. No one from Cambridge has been contacted."

"What time is it?'

"Two o'clock in the morning."

"How bad do I look? I don't feel a thing. What's that bag on the side of your bed?"

"It's for my pee. You got one, too!"

"What happened to Mark and Rick? I hope nothing happened to his fine face."

"He only got a scratch on his stomach. Mark, on the other hand, broke his back. They airlifted him to a different hospital."

"How long have I been sleeping?"

"Sleeping?! Girl, you've been in a coma."

"What? How long?"

"Five days!"

"Oh my God! I'm beginning to feel awful. I feel like I've been hit by a truck. I got to see. I got to see!" I was trying to sit up and get a look at myself, but I was unable to move. I rang for a nurse, who promptly arrived. I asked her what was going on with me and told her I wanted a mirror.

"You'd better calm yourself down and wait till the morning. There are no doctors you can speak to until then. I'm not qualified. Try to relax. It's good to see you're awake."

Later that morning, several doctors came to see me. The pain was driving me nuts. I told them I wanted something for the pain and desired to look at myself.

"We can't do anything until we know who you are. And what we have been told doesn't seem to add up. We don't think you are eighteen years old, and we don't believe your name is Star."

"You've got to give me something for this pain."

"As soon as you tell us who you are. Where are your parents?"

I glanced over at Marian, and she nodded, giving me the go-ahead to at least come clean with my identity.

"My name is Sheila Robinson, and I'm seventeen years old." Much of what occurred at that time, having just awakened from a coma, is indistinct. I have pieced together events from fragments of memory and what others have told me.

Perhaps due to my confusion, I felt telling them I was seventeen would somehow make a safer escape for Marian if she wanted to stick to her story. "I want my mom. Can I call her?"

"We will call her for you."

I struggled to give them the number, and, after about fifteen minutes, I was handed the phone.

"Sheila?"

Hearing my mother's voice, I started to cry and became a sixteen-year-old girl again. I was tired of pretending to be grown-up. Look at where it had gotten me—the dumbest thing I had done in my life.

"Mom," I mumbled in a little girl's voice between the tears and sobbing.

"Oh! It's my little lamb. Don't even try to talk, baby. I am on my way right this minute. And the doctors will give you whatever you need until I get there. I already talked to them."

"Okay, Mom." I was crying like a baby as I released my grip on the phone.

After I ran away from home, everybody in town was asking my mother why she hadn't reported me missing. "Why don't you report her absence to this agency or that agency?" My mother said, "I'm leaving it in God's hands."

The exact minute of my accident, a voice entered Mom's mind and said, "Sheila is dead!" It woke her from a deep sleep, and she sat straight up and said, "I rebuke and denounce that in the name of Jesus Christ!" My mother claimed it to be the voice of Satan. The hospital did all they could to keep me alive, but, truth be told, I believe it was all God's doing keeping me safe. The doctor told Mom over the phone, "We don't know how she is still alive. You'd better come immediately."

When Mom entered my room, she had the most beautiful white, fluffy robe over one arm—under the other, a huge, white, furry lamb. Before Mom or Aunt Cathy said a word, they both gasped for breath and began crying. They just cried and cried. The depth of their tears confused me. I did not understand why they were so hysterical. I imagined I must have looked like a mess. I wanted to see but could barely move with bedpan, catheter, IVs, splints, and monitors. I had given up on the idea as a lost cause.

The doctors came in and quickly left with Mom to talk outside the room. They returned and told me I was going back home with her. Afterward, the nurse came in to undo my catheter and hooked me up to a portable IV. It wasn't much later I needed to go to the bathroom. I told Mom, and she went to get the nurses. I had to be lifted up, wheeled into the bathroom, and helped out of the chair onto the stool. It was pain beyond anything imaginable, a pain that few learn the human nervous system is capable of inflicting.

I really wanted to look at my face. *How bad could it be?* I thought. *They're letting me go home with Mom.* Before returning to the wheelchair, upon my insistence I was assisted up to the mirror above the sink— immediate shock. Though I had a temporary cast on my leg and arm, there were no bandages on my head or face. The teeth that remained in my mouth were loose. My head was swollen twice its normal size and cocked to one side. My jaw was broken and my nasal cavity crushed. My right eye was down inside my cheek. It was grotesque. Imagine a wax sculpture of a face twice its normal size that had been tilted to one side and gently warmed to allow gravity to pull the swollen mass of material downward. Deformity? *I look like I should be dead,* I thought. *Why didn't anyone tell me? All I heard was they were letting me out of here, thinking it can't be that bad. I was getting on a plane? First class!* I was very angry.

I was starving. Mom could not believe it when I told her I had to eat something. I don't think she realized I had been out for five days with nothing to eat. Mom said, "Your teeth are swinging, and your jaw is broke, nose and cheek. Are you nuts?" I was provided soup through a straw.

Mom was somewhere outside of sanity. Her mental acuity was less than mine, and I had been on Demerol. When we arrived in Cambridge, she brought me home with her. Without medication, no pain pills, I was going into withdrawal and having sweats, and the pain was starting to kick in. The next day, Mom called Onslow Memorial Hospital to find out what to do, and the representative at the hospital said, "My God. Did you take her home? You have got to get her to the hospital! When you told us that you were taking her home, we thought that you meant that you were going to take her to the hospital where you live. Get her to the hospital now!"

Mom said, "You all didn't instruct me to take her to the hospital in Cambridge. I told you I was taking her home!"

Mom called the hospital in Cambridge and told them she was bringing me in. The hospital told her, "Stat." She called Aunt Cathy to pick us up. The doctors at Onslow Memorial had only set my pelvic bone so they could place a catheter in me. My broken bones all had temporary splints, and I had broken pieces of teeth in my face. It was absolutely ridiculous. To this day, I have no idea what my mother was thinking. I can only assume that she was in a state of total shock.

While Mom was getting a few things together for my stay, I had to use the bathroom. I got up on my own and fell, slipping on the wet bathroom floor with a broken leg and broken arm. I was incapable of moving. My left arm lay up against an electric heating unit that ran along the floorboard, searing my flesh. I screamed for Mom as my arm burned, unable to move or take any weight off it. I was delirious from pain. Mom moved me from the heater but could not lift me from the floor. She immediately called for an ambulance and waited until the paramedics came. That is how I made it to the Cambridge hospital.

Once admitted, I was immediately put on a morphine drip. I was in such pain I couldn't even cry. It was excruciating. They had to set my bones—my arms, wrists, legs, and nose. That's when they discovered all of my sinus cavities were shattered. I could not breathe though my nose. Mom snapped out of her shock and began fighting for me. She called an attorney and made the effort to reach Ray. All hell was about to break loose.

The surgery was performed in Cambridge by Doctor Shrikintea, a specialist the hospital had to call in. My head was like the Elephant Man's, and my right eyeball had dropped down beneath my cheekbone.

Doctor Shrikintea came in before the surgery and said, "You will be deformed for the rest of your life. I am telling you this because it is necessary for you to be prepared for this reality. We are going to put a plate under your eye that is necessary for the facial bone reconstruction, and we will put a sinus window in place that will allow for the sinuses to drain. I am confident you should be able to breathe normally."

Breathe normally, I thought. *I am going to be a freak!* For me, life was at its end. There was nothing left for me to live for. Up to that moment, the seriousness of my condition had not fully sunk in.

Mom called "Chucky"—Chuck Simpson, Mom's favorite cousin in Cambridge and one of her best friends. He was a minister.

"The doctors are saying there is nothing their hand can do. But I believe a Higher Power can assist you, Sheila. Do you believe God can heal you?" Chucky said, "Do you believe in Jesus Christ?"

Well, what could I say but yes?

"Do you accept Jesus Christ as your Lord and Savior and that he died for your sins, and through Him you will have eternal life?"

"Heck yes!" I exclaimed. "Of course I do!"

My mind might not have been right with this, but my faith was real. I knew if a specialist was telling me he couldn't fix my face, I sure needed something greater than man on this one. If God is who He says He is, now was the time for Him to show me. As a child, that's how I was thinking. It was innocent. God says don't test Him. I wasn't testing Him. I was just saying, "Let me know if You are real."

The surgery lasted nine hours. I don't remember much of anything for about a week afterwards. I was completely out on morphine. I had to keep my head in one position so the bones could have time to heal together. My entire head was wrapped in gauze except for a portion around my mouth and left eye. High school friends would come and visit, but there wasn't much I could do to respond to them, yet I was happy to see them. Two weeks elapsed before I was coherent enough to know what was going on. It was about six, maybe eight weeks before they came in and told me it was time to remove the bandages.

After they unwrapped my face, they had to pull tons of gauze out through my mouth and nose. It hurt severely, and the plate inserted under my eye was sensitive and sore. I wanted to scream in pain but could not because of all the gauze in my mouth. It was horrible. Doctor Shrikintea stepped back and said, "It's a miracle. You're perfect. You are simply perfect."

"Praise God!" a nurse said.

"It wasn't God—it was my hands," said Doctor Shrikintea.

Though I really didn't understand much of what was occurring, I knew God was real and how much He loved me. When I emerged from the surgery room, Mom, Aunt Cathy, Kevin, everybody was praising God. And that's the day I knew my relationship with Him was all about me, where I stood with Him, not where He stood with me. But I was young and fearless, without any option but to make a stand as a lover of God. I would soon forget such a blessing and take it for granted.

I remained in the hospital for another four months. They would repair my teeth later. I spent an additional four months in the dental chair with reconstruction wires in both my upper and lower jaws. That was worse than the hospital. I almost didn't want to have the work done. I wore partial plates as long as I could, but when I got back into the dating scene, all that flopping around caused me to decide it was time to get something secure. The perms. Enough of the flopping while you're talking.

A friend of Mom's told her to take Ray back to court to increase child support payments. Mom went to Los Angeles for a hearing when Dad would learn for the first time the details of what had been happening in both of our lives. Those who surrounded Dad shielded him, kept information from him. He broke down in the courtroom and cried.

I had never looked at it from another pair of eyes before, but now I was seeing and feeling the horror my actions had brought to my mother. I never imagined anything like that happening to my children. I could not survive walking into a hospital emergency room seeing Jeanna in that condition. My heart cried for my mother, "Oh, Mom. Forgive me!"

*   *   *

Such a past was present with me as I sat in the prison commons area, head held down with acid in my stomach, hoping and praying I would hear something from the outside about Jeanna. Like my mother, I could do nothing but place her fate in God's hands.

"Sheila Robinson."

I almost fell out of my chair as I bolted to grab my mail. It was a letter from Jeanna. As I tore it open, tears were streaming from my eyes. Jeanna had tracked me down through Kevin. She had run away from the foster home and was in juvenile detention, but she was okay. Once again, she reached me and told me how much she loved me and how much she wanted a relationship with me. I was a crackhead in tears, a poor excuse for a mother in federal prison. But I was breaking that chain to my past and knew the bond between mother and child yet existed. I was awash with love for Jeanna and all my children.

Why did I take it out as far as I did? How did I lose sight of all that was merciful, holy, and pure? Why did I allow the world to draw me away from the goodness of God, from Jeanna's willingness to give me another chance, my miraculous recovery from my accident? And no matter how far you take it out, as long as you are willing to receive God for who He is, He will intervene with this world. That much I am privileged to know.

Before church service the following Sunday, the chaplain approached me. "Sheila, if you still want to perform this play of yours, it will be all right. You can go forward with it."

"Thank you," I said. I was on fire. Ecstatic!

"I will make an announcement toward the end of the service and call you up to present it to the congregation."

As I stood in front of the congregation, I talked about the circumstances surrounding the inspiration for the play.

"The connection with the divine—what is happening with me—God slides so smoothly and lovingly in. The whole time I was out in the streets I could not bear to hear music—it was too close to my soul. Whenever I was around music, I would go into the bathroom and cry. I would turn off the radio, or I would just get up and leave. It was too close to me, and I could not bear to be without it, so I would remove it. In that way, I could not feel its painful reminder, its call to me, my soul, my life. I was living absolutely contrary to my heart and knew it. Music was the only thing that could overpower the high of the drug, cut through the artificial coma. Music is God's gift to me, and it always reminded me of the hell I had abandoned myself to, the hell I was in.

"When I first started writing lyrics inside prison, I thought they were poems. When times of trouble started to occur in the jail, melodies to the words I had written sprang forth—the songs manifested like that—and all of a sudden, I started to sing. It wasn't something I was thinking about. It just happened effortlessly.

"There was something genuine going on inside of me, not just in the spirit—in the physical. One thing you should know—my hand was broken in a car accident when I was sixteen. The bones never grew back together properly. I can write only about two or three minutes at a time before my hand locks up, my fingers go numb, and I can't feel the pen between my fingers. While writing during those fourteen days in lockdown, I never felt that pain and was able to write for hours on end. I could tell during that time I was being guided—felt it physically, knew I was within a place above the physical reality in complete love and comfort. The best way to describe the place where I was when I wrote this play is like this: on the coldest night when you were a little kid outside and playing, and you came inside, and your mom or dad brought you into their arms, and they would rub you all over, and you were in complete love and comfort, secure. Solid ground—engulfed by the love package unwrapped. Right there behind a locked cell door, inside four concrete walls, a toilet, and mattress. Prison had become my monastery.

"The first thing I did was to turn to the Bible. The Lord says, 'Wait for me.' And with that thought inspired from Psalms, I wrote down the words to "Wait on Me," and I started to cry. These were words to myself. I started to sing, and the melody just came out. The first time it was broken, soft, and tearful. My heart felt as if I were about to hemorrhage my life's blood—it's almost as though it wouldn't come out—as if there was resistance between God and me. Almost immediately thereafter, I sang it again. The second time, however, I sang it *to* God, and that is when the other inmates heard me. I sang it with absolute conviction, screaming these words. REMEMBER ME! LEAD ME TO THE TRUTH! THIS IS WHERE I NEED TO BE!

"That is the story of this first song in lockdown:

Remember thy tender mercy
Remember no sin from me
Lead me to thy truth and comfort me
My guiding light
Yes, I'll wait for thee
I will wait on thee, my Lord
Yes I will wait on thee, my Lord
Yes I will wait on thee, my Lord
My guiding light
Yes, I'll wait for thee

"For the first two days, that's all I sang and all I did. That one verse and the chorus—what God gave me—what I needed. I realized He was saying, 'Hang on, sister.' Inspired to sing during a moment of abandonment, it is all I could think of doing. It is all I had. I kept saying over and over and over, 'Okay, God. I am waiting on you. You hear me singing. I'll wait for thee. I'll just keep singing.'

"During that time, some of the inmates were slipping me notes under the door. They wrote about how my singing was affecting their lives. Someone would occasionally shout, 'Shut up!,' and the rest of the inmates would yell, 'Who cares whatever she is saying? Don't stop. Don't stop.'

"I didn't care what anybody else thought at that point. When David was repenting, he would write beautiful songs. He was an outrageous person and considered a man after God's own heart. His love for God was unbelievable, and that's why I know what we think is *good* and *bad* is so unimportant to God.

"The idea I had pounded into my head for years was simple: I was condemned. Can you imagine living with one thought continually reverberating in your mind, 'You are condemned; you are condemned?' For years, I lived with that. What keeps it on you? The thought that you are garbage, and the answer to that condemnation: 'Smoke some crack, and you won't hear or remember the thought.' But there is good in everyone; no one is entirely rotten. Everybody in the Bible God used for the greatest of the greatness was all messed up. The pity party in your mind forms the gates of Hell. Once you go there in your mind, you lock Spirit out. You lock God out, and God completely broke me down.

"God met me where I was, and I needed to feel good about myself within the interaction with the other inmates, and they were being affected while in prison with me. It lifted me, brought me a sense of self-worth that I had not had for many years.

"Prior to my lockdown, I had briefly conversed with an elderly inmate who shared some of her story with me. She had met a white guy—a farmer. He took her way out into the country, way up north to his property. She was from Chicago and straight out from the hood. She rocked his nation up at the farm. He left her there to go help his daughter in the cities, and back at the ranch, she wiped him out. She got caught when he called the police, and that's the reason she was behind bars.

"She slipped me a note during my third day of lockdown: 'Yeah, girl. I used to be in the church. I used to love the Lord, and he loved me. But then I started backsliding and stuff. Now I am out of God's grace.' She went on to say how the song had affected her and had brought her back to wanting to reestablish a relationship with God—how she wanted to find her daughter and talk to her.

"I had no intention to affect anyone else. I was simply responding to me—to the God in me. Now I know for sure that everything we do affects everyone and everything else. My understanding is childlike, and God's power great. After that, other songs started to come—and finally the ideas and visions of this play, *Prodigal Praise*.

"That's my story about this play that I—we—have received permission to perform. I invite anyone interested in participating as a member of the cast, choir, or production crew to meet with me after the service. We will have an organizational meeting Wednesday night and get the show on the road."

After the service, I was pleased to be greeted with enthusiasm by eighteen members of the congregation and gratefully took their names. I had no intention to play any role personally and held hope the production would affect the hearts of the audience and cast I would direct. I had been thinking about casting from the moment Helen saw it as a viable project. With the final approval, I went to inform those I had in mind for the leading roles. All were outside the church.

CHAPTER 16

RECORDING
WITH DAD

Victory comes when we learn to love people
And use things
And not get those two things mixed up

—NEIL T. ANDERSON,
THE BONDAGE BREAKER

"WHERE YOU GOING?" Marcia asked as we left the chapel that Sunday evening.

"The smoke pad."

"Why are you going out there?"

"Just to hang out."

"Don't separate from the love of God."

"How can I do that? That's pure crazy! I love you, Marcia. Don't worry about me. I'm not going there to smoke." But I was the only member of the congregation making her way to that area.

Smoke.

I had been inhaling it for as long as I could remember. Tobacco, marijuana, and cocaine were the progressive wisps of my preference. Surrounded by cigarettes as a child, I regarded smoking as something most adults did, something from which children and most grandparents abstained. It was natural, then, to view the habit as an icon of adulthood—

virility and fertility. I reached puberty early and started smoking young. In high school, we did it outside on a rutted dirt road on the far side of the football field that melted into tall grass and then—brush, brush—we would rip through when someone decided it was time to keep us honest to school policy, unwilling to bear the wrath of angered parents, of which my mom would be one. And so, in that manner, the habit served the rebel within me. The most effective way to get me to do something has always been to forbid me from doing it. That could very well be an inherited trait from my father.

Mom told me a story about when Dad took a tape of his music to the head of a small record label in Texas. After listening to the demo, the executive told Dad, "Get yourself a cup and some pencils and open up shop on a street corner because you sure aren't going to sell any records." Dad brought his first gold record to him, thanking him for making such a pronouncement—it made him try harder. I can't claim to know his motivation or if there is any truth to the story, but it sounded like something both Dad and I would be inspired by. And when it came to other similarities, Dad smoked like a chimney.

As I became familiar with music and nightlife, I would learn that bars and nightclubs not only were synonymous with the liquor industry, but also that smoke was the atmosphere of such establishments. Nicotine and alcohol went hand in hand, perhaps not a symbiosis made in Heaven, but the two are married nonetheless. Hollywood did its best to oblige Big Tobacco, and my family and those who surrounded me did their best to support it.

Like a single tent sheltering an entire band of gypsies, a two-bedroom Bugs Bunny apartment would be filled by the Betts's entourage, all sharing the common religious commitment to cigarettes, simultaneously celebrating Mass: grandparents, aunts, uncles, brothers, sisters, and the inherited stranger taken into the family. On a holiday or special occasion, twenty or thirty would light up and fill the air so thick that even the most ardent smoker would get teary-eyed—grateful for a break into fresh air, even if such a breath was to be found in subzero weather.

Whatever the forces that bound me into such a relation with smoke, I was schooled early to its use, well-versed in its etiquette. I would have to condemn just about everyone I had ever been close to—certainly most of whom I call family—to a life of eternal damnation were I to claim that God could not be known nor salvation found within one who smokes.

I can only guess it was the butts discarded everywhere about the prison grounds, coupled with the growing disfavor of secondhand smoke, that led to the change in smoking policy. Prior to the designated smoking areas—dubbed smoke pads—smokers were free-roaming. The policy change was assured a mention in the prison rulebook, and its effect on the grounds during recreation and free time was quite remarkable and immediately visible.

The main smoke pad was centrally located between the four quads, equidistant from the exercise area, sharing a common terrain that was perfectly flat throughout the prison campus. It was nothing more than a two-dimensional, twenty-by-thirty-foot slab of asphalt and, when the grounds were unoccupied, it was unremarkable. Were it not for the coffee cans distributed on its surface to collect the butts, I dare say it would go completely unnoticed. However, during recreation time, what was of two dimensions became three, a rectangular solid formed of inmates now forced to feed their habit within this little area.

In prison, cigarettes are money—at least to the smokers. When considering the hourly wage could be as little as twelve cents, one cigarette could represent nearly two hours of work. When I was young and hanging out in school, most of my friends had no problem flipping me a square, but it wasn't like that in here. Every little favor implied something in return. To witness an inmate offer another a smoke was as unusual as seeing a crackhead offer her pipe to a stranger, as godly an act for addict or inmate to be known. Unconditional love meets the smoke pad or the crack house. It is a rarity. But such legends have their origins in fact. Unless one has been so reduced by an overpowering addiction, you simply cannot comprehend the depth of such a selfless act.

So the smoke pad became another church, one that had its own self-appointed ministers and proselytizers. The language of their sermon was one of the street, in your face, and often quite hard, cold, and unyielding. Different groups clotted in little areas upon the pad, and the smokers' church was filled with its zealots—especially right after ten o'clock count on the weekends when its doors were open until 2:00 a.m. If you intended to worship, you'd learn quick to bring your own pack of squares. Within this congregation, I would find Poke.

Her name was Deborah Polk. I had become acquainted with Poke on the pad weeks ago. I found so much of her personality to be like mine: playful and silly, and she loved to laugh. She was the first one I asked to be a member of the cast if the play's performance was approved—the leading role. She was rather thin, which accentuated her six-foot frame. I instantly had my heart set on her playing my character in the play—the character named Monee.

Once I found out that she could sing, I lost my mind. We would get out there and sing old songs from the Stylistics and the Spinners. Poke was twenty-four years old and knew all those songs the same way I did, from her mother. "Why don't you join the choir with me? I just did. The girls are singing their asses off."

"Because everyone knows I have a girlfriend. I don't want to put up with that stuff."

"It's cool with me, Poke, but I know what you mean. People in the church are freaking out over the relationship I'm having. Everyone has a completely different point of view about it. Far as I am concerned, it has nothing to do with my relationship with God."

It was no secret Poke was bi, into the jail girlfriend/girlfriend thing and all that stuff. I was the last person in the world to be concerned with that. I didn't care. The more I got to know her, the more I knew that she was me. I wanted her for the leading role in the play. She was remarkably talented. If the world knew of the talent that was in prison, it would make you cry. I wanted her for the play, and she had already agreed. I couldn't get to the smoke pad fast enough.

"Poke! I got permission to do the play. We're on, sister!" "All right, girl. Let's get it going!"

"Wednesday night at the chapel is the first meeting. We'll get the lowdown from the chaplain and the bosses and set up rehearsal schedules and stuff. I am so excited. Have you seen Joe-Joe?"

"I just saw her on the other side of the pad."

Joe-Joe was a girl from my quad—young, maybe twenty. She looked like a cute Mexican guy, perfect white teeth with long black hair and the sides shaved like the boys do. She was always in trouble, always making me laugh. I was either counseling her on the stupid stuff she was doing or listening to her stories and cracking up. Her little clique did crazy things like switch places with one another and spend the night with their girlfriend in another quad! After one such outing, they all overslept and got busted. Usually, one was shipped out for such a violation. There was zero tolerance for sexual interaction, and being out of bounds only added to the offense. In the captain's office, pictures were posted on a huge bulletin board of all the known couples within the inmate population. My picture was never up there, though it could have been.

Most of the lesbian relationships brought fights and disruptions to the prison environment. Joe-Joe got off light, a week in solitary confinement. My heart was set on her playing the part of the main dope dealer. She was Hispanic and rough like that to a T, and she liked the idea of playing a guy. She was the second person I asked to be a part of the cast, and, like Poke, she agreed. Poke and I found her with her girlfriend, and the three of us held the first unofficial production meeting. It was wonderful.

The next evening after dinner, I was with Sharon, sitting on the bench near the athletic field. We had agreed to meet to practice with our flag football team, but I wanted to heal the rift that was developing between us. With play rehearsals about to begin, my time would be less accommodating to our relationship. I wanted her to understand why it was such a big thing for me to see this through.

"You see, Sharon, this is more than just something to pass the time in here. All my life, I have been told I was good at writing and singing but not good enough to ever get things off the ground. You need to understand how it was for me. I have started many things and completed nothing, just like my mother, who started so many wonderful things and never completed them, incredible ideas put in motion but no follow-through. I need to break that cycle. The self-destruct thing—it was taught, and a habit formed. I would get right to the point where something good was about to happen, and, consciously or subconsciously, I would sabotage the deal.

"I was the artist of the year, front page of the variety section. Mint Condition and Next were opening for me. That was in 1988 when I got to Minneapolis. I didn't even show up because I didn't feel worthy. There wasn't any true success in my life, no peace or harmony. Look at all the things that happened to me. And those who wanted to see me successful saw it in some way as their success. I felt that way about my mother and so many more. It had something to do with my father, and I hated it. So on the award night, I went to the crack house. God finally made my heart overwhelmingly peaceful right here in prison so I could receive His Love. He showed me His love and grace was sufficient. I decided to walk out proud and strong and do this thing, and there is nothing that will stop me. I am seeing this play through to its completion."

"We all have to look out for ourselves, I guess," Sharon said with an attitude. "I need someone who cares about me. See ya."

She left me there, sitting on the bench in the exercise area with thoughts and stories I wished to share with her . . . .

After my accident and recovery, I received a settlement from the insurance company. I got my GED and went to Ohio State as a music major with a minor in child psychology. I was eighteen. Had a new car and a motorcycle. For a year and half, I was doing well in college; then it became all about the parties, drinking, and smoking weed. And one day, I just stopped going to school. I stayed in Columbus, kept the apartment, and started going to the clubs. I was nineteen. I finally burned out of the party mode. Behind in rent, car repossessed, and unable to take it any further, I, Mom, and Kevin moved back to Cambridge, and shortly thereafter, Uncle Jerry called Mom.

Uncle Jerry had a contract to do food for a health spa in Denver, and, just as before, I was having trouble. Mom was thinking I needed a father figure, and no one could make a sandwich like her. In her mind, the deal was perfect; we could both work for Uncle Jerry. We moved, and things were further solidified when Aunt Cathy arrived with her boyfriend, who was born and raised in Denver. Mom's intention was to hand Uncle Jerry the reins when it came to me, but I found my own job and got an apartment with Mark King, my high school sweetheart. We reconnected after I had moved back to Cambridge from Ohio State. Mark found a job, and after several months, we had established a solid financial base, meeting our bills and expenses with some additional spending cash to boot. We went out together for drinks one night. At the bar, a girl came up to Mark and said, "Bud. Oh, Bud. What are you doing here?"

I was looking at Mark; she was looking at Mark; he was looking at both of us. He was turning every shade of red as she ran to him and gave him a big kiss on his mouth. I grabbed her and said, "Who are you kissing? Are you nuts? This ain't Bud! This is Mark."

"Well, sister, his name was Bud three nights ago!"

Mark took off running around the bar. I found him way back in a secluded corner lighting matches, throwing them on the floor and table. He had a habit of doing psychotic stuff when he got in trouble. I knew he had been with the mystery girl who worked as a waitress at that very bar. I returned to the bar, found her, and was about to go after her with a vengeance, but the bouncers held me back. The chaos and noise we both were creating turned everyone's attention away from Mark. In his state of delirium, he started the place on fire, and the bar had to be evacuated. I told Mark to take the motorcycle, pack his stuff, and leave. I have never been one to hold a grudge, but our relationship had run its course, and fate was about to lead me out of Denver back to my father's door.

Mom and I went to one of my father's concerts in Denver. Afterward, in the lobby, my mother was talking to someone in the local music business. She grabbed my arm. "This is Ray's daughter, Sheila." *As though you have little to do with me, Mom,* I thought. *Like I'm not your daughter.* I laughed and said, "Hello, very nice to meet you."

There were a handful of reporters around, and one approached us. "I'm Tony Winfrey. I couldn't help overhearing your conversation." He turned to me. "Can I take some pictures of you?"

"Sure!" I said.

"Of course," Mom said. "Now, Sheila is a singer, twenty years old, and we just moved here to Denver."

The conversation continued, and Tony told us his credentials. He had managed Prince, Earth, Wind, & Fire, and so on. Tony was a very nice-looking guy and very smooth. It was an easy pull for him to rope Mom into some kind of deal or for her to rope him in. For the next couple of weeks, Tony worked on an image for me—the way I dressed, how I was wearing my hair, stuff like that.

We moved to Los Angeles, and Tony began taking me around—the BRE Convention (the Black Radio Exclusive), Janet Jackson's birthday party out on her yacht, party after party of the who's who in the industry, Tower of Power, Don Myrick—and everyone fell in love with me. I was Ray's daughter, a big thing in Hollywood. Tony put out a cattle call for musicians to form a band around me. I was talking to my dad and told him what I was doing—that felt so good. I had a couple of opportunities to see him in his office. He listened to a couple of demo tapes and said, "This is good, but it isn't quite there yet." For me, that was as encouraging as anything could be.

Tony asked me, "Have you ever written anything before?"

"I used to write poems."

"Well, a song is just like a story. You have a beginning, middle, and an ending. Usually it's about something you have been through."

"I got a whole bunch of stories!"

The first song I wrote was "Pleasing Fool," which was about my mom and dad. We recorded that right away. "You say that you love me, but how could I know, that you were going to leave me before our love could grow. What was on my mind? Was it that I was so blind? To know you're only teasing me, what kind of pleasing fool am I?"

Mom was like, "Oh no!" and immediately brought it to my father. Dad said, "Sheila did not write that. That is too over her age!"

"There is no way you wrote that song at the age of nineteen," Dad said to me.

"Well, Dad," I said, "I was just talking about you and Mom. It wasn't that hard!"

That was the truth. I watched my mother jump through every hoop Ringmaster Ray threw into the center ring. It was ridiculous, but the amazing thing is she jumped clear through them all. That song was easy to write. I wrote "Love Sensitive" after I met my next boyfriend, Oscar. And then I just kept writing and writing. Tony thought it was great. We put together the band and started rehearsing. We called it "Sheila Raye and the Evidence." The band was off the chain, and we were the evidence of continuing the legend of my father.

After three months of writing and rehearsals, we had put together an hour-and-a-half show. The buzz was starting to get around Hollywood. I did Carlos' n Charlie's; everybody was there—Eddie Murphy, El DeBarge, Tom Selleck, all the L.A. Lakers, Buddy Rich. Then I did a song at the BRE convention. We were getting great feedback. Tony came and said, "Okay, it's time to do a showcase at the Roxie."

Shortly before the night of the showcase, Warner Brothers had called Tony in from the show at Carlos' n Charlie's. At that time,

Prince was the head artist. When Tony and Mom went in with our music, Prince was there along with the head of Warner Brothers Records. Prince said, "No. We will not deal with Tony Winfrey!" Unknown to my mother and me, Tony was blackballed in the industry. He was freebasing the whole time—a big, big cokehead. He had tried to rip Prince off for three million dollars. Tony cried right in front of the head of Warner after they said that they were not going to deal with me. Tony said, "Look, you don't even have to pay me to get out of the contract that I have with her. Don't do this to these kids. She has worked so hard."

Prince said, "You should have thought about that before you tried to mess with me."

Mom told me Dad was always watching me and checking into what I was doing. I never believed it until after the show at the Roxie. Jimmy Spurgin and I did a duet of "You Don't Know Me." Spurge was a guy with long blonde hair—a white brother with so much soul, it wasn't funny. After the show, the owner of the Roxie told me never before on a Wednesday night had he seen an artist fill the house to standing room only. All the record company heads were there— except for Warner Brothers. Their rejection could have let the air out of our tires, but, instead of rolling over and dying, we rose above the occasion and smoked the performance. We brought the house down at the end with "You Don't Know Me."

The next day, Dad called. "Sheila, get over to my office right away." It was an unexpected invitation. After telling Mom that Dad had invited me over, I went immediately to his office. I was a bit nervous and didn't have a clue what he wanted. I got into his office, and he told me to sit while he plopped in a videotape.

"Well," Dad said, "you did, a-a-a-ah, pretty good, now! I-I like that!"

"Dad," I said excitedly, "you were there?"

"No, no. Now, baby," he said, "I wasn't there. But I-I-I had Carl over there, and he was checkin' it out and recording it."

He fast-forwarded the tape to "You Don't Know Me."

"Now, who is that—that singing with you on that?"

"Jimmy Spurgin."

"Whose band is this?"

"My band. The Evidence band! Now, Dad, you always said that I should get the best people I could around me. I'm the baby in this group. These guys are all more seasoned than me."

"Now you doin' something right here, darling.'" "Do you really mean that, Dad?"

"Yes, mama! You did just fine!" he said with the biggest smile, hugging himself and rocking back and forth. "Now, I have a few ideas. This is what I want to do. I want you to pick five songs that you want to record. I am going to pay you all to come in here and record with me. I'm going to produce this for you."

I had never been more excited in my life. The first thing I did after telling my mother what had happened was to call a band meeting. The band was ecstatic. Just to able to say we had recorded on a project Ray produced took them to a new level—it would be more than a feather in their caps.

Dad loved my band. My father was a perfectionist. Everybody in the band did everything perfectly in one take. Except for me. I was a nervous wreck! He was professional, and whatever father thing he had, as slight as it may have been, went out the door when we were recording. I became an artist, and it became a professional relationship and very impersonal. I kept messing up this one song. Dad wanted to hear one particular vocal sound I just couldn't get. We went over and over and over one section of a song, and it made me feel incompetent.

The songs I had written were beyond my years, but I lacked the strength vocally to bring out the feeling he was looking for. At that point, I didn't care about a record deal. I was just a little girl trying to please her father. Whatever it was to get that thing that he was looking for, I was willing to do. I wanted his approval. For two days, I worked on one phrase in one song. I wanted to do it so bad for him, but the more I tried, the worse it got. I was sweating blood over it. Dad got so frustrated, after two days, he finally said, "Forget it! Just sing it your way!"

I started to cry. He called me into his office. "Now, baby, what's wrong?"

"I—Dad—I don't know what you want. I'm nervous. I'm scared."

"Now, when Aretha came in here, she said she was nervous, and I can understand that. When Gladys came in here, she said she was nervous, and I can understand that. But you are my baby. You are MY DAUGHTER! I'm just your father!"

I thought, *REALLY?! You are just about killing me here with your barbaric crack-the-whip recording ethics.*

"Yeah, you are my father," I said, "but I have never been in a professional studio with someone as great as you! You are Ray Charles! The living legend! The genius of soul! You can listen to a song once and tell every note that's played and if it's wrong or if it's harmonically correct."

Once we finished, Dad said, "Baby, I am going to send this around to a few people. You know, I got a few friends in the industry who just might want to hear this—I think I'm going to start with Quincy."

Dad had us on hold, waiting to see what he could do getting us a record deal. We had no money, were hanging around in Hollywood, and were paying two thousand a month for rent, not to mention food and stuff. Tony came up with some money for us to hang on for a while, but when nothing materialized, my entire band left me. The crash from that high was unbearable.

Dad called me and said there was something that he had to tell me in person. He asked me to come to his office. I told him I wanted to bring Geno, my musical director, bass player, and only musician who stayed loyal to me, and he agreed. We brought a demo of "Goodbye," a song Geno and I had written, and played it for him. Dad liked it. He liked it a lot. Then he began.

"I want to give you this advice: in this industry, you have to be careful. When you find a manager, you will know if he is the right one if he is willing to give you everything that he has and owns in life because, once you make it, he will be living off you for the rest of his life. If someone claims he wants to be your manager and asks you for money, that has to be the quickest good-bye you could ever say. Now, you will read about this in the papers tomorrow, a merger in the industry and a huge billion-dollar deal involving Michael Jackson. My label let me go. They are not taking any new artists and are canceling contracts right and left. They are not renewing mine. I no longer have a recording contract. I am in the same boat as you are right now."

"I can understand the idea of not signing any new artists," Geno said. "I can get not renewing some of the artists out there. But I can't understand why they would let you go, Ray."

"Geno," Dad said, "that's because they don't know what in the world it is they are doing."

"So what does that mean, Dad?" I asked. "Just another 'see ya later'? I am not in the same boat as you."

"Things happen in this industry. It's just how it is. I need to make moves and get my feet back under me."

I was convinced I was on my way—I just didn't know I was on my way to nowhere and, after a long trail ride, federal prison. Till the day he died, Dad said that was the best music I ever produced. He was Ray Charles, my father, and he never did anything with those songs. It destroyed my whole life. At least he thought I had talent. I don't know to this day if Dad ever let anyone hear them. I couldn't understand why he did it. It made absolutely no sense to me. If the industry leaders Dad approached didn't like them, why wouldn't he tell me? Why leave me in limbo?

I became aware of my surroundings once those questions came to mind. I stared out into the recreation area blankly, watching a dozen inmates on the football field kick a soccer ball and this group and that group mill around. I wondered how long I had been engaged in this useless reverie.

Snap out of it, Sheila, I told myself. *You've got the play to be concerned with and the first meeting tomorrow night.* I pulled myself together and did my best to leave Sharon, Dad, and all the questions behind in the setting sun as I headed in for bed count.

Wednesday night after dinner saw Helen and me walking to the chapel. She was coming to assist and oversee the play with me. When we arrived, people were starting to come, and a genuine excitement was in the air. The chaplain was there with Ms. Keller to lay down the law. Five members of the choir showed up, a dozen or so girls in the congregation, and Poke, Joe-Joe, and Joe-Joe's girlfriend.

Once I told everyone to take a seat, the chaplain stood in front of the cast. "Good evening. I'm Chaplain Mike, for those who don't know me. There are set rules in church, and you will be rehearsing here as our schedule permits. But these rules should also apply when you rehearse in another building. We have received permission for you to use the education building as well. No horsing around, no disrespect, no cussing. But the main concern from the administration is that some of you girls will sneak off and fraternize. There will be no sexual activity during these rehearsals. If you have a girlfriend, better leave her behind. Everyone must take this seriously. The rehearsals will not necessarily be supervised, so we trust you will police yourselves."

Miss Keller chimed in, "This is an opportunity to allow for such activity to be ongoing into the future, and anyone who messes this up will mess it up for those down the road. This is a privilege, and it should be regarded in that light. Sheila, you now have the floor."

I said, "After we're done, we'll meet and put together a rehearsal schedule that will work for everyone. I know some of you are in night school, and I intend to have evening rehearsals as well as during the afternoons on Saturdays. Choir rehearsals will begin a little later. Now, we are going to try to perform this in six to eight weeks. We will rehearse twice a week.

"The stories and events in this play are things I lived or witnessed in my life. My heart was opened to reveal true situations from my life, like going to church high on crack—and other situations some of you may have experienced, situations one rarely speaks about but ones that are real for the drug addict. Mama always said the Devil beats you to church. I needed to be free from these experiences of my life, and writing this play and talking about it now gives me that freedom. This play depicts life on the street, but it is not intended to condone such a life or look at it as a cool thing. It just was how it was for me, and I desire to be free from it.

"Now, I never sold my body for drugs. For some reason, I had the ability to hustle and flip the drug. I could get a hundred dollars from someone and, at the end of the day, have three or four hundred. You girls know the men in the game look at women as something less than life. Everyone thinks a girl will do anything for the smoke and looks at you as something lower than an ant on its knees when you're smoking. The dope dealers are selling the most poisonous stuff on the planet, and they're talking about you like you are a dog—like they are somebody. If I was a dog, then they were dogs, too! I bring this stuff out in the play."

It was a good meeting. We set the first rehearsal for Saturday night, but everyone wanted to start rehearsing right then. I sent a letter to Mary Lou through one of the other girl actresses, Juanita. I noticed on her information sheet she was in B1. She had shown up to volunteer for a part, and I assigned her the role of one of the gang members. I wrote to ask if she would play the part of the girlfriend of a drug dealer whom Joe-Joe was playing. B1 was also where Sharon was located, and I walked back with Helen.

"Mary Lou!" Juanita yelled out in the commons area of the quad. "I got a message for you from Sheila!"

A moment later, Mary Lou responded, "I'll be right there."

Sharon stepped out of her cell and headed for Juanita, arriving in the commons at the same time as Mary Lou. Sharon said, "What's the message?"

Juanita said, "It's a . . . "

Mary Lou stepped in. "None of your business!"

Sharon later approached me, furious. She asked with serious attitude, "Why are you playing games with me? Sending Mary Lou a letter!"

"What are you talking about?"

"Oh, I saw the letter, Sheila."

"Well then, you should know I . . . You know Sharon, I've got to be asking myself right now what the ____ am I doing? I spilled enough of my guts to you. I really thought that you would understand."

"What does that have to do with you sending letters to someone else?"

"You know, you're right! I forgot that I had another letter to write her. Maybe you would like to deliver it for me?"

Fifteen minutes later, over the loudspeaker: "Robinson, report to the captain's office immediately."

Now what? I thought. *It must be about the play or someone in the play.*

"Yes, Sheila Robinson reporting as ordered."

"Well, Sheila, there is problem, a communication problem with you and Miss Fischer."

"What are talking about? We were just having a conversation fifteen minutes ago, and we were communicating just fine."

"Well, it appears that she has asked you on more than one occasion to stop trying to talk to her. She just wants you to leave her alone."

"She was the one who sent someone into my quad to tell me she wanted me to come out and talk to *her!*"

"This is the reason, Sheila, that there is zero tolerance for this type of relationship on campus."

"What are you saying? We are good friends; that's all."

"Here's the long and short of it: to keep you both out of lockdown, you need to stay away from her. We'll advise Sharon to stay away from you, too! You can go now, Miss Robinson."

As I was walking back to my quad, Sharon was walking back to the captain's office. As we crossed paths, it was clear that I was mad, and her face was beet red with embarrassment. They had immediately called her as soon as they had talked to me.

This was interfering with my effort to have the play performed, and I could not afford to get into trouble when I was the one putting it all together. When I got back to the quad, everyone wanted to know what the deal was at the captain's office and why Sharon was heading for the medical facility.

"The medical facility?" I responded in dismay. *Oh, clearly she has lost her mind*, I thought.

"What happened? What did you do?"

"It's cool, but I don't want to talk about it. I am going to my room." If this dog-and-pony show Sharon was bringing to the center ring was to continue, one of the two productions had to be terminated. I was determined to see *Prodigal Praise* through to its performance. Sharon had gone psycho; that was that.

CHAPTER 17

RECORDING WITHOUT DAD

It is better to eat a dry crust of bread
In peace and quiet
Than to eat a big dinner
in a house that is full of fighting

PROVERBS 17: 1

THURSDAY NIGHT brought another guest speaker to the church. I attended the service under the weight of obligation as much as my own desire. I was not feeling well and thought about staying in bed that evening. As a member of the choir, I was expected to be part of the scheduled rehearsals and services, but I felt eyes were now watching me as rehearsals for the play were about to begin. Though it was never spoken directly, Helen certainly would voice her concern if I did not attend. As it turned out, I was pleased I made the effort to go.

After the service, I had a few questions for Chaplain Mike and waited while he conversed with a new inmate. Overhearing a portion of their conversation, I understood her desire to immediately become involved in the church. The chaplain thought she could help with the choir in an upcoming special program. He proceeded to introduce her to Miss Sharon. I observed the new inmate. She was a very meek, older lady, but she carried herself with a great deal of confidence. She appeared strong-willed with a loving heart, very Baptist, and she had an aura that let everyone know she insisted on order. Her mannerisms were motherly and wise.

I concluded my discussion with the chaplain regarding the first rehearsal on Saturday and turned to stand face to face with her.

"My name is Vanessa. I just arrived and was talking with Chaplain Mike and the choir director about getting involved here, and they both told me about you. Is there anything I can do for you in the play?"

"Well, if you aren't a godsend! I was looking for someone to play the part of the mom—it's one of the main characters. You look to be made for that part! If you are so willing, first rehearsal is Saturday."

"I'd be honored," she agreed. It was a perfect fit.

* * *

I was very excited as I addressed the group during the first rehearsal. "The main focus of our initial rehearsals will be the meat of the play, the part of Monee (Poke) getting turned out with the crack and the way one is disrespected on the street as a woman on dope. Also the scenes that involve Poke, Vanessa as the mother, and the part of Johnny, who I have yet to find an actress for. I will be reading those parts until we find our John."

All the girls began laughing at my unintentional pun, and the moment I got it, I started laughing, too. Helen shot me a quick glance, and I pulled myself together. "Mary Lou, girls with minor roles, and extras—if you will be patient, we will begin with the opening scene."

I had already assigned one of the members of the congregation from church the job of putting together the stage props and directing that part of the operation. She directed the stage crew to one end of the room as I pulled the actresses over to the other.

"Let's begin. The opening scene finds Mom at the dining room table alone. She is very upset and concerned, praying under her breath in a whisper. She's reading a letter and is angered at the information it contains. As the door opens, she slams the letter to the table. Johnny and Monee enter, set their books down, and move to the dining table."

Johnny: Yo, 'sup, Mama?

Mom: *'Sup?* I need both of you to sit down. I have something to talk about right now.

Johnny: Too bad. I can't, Mom. I'm hookin' up with Amy. Then I have to go meet up with my boys to make up some words for the rap show at school next month.

Monee: Yeah, Mom, I've got to go with Melissa to the Mall of America to get some new clothes for the rap-off.

Mom: Sit down! (*with attitude*) There won't be no rap-off, but there will be a smack-off if you don't come over here and listen to what I have to say. And don't say a word till I'm through!

(*Mom turns to Johnny*)

Mom: I got these letters today from your guidance counselors. They tell me that you have missed twenty thousand days of school, and, when you do show up, you are disruptive. Harass the other students, disturb classes. And are doing all that rappin' in the halls!

Johnny: Mom, first of all, there has only been seventy-five days of school.

Mom: Well, he is counting the ones from last year, too!

Johnny: Second, Mom, I ain't harassin' nobody, but they be gettin' on my nerves. Always gettin' up in my face. And as for rappin' . . . it's my gift.

Mom: Yeah, and I am getting ready to take it back for a refund.

Monee: Mom, everybody loves it when Johnny raps. Everybody gathers around, all the fine guys.

Mom: You know, Monee, that's what it says right here—you're too busy trying to follow in your brother's footsteps. Clowning at school. And what do you mean, shopping for the rap-off?

Monee: Mom, I want to go to the rap-off to see my brother rap against the other guys. And I want to look cute!

Mom: Well, I don't know if either one of you will be going to the rap-off.

(*Monee and Johnny sigh loudly in exaggerated frustration.*)

Mom: You have broken my trust, and you know how I feel about that. Johnny you are grounded for a month.

Johnny: What? (*loudly*)

Mom: And so are you, Monee. You have to ask me to go to the bathroom! Also, I will be calling the school to check on your attendance and behavior. If you miss one day, you won't be doing any show.

(*Johnny goes to his room and slams the door.*)

Monee: What about me, Mom?

Mom: Same goes for you.

(*Mom leaves for her bedroom and kneels beside her bed.*)

Mom: Lord, please help me guide my children better. Help me show them the love they need. And Lord, let Johnny win that concert next month. Amen.

Everyone was upbeat and excited as Vanessa and I left the rehearsal together. I could not have been more pleased. "You did so well, Vanessa."

"I am just glad to be a part of it. So what are you in for?"

"Drugs. Crack. The play is pretty much about me."

"I've heard it whispered you have a girlfriend inside."

"They whisper a lot about me."

"I'm gay, Sheila. Always have been gay on the outside. I was the choir director at my church. Everyone knew, and it wasn't easy for me."

"That's the primary topic in here."

"Church inside is worse. The administration, their whole thing is holding down the sexual interaction. Sure isn't a secret they gave the male population saltpeter years ago to try to control it. So you have a church led by the chaplain who is part of the administration and other members of the church council who are inmates and convicts trying to understand how to get right more with the program than with God—least that is how I see it. God is about love."

"Now you are talking my language. If I am not feeling the love, I'm not feeling God. Besides, God does not think the way we do. Members of the church are the first to condemn those who are gay for the stay or just out having a cigarette."

"Probably the ones thinking about it the strongest are the ones who are saying 'don't do it' the loudest. It's their own fear that drives them. To tell you the truth, Sheila, I think we are all just a bunch of frightened little kids. Besides, there probably is not one inmate on the prison grounds who hasn't considered such a relationship."

"Vanessa, my life has been nothing but up and down and filled with disappointment. I do have a girlfriend, and she is going crazy, you know, about me going to church and the play and everything. "

"It's hard enough having a relationship on the outside."

"One's life must be transformed if the message of love is to be real. I will never say that the love within a gay relationship is not genuine or that God doesn't see that love. I have seen love expressed in that type of relationship, and how can anyone say that love is false? But I am beginning to think it's not what God wants for me. That's all I have to say about it."

We continued to talk in the afternoon sun, and I noticed Roberta approaching. "I have someone I need to speak with. Will you excuse me?"

"Sure, you go do your thing, honey."

"See you in the morning, Vanessa."

Roberta said, "Hey, Sheila. How did your first rehearsal go?" "Great! Thanks. Roberta, Sharon went psycho."

"I saw that coming. Told you so."

"Have you seen her?"

"Yeah. She's at the pad. You should have picked me."

I could do nothing more than say, "I love you, too, Roberta. Maybe I'll see you after dinner." I turned around and made my way to the smoke pad. Four days had elapsed, and I could not hold a grudge. I had passed Sharon several times without saying a word. I had been ordered not to. She would look at me, and it led to smiles. The both of us knew the whole thing was stupid. The weekend was here, and there was no way I was going to be around her and have to be quiet, pretending I didn't want to talk to her. I still felt love in my heart for her.

Sharon was sitting with a new inmate who had just arrived. She was tall and slender with sandy blonde hair. They were sitting talking, and that ruffled my feathers. The sexual attraction was there, and I was in a serious state of confusion. I could think of nothing but to go over there and protect what was mine, but I refused to do so. Sharon saw me, and I turned right away. I waited for the new girl to leave.

"Can we walk for a little bit so we can talk? Walk around the track with me." She smiled at me. I knew it pleased her I was the one giving in.

"Sheila, I have to be honest with you. I am very jealous of your play, especially when I see you talking to other girls. I have to admit it was really stupid of me to have gone to the captain's office. I guess I just wanted your attention. But you're a short-timer now, Sheila. You have five or six months to go. I'm still looking at years."

"Oh, Sharon. Of course I want to spend as much time with you as I can. But I can't turn from this. It is deeper than me, or you, or prison, or getting out of prison."

"I just wish I could feel like I was a greater part of your life."

"I wish you felt like it was something you could be a part of."

My sincerity must have reached her. I saw her willingness to make peace. "Is there a chance you have some time this afternoon? You know—the rec trailer?" She looked at me with those eyes. Make-up sex.

"I think that's possible," I said with a smile, and together we dipped on in.

The weekend quickly passed. I felt that the human touch did me a world of good. Monday, work arrived at the warehouse and saw me standing around a few minutes before lunch break. "I Call Your Name" by Switch came on the radio. Roberta approached me.

"How's it going, girl?"

"Wow, Roberta. This song is a trip. Bobby DeBarge. That whole album was nothing but hits."

"What?" Roberta said as the lunch bell went off. "Do you know him?"

"Yes. We were on the road with them, touring. My brother Kevin and I—we opened the act. After my dad recorded my band, we were hanging out, waiting for him to do something with the music. Bobby and Switch had already recorded that album sometime before I met him. The band split up, but I don't know why. El DeBarge lived across the street from Mom, Kevin, and me on Sherman Parkway—they called it the valley.

"Kevin had met El through a girl who was across the street or something. At that time, El was big time. He had hits on the radio and had left DeBarge a year or two earlier—'Rhythm of the Night,' 'Secret Garden.' From the first moment, Kevin and El just clicked and got close right away.

"They started hanging out together all the time. We were living across the street in a posh apartment complex. Mom had it looking like something out of Beverly Hills. El walks in and says, 'Here's the ex-Mrs. Ray Charles,' and Mom said, 'I am not the ex-anything. We are still doing the do!' That's how it always was—Mom was always the star, no matter what. And then I am again back being 'the daughter of Ray Charles.' I was young and feeling like I had to play the role of being Ray's daughter—like, what is that? I am hanging out with all kinds of people—Parliament, Ben Vereen's son Bootsie—and I was feeling on the verge of success."

As we walked to lunch, I continued with my story.

I asked El to write me a song. He said, "Okay." He sat right down at the piano and started to play these beautiful chords and put me on the spot. I was so nervous. I wanted to tell him I didn't mean right now. I was all thumbs with my voice. I don't know why, but my nerves took me right out of the game. I was thinking, *This is El DeBarge!* And was he thinking, *This is Ray Charles's daughter?* "Sing this part with me," El said. I was shaking inside. He told me I was tone deaf and tagged it with, "You know we DeBarges are the kings of harmony. America's first musical family—it was not the Jacksons."

Occasionally, one of the DeBarge family would come over—Randy, Marty, James, Bunny, or Bobby—to find El or Kevin or whoever. One night, all of them showed up, and I was thinking that this was divine order. Mom started to ask them questions about their family, and they were taken with her. They were obviously high and began getting weird, doing sexual gestures to each other. One of them said, "This is what our father did to us." Really stupid stuff. And they referenced everything they did to the Jackson family. James was married to Janet, and it was no secret that there was animosity there. What I got from their behavior was that either they were molested as children or they were making fun of the Jackson family. Apparently, sexual abuse and insanity are ever-present. There was something haywire in their past, abuse inflicted by someone close to them.

They opened up to Mom when she asked, "What are you on?" Everyone felt as if they could tell Mom anything. The DeBarge family shared many issues from their childhood with her, and she was deeply concerned for them. They loved Mom, and she loved them back. She would talk with them for hours and hours, and the next day, they would come over and say, "Oh, Mom, thank you so much." They were very grateful for her ear and her input, her wisdom, and her love. They told her their darkest secrets—everyone did—and I never knew Mom to use something like that against anybody except Kevin and me. Mom would unload on us after we would reveal our stupidity to her; if not at that moment, she would file it away and hit us with it when we least expected it.

Mom got the idea to start Youth Against Drug Dependency (YADD). She found an investor, Bob Chambers, an old friend from Ohio. Kevin and I were to open the show, and the Debarges would be the headline act. Bob and Mom started to put together the tour. We knew everyone had issues with drugs, but everyone claimed they wanted away from it. The DeBarge family had been using coke, and loads—Randy, Marty, James, Bunny, and Bobby. Loads create the heroin high. They would be doing the nodding and break out in hives. They were into smoking crack. They were doing everything.

We all left Los Angeles and moved to Columbus, Ohio. Bob, the investor, had a huge ranch and facilities there for us to rehearse and put the show together. Our first bookings were in Ohio, and "the ranch" was home base. I was excited. One of the things Dad said to me that I took to heart was, "One of the best things that you can do is to surround yourself with people better than you or people who can in some way enhance your career."

I thought this was a wonderful opportunity to put together a new band. Geno Lopes had agreed to be my musical director and do the tour. He had called the players he wanted, and everyone flew to Ohio for rehearsals. I also had the greatest respect for the DeBarges' musical talent and saw this as nothing but an opportunity to get my feet under me as an artist. I was grateful I had the very best around me. I was thinking, *I am on the road with DeBarge, and I am going to learn the real side of music.* They took me in as part of the family until they heard me with my band and discovered "little baby girl" had some juice. I don't know why they were expecting anything different, but, then again, I was expecting something different as well.

There was little if any money. The accommodations were crowded, to say the least, and, when I arrived, the DeBarge group was camped out on the floor. Bob was gay and not only was providing money but his residence to spring the operation. He had a gay ex-con working as a chef who couldn't cook and another who owned the title of "driver.'" Gay porn videos were frequently playing in the main house night and day.

Geno had cleared a rehearsal space for my band in the barn next to stabled horses. Bobby claimed the DeBarges needed the rehearsal space in the garage by the main houses to put their thing together. And after a few rehearsals, Bobby and the rest of his group arrived at the barn to hear my band. The band Geno put together was smoking and sounded better than the DeBarge band. Later that day, Bobby called a meeting with Mom and Geno. "I do not want Geno to play in Sheila's band because he is white. I am flying a black bass player in from L.A. to play with Sheila." He was a good player but clearly bisexual, and everyone soon was aware he was one of Bobby's lovers. He stayed for less than a week, and I was back with Geno. As my dad advised me—stick with the best.

The first concert went all right, but the band was high. The second night, they got into their groove and smoked the show. Bobby freaked when he walked out and saw a crowd of people going around the block waiting for autographs and nobody was giving the DeBarges any attention. A few people here and there, but nowhere close to the attention my band and I were getting. Two shows and they threw in the towel on me.

El was the one everyone wanted to see. People expected El to be there. Though Bobby was the innovator and could smoke out El singing, it was not good marketing. They called it the New DeBarge with Bobby DeBarge. He was a nice-looking guy but wasn't El. Bobby and the rest of them were not appreciative of my band.

In reflection, maybe it was something that wasn't supposed to be. We were on a Youth Against Drug Dependency tour or promotion, and the concept was beautiful, but the headliners on the bill were stoned out of their minds, to the point people were booing them. They were cussing in the middle of their songs. They were staggering around. Maybe it was no big deal to them, this little nightclub, but it was to me. I was trying to break out. They felt it was beneath them, and they felt they were bigger than that. It kicked their butts, and ego is a hard thing to deal with.

An engineer from Paisley Park, Prince's studio, approached me after the concert about recording in Minneapolis. He wanted to produce four songs with me. I was very excited about the opportunity. Additionally, my mother had hooked up with an author from Minneapolis to write her story about her life with Dad. The DeBarges were not grooving on that at all.

The next day, the band and I were sitting in the kitchen. Bobby came in, went to the refrigerator, and pulled out a bottle of orange juice.

Bobby said, "Ohhhhh! What's this! Who opened my orange juice?" He hawked up a glob of phlegm, spit it into the bottle, and continued. "I bet none of you suckers will drink it now!"

And then he drank it in front of us. Oh, it was nasty! I didn't know if it was my band member or his band member who had had a drink of orange juice, but I was thinking, *This man is nuts!* His attitude sucked, just made me want to puke, but I refused to give him the pleasure.

Later that morning, Bobby came down to the rehearsal barn where there was a large stage constructed. It was a shared space. If my band went down first into the big rehearsal space, we were supposed to switch. We had been rehearsing for twenty minutes, and he came in and shut the power off! He said, "We are the main act. You guys are just the opening act. You have to go now. I need this space!"

Up until those shows and rehearsals, I don't think they ever really heard me sing. I had my band, and I was comfortable. I was doing my own thing and had my core people around, the guys whom I had gone with into my father's studio. I knew he loved the talent I had surrounded myself with. I was feeling my groove. I can only assume that the problem DeBarge was having with me was that they were being upstaged by their opening act.

Later that afternoon, Bobby approached me. "This isn't going to work. Kevin has the zeal and the thing that we want. He can open up for us. But Sheila, you and your band, well, it just isn't working out."

I let loose with, "I don't give a hoot! You guys ain't nothing without El, anyhow." I couldn't help it. I was hurt.

Bobby talked Kevin into staying. He was young, stupid, and fresh, still perfecting his craft. He was not the artist he is today. He was eighteen and could make his own decisions. They were going to continue to let him open up the show. Kevin wanted to stay. It made him feel good that they wanted to keep him or whatever, but I questioned their intentions.

It got ugly. I couldn't figure out why Kevin wanted to stay, anyway. Marty chased me with a bat, and I was six months pregnant. He chased me to the car, running me off the ranch like that with a bat. It was beyond the claim they no longer wanted to work with me. They couldn't let the tour just be because we were smoking. My band was killing it.

Mom and pregnant me were heading down the drive, ready to head back to Cambridge to stay there before we moved to Minneapolis. The drive to the main road off the ranch was a good mile, maybe two before we hit the front gates. Before we got there, I was crying hysterically. "Mom, we cannot leave my brother. Not with them." I was crying so hard, it's surprising I didn't go into labor right then. That is how intense the emotional calling was for me to go back and get Kevin. I had a tantrum. "I want my brother right now! He is either going to get strung out on the drugs they are on or they'll take advantage of him—the crazy sexual habits they are into or something."

I saw a flash of that in my mind. "Turn the car around."

Mom said, "Are you crazy, Sheila?"

We turned around and went back. I lost my mind, and Marty chased me around the car again. Marty was saying, "Forget this girl!" Mom was saying, "Kevin, get in this car right now! Your sister is pregnant! You don't need this." The DeBarges were saying, "Stay here with us, Kevin. Forget your people."

I said, "Forget you, Marty. Kevin, you're my brother. I don't care what these people are saying; you are coming with me. I'm not leaving without you."

Kevin reluctantly came with us, upset with me that I wouldn't let him stay, that I insisted he come with me. Had he stayed, it could have changed the course of my brother's life.

*   *   *

Roberta and I were returning to work after lunch as I was finishing the story. She turned to me and offered, "I thought my life was crazy."

"Yeah, and it wasn't much longer after that I placed my life in the hands of a crack pipe."

Play rehearsals, choir, and work occupied my time over the following weeks. It was amazing to me what was happening during rehearsals. I made it very clear it wasn't a requirement to become a member of the church to participate in the play. I recruited Mexican girls to play the male dope dealers and gang members. They had lived that life and were well qualified to play their roles; however, in the play, instead of being the peon just running dope, they got to be the big dope-dealing cello. The cast saw the play as being about them. As such, they approached it with a personal interest and a great deal of excitement. The Hispanic actresses bonded with each other immediately and initially stuck together in their own clique. They made up almost half of the overall cast. They would say their lines in English and then add something in Spanish, improvising within the script—something I had not anticipated. There was a lot of crying as inmates relived hardships from their past.

It was becoming real to me, what was happening to the people involved, and I felt so good about it. I was getting so absorbed in thinking I had something to do with it. Through the play, people who normally would have been going out of their minds with affairs or dwelling on the recurrent, inane prison drama began to see things in a whole different way. I saw it as evidence I was doing things the way God wanted.

When it was time for rehearsal, Poke was the first one out the door. When you saw her going to rehearsal, you saw me—we had the same energy about it. She had a church background and knew how to respect the church. Others such as Joe-Joe did not. She refused to do anything but keep it real to the street and had no problem inside the church saying "F__ this or that."

My mentor, Helen, was getting upset because of what they were bringing to their roles as drug dealers. She felt it was taking away from the message of the play. They were cussing in the chapel, and it was very disturbing to her. She felt that energy should not be brought into God's house, and the central message of the play should be surrendering to Christ. I felt she was a preacher with a *cast thee down to hell* perspective on God's embrace.

Poke's part was equally disturbing to Helen. She had to act tweaked out on crack in church. This caused a lot of laughter. Most could relate to being high somewhere—if not in church, in some circumstance where you could not take a hit even if you had the dope on you. Helen looked at the laughter as debasing the principles of Christianity. She was getting very upset. It created a conflict between us, and I had to bring it to Helen.

"First of all, the story is a semi-autobiography. The climax is when Monee overdoses and is taken to the hospital on the edge of death and connects with God. You don't think it's a valid bit of my life experience and, more importantly, a story that delivers the message of God's unconditional, without question, unbelievable love—not to mention what is happening in the lives of the actresses? That message is being received on a very real level. I feel justified bringing it this way—the way it is going down. Some church members have the audacity to say some of these people ain't nothin'—the lesbians, that they're going to hell—not realizing the street attitude they bring to the church in that way. If you claim the Spirit within you says that is okay, then, why good gravy, proclaiming knowledge of God without tolerance for another's idea is an idea you need to get rid of.

"We are all in this together, for His Divine purpose. Whatever that is, some of us are born only to die in a matter of hours. I do not understand that. All I know is while going through the process of finding out what it *is* all about, which I am yet far from, that if looking at your neighbor, or another person who seems foreign to you, or someone you don't understand—if you discover such a view creates fear within yourself, then maybe there is a darkness inside you that hasn't been fully discharged. If you can't see the brilliant light of love, then you should not profess any understanding of God or Christ. What delivers the Truth? The Truth. The true relationship with God comes from within you directly. The light of love must shine no matter what the circumstances. I have seen that in you countless times. Come on, man, what is all this suffering about—to learn a bunch of stupid-ass rules and forget about love? The smoke pad people have more love for the church people than the church people for the smoke pad people. If you believe in the divine law of love and grace, none of that stuff matters, and what man does cannot even be equated to the Spirit. When Mom was checking out of here, she went to a love thing different from any other love thing she ever had.

"Mom would say, 'Why you lookin' at the sty in someone else's eye when you got a log in yours? Get over yourself.' Everyone is looking for the love. It is found in you. It is of God. End of story."

After my tirade, I went to the pad and met Tyra. She was perfect for the role of Johnny. Just like my brother Kevin, she was silly and had me cracking up, and she could rap her butt off. I asked her to join the cast, and she agreed. She fell right into the part in two seconds.

Toward the final rehearsals, Poke was acting the part of the addict—having sex with the dope dealer so she could get some dope; then he turned her down with the words, "You ain't getting nothing more from me. You are just another ho out there as far as I am concerned—just like everybody else. Get out of here!" She cried real tears! It blew me out of the box. She was acting her butt off. It was more than acting—she was reliving a part of her past. The acting was unbelievable—these people, prisoners of life.

CHAPTER 18

NEVER GOOD ENOUGH

In my anguish I cried out to the Lord
And He answered me by setting me free
The Lord is with me—I will not be afraid
What can man do to me?

PSALMS 118:5, 6

THURSDAY MORNING delivered the promise of a great day. Elated with last night's rehearsal and excited about the approaching performance, I walked to work with a spring in my step in the early morning sun. I was singing to myself as Linda, a friend and cellmate of Sharon, approached me.

"Sheila, you won't believe what Sharon told me last night. She has a thing going on with Doctor Hanson. She has been seeing him frequently."

"What? That's weird." *Payback is tough,* I once heard Sharon say. Collecting myself from the initial blow of her pronouncement, I asked, "Are you sure?"

"Sure. She told me last night. Me and Liz. Something is going on between them. She got money on her books and claims it's from him. Just thought I should tell you. See you later."

I was struck by a sickening sense of betrayal, a feeling of being violated. *Money, it always comes down to it. It buys you anything, and when you got it, everyone is your friend. Money and drugs.* The personal nonsense of my life immediately clouded the morning sunshine.

Roberta opened the door to the warehouse and held it open as I approached. "Okay, Sheila, what did she do this time? The only time you get like this is when you and her are fighting."

"Linda just told me she heard Sharon tell someone last night that she's having an affair with the doctor."

"Oh, now, that would be stupid!" Roberta paused contemplatively, "But she could have just been saying that with the intention it got back to you to piss you off—playing the game. We both know she's capable of such childishness."

"You know how you get the feeling that something's up? Over the past several weeks, ever since she freaked out and went to administration with the harassment nonsense and then went to the doctor . . . " I paused. "He put her on those blasted antidepressants after her psycho routine a few weeks ago! She gets high on those meds. I've seen her going through the line, talking to him at dinner. She was coming on to him, and he was touching her arm, glancing over at me when that was going on. I just got that feeling something was up."

"It might be nothing more than Sharon trying to get a rise out of you. It's stupid."

"Stupid or not, I certainly don't need this right now. My final two rehearsals for the play are tomorrow night and Thursday. We do the first performance in one week. You know how much this means to me. I think there's something to Linda's story."

"I guess I know where you're going on lunch break. Don't do anything crazy now, Sheila. You are close to getting out of here, too close to allow some nonsense like this to mess you up. I told you— you should have stuck with me!"

"All right. I suppose you can give me the 'I told you so' thing. But I just don't need to hear it right now. See you later," I said and turned to report to my station.

"Sheila, keep it together."

With the spark of my frustrated ego stirring the fire of anger within, I made a beeline for the door upon hearing the lunch bell. I found Sharon outside the mess hall, milling around as though she was expecting me.

"Sharon, what is with you and the doctor?"

"What are you talking about?"

"You know, it's really amazing to me—out of all the people you might confide in, it would be Linda. You knew very well she would come and tell me! Linda and I have been tight, one of the three people we allowed to know anything about us. She couldn't wait to come tell me about the doctor. She told me he has been putting money on your books and all the rest of it."

"What do you expect me to do? My husband deserted me, you've only got three or four months left, and I'm at my wit's end. I have no cash coming in. My job sucks. I'm making thirty cents an hour."

"Like I don't know that business! Where do you think I've been? That's not the way to do it. You can get a charge and additional time! On top of that, he's a married man. So what if he has his own private office and examining room? This is all just to get back at me."

"Oh, Sheila! What are you talking about?"

"You do not go to see the doctor after hours, Sharon. How stupid do you think I am? I know that's a *special* appointment, now, isn't it?"

"Quite frankly, Sheila, it's none of your business. We have severed ties. You're going your way, and I'm going mine. You're doing your thing. I don't owe you any explanation at all."

"What? You know my heart is involved. If you really wanted to keep this secret from me, you wouldn't have told Linda. You wouldn't be trying to mess with my head. How unfair is that—right before the play, you do this? It was no secret between us that when we discussed our thing being over that my heart was still involved, my emotions, my spirit. Missing you was kicking my ass!"

"Well, you're a Christian. Go pray about it."

"That's exactly what I am going to do! For both of us! Oh, and by the way, forget you two—and you, too!"

I didn't eat lunch, just paced around the rec area for thirty minutes and returned to work.

At the warehouse, Roberta looked at me. "Yeah?"

"Yeah!" It was all I had to say.

"Let's try to have dinner together."

"Right now, I'm not thinking about eating, but all right. I'll look for you then."

We met for dinner. Sitting at the table with Roberta, I watched as Sharon passed through the line and stopped to do her thing with the doctor.

"I told you, Roberta."

"I'm a believer."

After dinner, I walked the track with Roberta and turned in early. I checked the morning call-out sheet. Robinson, 9:10 a.m.—Doctor Hanson: complete physical.

It is undeniable, I thought. *My life is scripted.* Synchronicity, fate, destiny, the trials of God, whatever—the drama was beyond chance.

As I walked toward the medical facility in the morning, I had to ask myself more than once, *Does it work like this for everyone?* I tried to get past the Sharon thing. I was heading for a blasted physical, and I never was comfortable with a male doctor performing a gynecological exam. Furthermore, I realized that, after Sharon freaked out, Doctor Hanson learned about our relationship. She told him everything. The three of us knew each other as points of a twisted triangle. As I sat in the waiting room, the emotional mix had me literally shaking. In a few moments, Doctor Hanson would ask me to drop my pants so he could stare further into my privacy while I wanted to strip him down and tear him a new asshole. We were in the same closet together with the door wide open. I stewed with the question whether he regarded me as the other woman or the other man.

"Miss Robinson." The nurse led me back to an exam room. Doctor Hanson walked in with his huge, abnormally elongated teeth, their brilliant whiteness accentuated by the Hispanic hue of his skin and coal-black hair. He looked me up and down with abnormally large, dark eyes. He was a vision of deception personified, a total invasion of my world. Absolute penetration. My ability to respond from a detached emotional posture had completely evaporated. In its place, all the defense mechanisms of the street returned with the tenacity of a repressed urge to be exorcised—a frustration to be purged.

As he sat down, he said, "Miss Robinson, how are you today?"

"Well, actually, not very good." The final thread snapped to the leash holding a rabid dog at bay.

"Well, what's the problem?" He responded with a smile that clearly conveyed he knew I knew. Equally aware the closet door was wide open, he expected I would leave and close the door behind me.

"What's going on with you and Sharon Fischer?" I inhaled the vapor of my emotional fuming. "I will tell you. It's nonsense, that's what!" And I flexed the street muscle so long held down.

"Really!" He smiled again, as if trying to provoke me.

"You can cause her to lose all her good-time, not to mention the repercussions that could rain down on you. She's my girlfriend. Why are you messing around with my girl? It can't be worth it to you. I think you'd better leave her alone." The moment it came out of my mouth, I realized how inflamed I was over something I could never justify. Yet the anger was there, genuine—my personal insanity revealed. I offered no excuse or apology. Reduced to anger, I was incapable of embarrassment.

Maintaining his cocky smile, he repeated, "Really!"

"Did she tell you about me?"

"Oh, yes, she told me about you. She claims that you have been stalking her, and she has come to me with all the sordid details about your relationship. She claims she doesn't want to be in such a relationship with you. At other times, she claims she is very depressed about the break between the two of you. Sheila, what you need to understand about 'your girlfriend' is the truth about Sharon. She's bipolar and has symptoms suggesting multiple personality disorder. She is not well. On one side, she has an attraction to older women; on the other, an attraction to older men. She doesn't have the ability to recognize the distinction between the two opposing sexual desires, not to mention her emotional needs. What you need to do is focus on your life outside of prison. You are getting out in less than three months."

"Oh, really, good doctor?! So if you as a professional know she is disturbed, has some preexisting mental condition that you are supposedly helping her overcome—I mean, with the knowledge that she has to seduce every being in her life—why would you succumb to her advances?"

"I don't know what you are talking about. I have not . . . "

"So then, you are not putting money on her books?"

"If you repeat that, I could get in a lot of trouble."

"Then you need to stop doing it so you won't get in any trouble. You need to leave her alone. If she *is* mentally disturbed, why would you make her condition worse, taking advantage of her? Are you going to stay with her, stick with her when she gets released in five years? I don't think so."

"We have an exam scheduled, Miss Robinson. I suggest we get on with it."

"If you think you are sticking your fingers inside me, you've got another think coming! I want a female doctor!" I got up and walked out.

It was Friday night after dinner. Sharon was outside in the recreation area. I was furious and had all I could do to contain myself. I approached her with but the single commitment to finality. "Sharon, we are tha-rough!"

Sex! It never brings lasting happiness. If it did, we would have only sex once. That was my thought as I returned to my cell. I rewound the events of the recent past with Sharon and witnessed my behavior in the theater of my mind. I silently watched my connection with what I thought was love fly out the window as anger and jealousy invaded me. I did not like it. The habit of self-absorbed need, allowing my inner peace to be dependent on someone else, placed the condition of happiness in the hands of my mind and flesh. It is like that with anything of the world, whatever or with whomever that relationship might be.

I have always had insane encounters with sexual partners, relationships that were often abusive. Over the past months, I had tried to break free from the pain and confusion I carried from those experiences. In sexual relations, when you become intimate with someone, you share a part of yourself and vice versa. I could feel my personality changing because of my relationship with Sharon. There were elements within our relationship that had felt wonderful. But, no matter, I now knew I had played with fire; I accepted the burn. There were two forces acting within me, and I wanted there to be but one.

I was directing myself to put the energy I felt so strongly with Sharon back into who God had created me to be, to have a personal identity with the very spirit of self.

Such an identity in Christ is sufficient. One does not need anything beyond that. There is no greater joy, and I wanted that joy to be my guiding principle, my yardstick to measure my action. It is not a joy of the mind, nor is it obtained by following a set of rules of dos or don'ts. The danger within such an unfettering is the confusion and the noise created by one's own mind and the desires it creates. The principal yardstick must be this joy. I was going the way of Spirit this time, stronger than ever before, and I asked God that my personal attachment to Sharon be released with love and grace.

Saturday morning found me in a slightly improved condition, making my way to the smoke pad after breakfast. I found Poke and told her about the fiasco with Sharon and the doctor. Poke could do nothing but laugh, and, in that manner, I was healed completely of any personal hurt.

"Thanks, Poke. You're a good friend," I told her while inwardly thanking God and His presence.

"That's right, girl. Don't let that nonsense rattle you. Besides, sister, rehearsal tonight at 7:00 p.m. Right?"

That one question triggered my thoughts back to the play. "Oh, I forgot. I have to confirm rehearsal tonight with the chaplain. I've got to go. See you later, Poke."

I maintained a quick pace to the chapel and found the chaplain. "Rehearsal still okay for tonight, chaplain?"

"The chapel will not work tonight, Sheila, not for play rehearsal. But I knew you planned a rehearsal for today. The only time and space available is this afternoon over in the education building."

"Oh no! We need to rehearse today. I've got to get moving and let everyone know we're moving the location and the time ahead."

I ran back to the quad, out of breath and frantic. I do panic like nobody else; I was raised on it, and I had juice to spare. I flung open the doors and yelled for the guard. There was no one at the guard desk. I stopped the first person I saw. "Where's the guard?" I was screaming. "The guard!"

"What's got your pants on fire?"

I ignored her and approached another inmate with the same question.

"I saw the guard walking over to Brazos II."

"Thanks," I said over my shoulder as I headed for the door. Running once again, I threw open the doors to the neighboring quad and entered the commons area. No guard to be found. *What is this?* I thought. Were there any concern that I was out of bounds and in direct violation of one of the cardinal rules of my internment, such a consideration just flew out the window. In my mind, I was justified in this violation. I had an emergency on my hands and very little time to deal with it. I ran up the stairs to the second tier, making no effort to conceal my presence. I was hollering for a guard, and the commotion I made was rewarded with a guard descending the stairwell toward me.

"Oh, thank God you're here! I have to get a communication out over the loudspeaker for the people involved in my play's dress rehearsal."

"What're you doing here? You are out of bounds."

"Looking for a guard. I have an emergency!"

"What emergency?"

"What emergency? What do you mean? I just told you."

"Don't sound like an emergency to me!"

"Look, you know I'm doing my play next week. I was just informed of a change in rehearsal time, and I have to get a message to everyone involved to meet me outside on the recreation grounds to pass the word about the change in schedule."

"I can do that for you, but I still have to write you up."

"Oh, please. My intention was to find a guard. I wasn't looking for anyone but you."

"Sorry, got to do it."

The guard made the announcement, and I had to continue with my mission. I was convinced everything would work out in the wash once the guard explained the reason why I was out of bounds in the neighboring quad. With the exception of a few extras, the cast and crew were informed about the change, and we rehearsed that afternoon. I was pleased with how things went. It really did run smoothly, a flow that was unstoppable. Everyone from top to bottom in the administration knew I was putting this play together.

The chaplain gave a beautiful announcement during Sunday service regarding the forthcoming performances Friday and Saturday night. The buzz was reaching a crescendo, and I was on top of the world. The next several days passed with little incident, and Thursday morning arrived without a word about my violation. The final dress rehearsal was only hours away and then the following evenings' two performances. It was late morning, almost lunchtime, when over the loudspeaker the command was given, "Robinson, report to Miss Keller's office."

On my way over to the quad, I was hoping this was over the out-of-bounds violation on Saturday and not a problem with dress rehearsal tonight. I walked into Miss Keller's office and said politely, "Hello, Miss Keller." The captain of the guard was there also.

"Miss Robinson, I have been ordered to give you three-day room restriction, and you may have a job change as well. It depends on what Miss Crenshaw decides. She has yet to inform me what she wants to do."

For the briefest moment, I lost the ability to breathe. "Wasn't it explained to you that I was just over in the other quad looking for a guard? The guard in our quad wasn't present. I had an emergency. I didn't want to miss the opportunity to rehearse. It was the first of two dress rehearsals, and I had to get the word out to the people involved that the rehearsal had to be earlier than scheduled."

"It doesn't say anything about that in the report. It just says that you were out of bounds, and the guard reporting the incident won't be back on duty for the next two days, so, whatever, like it or not, room restriction begins as of now."

"You mean to tell me that you are putting me on room restriction for the final dress rehearsal and the only two nights of the play? You know how hard I have been working on this. I had to come to you to even start the process. How could you do this to me?"

"It's protocol. If I let you get away with it, everyone else will think they can get away with it."

"I'm not going to say anything. Why not start me on restriction after the play is through?"

"As of right now, you are on room restriction. When you go through the line tonight at dinner, you can talk to the warden."

"Good-bye," I said and opened the office door with the thought that, if I had to, I would sneak out and go.

"And don't even try to go to that fool play!"

I reported back to work, diminished by the news with the single thought of throwing myself on the mercy of the warden. Roberta thought the warden would overturn their decision. "They just wanted to put the fear of God in you," Roberta concluded with a chuckle.

Roberta had spun a thread of hope, but I knew it would have to be something life-threatening for the warden to override the disciplinary measures of her subordinates. Nonetheless, I held out for the miracle as I approached her at dinner.

"Warden Winters, I have just been put on room restriction for three days, and I won't be able to see my own play. You know how much effort I've put into this thing. I mean, we've worked on props and wardrobe and everything. The guard who wrote me up is off for the next two days, but she knows the reason why I was out of bounds."

"I don't know anything about it. I'll have to investigate and look and see what happened. I'll get back to you."

There could not have been a bigger mind-bender than the current circumstance. That is the way it was for me. Rehabilitation? The people in charge of the inmates were yoked within the same mental attitude. Well, if this was meant to piss me off, provide inspiration to never want to return to prison, the system had succeeded.

I went to my room and cried. *God! Why? What is this about? Not now, please. You are aware of all the fear and insecurity I had to overcome to cause this play to happen. Help me understand whatever it is that I am to learn from this. I can only know that the outcome of this will be Your perfect will. If it is Your will, then I will be at that play.*

I went to the chaplain and captain just to see if I could get a pass to watch it. They were unable to help me, and Friday night arrived with me confined to my room. Helen made a point to pass by my cell and tell me that it went well, but there was no further feedback; the performance that night was held for the boot camp girls. There was still a ray of hope—tomorrow night's performance for the inmates.

In this manner, I was able to sleep. I held hope for tomorrow. And through the course of that day, I maintained the idea that God would not forsake me. At dinner, I approached the warden, and, before I was able to speak, she dismissed me with, "We are still investigating the situation. As I've said, I will get back to you."

It was clear there was no intention to grant any clemency in this affair. I lay in bed inside my cell and cried again. "Okay, God, it's time for me to know," I said. I stood up, grabbed my Bible, and threw it open. I thought of my brother and my good friend saying, "If man is the one doing the crowning, we are the ones doing the clowning." And

I realized God needed to humble me. I thought the effort was all about me and for me. God works through everybody, whether they realize it or not. I needed to learn not to take pride in what I accomplish in life. I placed a crown upon my head that did not belong to me. It belonged to God.

At Sunday dinner, I received word I was off room restriction. Perfect. The inmates who attended the play and those involved in the production began telling me about how the play and music had given them hope, how it had changed their hearts. I was grateful for hearing such things. I had learned that lesson, for I would respond to everyone, "Give all the glory to God." *Well,* I thought, *the play went well. We got that done. Thank you, God.*

I checked the work sheet. I was transferred to the kitchen and back to twelve cents an hour. I was to report at 5:00 a.m. to Mr. Reynolds, a guard who was also a certified chef. Within that first orientation to kitchen detail, I was struck with the seriousness he emphasized, the FDA stuff, and a whole lot of other acronyms for this and that. Some inmates were there because they signed up for the duty, but most were like me, assigned because someone had to fill those positions.

After the hour meeting, I was assigned the duty of egg cracking: ten thousand eggs, two other girls and I, three large stainless steel containers containing shelves and shelves of eggs.

Cleanup could take hours after the end of a meal, as the beginning of the next meal would start as soon as the previous had ended. I finished cleaning the grills used to cook pounds of bacon. Feeding over three thousand people creates a big mess to clean up. As soon as we were done with breakfast, people were already working on lunch. There were about twenty inmates running around in the kitchen area at any one time. Between cooking and preparation, serving and cleaning, it was a madhouse back there. There was no administrative cook—the head chef was someone who was a longtimer and had served in the prison kitchen for some time. After lunch, I was again cleaning up while the crew was already working on dinner. The morning shift ended at 2:00 p.m., and I was anxious to get out of there—it was only my first day.

For me, at least, kitchen detail was definitely a punishment. I hated it. It was a lot of work, it was hot, and there was grease and crud on the floor that made it slippery. If you didn't have the right shoes, you could slip and break your neck. Most of the new inmates were assigned to kitchen duty.

I was sweeping the floor as fast as I could and ran the broom over one of the other worker's feet. She was from Africa and ready to fight. She started twirling around, throwing salt over her shoulder, and then she began making crosses with her fingers, all the time hooting and hollering like there was no more tomorrow. I thought she had lost her mind.

"What is that all about?" I asked another African.

"Seven years bad luck," she said.

"For running a broom across her feet?"

"Yes, ma'am!" she said looking at me like I was nuts.

"I ain't having none of that. That's superstitious nonsense."

Texas was right around the corner from Louisiana where all the voodoo stuff was, and some of the inmates coming from there were deep into that dark scene—the devil-worshipping stuff. I knew enough of it to know that it worked on those who were subject to such things. I wasn't afraid of it. I just did not want to be around it.

I knew right then it was time to get out of the kitchen and put in for a transfer. The kitchen was a little too weird for me. The landscaping crew had openings. I could make it for a week or two until the transfer kicked in. The excitement over the play had died down, and I was content knowing I had but a matter of weeks left in the joint. The final three weeks would be in a halfway house on the outside.

A few days into the routine, I was called upon to prepare potato salad. I was working with what I remembered of Mom's recipe. There is something about such plain and simple food; it doesn't have to taste that way. My mother was an expert at turning such dishes into something more than just something to eat. Everyone was raving about it, and I felt a connection with her. It was one of the few moments in the kitchen I enjoyed.

It occurred when you least expected it, at the most inopportune moments: a surprise inspection. It was the fourth day of kitchen duty after lunch had been served. I had been on my feet all day. It was extremely hot, and, on top of that, everyone seemed to be suffering from the same thing— that time of the month. Apparently, we had been living and working together long enough for most of the girls' biological clocks to become synchronized. I just wanted to get outside and cool off in the afternoon air. I had ten minutes left to my shift, and now I had to hang out in the heat of the kitchen, wondering how long all this was going to take.

The guard had an attitude as she stopped everyone to announce the inspection. Apparently, the biological merging did not make distinctions when it came to the color of the uniform; she clearly was right there with us all.

"You people make a mess. I'm doing inspection now. You know the program."

We lined up, compressed into a small open area of the kitchen. Once it was confirmed that everyone was accounted for, we watched as she checked in boxes, behind doors, under tables, and inside the lockers. Her last activity was to enter the bathroom. After several minutes, we heard, "My God!"

The guard emerged from the bathroom with something concealed behind her back and approached the front of the group. "Look what I found in the paper towel dispenser!"

She thrust her hand up above her head, holding two cucumbers end to end within a pair of pantyhose tied in such a manner to secure them in that position with a pair of oranges, equally secured at one end. The entire apparatus was wrapped in a plastic cellophane wrap. Instantly, giggles and laughter erupted. The guard proceeded to erect the object on the tabletop beside her in a freestanding display for her forthcoming inquisition.

"What is this?" She was cracking up but clearly angry, an unpreventable reaction to the display. "Oh, I've got to go show the warden this. Everybody on the compound is going to see this, and they are going to know that one of you lovely ladies in the kitchen has some kind of perverted idea of what a woman needs or wants. This is pathetic, and you are cooking everyone's food?"

Every inmate in the kitchen knew it belonged to someone we were working with. That thought alone was cause for laughter. It was impossible to take it seriously, and that mood was only fueled by comments such as, "I would go sit on that right now. I haven't had a man in years."

"Who belongs to this . . . artwork?" The guard just had to say it, knowing full well no one would ever make the confession. "It's the plastic over this that makes me think it's not a prank."

The inspection extended beyond the kitchen. It was an entire sweep of the compound. Cell inspection was intensified for all who worked in the kitchen that day, and the guards tore our cells apart. In my cell, they located two oranges and an apple that had fallen behind a box in my closet. I forgot that they were back there. They had become moldy and were fermenting. I had to respond to inquiries into moonshine-making skills. Fortunately, I had my receipts from the commissary and avoided any disciplinary action.

Had I not already put in for a transfer to landscaping, that event would have been the clincher. I reported Monday, receiving the information that my work transfer would occur next week. I was a little more relaxed in the kitchen knowing I was not much longer for that detail.

Every other day within the prison, there was someone with a birthday or a going-away party. That week, we had planned a birthday party for Jeanine, one of the girls from my quad and a member of my crew. It was decided we were going to have a fruit salad at the party. Someone said, "Sheila, you work in the kitchen. You can do this for us; get us the pears." Without giving it a great deal of consideration, I said, "Yeah, okay, we got canned pears."

The day of the heist arrived. Only at the moment I had crammed two plastic containers filled with pears and juice down my pants, cellophane wrap serving as lids, did the thought of getting busted enter my mind. I drifted to the cucumber incident and the severity of that situation. *I'm a person representing the God within, and if I get caught stealing, that will negate whatever it is I have been mentoring and counseling to other girls. If I get caught, it's a federal offense. But how could it be stealing? They are meant for us to eat, right?*

At the four-way, a guard was conducting a random search of an inmate. It was "Big Man," the compound's guard who bore the distinction of being the largest living being who existed within the confinement. He approached seven feet in height and four hundred pounds. I went around him quickly and started a squeezed-cheek racewalk pace to the quad.

"Hey, you. Come here. Come back here!" he said while finishing up with the other inmate.

I picked up my pace, pretending not to hear him. I did not want to break into a full run, afraid I would spill the pears.

Big Man yelled, "I said HEY!"

At that point, I went into a full run, breaking cardinal rule number one: no running! I wrote off the pears. I could hear his footsteps pounding the sidewalk after me. I was thinking, *Oh my God! Sheila, you are not going to get busted with the pears.* I threw open the quad doors and ran up the stairs as the juice spilled all over my pants. In the bathroom, I threw the pears into the garbage and covered them with paper towels, pushing cup and pears to the bottom of the trash. I flushed the toilet quickly and walked out the door. I pulled my pants up with one hand and ran the other across the top of my forehead. With a gigantic exhalation, I said, "Phhhheeewww! I had to pee!"

Emerging in such a Broadway manner to illustrate to all who the actress diva of the compound truly was, I came face to face with Big Man and about a dozen other inmates who had gathered. My mad dash and Big Man's pursuit were telltale signs something was going down.

"All right, Robinson, what you doing? What happened? What you got, Robinson?"

"I don't have anything," I said with a chuckle and a smile. The crowd was whistling, and I started to laugh because Big Man knew I knew he knew I had taken something from the kitchen.

He entered the bathroom and came out with the pears and the cup. "I bet these pears aren't yours."

"Pears?" I exclaimed. "I don't even eat pears. I don't know what you're talking about. I don't have no pears; ain't seen no pears; don't know no pears."

"And I suppose that ain't pear juice on your pants, either."

"Pee," I said. I'd rather say I peed my pants than say I had those pears.

He was good-natured about it, and I had been counting on that. "Robinson, all joking aside, if I were any other guard, you would be in the hole right now. Don't ever run from a guard. I don't care if you have to pee; then you stand in front of me and pee."

For several weeks thereafter, I was known as Pee-Dee Pears. On Monday, I reported to landscaping. It would be hard to get into trouble doing outdoor physical labor, and the silent communion with plants appealed to me. I recalled a quote from Aldous Huxley: "Next to silence, the closest thing to expressing the inexpressible is music." I knew music as the key to my soul, but, at that moment, silence was calling me.

CHAPTER 19

SNOW IN TEXAS

As a prisoner for the Lord
Then I urge you to live a life worthy
Of the calling you have received
Be completely humble and gentle
Be patient, bearing with one another in love
Make every effort to keep the unity of the Spirit
Through the bond of peace

EPHESIANS 4: 1–3

IT WAS AROUND 8:00 P.M. Sunday evening as I headed for the shower with my Bob Barker shampoo. Having been reduced to twelve cents an hour, I could no longer afford brand-name toiletries nor feed my love for candy. But I looked at it as a small sacrifice and took it in stride. The play had created a bond of sisterhood among several of us inmates, and we began meeting every night at nine for about an hour before bed count to talk, stay connected. After my shower, I made my way to the commons.

"I start my new job on the landscaping crew tomorrow," I said as I took a seat among the group.

"I am sure you are happy to be out of the kitchen," Uhuru said. "Being within this group really helped me."

Uhuru had been coming to the meetings for about a week. She was six-foot-two, very slender, her skin coal black. She spoke English with a thick accent expressing a soft, loving tone. The dark eyes behind her glasses revealed a meek and humble soul who had waited in Africa for seven years while her husband and child in the U.S. became citizens. She had been in America only for two years when she was thrown in prison. The government claimed she had not been cooperative. She owed federal taxes.

Women from Africa, Southeast Asia, and Mexico who were not U.S. citizens began appearing in the federal prison system in great numbers after 9/11, no matter how inconsequential or minor their violation. One girl from Africa was incarcerated because of an unpaid traffic ticket; she had lived in the U.S. for twenty years. Many women were in for ridiculous reasons. I was ashamed of our government, stripping mothers from their children for little reason. The African women were tight with each other. Their English was not very good, and they often spoke in their native tongue amongst themselves. The American culture was a new experience for many of them. Little bonding occurred among them in their own culture. They were blacker than their black American counterparts and ridiculed by many of the black American sisters inside the prison. I felt a great deal of compassion for them, suffering abuse from all angles.

Uhuru disclosed things about herself and the part of Africa she was from. The men did not show affection toward women, and the women from her tribe were circumcised at the age of twelve to limit any sexual pleasure. It was mandatory. I found the idea barbaric— insane. Her parents and grandparents accepted such practices as perfectly natural. The men treated women as something less than human. She felt very unloved.

"Isn't this ironic? I was abused—imprisoned, in a manner of speaking, by my culture—simply for being a woman, and now, after only two years in America, I'm in prison because I'm African, and I didn't know what to do. I guess God doesn't love me very much."

We spent an entire week in the group trying to help her understand that it wasn't God who was punishing her. She felt it was wrong of her to feel negative about the customs of her tribe but also did not feel right about her husband—he was controlling and abusive. While in Africa and separated from him, she was exiled by her tribe because her husband and son had immigrated to America. We would hug and embrace each other, an experience that was foreign to her. We talked about God and her deportation as an inmate approached our table.

"Why would you be talking to that skank? She ain't nothing. I'm the one who's 'all that.' I jacked some stuff up—she didn't. She ain't nothing! I'm the one who makes it happen up in here!"

We all looked at her blankly, and she responded, "Whatever!" and walked off.

"What can I say, Uhuru? Had I not connected with the God in me, I would have gone crazy on her. How can you respond to that ignorance? I apologize to you for her. I have a few things to do back in my room. You can stop by later if you wish."

An hour later, in my room writing a letter to a good friend, I looked up at Uhuru in my doorway.

"Can I talk to you?" "Sure. What's wrong?"

"I got a letter from my husband. He's thinking of leaving me."

"What?"

"I tried to call him, but the phone was disconnected."

"Your husband is nuts!"

"If God is so good and loves me, why is all this happening to me? If God is all-powerful, then why does He make me suffer?"

"God has a purpose for it."

"I have never felt loved. You say God is all love. It doesn't feel like that to me."

"God isn't a feeling. He is an empowering Spirit. You have to know He is in control and whatever is for the betterment of you and Him. Your story of God will be great."

"I wish I could know that."

"Your elevation from this situation will be great because you will have a great story to tell. God does things for His glory. Don't worry about it; just stick with me. As long as I'm here, I will stand by your side."

"I have had nothing in my life to love. Mine was an arranged marriage to a husband who showed me no love or affection. My child has been stripped from me for seven years, and now I am here in prison and I have done nothing wrong!"

"I understand."

"Why would you make a woman come to a place like this? You have no dignity. They make you feel so filthy."

I knew what she was talking about. We had all been hosed down.

"Why would I be placed in the same place with someone who robbed a bank with a gun or a prostitute or drug addict?"

"Underneath it all, no matter what our cultures may have taught us, we are all of the same Spirit."

"Pray for me, Sheila."

"I will, Uhuru."

She left, and that was the last I would see of her. The morning delivered the beginning of a landscaping assignment, and I discovered the girls on my crew were hardcore. I could not stand them. It was too much of a mirror into my past. God said to love your brothers and sisters, but it was hard for me to make a stand of love with them. The head girl on the landscaping crew, Shaqueena, had it in for me. She came from Texas Steel, the state prison system with its chain gang, and took pride in the fact she called the cadences on the gang. Shaqueena liked to work hard, and she was rough.

I went from a sweet job at the warehouse as a clerk to the heat of the kitchen, and now I was working like a Negro slave on prison grounds. Humbled by recent experiences, I was looking at everything in a new way, aware that God was present everywhere, responsible for everything. I held respect for all living things and made a stand of love over a defenseless tree. I decided to take on Shaqueena and her girls.

It was a most beautiful tree. In the springtime, it would bloom wonderful white flowers. It had become so big that it was blocking the view of the warden's window, a window that allowed her to see the entire compound from her office. The order was given: "Dig a hole and plant it somewhere else." It wasn't small by any means. The trunk was about ten inches in diameter, and it was probably fifteen feet tall.

I watched as Shaqueena supervised an execution squad brought to bear upon the tree's roots. They were taking out revenge on that tree and had become living anger and hate. I was feeling the pain of that tree, and my connection with it told me they were destroying its life, a life that meant nothing to them—their own lives seemed to mean nothing to them. Their actions spoke of one accord: *"To heck with life itself!"*

I went to the head of horticulture, Mr. Dean, who was a professional and taught horticulture at the prison. I reported to his office and said, "Look at what they are doing to that tree!"

"I just took a look at it, Sheila. That tree is going to die. They beat it up so bad, it will not survive. Don't worry about it."

"Please, can't we do something for it? You know what? I'll dig the hole myself and replant it. I don't know why, but it's very important to me to replant that tree."

Through my pleading, Mr. Dean's position with the tree was altered. I caused so such commotion that Shaqueena and her death squad got in trouble for not attending to their job with care.

"Sheila," Mr. Dean said when he came to me, "I want you to understand that I am doing this strictly on the basis of their actions. It's not about the tree. I don't think the tree is going to live. It's probably going to rot and die, but it will be a lot easier to pull it out and get rid of it. If it has any shot at all, it will have to be heavily watered every day."

"I'll do it, Mr. Dean. I'll water it every day."

"You guys will not only dig that tree up from the roots, but you will dig a hole and replant it! A hole six feet deep and twelve feet in diameter."

I was now a "psycho idiot" who had to have this tree replanted. Everyone was mad at me and would get really ugly, purposely trying to destroy the bushes they were trimming and make them look ugly. It was heartless and cruel.

The hardcore gals were now calling me "Mother Nature," "Miss Can't-Hurt-a-Bush"! I was on everyone's radar screen, but a great peace overcame me by moving the tree. I faithfully watered it every day for three weeks. I went there for the last watering to discover it was blooming. I got on my hands and knees and thanked God for the understanding that all life, every tree, was significant to Him. I found Mr. Dean to report the miracle.

"That is probably a bloom from its old life," he said emotionlessly. His response only increased the significance of my personal connection with the tree. If we are His most precious and prized possession and can love a tree that much, who am I not to allow His love in me so I may love myself enough to remove the ignorance within me? I was not willing to see a tree suffer but willing to let myself suffer. That was ridiculous. God lives in me! I was ecstatic with my new energy, but none could grasp it. When I was confronted over the tree, my response was, "It's alive, a living thing! It cannot be separate from God!"

I went to bed filled with a commitment not to my life and my love but a commitment to Life and Love. There is a great difference, and I slept with a great peace until 3:00 a.m. when a guard appeared at the cell door. "Robinson. Up and at 'em! You've got fifteen minutes to report outside the quad to lay salt and sand. We are going to have a snowstorm."

"You have got to be kidding me!"

"Fifteen minutes! And dress as warm as you can. It's ten degrees! Darn cold—freezing."

"This ain't Minnesota. It's Texas. Who has clothes for this cold?"

"Get yourselves up! You've got fifteen minutes!"

Commissary had work boots for seventy bucks a pair, but what good does that do somebody at twelve cents an hour? One did not have to be a rocket scientist to figure out that no one was prepared for this. I reported to the sign-out area in tennis shoes and a light warm-up jacket, no gloves, and a baseball hat. Most of the other inmates were dressed like me; only a few were dressed for the weather.

"Okay," the guard said, "we have to make the best of this. We've got to get salt and sand on all the walks. The ice is everywhere, and it just started snowing. We've got some old work boots if you want 'em."

I looked at the boots—worn, torn, and funky. They didn't look any warmer than the tennis shoes I was wearing. There was no way I was putting those nasty things on my feet. Some of us had to get up on the back of a pickup truck and shovel the sand and salt out the back. Others had to distribute the mix of salt and sand on walks with buckets. We finished at 6:30 in the morning and covered the entire compound the best we could. As soon as we finished, it started to snow heavily.

We were given four hours to get some sleep and ordered to report at 10:30 a.m. to shovel snow. We got to eat lunch early with the boot campers. We all got dressed and went outside. Marcus, the morning/afternoon guard was cool. He let us call him by his first name. He liked me and knew about the tree thing. We laughed and joked all the time.

Once we began shoveling, it was obvious some of us could easily get frostbite. Marcus said, "Every thirty minutes, go ahead and take a five-minute break and go in and warm up."

Native Texans and Mexicans had nothing to protect themselves from the cold. They had no hats, gloves, boots—nothing to keep warm. It was 3:00 p.m., and we were inside taking a third warm-up break when the guard change occurred. Officer Brady came on duty and entered Brazos II. We had just started making coffee.

"Where's your sign-in?!" Officer Brady was pounding his finger at the sign-in sheet. "Who told you it was all right to be inside?"

I said, "Marcus said we could come in and warm up. We aren't properly dressed for this."

"Oh no! Get outside. You are on my time now. Marcus is no longer in charge of you. You're on my time! OUTSIDE!"

"Mr. Brady," I said, "it's freezing out there. Some of us don't have gloves. We need to warm up. We're doing manual labor out there— it's freezing rain. You have got to have compassion."

"You're on my time! MY CLOCK!"

You Aryan Nation prick! I thought. "You know what? Marcus said we could come in here," I said. "Some of us don't have boots—some of the girls have holes in their tennis shoes 'cause they can't afford them. They're wearing shoes that are hand-me-downs. Their shoes are missing part of their sole! We are not prepared for this! That's it. I'm going to the captain!"

I headed for my room right then! Inside my room, I put my coffee mug and stuff inside my locker and turned around. Officer Brady was standing in my doorway.

"So what are you going to do, Robinson?"

"I am going to the captain! We were told we could come in and take a break. I'm reporting you. I have a right to report any officer."

"So you're going to report me?"

As soon as he said that a second time, I said as loud as I could out into the quad, "HEY! DOES ANYBODY SEE ME?! THIS IS SHEILA! I'M IN ROOM 26! SOMEBODY COME OUT! I NEED SOMEBODY TO WITNESS THIS!"

All of the inmates who were inside, the people who worked the morning shifts, all came out and stood around the pier.

"I NEED SOMEBODY TO WITNESS THIS!"

I already knew it was on! When I tried to leave my room, Officer Brady leaned into me as I was trying to walk past him.

"Oh," he said. "So, now . . . okay, Robinson! So you want to hit an officer! Well, I'll show you!"

He took me and put me up against the wall and handcuffed me! "Someone go to the captain. Someone go to the captain!" I said.

Two inmates took off running to the captain's office. Brady spoke into his radio. "I have an inmate here who has assaulted me. I'm bringing her down."

Three other guards showed up to assist with the escort because everyone thought I was deranged! I didn't say a word the whole way down. The other inmates were in shock and knew I was fighting for them more than I was for myself.

Arriving at the captain's office, an inmate passed by and said, "Don't worry, Sheila. We gave our statement. We told them you didn't do anything. We saw Mr. Brady purposely get in your way!"

The captain was not in. The second-in-command was on duty and was already sick of me because of the Sharon stuff. It was rumored her husband was once a guard at Bryan and divorced her to marry one of the inmates. She had it in for every girl inside the prison.

She took my story. I had to write a full report along with Officer Brady. I told them that all I was trying to do was make sure the others were not mistreated, and, as far as I was concerned, they were being mistreated. I was placed in lockdown, standard procedure when an inmate is accused of assaulting an officer. This was serious. If the assault charge were to stick, I could get five years added to my sentence and be classified a felon.

I recalled the old-timers telling me, "We've seen it happen too many times. You're getting short, just about out of here. That's when stuff starts happening—the kind of stuff that will make you get more time."

Twenty-five inmates came down and gave the exact same report. "Mr. Brady is full of nonsense. Sheila wasn't trying to do nothing. She just told him she was going to the captain's office to report him!"

Within less than an hour, I was informed special investigators had to be called in from Houston. I was now classified a violent criminal, at least during the course of the investigation, and that required complete separation from Brady. I was back in shackles to be transferred to Houston. Because of my new classification as a high-risk inmate, I wasn't even allowed to go back to the room and pack up. They threw all my possessions into a bag. I would never walk through the compound again. An escort was coming for the two-and-a-half-hour drive. I would be in maximum security by 8:00 that evening.

CHAPTER 20
MAXIMUM SECURITY

The Light shines in the darkness
And the darkness has not overcome it

JOHN 1: 5

SHROUDED WITHIN a heavy blanket of doom, a dark rain stretched into the flat Texas horizon, bringing a strange soothing—the harmony of nature and mood. As I rode within the escort, chained once again, my stomach was so far up my throat, I could almost chew on it. Where or what was the lesson for me this time? Try to love my neighbor all the way to Dallas-Fort Worth Maximum Security Facility? Find the moxie to lead the girls in a couple of campfire songs? *God, what is this all about? I was supposed to have my last three weeks in a halfway house.* My heart was hurting, my mind was confused, and my spirit had all but disappeared. Once we arrived at the prison gates, the guard tower overhead became an iron fist squeezing my anger and despair into black rock. *Please, God! Not again,* my heart cried out. It was the spitting image of Oklahoma City, steel-gray truth.

"This one assaulted an officer."

With one exception, the treatment was worse. Another unshackling, strip-down search, hose job, a new uniform, and a fresh supply of Bob Barker toiletries were unavoidable realities.

No matter what situation I was in, my life was one continuous example that circumstances can always get worse. Go with the flow?

There was no flow and nowhere to go within granite. The hardcore were all innocent victims. I had to be included on that roster, but I was different. I *was* innocent. The only joyful sound was the silence late at night!

I was back to a locked door and a toilet next to my bed. I spent my first few days in complete solitude like a little turtle withdrawn into its shell. I decided to peek my head out and have a look at the new waters. I made my way to the TV room and took a seat in the rear with the intention to melt unnoticed into the surroundings. There were a few inmates scattered about. My attention was drawn to a white girl intently watching a program in one of the front seats. I had observed her several times during lunch and dinner and classified her as a serious contender for the angriest human being in the world. On top of her general abhorrence of all life, she unabashedly advertised her ignorant bigotry—every other word that came out of her mouth was "nigger this" and "nigger that." A black girl came in and sat down in front of me next to another sister. They knew each other.

"Hey, Sasha, what's up?"

"What ya watching?" Sasha asked as she sat down.

Instantly the white girl turned and glared at both of them. "Shut up!"

"Forget you, Missey," Sasha exclaimed.

The air thickened with hatred. A few girls got up to leave, aware of what was about to go down.

"So what is this jacked-up program you're watching?" Sasha goaded Missey.

"Don't even think about changing the channel, you black loser!"

Sasha turned to her friend. "That Aryan witch going down!" One of the exiting inmates walked in front of the TV.

"Get out of the way, trash!" Missey said, and added, "You dumb nigger."

At that moment, there were but the three of us. Those who had exited the room had posted up in the doorway. The first peek I had taken into the new pond left me with a ten-second window to either say something in an effort to stop the current momentum or join the group at the doorway. I spoke up.

"Chill! You guys are already in maximum security, and you're about to be shackled and taken to solitary. What sense does that make?" It was wasted breath; they were already into it before I finished with, "It's not worth it."

Sasha beat down Missey with a vengeance that had been stewing inside of her for most of a lifetime. After the guards questioned us, I left and emerged into the commons. Near one end of the room stood a very tall black woman in civilian clothing. She had her hair pulled up in a ponytail that allowed the loose hairs to fall down around her face. She was full of light and love. "Bible study, anyone?" she said.

Bible study? Sounds good to me! She could have said *Mister Rogers' Neighborhood* and I was going. Quickly I went to grab my Bible and made my way to the room that doubled as a study classroom for the school held within the prison. I took a seat at one of the school desks with some awkwardness, desks from a simpler period in time and identical to the ones in grade school when thoughts of exploring magical, far-off lands filled my head. Now I was left thinking, *With the money the feds get for harboring these people, they could at least get some chairs you could sit in without dragging them halfway down the aisle when you tried to get out.*

I was completely blown away at the number of girls who started to enter, surprised by the appearance of several inmates I had assessed earlier as unreachable. I took a moment to study the lady in front of us. There was a brilliant light about her spirit.

"My name is Maggie, for those new to the group," she said. "How about we start with a little singing? Anyone have a song in mind?"

One girl screamed "Amazing Grace," another screamed "Jesus Is on the Main Line," and a final contestant offered "This Little Light of Mine."

"And what about you?" Maggie asked, looking in my direction.

I did not respond immediately. My heart was still hurting. I was confused. I had not considered singing and did not know if I felt like it or not. "'Draw Me Close to You,'" I said. "I heard this song in church back in Bryan, when everything in my world was separate from God." When the choir began to sing it, I knew I'd keep those words close to my heart. And I would learn to sing that love-song to God. "Sure, I have a song—'Draw Me Close to You.'"

"Well, we'd love to hear it."

As I stood, I could feel my knees quivering. My choir experiences at Bryan had allowed me to overcome any nervousness, but this was completely different. The violence I had just witnessed created a personal sense of purpose! The words started to flow from my mouth, and love took over my heart.

> *Draw me close to you, never let me go*
> *I'd lay it all down again to hear you say you are my friend*
> *You are my desire, no one else will do*
> *For no one else can take your place*
> *I need to feel the warmth of your embrace*
> *Draw me close to you, never let me go*
> *You are all I want*
> *You're all I've ever needed*
> *You're all I want*
> *Draw me close and never let me go*

—KELLY CARPENTER (1994)
MERCY/VINEYARD PUBLISHING

I felt God providing me the strength to sing through worn and tired vocal cords and, once again, every woman in the room was opened through my song. Tears of joy, love, deliverance, and complete acceptance enveloped the room, indeed a place and space in time when humanity was in one accord under God. It was miraculous and something not of me.

The meeting was over all too soon, but among the girls present, a bond had been formed. During the next several days, the buzz about the girl who could sing got started, that I was a great person to talk to. I returned to reading the Bible and found I was sharing the goodness of God's love with those who were in distress. Hope sprouted within the concrete, and moments of laughter began to occur with a will of their own.

Maggie's Bible study group strengthened, and it became a normal routine to open up with "Draw Me Close to You." It quickly became our theme song, and within one week, the group had swelled to three times its size.

"I can't begin to express the gratitude I have to God for His mercy," I said to the girls at one meeting. "This is one of the reasons I know

Christ's death has truly given us grace, and his resurrection has truly given us life. If the wages of sin are death and my sins weren't forgiven, I would have been dead in sin long ago. I praise You, Lord!"

I was beginning to relax a bit from the anxiety and uncertainty about the assault charges and ongoing investigation. While standing in line for lunch, Chanelle, a girl from the group, confided in me. I listened as she told me a common story inside the prison walls. She had been busted selling meth. I knew she was making an effort to turn her life around and decided to look out for her.

"Sheila! Sheila Robinson!" someone shouted, sounding as excited to see me as if I were one of her longtime friends from childhood.

Who is that? I thought as a dozen other inmates turned in her direction.

"Bonnie!" I exclaimed with an enthusiasm that stemmed more from identifying the stranger than being thrilled to see her. I knew her casually from working on landscaping, but her reputation was huge at Bryan. She was one of the inmates who was gay inside and out, African American, exotic in appearance, and strikingly beautiful. She had a large gash above her eye.

"Oh, girl, what's up?" Bonnie exclaimed, continuing in a voice that gathered a crowd of ears. "You are the talk of Bryan. Girl, everybody is talking about how you got in Mr. Brady's face, and they're saying you cursed out the warden. And that you did it all for your girlfriend, Sharon!"

Oh my God! Why are you screaming, and, second, why are you exposing my life right here in my face? I thought. Sharon was never involved, I had not cursed out the warden, and the only "friend" I had when that incident occurred was an imaginary one in my mind. I did not assault an officer, either. There was at least consistency in the fact everyone had it wrong. My initial impulse was to go off. Thankful for Maggie's presence and my reconnection with who God meant for me to be, I knew that no matter what I might say, to correct her story would simply propel it to greater heights.

"Really?" I responded innocuously.

"Does your dad know they transferred you in here? Maybe he can do something to get you back to Bryan."

"What are you guys talking about, Sheila?" Chanelle asked. "Who is your father? How can he help you?"

"Don't you know who you all been hanging with? This here's Ray Charles's daughter."

"Let's not talk about that, Bonnie! I'm more interested in what happened to you," I said, looking at her wound.

"Jackie."

"What caused her to go that far?"

"Sheila, you won't believe it. Jackie went off on me. She caught me messing around with another new girl—you know I do it to them every time. It's the sex. It's the sex. I am just the bomb at the sex."

It was no secret that Bonnie's self-identity was strongly rooted in her ability to seduce a straight girl and engage in a sexual relationship with her. Chanelle represented herself as being a staunch Christian and had become part of the conversation. It was immediately apparent that Chanelle had little education and came from poverty, drugs, and crime, and I had taken her under my wing. Bonnie immediately began her pursuit. Chanelle was the perfect conquest, and Bonnie's conversation immediately headed in her direction. I knew the entire scenario about to play out. It was a match made by the Devil.

Later that evening, I went to Chanelle. "Be careful with your relationship with Bonnie. She is known for turning girls out, known for accepting the challenge of making a girl cross over to the lesbian style. When it comes to that, she ain't nothing nice. She has a girlfriend back at Bryan. I've been there and done that, and it ain't worth the repercussions you have to deal with."

The following afternoon, Bonnie approached me. "Why are you in my business? Why are you bashing me? Chanelle told me. Let me do my thing. You're a Bible-thumper—you do your thing; let me do mine. I ain't with Jackie anymore. We broke up."

"All right," I said, "I won't say another word to Chanelle." I turned and walked away with the thought, *Isn't that fabulous, Chanelle?!*

As I passed the concrete block wall that partitioned the walk from the solitary confinement cells, I could hear whimpering coming from the hallway that led to the four side-by-side isolation chambers. Accessible off the walk, it was an out-of-bounds area to inmates, a restriction that previously prevented me from investigating the perpetual crying and pleading I heard coming from Missey. It began the very first moment she was confined. The small area had its own showers and remained completely isolated in that manner. I'd had enough and snuck back there.

"Are you all right?" I asked. "You sound terrible. Is there something that I can do for you?"

"I'm claustrophobic. Just leave me alone."

"I'm just trying to help you out and let you know that my love is real. I don't care about that black–white thing."

"If you really are serious, I could really use some ice."

There was a little ice machine back by the showers. I slipped some ice under the door in a plastic bag. "Thank you very much. Sorry about being such a loser."

"I got to go before they figure out I am back here. I'll try to sneak back again sometime."

The following morning, as fate would have it, Bonnie was moved into my cell. It created little problem with me. However, living with her, I became aware of Bonnie's lies regarding her claim that she was through with Jackie. Bonnie was writing and receiving letters from her daily; they had been together for almost four years at Bryan. I couldn't continue to talk to Chanelle about it; she had already broken my trust after I had spoken to her in confidence, and Bonnie and I had come to an agreement. *You do your thing, and I'll do mine.*

Within two weeks, Bonnie had turned Chanelle, and she was walking around with her nose wide open—cuckoo for cocoa puffs. And within two days after the completion of her project, Bonnie approached me again.

"Sheila, this woman is crazy! Chanelle is stuck to me like glue. I can't breathe. If I want to go downstairs and watch some TV with friends, she is right there. She is driving me crazy!"

"I ain't even trying to hear none of that stuff. You pick the most homophobic one—that's your whole game, your big victory. You feel like you accomplish something when you take a Bible-thumping I-will-never-be-gay girl and turn her out. And now you don't want anything to do with her. I don't want to hear it. That's your thing."

"Sheila, Chanelle told me that if I ever did anything to hurt her, she was going to kill me."

"Well, there you have it, Bonnie. Congratulations."

One principal difference between maximum security and Bryan when it came to Bonnie's game—it is one facility, one space; there is no place to run and hide. In Bryan, if something like this went down, she could say to Jackie, "That chick is crazy. I am moving out of this quad." It was easy; she could just tell the administration that someone was messing with her, they would move her, and that would appease Jackie. Bonnie had everyone fooled.

Chanelle was not letting Bonnie move around. Coming in at lockdown was the only peace she would get. Finally, Bonnie came to me one morning. "I can't get up and face this witch. What am I going to do?"

"Pray about it."

* * *

Missey had been in solitary for fourteen days, and the afternoon of her release found me at dinner. She dropped her plate next to mine and immediately began. "Sheila, what am I going to do with my life? Who do I turn to? If I don't go along with the feds, cooperate with them, I'm in here for twenty-five."

"That don't sound pretty. What do they want from you?"

"Me and my boyfriend were major meth dealers. After I got busted, the feds wanted me to set people up in the street. I refused to do it, and they threw me in here. I think they just wanted to see how we were cooking it up—see the process we were using. There is a new formula for the stuff every month, and most of the ingredients are easily obtained. They can't get a grip on it, control it. It isn't that they really care about the people who are having their lives destroyed; it's just that they aren't getting their cut of the action.

"I'm looking at twenty-five years, Sheila. I'm nineteen. I don't want to set up the people in my circle. If they ever found out, I'm as good as dead. What kind of choice is that? Like those feds are going to protect me. I don't know what to do, but while I was in solitary, I thought of just saying forget it and do what they ask of me."

"Missey, I sit here and listen to you, and I got to say . . . DARN! Let me tell you. I was raped at the age of seven or eight—I can't remember exactly when. I didn't meet my father until I was fourteen. Been close to death. Smoked crack for fifteen years and sacrificed all my time and rights as a mother. But I want you to know, and I mean this from the deepest part of my heart, I see what you are facing, and I have to look at myself as being fortunate. Now, I don't know if I even have the right to tell you something about what I think you should do because what you're looking at is something I can't imagine. Twenty-five years in here would be something worse than death, but I want you to know there is a God, and He loves you.

"He knows what you are going through, and He doesn't want that for you. And if you bring yourself to Him, He will intercede on your behalf, and there is no man or institution of men that can stand in the way. I'm not a miracle worker, but I believe in them and the One who works them. I have known miracles in my life, and that is all that I can tell you. As He loves, I do. Believe that, Missey. It is true. I had a choice, but I see none for you except that you go ahead and cook for the feds. Would you let me pray with you?"

"Yes, of course. Would you really do that for me? I was hoping that you would say that."

"Hold my hands. God, my Heavenly Father, King of all Kings, Ruler of Heaven and earth, this child, Your child, is in a dire circumstance. Her heart is hurting, and it is not right for her to have no hope. I know how that feels. Reveal to her the mistakes she has made. I am praying You lift this burden from her, and she will change her life and listen hard to You. Guide her and be with her. In the name of our Father, Amen."

Missey broke into tears and said thank you. "I have never felt this free in my life."

"I feel free, too," I said. It was time to return to our cells.

Bonnie was waiting for me. "Sheila, not only am I having a heart attack over this Chanelle but Jackie got into it so hard with someone at Bryan, created such a disturbance, that she is being transferred here with us. If she ain't already here, she'll be here within a day. I'm in deep trouble."

"Leave me out of it. I am still waiting to hear about my assault charge."

Jackie arrived the next day, and Bonnie made every effort to conceal the two relationships from each other. Within less than twenty-four hours, it got back to Chanelle that Jackie and Bonnie were talking about getting married on the outside. Chanelle snapped and stormed Bonnie while she was standing with Jackie in the dinner line. "I told you, loser, if you ever did anything to hurt me, I was going to kill you. This witch intentionally messed someone up at Bryan just to get in here to be with you?"

In turn, Jackie freaked out. As soon as the ruckus began, a nearby guard intervened and squashed it. Later that evening, Chanelle put two cans of tuna fish into a sock and took it to the shower. While Bonnie was in the shower shampooing her hair, Chanelle beat her down in the head with the two cans of socked-up tuna. The entire facility was going crazy in an instant. By the time the guards stormed the shower, blood was everywhere. They secured Chanelle and immediately escorted her to solitary to be removed to another facility. At that point, Chanelle had snapped, nothing short of a babbling idiot. Jackie learned what happened and arrived with the intent to kill Chanelle, but she was already in lockdown, facing charges for attempted murder. They brought Bonnie out in a gurney, her head gashed and swollen. Her nose was halfway inside her head! She was taken to the hospital. Jackie became hysterical when they refused to allow her to go to the hospital and see Bonnie.

"Do you realize that you are in prison?" the guard said to Jackie. "Have you lost your mind?"

For the next several days, Jackie was on the verge of going to the asylum, completely out of her mind. The authorities decided that Jackie had to go and would not let Bonnie return from the hospital until there was no possibility for further violence. It took six guards to remove Jackie to another facility. She fought them tooth and nail, screaming and hollering as if she were out of her mind.

Several days later, they released Bonnie from the hospital and she was back in the cell with me. She looked like the Elephant Man, and the only person she wanted to talk to was me. "Sheila, there is no way you can tell me that this is any good. I am not messing with another woman again. Sheila, I don't know what to do."

"Maybe it's time to let go and find something else."

"Wait now, Sheila. You don't know the half of it. I do love Jackie. Four years I have been in prison with her, and I feel for her, but I have a real wife, a wifey! I have been with her for fifteen years on the outside."

"Oh my God, Bonnie." I said.

"My girl on the outside knows the drill. She knows that I needed some companionship. She told me, 'As long as you still love me when you get out and we remain together, it's all right for you to find someone on the inside.' I am getting out in four months, Sheila. I told her about Jackie, but I never told Jackie about her. I introduced Jackie to my family members."

"Bonnie, you took it too far out there."

"I had Jackie write my brothers and others when I would go to the hole for fraternizing with other girls. I couldn't tell Jackie about my girl on the outside because I didn't want to risk Jackie going off the chain out there, crazy, and I was obviously right about that."

"For crying out loud, Bonnie!"

"There was a time when I knew God in my life, before I came into all this messed up life. I have to get back to Him before I get killed. I almost did."

"What are you going to say to your girl on the outside, your wife?"

"I don't know. I get out in four months, and Jackie gets out in four and a half. Jackie knows where I live. She will find me. I don't want to go back there because someone is going to get hurt."

"There is a place inside where you can go where none of that matters anymore because you recognize where you have been is not even real. That place is one of unconditional love and a far greater joy than being the one able to turn a straight girl into a gay one. For you, a part of what kept you surviving in prison was that game. Do you know that they used to place bets on a new girl coming in, whether you or Joe would get there first? Joe was the one I put my money on at first; she looked more like a guy. It wasn't even funny. I suppose I had to give it up to any girl who could grow a goatee. I guess you thought you had to live up to that reputation. Besides, anyone reporting to the captain's office saw the big pictures of you and Jackie. You guys were the husband and wife of the compound."

"God, Sheila, you're right. How I did it with Jackie on my back all the time, you can't imagine. It was a lot of work. I had people hiding me in the bathroom and here and there and dodging her all the time. It was sick. The hassle was crazy, sneaking and dodging, ducking and dipping."

"Well, Bonnie, look at it this way. If this is what your life was meant to be, then how come there was so much pain in it? Why weren't you ever truly happy or didn't have any inner peace? Living that life will make you feel like there is no God at all. Every day was mental torment. Women are so emotional; there is no way that it makes any sense for two women to be together. Let's face it, Bonnie; we are the worst when it comes to jealousy. Bonnie, Sharon was having an affair with the doctor at Bryan, and I confronted him—I never felt that intense anger over a man. It is crazy. In any intimate exchange, we acquire each other's karma or psychic garbage."

"Sheila," Bonnie said as she broke down crying for a moment and then continued, "I can't believe anybody would tell me these things. In a minute's time, I can see inside of them. I can tell if they are going to hold on to their homophobic stand. I had that ability, and I used it to get some. I just never understood why they all went psycho afterward."

Bonnie broke down completely. As I held her in my arms I said, "The only thing that anyone is looking for is love. People don't realize they already have it. This messed-up world tries to trick you into thinking that you've got to have this or be that before you can be loved. There is a great secret this life made clear—there is nothing that you can do to further your qualification with love. It is the natural condition of your soul and comes directly from God. If you haven't connected with that truth, why would you want to be in this world?"

I broke down and started crying with Bonnie, feeling her pain. And between my tears, I said to her, "Sometimes I ask, 'God, what does it all mean? I don't know if it is right or fair or what. You've got all these Heavens, somewhere up there, where there is no crying and there is no pain. There is no hurt, and we are all in love with You and each other. Come on. All I know is I've got a bunch of questions for You. There is so much suffering here. I don't think this is right!'"

We collected ourselves as other inmates were passing by. It was dinnertime. "Let's get something to eat," Bonnie said.

"I think I'll pass on dinner," I said. "I'm not much in the mood, but you go ahead. I might find you later. I'm too wiped out right now."

The days were drawing close for my release. I had not yet heard from the committee about their investigation with Officer Brady and the assault charge. I was nervous. I prayed God did not have a lesson for me that would end in my continued imprisonment. Because of the spiritual battles being played out, I knew I needed to be alone with God. I kept it to myself. The spirit of jealousy rang through the air when it was time for an inmate's release. I had been in maximum security for over four weeks and still knew nothing of what was to become of me.

Bonnie returned in an hour with a smile on her face. "Have you seen Missey?"

"Not for a week or so. Why?"

"She is a totally different person. She is saying hi to everyone, playing cards with other girls. Everyone is wondering what happened to her."

"Well, isn't that some kind of a miracle? You seem to be feeling better now."

Before the conversation could continue a moment longer, "Sheila Robinson to the officer's desk" blared out over the loudspeaker.

"God, what now?"

Bonnie looked at me as I left the cell. "Good luck."

I looked over the rail and recognized the investigator standing at the guard desk. My heart was beating so fast, I could feel the tops of my ears burning and thought I was going to faint. I presented myself to both the guard and the investigator, unable to speak. I stared at her dumbly.

"Well, Sheila, after a great study of your character and the incident, I have come to a decision. Sheila, you have been found guilty."

"Oh no! Oh NO!"

"Now, just wait a minute. Hear me out. You are guilty of two things. You need to let others fend for themselves, and you need to learn that if you're going to have someone reprimanded, you don't give him fair warning. Therefore, you are guilty of talking too much," she said with a smile.

My tears had turned to joy. Reduced to silence, I thought, *I do know two things. I will never stop fending for others, and I will never stop talking of God's goodness! NEVER!*

"Get yourself ready to be released. They are releasing you day after tomorrow."

"Thank you, Jesus . . . again!"

The investigator continued, "Never before when conducting an investigation have I known so many inmates to stand up for another inmate. They all had the same exact story. You are a special person, Sheila. Do something with your life. You are a day from being out of here."

I floated back to my cell. Bonnie asked, "So what's up?"

"The investigator discovered I was telling the truth. I will be released soon."

"Do you think I can change like Missey?"

"You already have. I only hope someone steps up to the plate to help her because it's easy to get dragged back into the nonsense so fast you are in way over your head before you even have time to think."

Love changes people.

CHAPTER 21

FREE AT LAST

Let no debt remain outstanding
Except for the continuing debt to love one another
For he who loves his fellow man
Has fulfilled the Law

ROMANS 13: 8

AT FOUR IN THE MORNING, I awoke to a guard pounding on my cell door. "Robinson, roll up and wait by the cell door."

With everything from my cell in my pillowcase, I stood in federal orange next to my steel door in no time flat. A guard arrived to escort me to the administration building. I was thrilled.

I was handed the clothes Kevin had sent me. I was in street clothing for the first time in over eighteen months. It was psychologically unnerving. I emerged into a room where I sat and waited with other inmates being released, but I made no attempt at conversation. A few of the girls had clothing that did not fit and was horribly out of fashion, leaving with the clothing they came in with years earlier. Though fashion was the last thing on anyone's mind, I was grateful for the two-piece jogging outfit Kevin had thoughtfully provided.

A guard ordered me to stand, and I was placed in cuffs. Another girl and I were taken to a van from Bryan. Had there been time left on my sentence, I would have returned there, so my release had to be overseen by Bryan officers. I took a seat in a minivan with several other women. Passing through the prison gates into a new day, I was leaving with a greater part of myself. I didn't mind the customary handcuffs. I felt as free as the lightly falling morning rain.

"It will be about a three-hour drive, ladies."

There was anxiety inside the van, positive tension. Everyone was on pins and needles, holding her breath. No one wanted to talk to anyone.

A little fight, one little breakout, and you were going back. Most of the other girls were still on parole-probation. Due to the recent assault charge against me, my case had been given local jurisdiction. I would not have to fly Con Air and return to Sherburne County for my release. I kept that information to myself.

We pulled into a gas station. Both the driver and the guard in the front seat got out. The side door opened. "Time to take off the cuffs. This is it for you guys."

The door closed, and we were hands free. It looked like a scene from *The Dream Team* where four mental patients are outside the institution for the first time in years, abandoned in their van for hours, waiting for their doctor to return. We looked at each other in silence and came to understand our freedom. The ice broke, and mayhem ensued. "Where are you going?"

"Home."

"Where is that?"

"Doesn't it feel great?"

"Weird."

It continued, and we learned about each other within the rhythm of tires, road, and rain.

"Anyone hungry? We're stopping for lunch at McDonald's. The last meal on the house."

The rain had stopped, the clouds were clearing, and the sun's rays were visible in the sky. It was a picture-book image. We pulled into the parking lot. The driver and guard got out and headed for the door. One of them turned around and said, "What? You forgot how to open a door?"

We piled out, stepping into fresh air enhanced with the smell of summer rain. Though we had open air at Bryan, there was a perceptible odor to our confinement. My final weeks of incarceration at Dallas-Fort Worth were without outside air whatsoever. Now, the air of freedom revealed itself. Observing people in clothing of varying color and style was foreign. All I had seen were blue, gray, and khaki for almost eighteen months. I so much wanted to tell someone I was free but thought better of the idea. Ronald McDonald would have little interest.

I salivated over a hamburger and fries and made an effort to resist stuffing it in my mouth, only to qualify the effort as vain as I released myself to the experience. We all did, tearing through the food as if we had not eaten in weeks. It was nothing but a hamburger and fries, but it was the first thing we had all eaten on the outside.

I was dropped at the Greyhound depot and handed the exact amount of money for a ticket to Minneapolis with an additional $25 for expenses along with the parting words, "Hope we don't see you again."

I immediately grabbed a pay phone and called Kevin—no answer. I needed to tell someone that I was free. I called Patrice, Spud's sister. She had taken care of Mom toward the end, before her final hospital stay. At that point in her life, Patrice had cleaned herself up, and Mom wouldn't eat anyone's cooking but hers. There was not much to say except that I was out and glad to know she was clean. It was a short call, but it fulfilled my desire—I told someone who knew me that I was out.

Within moments, I was getting on the bus. I found a seat, settled in, and considered my return. I recalled the last time I was released, returning from Bryan. Pat had picked me up with thirteen cents in my pocket and allowed me to stay with her. She had a business called Loyalty Card, where one purchased a card and after so many purchases, the card provided deep discounts to the products or services offered by participating companies. She now offered me a job as the business receptionist. While at work, I called Dad and asked him for a few dollars. I told him that I had a job, that I was calling from work. When he returned the call, I answered saying, "Hello, this is Loyalty Card. How may I help you?"

"Ah-ah-ah—now, that's what I'm talkin' 'bout."

"Dad!"

I needed a place to live and some clothes. It was good to talk to him, and he agreed to send me some money. In the past, Dad would give me money if I was working, but if I was out of work or desperate, he was often unresponsive. There would be no such generosity this time, and it hit me.

Would there be forgiveness in the hearts of my loved ones? It had been almost four years of incarceration and about ten years of crack before that. Would there be forgiveness in my heart for me? What would I see in their eyes, and what would they find in mine? Doubt flooded me. Were my efforts in prison vain expectations, unrealistic hopes for a future? The very things I had warred with—the wrong and hurt I had witnessed as a child that I had unwittingly served—struck fear into my heart and removed the joy of my freedom. I stared out the window. Now what? Uncertainty.

It was late in the evening, about eight hours into the ride, when a young black man entered the bus at one stop. He was very attractive, and our eyes connected. Four years behind bars with females improved every man's appearance. He went to the rear of the bus where there was an available seat

Later, as the bus emptied, I moved to a pair of empty seats across from him to stretch out and catch some sleep.

"We are pulling into a stop, last one in Texas." The driver came over the speaker. "We will be here for an hour. There is a cafeteria for breakfast."

We both awoke slowly to discover daylight was breaking. Our legs had become intertwined in the aisle, and we looked at each other awkwardly, simultaneously withdrawing our legs from the aisle and apologizing.

"Excuse me. Excuse me," he said.

"Excuse me," I said as we both started to laugh.

"Are you hungry? I'm getting off the bus for something to eat." "Absolutely. At least some coffee and to stretch my legs." "Come on, then," I said. "Let's go."

We started talking and getting acquainted. His name was Travis, on his way to Omaha to stay with his brother. He wanted to go to school and had just gone through a mad breakup with a girl he had been living with. He told me he really enjoyed being a father to her kids and was hurt at having to leave the relationship.

I asked, "How old are you?"

"Twenty-four."

"You are certainly mature for your age."

He asked, "How old are you?"

"Twenty-nine," I said, laughing. "No, really, I'm thirty-six."

I was happy to have someone to sit with. Over the next twenty-four hours, we became friends. I told him about prison. We played cards together, little word games and crosswords, and talked, becoming closer and closer. We laughed at people coming onto the bus drunk. I liked his personality and found him to be a gentleman. At each stop, he asked if there was something I wanted, if he could get me anything. Our conversations were beautiful; he was very respectful, and I found that romantic. We decided we would see each other again. I gave him all my numbers, Kevin's number, Pat's number, and he gave me his cell phone number. We reached Omaha, and it was time for him to get off—we had a forty-five minute layover. His brother's wife had arrived to pick him up. Travis introduced me to her. We kissed and said good-bye.

My attention turned forward to my arrival in Minneapolis. The bus terminal's pay phone produced Kevin this time. I told him how wonderful it was to be out and asked if he could meet me at the depot upon my arrival. "I'll be at work. Sorry I can't meet you. Just take a cab. The landlord, the owner of the property, lives below me; he will let you into my apartment. The money for the cab will be on the bed. Can't wait to see you."

Boarding the bus once again, I was saying good-bye and hello to Kevin in my mind. *Just take a cab? I guess I could manage that.* It left me uneasy nonetheless. It wasn't Kevin's follow-through I questioned; it was his landlord that had me freaked out. *It will be fine, Sheila. Just go with the flow.* I walked off the bus in Minneapolis with nothing. Not a dime, no driver's license, no one to greet me, nothing but the clothes on my back and faith all was going to be right.

I grabbed a cab and gave him the address, and we arrived in no time. "If you would please be patient, I have to get inside to get the money to pay you."

I got the landlord as Kevin instructed, and he let me in without question. I located the cab money on a bed along with a pile of new clothes. I was so excited, and it meant so much to me. I forgot about the cabbie waiting outside until I heard him honking his horn. I hurried out the door with the cab fare, crying.

"I'm sorry you had to wait," I said through my tears.

"What's the matter?" he asked. "Are you all right?"

"I'm just happy. Never been better. Thank you so very much." The phone was ringing when I got back into the apartment. *Should I answer it? Why not?*

"Hello. Kevin Lambert's phone. This is Sheila."

"Great! So you made it in," Kevin said.

"Oh, Kevin. I can't tell you how grateful I am to have you as a brother."

"It's all good, sister."

"I can't say thank you enough!"

"Just relax. Take a bath or something, and I'll see you when I get home."

I said a long good-bye and hung up the phone. *A bath?* The thought was foreign—unless there was a medical reason to take a bath, and that was in a completely different facility, you showered without privacy. *Privacy? Bath?* I took an hour-long soak.

I put one of the outfits on, took it off, and tried every other outfit on until I was on my second round. Everything fit perfectly. *My brother is the fashion king,* I recalled to myself. It was just wonderful, the look of new clothes, the way they felt—I was merging back into a free society away from a social order that knew uniformity as its dress. I became aware that the ingrained routine was not easily released no matter how disparaging or dark. And I was emerging from darkness and change. Though welcome, it was mired in uncertainty. Insecurity.

There is a conditioning, the biorhythm that you are accustomed to. I was getting hungry but did not even consider going to the refrigerator or looking for any food.

Kevin and Torrie walked in the door together, and after endless hugs and tears, Kevin said, "I'm hungry." Looking at me, he asked, "Are you hungry?"

"I'm starving," I said.

"Why didn't you make yourself something earlier?"

I considered it for a moment and realized how deep the programming was within me. Of course, my heart knew it would have been all right to make something—this was my brother—but I did not even consider the idea of responding to my hunger; my mind would not acknowledge it. There was sadness in my eyes.

"Come on," Kevin said, sensing my quandary. "Let me show you your room, and we will fix something to eat right quick."

"I have my own room?"

We hung out in the kitchen and fixed dinner. Later that night, we talked about things after Torrie had gone to sleep. We talked about Mom and some of the experiences from our past.

"Kevin, the only other time I saw Mom turn money down was when I was making serious cash selling crack. Like a cat bringing a mouse to the door, I brought Mom several thousand dollars and slapped it down on the table, and she said, 'Get that money out of my house!'

"That was my offering—I wanted to come back home. So I said, 'Well, you're sitting here broke, busted, and disgusted—isn't it all the same? I know some of your schemes could easily be questioned as to your motive.' I felt so completely rejected, I walked out the door with, 'I'm going to the store.' It was my favorite escape line. You know the one, Kevin."

I told him that my most difficult trial in prison was knowing he was in trouble, more trouble than he ever realized. I was worried to death about him. While he was out in the streets, Kevin had witnessed a stabbing and had brought the victim to the hospital. I knew the people involved, and they were after Kevin. If the girl died, Kevin was the only witness to the murder, and everyone involved knew Kevin was not cool with it. I heard of the incident through the grapevine while in Bryan and placed a call to someone close to the affair. I told her to call the dogs off my brother, and she assured me such a command would be given.

Kevin said, "Yeah, whatever, Sheila."

He hated that I was involved in that life, that I even knew those people. Whenever I exposed my connection to the reality of drugs, Kevin played it as if I were just making the stuff up. I looked at him in a manner that communicated the truth of what I had just revealed, and we hugged each other with an endearment I had felt but a few moments in my life.

The following morning after breakfast, Kevin left for work. Torrie said, "Auntie, you were the coolest aunt. You were always there, and when you left, no one understood why. All of a sudden, you just left. We were really hurt when you weren't there."

"Torrie, there are things that happened to me when I was real young." It had been less than forty-eight hours of freedom, and I was in the thick of it. "Your dad has a hard time with this. Do you think you can handle it?"

"Yeah, I can."

"I don't know if I can."

"It will be all right. I want to know."

"I had broken away, Torrie, because, for me—this is how it was—like this all my life—Sheila was the one who was going to make the world a better place for all of us—the one to make it happen for everyone—the one who was going to make the big break. Everything was about Sheila. I didn't want that for me. So when I snapped, it put the fear of God in everyone. It was like our entire family fell apart if I did, and they didn't have to know I was falling apart in the street. What they didn't know wouldn't hurt them— that was the thing I was working with. Life goes on without Sheila. Go out there and do something with your life."

"What do you mean, Auntie? It wasn't any secret you were falling apart, that you had problems with drugs. Why didn't you come to us, to me? The ones who really love you?"

"It wasn't because I didn't love you. In a screwed-up way, it was because I did. Drugs are not the problem; they are the symptom, and, after you become addicted, they become your life."

I stopped for a moment. I did not know where to take this, how to bring this to him—to any of them. I was in uncharted water and holding the hand of a seven-year-old girl who yet lived inside me. I froze as a tear rolled down my cheek.

"Auntie?"

Into a young boy's eyes of compassion, I said, "I've got to keep it real, Torrie. I don't know exactly how or where to take this, but I have to get there somehow. I will need your help, you see. If I don't—I am afraid the only life I have known has been one turning my back on something and running since I was seven or eight years old—something ugly. Now that we started this, if I don't finish it, I'm afraid I will end up back there in the street. It happened before, and I don't want it to happen again."

"None of us do, Auntie."

"It was easier to talk about this with people in prison. Most had similar experiences, and many had a life far worse than mine. I could talk to you about God, but the truth is, you will have to find out about God for yourself. I can tell you He loves me just like He loves you, and we are something—each of us—something of the Greatest Beauty. What I am about to say is not to please God or do something for Him. He has already shown me He loves me without me having to do anything and in spite of all the bad things I have done. Now, what I am about to tell you is for me! Something I have to do for me so that I may begin to stand up for me, not for someone else and not for God. He doesn't need that from me; I do."

"I kind of know what you mean, Auntie. I get to school and look around, and it scares me. I don't have a clue what is going on, and no one else seems to, either. You're doing great. I think you can tell me now."

I thought to end the conversation right then and there. For the last fifteen years, drugs and prison were all I had known. As far as commitment, that was what I was committed to—the drug use and that way of life. I got so good at it, such an existence became natural and was burned into me. Aware there was a part of me drawn in the direction of the past, I needed to be able to walk away in the right state of mind. An uncharted future won the inner conflict that day.

"I began having flashbacks about being raped and molested and abused as a kid—by people from our family. How do you bring that to anyone? They had a big intervention for me one day at the house with Mom and Aunt Cathy and everybody. They just kept jumping on me, and, finally, I told them—just let the cats out of the bag one by one and told on everyone. Mom said, 'What did you do to bring that on?'"

I broke down and started crying. Torrie held my hands.

"Well, I couldn't handle that—that completely messed me up— threw me clear out of the loop. She couldn't accept that my dysfunction went deeper than her Ray thing, that this was part of her entire life. Sandy did not want to accept any responsibility for what had happened to me. She couldn't bring herself to that, and I have felt guilty because I told her. Do you understand? No one in this world loved her more than me, and I knew that was how it was going to go down! It is why I never said anything about it in the first place. I was nothing more than a scared little kid needing a mom and dad, and I had neither."

Torrie came and sat in my lap, and we cried and said nothing to each other for the longest while. He broke the embrace by standing up and saying, "It's good to have you back."

"It's good to be back."

"I got to go to school," Torrie said and left.

I had yet to connect with my children, Pat, and my close friends. Torrie and Kevin were enough for the next several days. I decided to eliminate everyone until I knew I wasn't going to fall back in the trap again. I couldn't afford to disappoint myself or the people I love, not another time. I was about to face the challenge of breaking the security of prison life, where the street life and its temptations did not exist. I had yet to adjust to physical freedom and knew it was going to be a tough road. I found contentment just waking up to say, *Thank You, God. Thank You for today because I have no desire to go to where I was in the past.*

Another morning arrived, and I was thankful. I took a walk to a neighborhood park and said hello to a few strangers. I returned and gave Pat a call. She had lost trust in me, and it would take some doing to bring her back into my life, but that was my intention, so I suggested lunch. She agreed. I was excited just to talk with her.

That evening, Torrie called Jeanna. She was in foster care. She and Matt could not get along, and she kept running away. In her mind, she was reaching out to me. I could not call her directly. The restraining order Matt and the authorities had in place prohibited Jeanna's foster parents from allowing me to speak with her, though they told me they did not agree with it. Instead, they felt it was healthy and good for Jeanna to have communication with me. After Torrie spoke to her for a minute, he handed me the phone. None would be the wiser as long as Jeanna was careful on her end.

"Mom, I miss you so much."

I told her how much I loved her, how much I wanted to be together, and I was working on making that happen—someday soon.

"Mom, Matt told me he doesn't want the other kids to even hear your name. He takes them to see everyone else in the family but doesn't want them to know about you."

"What kind of crap is that?"

"They can't see any pictures of you, Mom. It doesn't make any sense."

We began to plan how we would get together. I told her I would begin to contact an attorney and see what I could do.

"Please figure something out, Mom."

"I will, Jeanna. I promise you as God is my witness. How is everything else?"

We continued our conversation. I told her I would have Torrie call again in a few days, and I would let her know then what I had found out. When I got off the phone, I turned to Kevin and shouted, "That little bastard Matt! Kevin, you won't believe it."

"Settle down, Sheila. What got you going?"

"They are as black as motorboat smoke kids, but they can't associate themselves with me at all? What does he think that does to their heads? My children? Matt is so ugly with it. You brought him to Mom, Kevin, but Matt came to stay with me after he got out of the Army. Now he has the courts agreeing with him, not allowing my children to even hear my name or see my picture."

"That is how the world is, Sheila, and it is not the way of love. You mess up, and there are no more chances. But the will of love has something completely different in mind."

"Matt told Jeanna you and I were parasites and would not amount to anything!"

"What? Now you got me wanting to hurt him!" Kevin paced back and forth for a moment and gained control of himself. "All the same, Matt is the only one who had the ability to care for them. No one else in the family could. I wish I could have done it, but everything was so chaotic."

"As angry as it makes me, it was in God's plan my children were placed in their care, and I do know they love my children as though they were their own. I created this mess, and it's not for them to clean up. That one is on me."

This is the harsh reality of the truth of drugs and addiction. I knew I had to push through such a recognition so I could heal and reunite with my children. It was a necessary part of healing to call Matt and confront him regarding Jeanna's allegation. I made an effort at civility, but I became undone when I inquired about the parasite statement. Matt's refusal to own up to it really made me angry. He claimed, "Jeanna is nothing but a little liar."

I was defending the integrity of my daughter at that point and hung up the phone. There was no raw nerve more sensitive than the one Matt just struck.

I called Pat. She told me to get over it. "Sheila, if I can recognize you are not in the same place you once were, others will as well. These things take time." She told me to let go of my anger and promised to help me find an attorney. "Tomorrow we meet for lunch and celebrate your release. Let it be a thankful and joyous time." I was grateful for Pat. She had always had the ability to allow me to see things in a different light, one that offered a solution rather than a hopeless problem.

About a year into my relationship with Pat, I did one of my disappearing acts. Pat had sought the assistance of my mother, brother, and father to find me. She did not know my history of disappearing nor my long involvement with drugs. My family did. When she could not get any support to search for me, she was very stressed. Finally, she became seriously ill and was hospitalized in the intensive care unit for cancer patients. The specialists were unable to diagnose her condition, and it was only after a holistic health specialist worked with her that she recovered. The woman told Pat later, "It is my opinion, Pat, that you made the decision to die, distraught over the complexities of your situation." Pat's son, daughter, and grandchildren and the rest of her family all had been affected by my actions. They could not understand why she went that far for me. My mother and brother could not understand, either. Pat did not know why she was so intensely connected but at a very core level KNEW she had to try to help me. It would be a soft walk back into Pat's life.

She picked me up at noon, on time and dependable as always. "Wonderful to see you, Sheila."

"God is so wonderful. I was so angry about the Matt thing and my kids, but I realized anger was not going to do me any good. Then I got angry for being angry. Then I said it was okay to be angry at being angry. Only then, I was not angry anymore."

Pat started laughing and said, "Now you really are learning."

"It's so good to see you, Pat."

"How is Kevin?" she asked as we pulled away.

"He's doing so good, and what a brother. He told me not to worry about anything and that he had it covered. 'I got you,' he said. 'Settle back into society.' When I came out, I was stressed about not having a job, not having a place to live, not having a car, clothes, and so on and so on. These things cause people to go right back to what they knew and end up right back in prison. Truth be told, it can be a setup for failure. They say they are reforming you, say they are getting you ready for a job, get you regimented into particular habits, being responsible, and then they simply cut you free. I am more than grateful for Kevin relieving that stress. He said he will kick me a few dollars whenever he can."

It was hard to talk with Pat—I had written her that letter, apologizing and asking her to be a part of my life. Her response was NO! I wrote the letter because I knew that I had hurt her. I had a history of letting her—everyone—down. How many times do you tell somebody you have changed before they look at you like the boy who has cried wolf one too many times? Zero credibility. But there was no way that I was returning to a musical career path without her.

"You know I want to establish a musical career and that I want you to manage it." It just came out as we pulled into the parking lot of the restaurant.

"I'm not ready to commit to any management position, Sheila," she said, "though I immediately saw a change within you."

We sat down for lunch and talked about everything. She was helpful and forthcoming with the name of an attorney to speak with regarding my children. I was grateful for that, but I was not through with her understanding my intention, and she was not through allowing me to understand hers.

"Pat, every moment up to this point, I have crawled like a child. I know the trials I have put you and so many others through. I want you to know I feel very blessed just to be able to get to this mark. Now, I am not saying that I will not have my moments in the future when I fall, but I have touched something inside of me so much greater than myself, and there is a real joy I remember, one that I know will bring me back to where I need to be. People get mad at me when I now wake up so happy. My life before was a living hell.

Coming from where I come from, I can't help but 'Skip to My Lou, My Darling.'"

"I am happy to hear that from you, Sheila."

"I'm between my old life and this new one, growing into an understanding of what God meant when He said, 'No matter what it is that you are doing, continue to do what I have ordained you to do, what I tell you to do.' That is the real deal. That is what makes God greater than whatever you are doing. Your personal desires—they are slowly being burnt away—dissolving into nothing—fading away, in spite of the flesh warring with the spirit. I know now there are two of me, and one has nothing to do with the other.

"Christ said, 'Man cannot serve two masters.' I see myself in this transitional period; sometimes I am serving the flesh, sometimes I am serving God and my fellow man. The old life raises its head from time to time and takes over, but I now know the other one, the joy of God that is so far greater than anything I can conceive myself. So when I come back to this awakening, well, there is no other choice. I desire the higher joy—the Highest Desire. And I am resolved to bring you back into my life."

When Pat dropped me back at Kevin's, I knew I would have to crawl like a child back into her life—into everyone's life. And I was surprisingly cool with it.

CHAPTER 22

MORTAL GENIUS— IMMORTAL SOUL

Then Jesus turned to Peter saying,
Get behind me Satan
You are a stumbling block to me
You do not have in mind the things of God
But the things of men

MATTHEW 16: 23

Over the first weeks following my release, I assisted Kevin by locating investment properties for his business and contacted an attorney to explore possibilities to reunite with Jeanna. Within short order, I had scraped the money together to retain his services and began to petition the courts to have Jeanna emancipated from Matt and Becky. She was so important through my recovery, a lifeline yet connecting me to all my children. Her sincere and heartfelt desire to develop a relationship with me gave me hope. I responded to her hope by reaching out to my father. I called his office without expectation to speak with him and left a message that I had been released. The desire to have a relationship with him lived in me as it lived in Jeanna to establish one with me—karma I was intent on resolving.

A month would roll by, and I made efforts to reestablish musical relations with some of my past associations. I reached out for an open arm here and there, hoping I had not burned all my bridges. I continued to work toward reuniting with Pat professionally. It was a slow road, but I had not returned to drugs and the street, a major victory. I got my driver's license and a car—a clunker, but it was mine.

Friday evening around ten o'clock, within the fourth week of freedom, I was driving to meet Travis at the Greyhound station in downtown Minneapolis. He had been calling every now and then since that ride home from Texas. We would talk about the smallest of things, and my interest in a relationship with him had intensified. I thought he was a great guy, and we were physically attracted to each other. We had great conversations over the phone—very romantic— that evolved over the weeks from huggy-kissy to hot and heavy. It had reached the "Baby, baby, can't wait to see you" stuff, and I wanted to know if this relationship was going somewhere. As I rounded the corner several blocks from my destination, I saw Chazz and his girlfriend on the street, heading into a First Avenue nightclub. I slowed to a stop and yelled out the window, "Chazz!"

Chazz and I had recorded a few songs together years earlier. My dad and his band came to town during that time. I took Chazz with me the night I went to see Dad's concert and introduced Chazz to his band and Vernon, my father's valet and very good friend of fifty years. Chazz developed a friendship with Vernon, and they kept in touch with each other thereafter.

I yelled out the window again, "Chazz!"

This time he noticed me and started jumping up and down as he hollered back, "Sheila! Stop! I got to talk to you."

I pulled over to the side of the street about halfway up the block. The traffic prevented me from opening my door. As he came running up to the car, I put my head out the window.

"Girl! I have been looking all over for you. Your dad has been looking for you. You've got to get in touch with Vernon or call the office. Your dad left all his kids a million dollars each!"

"No way," I said. "You've got to be kidding me."

"Yes, almost a year ago, your dad brought all the kids together, a family meeting. Everyone but you and Charles were there. Yes, he left all of you a million in a living will or trust or whatever you call it!"

"What? I can't believe it."

"Chazz, come on!" someone was yelling from the doorway of the club.

He turned and responded, "Yeah, yeah!"

A car horn sounded behind me. I was illegally parked, and Travis was waiting for me. I scribbled Kevin's number down on a scrap of paper and held it out the door.

"Chazz, I gotta get going as well, and thank you for the news. Call me later at Kevin's, and we'll catch up. You can fill me in further on what you know. I love you. It is so good to see you."

"I love you, too. I'll call you tomorrow."

As I drove off, my thoughts went instantly to the negative. If Chazz had the information correct, why didn't Dad or his people inform me? They sure knew where I was. Something that life-changing would have been communicated even if I was behind bars. If I was excluded from such inheritance, it was because of my actions, prison, and drugs. Mom had fought so hard for me to have the name Robinson, Ray's last name, and to be acknowledged by my father. Now, even after she had passed away, I felt as if I was continuing to destroy her life.

I entered the depot lobby, contemplating whether I had missed the boat. I threw off the anxiety the moment I saw Travis awaiting me. We rushed into each other's arms and carried on like long-lost lovers. As we released our embrace, the moment dissolved as quickly as it arrived, distracted by the recent news and the three bags of luggage at Travis's feet. *How long does he think he is staying? We had talked about him staying a week!*

On the drive to Kevin's, I told Travis the story Chazz had just delivered. It was incredible as far as I was concerned. I could not help myself, even though I knew there was nothing more sickening than listening to someone's tirade about money. He was very nice about it, and I finally burnt out on the subject, changing the topic with the most innocuous of questions. "How was your trip?"

Kevin was not home when we arrived. We brought Travis's luggage to my room, and I quickly discovered that there was little within the three bags he was carrying. One bag had a couple pair of tennis shoes, another housed a light jacket and windbreaker, and a third had several changes of clothing and a jogging outfit. *He didn't bring anything!* A long bus ride for him and the emotional high from the news I received had done us both in. We lay next to each other. I had not been with a man for two years. We hugged and kissed, but sex for me was out of the question.

The morning came, and I had no one to call. Dad's office was closed, and I was waiting to hear from Chazz. The news had consumed my thoughts and served as nothing more than a vexation. How would I use or misuse such a resource? Kevin arrived late afternoon. As soon as he came in, I hit him with the news. "Kevin! Kevin! You aren't going to believe this. I think Dad left me a million dollars!"

"You're kidding me."

"Yes. I mean, no. I'm so excited and confused. I just ran into Chazz on the street, and he told me. He's been in touch with Vernon. Chazz is going to call today and fill me in, catch up on things. I never got his number but gave him the house number here. I was in a hurry—he was in a hurry. Oh, Kevin, this is Travis. Travis, this is my brother, Kevin."

We hung out and talked. I was pleased to see that Kevin and Torrie both liked him, and it wasn't too much later that Kevin left on some business. Chazz called an hour later, and we caught up on a few things. He reiterated the story from the day before.

"Yeah, and they have been trying to find you to give it to you."

I said, "What?"

"They have been trying to find you."

"Well, that's nonsense. They knew where I was over the past year. I was writing Dad regularly. I called out there when I was released. Well, the office is closed until Monday. Do you have Vernon's number?"

"I don't have it with me and won't be home until late Sunday night."

"Fine. Call me when you have Vernon's number. It was great to talk with you."

Later that night, Kevin was in and out. He was with a couple of friends, going outside and coming back in. Finally, he asked, "What did you find out?"

"Won't know anything until Monday. Chazz didn't have Vernon's number, and the office is closed."

His whole demeanor had changed. He must have been drinking, and the fire was ignited. I knew Kevin was about to go immediately to ridiculous. "I think I deserve a third or at least $250,000."

"What?"

"I think I deserve a third or $250,000."

"Why you doing this, Kevin? Okay. Are you telling me that when your father passes away and you inherit the monies he has left for you and your brothers that I get a quarter or third of that?"

"After all you have put me through—all my life—all of your drugs and you being missing and stuff—I deserve that much."

"Kevin, I just got out of prison. I don't know what is happening with Dad. I have no money—no way to get out there. Now I've got to deal with the office! It's just the word on the street. I have yet to confirm any of this, and you immediately go nuts."

"Where do you think you are staying? Who has been taking care of you?"

"That is terrible! And I know you have been drinking because you would not have the nerve to say that sober."

"Like you got something to say to me about that!"

"Whatever, Kevin! Leave me alone!"

"Forget Ray Charles." He slammed the door and was gone.

Money is a strange beast, and its possibilities frightened me. I was no stranger to its allure. The answer to any problem always seemed to involve money. Mom always looked at money in a very strange manner that somehow revolved around Ray—a peculiar sense of entitlement or something. I never could put my finger on it, but one thing I know—she never respected money but was always around it. Mom loved and lived contradiction. She had unconditional love, but if there was money in the mix, she needed to control it. And Dad expected his children to make something of their lives without the need of his assistance. What was this inheritance about?

One hears about a winning lotto ticket altering relationships, changing the dynamic of families, and destroying friendships. In my life, there had been little graciousness when it came to money. It was associated with one of three things: crack, an attempt to establish a musical career, or my father. All three issues were cloudy and left me with a great deal of uncertainty. In the mind-set of a crackhead, a million dollars meant but one thing—an eternal high. I did not want to return to drugs, but such a habit called to me. Money would make for an easy fix and washes one clean of sin in the eyes of man. I did not know how much I believed in a musical career, a career others had always believed in more than me. And I questioned my father's motives. As petty as it may seem, I was using Bob Barker shampoo less than a few months ago, earning twelve cents an hour, and writing my dad every day while he gathered his other children to inform them he was giving each of us a million dollars. Why not write and tell me or send me ten bucks for some shampoo and tampons? Where does 'tough love' end and 'no love' start? I never wanted anything from him but his time—a father, but most of all his love.

And Kevin? He had an unbelievable ability to pull great financial deals together and then lose them as soon as they were within his grasp. It is not what he truly wanted. Kevin was born for the stage, and he always felt he had to play second fiddle next to me, the *daughter of Ray Charles*. He heard it as much as I did. A couple of days into the bottle, and everything went out the door. Self-destruct. My mom was the same way. They could pull things together, and then, all of a sudden, it was, "Now, who is that?"

It made me angry, Kevin jamming me like that. He was my brother. What was he thinking? I wouldn't look out for him after all he had done for me? What does that say about what he thinks about me? I knew it would not be long before Kevin was full-blown into relapse. I had to get away, and fate just has its motives. I was on trial again with my past: drugs and depression. What structure there was to my life had just gone out the window, and I was within a whirlwind of confusion with but a single certainty. The very suggestion of money was destabilizing. The only time I had control of it or knew how to control it was when I dealt drugs. Busted, jailed, tried, convicted, incarcerated, and freed, only to face the true trial of my life—iron irony.

"Travis, I'm sorry, but I am going to have to get out of here. Everything is going to blow up. When Kevin starts drinking, he gets violent. The last time he went there, we got into a big physical fight. I will not go through it again. It is kill or be killed. There is a great deal of anger in him. We're going to have to figure something out."

"He'll be okay in the morning."

"You don't know him, Travis. When he is drinking, he has no logic. None whatsoever. I have to get away from him and soon."

Kevin remained away over the weekend. Chazz called late Sunday evening and gave me Vernon's number. It was too late to call him, and in the morning, I called Dad's office. Valerie answered. I asked her if I could speak with Dad.

"He is not available at this time. I will let him know you called."

"Well, can you tell me if it's true that I inherited a million dollars?"

"I wouldn't say that. It's just not on me to give out that kind of information. You're going to have to talk to Mr. Adams."

I called Dad's office again in the afternoon and spoke with Yolanda. "I don't know anything about that. You'll have to wait until your dad calls."

Well, they didn't say that it wasn't true, I thought as I hung up the phone. I tried Vernon's number, but there was no answer.

Kevin returned the following day and wasn't giving me a break. He wanted me to call again, but I told him that it would do no good. I was being patient and waiting for Dad or Joe to call. I did not want to hound Dad or the office about it. Thursday arrived without any word, and it was time for Travis to go.

"Look, Travis, I have to get out of here. Tomorrow I will drive you to the bus station."

"I still don't have the money for my ticket. I am waiting for my brother to send me the money. He is waiting for his wife to get the money from her family so he can send it to me."

"I don't have the money to give you. I might be a millionaire at this very moment, but right now, I haven't a red cent to give you, and I have to get out of here. This is not healthy for me, and I am darn sure not asking Kevin for the bus money for you. You have to work it out somehow on your own."

I had begun to question everyone's motives. Travis began to appear as someone equally interested in me as an answer to his problems—the same kind of crap I was trying to escape. I questioned my own motives and asked myself if the only reason I was intent on leaving was to provide an excuse to call Dad's office with a new number and location. But when Kevin came in that afternoon with an attitude, drunk, disorderly, and talking a lot of ugly, I knew I had to leave.

I called Darlene and Ted. I knew them from the drug days, and I was heading into fire, intentionally avoiding them for that very reason.

But they were the only ones I could think of to call, and Darlene had been the head of finances for the IDS building for twenty-two years. Walking into great temptation, I rationalized, *If the rumor of such an inheritance is true, she would be a good person to ask regarding its management.* Even though I knew their lifestyle was not where I wanted to be, it was a lifestyle I knew, a place where I would be accepted with little expected of me.

"Sheila, where are you? We heard you were released. When can we see you?" Darlene's excitement shot out of the phone.

We talked about how good it was to be out, my circumstances, and my need to get away from Kevin. She was immediately on her way to get me after I accepted her invitation to stay with them. I told Travis I was going to the store and met Ted and Darlene up the street. Once we arrived at her house, I called Dad's office and left their number. No call came that day. I sat by their phone most of Friday and realized my life had once again been reduced to waiting for my dad's call. It was the same old pattern. Darlene suggested that we drive out to California to meet with Dad and Joe directly. I could not think of any better solution to my emotional quagmire. I called Dad's office and left a message that I was coming to see him. Darlene and I left the next day.

Over the drive, I learned from Darlene that she had nearly one hundred thousand dollars of equity in her house. She was trying to sell so she could get back on her feet. She just flipped out one day— had a complete nervous breakdown. She owned a big beautiful home, sports cars, the whole nine and just snapped. She was diagnosed as bipolar and put on some heavy kind of medication. I told her Kevin was into real estate and was sure he could assist her with her house.

A day away from Los Angeles, I called Valerie to inform Dad that we would be in tomorrow.

Valerie responded, "You might as well turn back because he is not seeing anyone. He is really not feeling well and just wants to rest up. I told him of your plans to visit him, and he asked me to tell you that he just wants to be left alone right now. He said to make sure and tell you that it is nothing personal. He just isn't seeing anyone."

I asked, "Will you let him know that I love him and really want to see him?"

"I promise he will get that message, Sheila. Regarding your question about an inheritance, your father told me to tell you Joe will get in touch with you."

"I so much wanted to see him. I love him so much."

"He loves you, too, Sheila."

I felt embarrassed when I told Darlene to turn around because Dad would not see me. Even if he was sick, it sounded like there was little connection between us. "He must still be mad at me," I told her. I would have hung my head lower were it not for the fact that there was an indication from Valerie that Dad had set something aside for me.

Upon our arrival in Minneapolis, I contacted Kevin to talk to Darlene about her house. It was an offering back to him and an excuse to reopen communication. Kevin told me he was giving Travis the money to go back home. I spoke with Travis, apologized to him for leaving so abruptly, and asked him to forgive me. I knew it would not work out, and there was too much confusion in my life as it was.

I began to accompany Darlene and Ted while they were looking for a place in the country, some kind of farmhouse or rural property. I became suspicious of their behavior—stopping every twenty or thirty minutes. They were obviously going somewhere to smoke and were making an attempt to not do it around me. I was grateful for that. I had yet to break down and say, "Give me a blast."

After a week, she found a house, and Kevin put her together with someone who would finance the new property. He required her to apply $50,000 to the new property, and if she missed one payment, he would snatch it from her. The house wouldn't even be in her name. Her response was "good-bye."

A mutual friend of ours, Jeff Peterson, brought a more equitable deal to her table through a real estate agent by the name of Colin. She sold the house and had two months to vacate her old property with $68,000 in her pocket. Darlene and Ted went on a complete crack binge. It was then I broke down and said, "Give me a hit." That is when things started to get weird, really weird.

Even though it was a familiar memory and my body welcomed that first hit, I was met with an unfamiliar reaction. It was not comforting, so I took another to further understand the present contradiction with my body's memory of the drug. I felt the rush, and yet the foreign feeling remained. I took a third blast, a huge hit to erase all contradiction, only to be amazed at the drug's impotence.

"What is this stuff?" I asked Ted.

"Some good stuff, ain't it?" Ted replied and then took a huge hit, held it in, exhaled, and smiled.

"It is?" I responded, profoundly perplexed.

Ted and Darlene let out all the stops now and proceeded to indulge themselves without reservation. I withdrew into discomfort, unable to participate in their exuberance and conversation.

My silence made my companions uneasy. "What's wrong, Sheila?"

"I don't know, but I'll be all right. I'm just going to lie down for a moment." I did not want to tell them their conversation was ridiculous and my spirit desired to regurgitate the few hits I had just taken. I did not understand my reaction, nor did I like it. Smoking crack had been a great part of my life, and now its call was weak, if it even existed.

I smoked with them again the following day. In a strange way, I wanted to like it so I would not regard my past as a complete and pitiable waste. I wanted to know its lie, unwilling to accept the truth. The crutch I had used in the past was unable to support me into the future, an awareness that made me insecure. I took several large hits and, to my dismay, was met with the same result. It did not interest me. The drug and Ted and Darlene's behavior repelled me. It was intolerable.

Ted began hiding a tape recorder in various places within the house before he left for work. Darlene was doing the same thing when she left Ted in the house alone. It was classic paranoid behavior. I awoke one morning to the two of them quarreling. Ted was playing the tape recorder, shouting, "This sounds like Daniel!" After a considerable length of time, Darlene admitted she slept with Daniel, if only to diffuse the wrath of Ted.

Ted exclaimed, "People told me about you two down in the basement for three hours by yourselves."

"It was one time, Ted, when we weren't even in a committed relationship."

"Well, that's like you having herpes and forgetting to tell me. How do you have herpes and forget to tell somebody you've been sleeping with for a year, you stupid, lying ho?"

"Calm down. He should be here to fix my car any minute."

Ted looked out the window and said, "There's that nigger, now. All white women who sleep with a nigger are nothing but trash."

Daniel rang the doorbell, and I answered it. I introduced myself to a man twice the size of Ted and invited him inside the house. Neither Ted nor Darlene even acknowledged his presence until Daniel ventured an interruption. "Hello."

Ted turned to Daniel and said, "I'll fix the car. You aren't working on her car."

Ted rewound the tape, pushed the play button, and turned up the volume. Aware the argument involved his affair with Darlene, Daniel looked at me and said, "Forget this! These people are nuts. How can you stand living here?"

"I no longer can," I said. Ted and Darlene moved their argument to the basement as an invitation for the both of us to make our departure.

"I'm going over to my daughter-in-law's. I live with my son and his wife and have my own room in the basement. Why don't you come with me? We're barbecuing today."

"Let's go." I love barbecues and needed a way out.

I met his family and had a great time. I babysat his grandkids while they went out for the evening. They came back late. I was already asleep on the couch in the family room, having made plans to go with Daniel to pick up a part for his son's car in the morning and figure out a place to stay. I woke up to someone banging on the basement window. It scared me half to death. The window was finally pushed open, and an intruder came sliding through the small opening, emerging from the shadows at the same moment Daniel stepped out from his bedroom doorway.

"What's with this creep?" she yelled, looking at me and then looking back at Daniel.

Oh my God, I thought, *straight up from the hood, ghetto stuff in my face. Out of the frying pan and into the fire!*

She came busting up to me and said with a serious attitude ready to fight, "Who are you?"

Daniel answered for me. "Sheila Robinson."

"Sheila Robinson? Are you the one who is supposed to be Ray Charles's daughter?"

"Yeah."

"Well, I heard about you! I know Spud and Patrice and all those people. My name is Carla!"

"Really."

She said, "Girl you need to get up out of here and go on with me."

"That's cool with me. I sure don't want any drama."

I needed a place to stay until I heard from Joe or Dad and had no reason to think her place was any worse than the current circumstance. We left together shortly thereafter. Carla told me she was on the outs with Daniel because she had caught him with other women.

"Well, that wasn't my reason for being there. He rescued me from Ted and Darlene's, friends that had gone out of control."

I left what I knew of Darlene and Daniel out of the conversation, but I was glad to have confirmation she was being truthful with me. Carla had a beautiful condominium in Brooklyn Center, decorated from top to bottom in a style similar to my mother's. The feeling I had found my place was further heightened by her genuine sense of concern over my well-being.

"Right now, I just need a friend and a little help," Carla said. "I just bought this real estate program that teaches you how to buy a home for no money down. If you help me with that, I'll pay you a couple hundred a week, and you can stay here. I got about seventeen grand in the bank, and if I can buy some properties, I hope to be financially independent."

I proceeded to tell her my story, and the moment I did, I asked myself what I had done it for. It was on. I left messages with the secretary for Joe, Valerie, or Yolanda, providing Carla's number.

"Girl, we are getting ready to make a road trip," Carla said and went online to obtain my dad's concert schedule. Soon, we were making arrangements to travel to his next scheduled engagement in Chicago. She bought me a thousand dollars' worth of clothes so I would be sharp. "You can't be coming out of prison and go to your father without looking like you are trying to do something. Just pay me back when you get your money."

Arriving in Chicago, we were informed that his concert had been cancelled. I called the office and was informed Dad was not feeling well, but he would be back on the road soon. Carla had family in

Chicago, and we stayed there for a couple days before traveling to Dad's next show in Kansas City. When we arrived, that show had also been cancelled. His next show was in Kansas City, Missouri—cancelled.

I called again. Yolanda said, "Well, your dad is going to have hip surgery. He is cancelling his tour for the rest of this summer. He will not be performing for an undetermined length of time."

"Is he okay?"

"He's fine. He just needs his rest."

"Yolanda, my friend and I drove all the way to see Dad, and she lost her wallet last night. I need some money to get back to Minneapolis. I'm still waiting to hear from someone about an inheritance that a friend told me about in the street, and no one is calling me."

"Look, Sheila, I don't care what you heard in the streets. You are not going to know the truth until you talk to your father or Mr. Adams. And, no, you have not inherited one million dollars. What do you need?"

"Just ask Dad if he could send me a few bucks so I can make it home."

I gave Yolanda the name of our hotel and, through Western Union, some money was sent. I picked it up, and we drove back home. I was bummed. I was indebted to Carla for the trip and the clothes. I'd better get back and get to work—easy street wasn't that easy.

When we arrived at Carla's, there were three calls from Ray Charles Enterprises on her caller ID. We checked her messages and heard, "Sheila, this is Joe. You need to call me."

I called immediately; he was gone for the day. Over the next several days, we played phone tag. When I finally reached Joe, he said, "I know that you have been trying to call and figure out what is going on, but you should realize you made these circumstances for yourself. When your father got all his kids together, you were in prison. He couldn't help that. This is what occurred: your dad decided to leave his children some money, 490,000 dollars each, after taxes."

"490,000 dollars?" I said in amazement.

"Yes. No. Excuse me. For you, it's 500,000 dollars. The rest of the children received 10,000 dollars at the meeting so they could start to learn how to handle a large sum of money."

"That's so wonderful. Can I talk to Dad?" "He is not available at this time."

"Will you tell him that I love him?"

"I'm the trustee over your money. The taxes have been paid on it—so the money you will be receiving is tax-free. Valerie will send you a paper to sign that stipulates you will accept the 500,000-dollar inheritance, and you will not fight the trust. If you don't sign this paper, you won't get it at all. All your brothers and sisters signed it a year ago."

"I want to talk to Dad."

"I will see what I can do."

"Thank you very much."

"He hasn't been talking to anyone—nothing personal. Your father said he just doesn't want you to blow it in one day. Now, I want you to go to a bank and open an account. I will send you ten thousand dollars like the other children received as soon as you call me back with the account number and you have signed and returned the papers Valerie is sending you."

"Thank you, Joe."

I hung up the phone and went through the roof. I was so pleased to know that I had not lost out on that part of my life. It took several days to receive the papers. I signed and immediately returned them. I followed through and opened an account sometime in mid-March, and, within a few days, there was ten grand in my account. I immediately paid Carla two thousand dollars for the trip and the clothes. Several weeks later, I borrowed Carla's truck and drove to visit an old friend, Scotty. He greeted me with a warm embrace and introduced me to his friend Paul. I thought he was the hottest thing since sliced bread. We had a good conversation but left shortly after another friend of Scotty's stopped over, Johnny Parson, a mechanical engineer.

Johnny was an older gentleman who made me laugh, and I truly enjoyed his company. When he asked me out to dinner, I agreed. We went out three of four times over the next several weeks until Johnny started getting overly attached and possessive—the "you belong to me" type of thing. I went over to Scotty's to talk to him about it because it was disturbing to me. As if it had been scripted, Johnny showed up at Scotty's door and inquired about me. I told Scotty to tell Johnny I wasn't there. "I just can't deal with it right now. He is getting too weird."

Johnny started going on about my car parked outside. Somehow Scotty was able to turn him away, and my suspicions were confirmed. It made me feel uneasy. Paul showed up with his roommate, Pat, whom I knew. It wasn't long before I revealed my uneasiness with Johnny to the two of them. Paul asked if I would like to come over to his place.

"Yeah! Sounds good to me. We can have a couple drinks and play cribbage or something."

At Paul's apartment, he told me we had met years ago while I was living in Minnetonka. My kids were babies at that point, and I had driven Spud to meet with Paul's roommate at the time. While we were there, Spud took my car and stranded me at Paul's for several days.

"I feel embarrassed for not remembering you," I said to Paul. "That scares me and only shows how out of control I was back then. I knew there was a reason it felt like I knew you!"

I now remembered how kind he was. He had taken care of me; he had been considerate and concerned over my welfare. That memory made me like him even more. He worked and had a sense of responsibility. Over the following weeks, we got really close. I would call and tell him what I was going through.

Carla's was getting chaotic, and the money from my dad was evaporating. I was asking myself, *How much do I have to give back? How much do I owe her?* I paid her for the clothes, bought a car from her I never did see, and lent her money. I had given her some money of mine to hold, and, when it came up missing, it was time for me to move. Paul and I saw each other every day. We went for walks and rides and went to his friend's house—the normal stuff people do when they are interested in each other. Paul's roommate, Pat, was doing renovation work on some properties, and, one day, Pat walked in with Colin. Reconnecting with Colin, Paul and I made plans to go out on the weekend with him and his girlfriend, Evette. We became a foursome, spending the weekends together.

Paul's roommate was upset because I was over there every day. Pat asked Paul, "Aren't we ever going to get to spend any time alone without Sheila?"

"Oh my God. Are you guys gay?" I asked.

"Oh no," Paul said. "He's just being that way because I have a girlfriend and he doesn't."

Pat decided to move out, so I naturally moved in with Paul. I called Kevin to let him know I was happy and in eternal bliss inside this relationship. I wanted Kevin to meet him, the guy of my dreams.

From previous experience in the real estate market, I was able to enter into a business relationship with Colin. I brought him some properties and refinancing deals through friends. We actually got Johnny's farmhouse in Princeton refinanced—fixed up the property and the relationship. My life was stabilizing.

Colin introduced me to Breedlove, a guitar player who had played with Al Green, the Temptations, and a list of others. Breedlove and I became friends and started to talk about putting a band together. I respected his talent, and we talked about contacting Dad about doing a duet with me, a lifelong dream of mine.

Several weeks into our acquaintance, Breed called me and said, "Look, I really dig you, and I am not trying to get any money out of this deal except to play with you and run your band. That is it. But this Colin is another matter. I would look out for him if I were you. He thinks he deserves some kind of compensation for putting the two of us together." He continued to inform me Colin was freaking out and trying to pull a scam to get money from me.

I confronted Colin, and he told me, "Breedlove has it all confused. I was just trying to tell him I put you guys together and wanted to help be your manager or agent or something. Why aren't you telling me what it is that you're doing?"

"That's the stupidest thing I ever heard, Colin. What do you know about the music business?" I responded. I thought Colin had lost his mind. I couldn't hold that against him and continued working on a lucrative real estate deal with him.

Leaked through the media, I learned Dad was having more than hip surgery. He was very ill. I began to suspect information I was receiving from his office was being filtered, which wasn't unusual. I had a feeling something was not quite right. But I still had the idea Dad was bigger than life, and, if he were ill, I knew he could afford the best doctors. I felt he would be all right in the end.

The very next day, I placed a call to Yolanda to speak with my father. When Dad would not talk to me, I had the feeling something was seriously wrong. I felt as if I were in the twilight zone, unable to understand why no one surrounding Dad considered his children's feelings. They were people placed in their position by him. Did they believe they had put themselves there, strictly of their own design? I always felt the attitude of Dad's employees was, "Who do Ray Charles's children think they are? Why would they possibly think they are important?"

I continued to call my father's office and ask questions, but no one would give up the real deal on his health. With every call, I heard the same response—"He's holding his own." I wanted to puke every time I heard Valerie or Yolanda say that. It sounded rehearsed. I knew our father was a man who got around. I also knew Mom's house was one of his spots, and she had given up her whole life waiting for him in the shadow of his music. As far as I was concerned, it was never the shadow of another woman. I was glad Mom wasn't around to have to go through this—it would have killed her.

"He's not receiving calls."

"What do you mean, he's not receiving calls? He's not receiving calls from his own children. That's insane! I don't believe it."

After three days of this cat-and-mouse game, panic set in. I had to talk to him one last time and let him know my life was changing. My life was different now. My thoughts went to Vernon, and he was the one who eventually hooked me up with Dad.

"Dad? It's Sheila." There was a long pause. "Dad, are you there?"

"Yeah, yeah, I'm here," he responded in a slow, labored voice. "I'm just so tired."

"Hi, Daddy," I said as I tried to conceal my sadness. "I love you so much. I want to come and see you."

"Okay," he responded ever so softly. "Okay, baby"—another response indicating he was weak and frail. "That would be great."

"No one would let me talk to you for the longest time."

"I'm just so tired," he repeated.

His voice was so frail and full of pain, I could not help but begin to weep. "I love you, Daddy." I think I must have repeated myself fifty times. "I will be right there" were the last words from my mouth as I hung up the phone.

I prayed he could read my thoughts, my sorrow. *I'm sorry I was a crack addict. I'm sorry I was not there for my mom when she was diagnosed with cancer. I'm sorry I'm an ex-con. I'm so terribly sorry I'm not there with you right now!* "I will be right there."

Little of the past months made sense to me; it was gray. I felt totally without structure—trying to merge into society, make it in the real estate business, make a move back into my music career, my father dying, removing myself from drugs, making good honest friends, reuniting with Jeanna and my children, attempting to see my father, and everyone except Paul backstabbing me along the way over some money! I had no clue what I was doing. Everything had twisted in on me.

People recognized I could be inheriting an incredible amount of money, and everyone wanted some. Kevin was continually calling, asking me about it. Jeanna was calling and wondering when she could see me. With the unsettled nature of life, I didn't want her to arrive and have everything in limbo. I was immersed in unimaginable craziness that stretched far beyond chaos, and only God prevented me from going back to smoking myself to death. I had lost my mom while in prison, and now I was forced to consider the question of what would happen were my dad to go. I didn't even know where he was exactly.

I called Yolanda to try to see if there was a way they could send some money for plane tickets to go see him. I asked to have $10,000 sent to the bank. I had mismanaged my money. My account was in the red with fees and overdrafts, and my banking relationship was bust.

The morning broke with a call from Yolanda informing me my brother Bobby wanted to call me. He wanted to meet with me when I got out there to visit Dad. I told her I would love to speak with Bobby and to go ahead and give him my number. She informed me she had yet to speak with Joe about the money but was working on it.

When Bobby called, the first question out of my mouth was, "What is going on with Dad?" He could only tell me none of us children were able to see him.

"How come he's been sick so long and you haven't seen him?" I asked.

He told me he had tried countless times to connect with him, but no one was permitting him to get to Dad. Bobby had no understanding of or explanation for the situation. I reaffirmed my intention to get to Los Angeles and told him I was coming one way or another.

Driving to and from appointments throughout the day, I kept hearing my father's songs on the radio. In the past, hearing him on the radio was an immediate *Change the station!* Now I had no desire to turn it off. It was comfortable to listen to him for the first time in years, decades! It still produced a bittersweet effect. I missed him. I wanted to see him and was worried sick over his condition. I remembered how sad it was while incarcerated, unable to be there for Mom in her final days.

As Colin and I were driving to meet Yvette, Dad came over the radio, singing "It's Not Easy Being Green." I don't know what it is about that song, maybe because I always felt it wasn't easy being me and he was singing that song to me—my own personal theme song. I had to turn that one off. I just couldn't listen to that, and it increased my anxiety to get out to Los Angeles to see him. Shortly thereafter, we pulled into the restaurant parking lot.

Colin, Yvette, and I met at the Eagle's Nest, going over the paperwork of a real estate deal. The closing was five days away, and I would be seeing about $6,000. I was very hopeful all would go as planned; the money would allow me to reestablish myself with the bank. We concluded the meeting with a feeling that the money was in the bank. No sooner had the three of us entered our house to pick up Paul and head to the movies than Colin took my arm and looked me square in the eye.

"Sheila, there's something I have to tell you."

"What?'

"Well, you know how they have been playing your Dad's music all day, every station we turned to?"

"Yeah, wasn't that something?" I said, thinking that he was about to say something about how great Dad was or something about him.

"Your father passed away today."

"No way! I talked to Yolanda today. She would have told me."

"I heard it on the radio earlier. I didn't want to tell you until we got through our business."

"What?"

I dropped onto the floor with my hands over my head and started to cry uncontrollably. I was hysterical. I didn't get to see him! My heart broke into a million pieces. *Why didn't Yolanda tell me? Am I some kind of psycho or what?* I never expected that my father was going to die. He was bigger than life, just like my mom. It was a selfish part of me that thought, *Don't let me down now.* He had the money to pay for the best doctors. The thought of his passing was never a question with me. He was immortal. *What was on his mind about me when he left here? Was I really his greatest heartbreak? Was he aware enough to remember our last conversation that I was out of prison? Or did any of that even matter to him at all?*

Paul turned on the television, and there it was, all over every station's six o'clock news. Ray Charles, the late, great jazz-blues genius of soul, had passed away. Half an hour later, I was able to pick myself up off the floor. Paul asked everyone to leave, and I was grateful. The phone rang. Paul answered and turned to me. "Sheila, it's Kevin. Do you feel like talking?"

"Yeah," I said. "Kevin, oh, Kevin."

"I'm so sorry for you, sister."

"I am crazy right now, Kevin."

"Everything's gonna be all right, Sheila."

We talked for but a few moments, and I told Kevin I had to figure out a way to get out to Los Angeles.

Breedlove called to offer his sympathy and proceeded to tell me Colin had called Joe Adams behind my back. He had left a message at my father's office, stating, "If you want the dirt on Sheila, I can provide her entire history with drugs and prison." According to Breed, Colin left his number and wanted to be paid for the information. I let the real estate thing just fly out the window. I freaked out hearing about that nonsense as the phone rang again.

"Sheila, this is your sister Raenee. Yolanda gave me your number."

"What? Who is this?"

"Your sister Raenee." I did not know of her directly, but she knew of me. I did know there were other children.

"Oh my God. I can't wait to meet you. It's too bad that we have to meet under these circumstances," I said and started to cry. She started to cry. Between the tears, I learned she was at a hair salon getting her hair done when she had heard about Dad. I told her a little of my day and how I had found out about Dad's passing.

"You wouldn't believe the stuff that's going on out here, Sheila. How dare they? We have to wait to hear about our father's death on the news. They did not let any of us have our last moments with him. The world knew about Dad dying before we did."

"Do you know anything about the funeral?"

"I don't know a thing. They aren't telling any of us kids anything. Joe controls every last thing. Who does he think he is?"

"Now I don't feel so bad. I thought I was the only who didn't know, like I was the only one not worthy enough, like I was so removed from reality that I didn't know."

She told me that Evelyn was the one who was supposed to keep the rest of siblings posted on Dad's condition—she never called me once.

"I can't wait to meet you!"

"I can't wait to meet *you*!"

I could not sleep, nor could I believe Dad was gone. I felt lost and didn't know how I would carry on. Why could I not have been there with him during his final days or have done things better with my life? I was grateful for the conversation four days earlier. I felt guilty for my selfish thoughts. *Now Dad is dead. I have no future whatsoever in music. Why could he not have helped me?*

I called Vernon, only to cry again. He told me he was in the room when Dad died. Joe threw him out the very next second. He never liked Vernon, maybe because Vernon was one of Dad's best friends, close as close could be. They did everything together, and Vernon was with Dad long before Joe. Vernon was always on top of everything.

Over the next day, I had several conversations with Raenee. I was a mixture of grief over Dad's passing while excited over meeting my brothers and sisters, my family. I told Raenee, "I'm looking forward to all seven of us being together."

"Seven?" Raenee responded.

"Yes," I continued for my own clarity, "I've met Bobby, Ray Jr., David, Evelyn, and heard of Corey, and now I know about you. If you include me, that makes a total of seven."

Raenee laughed. "There are a few more than that!"

"You're kidding."

"Five more, to be exact—Vincent, Retha, Charles, Robyn, and Alexandria."

"Oh my God," I exclaimed. "I wonder why Dad kept us apart, a secret from each other? I always wanted a sister."

"I'm sure he had some reason for it. At the family meeting, Valerie told me Dad was concerned about his children getting along. Dad paged Val to his office to simply ask, 'Are they in the conference room fighting?' Like, what made him think we would go at each other's throats or something?"

I was so appreciative of Raenee. Her concern and willingness to communicate with me was comforting. We talked about the funeral arrangements, and she asked if I would stay with her when I came out. I about cried over the love she felt for me.

I talked to Yolanda shortly after we hung up.

"Sheila, do you know that Matt Schuler, the man who has your children, called here yesterday? I cussed that bastard out so hard. Do you know that he said that if Ray's children inherited any money that it should not go to Sheila? 'Make sure she doesn't get it 'cause she's on crack and completely irresponsible!' Sheila, he told me that any money coming to you should go to him! Who is this Matt, and what is he doing with your children? Your father's body was not even cold! I told him, 'You little disrespectful asshole! *Sheila* hasn't even called here yet!'"

"What?! Oh my God, Yolanda!"

"Now, I got good news—we have the money together so we can get it to a bank. You have to get a bank together for us to send money into that account."

I called my bank, Associated Bank, where I had previously had accounts prior to going to prison. I had destroyed my accounts there. I told them Dad's people were going to send money to them to reopen my accounts. They told me that they would have to speak to Yolanda directly. They would require $1,700 and $2,000 to pay off the two delinquent and overdrawn accounts.

I called Yolanda back and asked her if she would communicate directly with the bank's manager. I told her what I needed her to do. She told me that she would have to talk to Joe.

She called me back later that night and said, "Okay, I'll call the bank tomorrow, and we'll take care of it." The money from Dad had yet to be deposited into my account. I had to borrow money from an associate of Kevin to acquire plane tickets for Paul and me.

CHAPTER 23

PRODIGAL DAUGHTER

Let us be earnest in what we do
And do the very best we can
As it should be
But may we be more interested in what we cannot do
In what God alone does and is doing now

—*GLENN SWANSON*, RETURN TO FAITH
SHOES OF THE SOLE MAN

I WAS WEARING a cream-colored linen shirt with brown trim and a matching pair of brown linen pants chosen specifically to meet my older sister Raenee. We used quarters from Paul's piggy bank to wash and dry the clothes recently tossed into two suitcases we acquired from Kevin on the way to the airport. I stepped out of the Chrysler LeBaron convertible, capable of falling apart any moment, and shut the door. "Hurry up, now, Paul. Just find the first place to park and get yourself in here. The plane is scheduled to leave in fifty minutes. Meet me at the check-in. I'll get the tickets."

Into the terminal's exquisitely orchestrated managed chaos, I walked to meet this final *coup de grâce*—picking up the tickets, checking in our luggage, and boarding a plane in under fifty minutes. I had no idea how to manipulate time itself; the nearest I could figure, it had something to do with redefining intensity.

Through the grace of twenty passengers and an airline employee, I got the tickets in under five minutes. Once they were in hand, I observed time in the frequency of seconds, an angst that was driving me nuts. Several minutes later, Paul approached. I unleashed on him. "What took you so long?"

"Look, Sheila, I understand you're under a lot of pressure, but just for your enlightenment, I need to tell you that you've become a witch. I was doing our laundry all night until two o'clock in the morning."

"Well, isn't that fabulous? You certainly aren't feeling any pain."

"It's not my fault your father died. I'm trying the best I can. Do you think that you could be a little nicer?"

"Yeah! Come on, let's go!"

Once on the plane, one would think there would have been a sense of accomplishment from doing the impossible, making a flight against time. Instead, I was breathing fumes of alcohol Paul consumed throughout the ordeal to cope with the stress. Were I a silver-spoon princess, I would be asking Mommy to go into her purse and flip me a couple of her Valium. As it was, all I could do was thank my mother in Heaven for the moxie to attempt such a thing and the skills to pull it off.

The moment we were seated, we heard, "This is the captain. We will be landing in LAX in two hours and forty-five minutes. Weather conditions are fair. Relax and enjoy your flight."

I turned toward Paul with the authority of revealing the Eleventh Commandment and said, "Paul, how much did you have to drink? If you are not sleeping in the next ten minutes, I'm knocking you out!"

I was thinking about meeting Raenee for the first time. I knew nothing about her. She had been kept from me, just one of many secrets, and I was filled with a wondrous anticipation as the flight attendant asked if we wanted breakfast.

"No breakfast," I told her, "but I could use a Bloody Mary. We both could."

We were in the air for only a few moments before Paul was out like a light. I managed to get about an hour of sleep. I awoke from a nightmare revisiting the Con Air flight to Bryan. Replete with loss and pain, I lay there with slobber on one side of my face and tears on the other. My father had been so upset with me, and for good reason. I was unable to tell him how sorry I was for having caused him pain, not just for him—for everyone. For a moment, I saw myself peering into a coffin and literally pinched myself to turn away from the emotional quagmire looming upon such horizons. I reconnected with the joyous anticipation of standing face to face with my sister in less than a few hours.

When we got to the baggage claim, I called Raenee and told her we had arrived.

"Oh, Sheila, I'm circling the airport right now. I am so excited." The enthusiasm and sincerity in her voice translated to an instantaneous love within my heart. "I love you. Even though this is a sad time, it is beautiful as well, a time for us—you know—a time for sisterhood, brotherhood, family."

"Oh, Raenee, I love you, and we have yet to meet! Okay, now, we will be outside the baggage pickup area in a quick second." I hung up the phone with an emotional lump in my throat. We got the bags and were waiting outside on the curb when a large black SUV pulled up. Out popped a bubbly black woman in shirt and jeans with long, wavy hair and the biggest smile. She was jumping out of her skin, and I could feel the love pouring from her. I knew instantly that it was Raenee.

"Sheila!" she screamed.

"Raenee!" I shouted in return as we ran into each other's arms. We held another for the longest time, a hug of genuine sisterhood.

"Sheila, I have waited so long for this. I tried to locate you in prison but just kept drawing a blank. No one would give me any information."

"Oh, Raenee, thank you for telling me that. You can't imagine what it means to me, and it isn't surprising to know the office wouldn't give you any information."

"Tell me about it, sister. I am so glad you are staying with us. Finally, I have a chance to be with you. How many of us have you met, again?"

"I have met Bobby, David, and Ray Jr. I met Evelyn only once, quite some time ago."

The drive went quickly. Entering the driveway of their beautiful home, a faint sense of balance and completeness began to arise within my heart, the fragrance of family. Greeting us at the door, a handsome man stood inside with a gleaming smile.

"Sheila, this is my husband, Kevin."

"Oh, Kevin, so nice to meet you. I can't believe it. I now have three brothers with that name!"

Raenee had spent more time with Dad than I had, a reality that had more to do with geography and where my mother was coming from. It was Mom's decision not to live in California. I was pleased to learn Raenee was on the same page with me when it came to playing down the fact Ray Charles was our father. The other siblings I had met, Della's children, had a demeanor that was different regarding Dad, and, for what it's worth, I understood why. I saw it as natural to the world we occupy. As we were talking on our way to a guest room, a very classy and sophisticated woman approached us.

"Sheila, this is my mother, Mae Mosely Lyles."

"Mae? Mae Saunders?" I exclaimed. "It's so very nice to meet you!"

"So nice to meet you as well, Sheila. Don't let me interfere right now. We will have time to talk later. Go freshen up or get some rest after your flight—whatever suits you."

"Oh, Mae, I don't know what to say. Thank you."

After Raenee and I were in the room alone for a moment, I realized the thrill of our meeting had erased the reality of our father's passing. "Raenee, I almost feel guilty that I am so happy to be with you. There's also such a great sadness in me over Dad's passing. I lost my mom several years ago."

"Oh, Sheila, I'm so sorry," Raenee said as Mae walked into the room.

"I cannot resist revealing a personal story to the both of you," I said, looking at Mae. "This is so weird for me. All my life, I heard a story my mom would tell—freaking out over someone she knew then as Mae Saunders. Apparently, Mae, you were registered in the same hotel Dad had my mother in. The manager told Mom that Mrs. Ray Charles just checked out and flew with Dad to New York. My mom went crazy and started to charge all kinds of stuff to her room on Ray's tab. That is all I knew about you, Mae. I didn't learn about Raenee until just a few days ago."

"Well, if I remember right, I found out about you and your mom in a strange way myself."

"Mom," Raenee said, "I thought I heard every story you had to tell."

"Oh, Mom," I said, as natural as can be. "I would so much like to know that story."

"Ray and I had an apartment in New York. Ray was at the studio, and I had gone there to meet him. Ray was singing 'It's Crying Time Again' in a manner that made me aware that he was feeling something down deep. Vernon entered, and I asked him, 'What's the deal with Ray?' Vernon responded, 'It probably has something to do with the paternity suit that Sandra is pulling.' I said, 'Paternity suit?' And Vernon said, 'Ray has a daughter with Sandra Betts—Sheila.' Well, that was the first of anything I had heard about you and your mother."

Instantly, I was calling Mae "Mom," and it was like listening to my own mother tell stories about Dad. This was a phenomenal healing for me, just as it was with my brother Bobby calling my mother "Mom." It seemed the way it should be, gracious and loving. But before this moment with Mae, that shoe never got on the other foot. Years earlier, when Bobby brought me to his family home, Della told Bobby, "Get her out of the house!" Later, I heard Dad tell Bobby, "What were you thinking, bringing Sheila over to her house? Sheila's mother is your mother's archenemy. She considers Sandra the reason we got divorced!"

Back then I was thinking, *Wow, now ain't that some piece of news!* At the time, for a brief moment, I experienced the smallest victory—a sad commentary on my way of thinking and my life. But what little bit of acknowledgment I could get, I took. I suspect we all did. Contrary to how the world tries to make us feel, we are not so different when it comes to certain fundamental things, the important things, the things that reach down home into your soul—such as knowing you are important, knowing you belong, knowing you are loved.

Raenee, along with the boys, had the ability to see Dad during his final years while I sat in prison. It raised a pain in my heart. I would learn from Raenee that our father helped Mae start a very elite spa. That hurt me, too. It cut deep as I recalled Dad's last words with my mother, intimately connected with her pain and the price she paid because of her incredible love for him. But God had already lifted a great deal from me, and I saw myself in Raenee, possessing the same need to claim what she could of our father. I realized how much more I loved her because of it. We held love for each other born from pain and a love spun of Spirit, our soul's connection to our father and God—the very substance of our being.

"Girl, we've got to talk." Raenee grabbed me by the arm and escorted me outside to be alone together. "Joe is tripping. We don't know the itinerary for the funeral. Dad wanted Bobby to pray over him and conduct the service. Well, it is just crazy—they're not being forthcoming with any information. We have no information whatsoever. I mean, it's ugly."

A mutual dislike for Joe Adams deepened the bond of sisterhood not just between Raenee and me; the dislike for Joe appeared to exist within most, if not all, of Ray's children. Whether the depth of that disfavor could be wholly or even partially justified was not the issue; it galvanized the family connection between us. It is not possible to understand that blessing unless one was to have such a common thread woven into the fabric of her life.

Later that evening, my brother Kevin called. He had made plans to come out. He had arranged tickets through Lee Roth, who would accompany him along with his daughter's mother and Kevin Newsome, people I knew as family.

"I am unsure of the arrangements that are being made," I told Kevin, "but, of course, you can come out. I see no reason why not. I don't know if I can get you into the large funeral production Joe has planned, but I'm sure that you can attend the family one." As I was talking, Raenee was nearby, and I looked at her. She was nodding her head. "It will be fine, Kevin. When were you thinking of coming?"

"Tomorrow. The flight arrives at 6:20 p.m."

"Just call when you arrive."

We continued our conversation for a few more minutes and hung up with love. I welcomed Kevin's presence; the thought of his arrival was comforting. I returned to the excitement of learning about each other. Kevin, Raenee's husband, had taken leave from his work during that time, and it appeared to me that he and Raenee had a perfect marriage. I told them both as much.

Another of my sisters, Robyn, was also staying with Raenee. Very small and petite like our father, she carried herself in the manner of a giant. Her shoulder-length hair and beautiful brown eyes accentuated the beauty of this young woman. She was there with her husband, daughter, and mother. She was living in Detroit. To think, several days earlier, I was unaware she existed. This day had become Christmas in June.

I was impressed with Robyn. When she told me she had a black belt in karate, I had to say, "Girl, I'm afraid of you!"

"Sheila, you know I've been pursuing a career as a singer. I so look up to you and would love someday to sing with you."

Robyn truly saw me as her big sister, and that was all it took to melt any fear or competition. Effortlessly, I fell into her vision of me. No longer was I the only child of our father attempting to pursue a career in music.

"Then we will do so together on the same stage, sister." And we danced around together holding hands.

Robyn's mom arrived as we were laughing and acting silly. She was a small lady, shapely, very attractive, and exuberant. She would be a standout in any crowd. Just like Mae, she was very accepting of me, and she reminded me so much of my mother.

We gathered for dinner as other brothers and sisters arrived: Bobby, now a minister; David, his wife, and children. The opportunity to meet and learn of one another was an incredible thing for me. My life of isolation and sense of abandonment had been instantaneously removed. I was living and breathing family. I can speak only for myself, but it appeared none of us got deep into the personal hurt we experienced through Dad's absence in our lives. I avoided it because the hurt yet remained in my heart. We all told our individual stories about Dad and discovered there were common elements to everyone's tales.

We all seemed anxious to dispel the myth that Dad's success was so intricately connected to Joe Adams. When he took over Dad's career, Ray Charles was already number one on the charts and considered the genius of soul. Joe just expanded on that. The one conclusion we all had to come to: Joe did not do anything Dad did not allow. If Joe fired someone and Dad did not approve, he would hire him or her back. We all had the feeling there were certain aspects of business Joe tried to keep Dad in the dark about—certainly I felt Joe tried to discount the relationship I had with my father.

I said to the group, "Joe can't tell me Dad didn't care about me. Every time I got into trouble or anything critical occurred, he was immediately forthcoming with assistance. Dad brought me into the studio and said, 'You are my daughter. I am so very proud of you.' As much as our father knew how to be a parent, he was—at least that's how I figure it. He did not have much to work with. The one thing he did remember was his relationship with his mother. He knew little of his father. Where does that put you on the fathering skill level? I believe he had a love for each and every one of us. I know he never got us mixed up. He never called my mom one of your mother's names. I know when he would talk to Mom, his voice was full of love. For whatever it is worth, that is what I am hanging on to."

Mae was always at Raenee's, from the break of dawn into the late evening. She would talk to us about how it was for her and Dad, on the road with him for years. Dad was having affairs with other women throughout the time she was with him, and Mae did not have a clue. On the surface, there was a good-natured sense of amusement as we all offered theories on why Dad juggled all these various women and how he was able to keep most of them in the dark about each other. But underneath that levity, I knew a deeper pain existed within each of us.

Another commonality to our stories was how it appeared as though Dad could see. He had the incredible ability, even in an unfamiliar room, to walk around as if he had lived there his entire life. Within a moment, he knew exactly where everything was.

"Another thing that made me angry was the way I heard of Dad's passing," I told my siblings. "I learned from others as I watched the TV news. I kept asking about how he was doing. When I talked to Valerie, she would tell me verbatim what I had heard before. 'Well, your dad is holding his own.' I don't exactly know what that meant, but it was frustrating. By the way, where is Evelyn?"

"I don't think she is going to make it, Sheila," Raenee responded.

The following day, Kevin called to let me know they had arrived, and his ex-fiancée, Erica, was in from Seattle. They had a daughter together and remained close. Lee and Juice had arrived from Minneapolis with him. Kevin came over to Raenee's with Lee and Erica. Juice preferred to stay at the hotel. Everyone was digging Kevin. He has that way about him. Everyone loves him.

Herb Miller, Ray's driver and good friend, stopped over. I was thrilled to have an opportunity to speak with him. "Oh, Herb, my mother had nothing but the greatest things to say about you. You look so good, so healthy."

Herb told me how much he loved my mother, how much Ray loved her for her innocence and the beauty of her voice, and how Ray was drawn to her love. It became a struggle to hear some of the stories because my mother sacrificed her entire life for my dad. Mom went to places in her mind that kept her from being who she could have been. Though she never said it, I feel my mom believed someday Ray was going to come and sweep her up on his white horse and just take her away. My mother could be in such wonderful relationships and opportunities; then, the minute Dad called, she would drop everything she was doing.

"I had to leave after Joe came on board," Herb told me. "Joe made it seem as though he were Ray Charles himself. I couldn't stand it. The only reason Joe got the gig was because he had the travel agency your Dad was using to book his tours."

The family funeral was the next day, and I was asked to write a poem for the service. I used the title of his songs to create a vision of what he was doing in Heaven. It was placed in the funeral program, and I was prepared with that for the service.

The weather was gorgeous as Raenee and her husband, Robyn and her daughter, and Paul and I were seated in a limousine. My brother Kevin, Lee, and Erica followed us in their rental car. It was a twenty-five-minute drive to the funeral home. I was glad to have Raenee, the love between us exceptional and rare. When we arrived, I realized I had forgotten my camera and asked the driver to take me to a local convenience store to grab a disposable one. Upon my return, people were milling around and obviously upset. I went to Raenee. "What's wrong?"

"Joe showed up here with the police and told Vernon he had to go. He wouldn't stand for him being present—told him he had to leave!"

We entered the chapel. From behind the curtain where our father's casket was located, Bobby emerged, crying. With anguish greater than grief, he exclaimed, "Jesus, forgive me. Forgive me!" He looked at us. "That bastard just took Dad's body."

Standing next to me, Herb Miller turned to me and said, "Sheila, this is why I had to tell your father good-bye after he hired Joe Adams. I could not deal with Joe's complete lack of anything resembling human respect."

Joe cussed Vernon out and had the police escort him off the premises—I figured because Vernon knew too much. Dad confided in Vernon. He always did. Vernon knew how much money he was leaving the kids and knew Dad wanted Bobby on the board of trustees of his estate. Joe was not having it, and Vernon told us so. Joe was forever firing Vernon, and Dad was forever hiring him back.

Joe said, "I don't want anyone outside of the family viewing the body." Joe claimed he had control over that, not us. David brought his wife, and Bobby brought his girlfriend. Kevin came to the funeral with Lee and Erica. *What do you mean, no one but the family, Joe?* I thought. *This is the family—this is my wife, Joe—this is my husband, Joe—this is my brother, Joe—these are our people, Joe. Our father's people. Family!* To use the police to solidify his crazy idea of family was nothing short of a slap in the face. Joe and the police left with Dad's body, returning it to the mortuary.

It was inconceivable! In front of an entire family gathered for a moment of final peace, someone would walk in and remove my father's body. I was speechless, a silent witness to the circus my life provided. Propelled once again by surreal circumstances, my spirit arose above all the commotion, and absolute peace descended over me. The rest of the family grew quiet. Dad had requested that Bobby perform the eulogy. The family knew that and pulled together.

Bobby arose and addressed the group. "Even though our father's body is not here, he is here in spirit. And we will pay respect to him in the manner that he wished, giving honor to a great man. We are his children, and no one can take that from us."

Like a book opened in the isolation of a dark room, Bobby's words were a light upon the final page, speaking of the common experience of being a Ray Charles child. Each of us had sought a child–father relationship with Ray. Ironically, his death brought us closer to a realization of family than what most of us had managed to achieve with Dad during his life.

In a moment of silent understanding, I read the words I had written in the funeral program. I felt I spoke for my siblings when I had written, *As we all know, to be absent from the body is to be present with the Lord. Though this knowledge is and will always be a comfort to me, Dad, your love and presence in my life will always and forever be missed. Your ability to bring such greatness to my life can never ever be duplicated. Dad, I love you.*

I then sang a song I wrote in lockdown, "Have I Told You Lately That I Love You?" After the service, Kevin said, "Sheila, it was like Heaven was shining a light on your face."

Following the ceremony, we went to Raenee's. Joe's antics were unbelievable, and our family's ability to persevere through such a moment was incredible.

"Can you believe what happened?"

"It was so amazing how we all pulled it together!"

At that moment, we realized that we truly were brothers and sisters, each mother's child but all Dad's. It was magical, miraculous, and spiritual. It was family. Dad's women, the mothers present, opened up to us all with more of their stories about Dad. Amazingly, each one of them felt as if they were Ray's special one. It clouded the faith I had in my Dad's love for Mom, while her love for him was unquestionable and extraordinary in my mind. It angered me. I felt Dad had misrepresented himself in that manner to both Mom and me—something that I felt unforgivable.

The following day, true to form, no family member had yet heard from the office over what arrangements were in place for us to view Dad's body. We had all become filled with anxiety; panic had invaded the camp once again. Joe Adams arranged to set Ray's body on public display, something I never thought my father would have approved, yet we, his family, had not been allowed to have it at our private funeral. There were media reports that Dad's family had actually requested the body be present at the public display, but to the best of my knowledge, no one from the family had ever been consulted upon that matter. My brother Kevin wanted to accompany me, but it was made clear to us by the office that a special viewing afforded the family prior to public admission was limited once again to family members only. Joe's definition of family was one that baffles me to this day.

That afternoon, we were picked up in a limo around one o'clock. Paul and I were permitted to attend the private viewing for family members and were chauffeured to the Los Angeles Convention Center. There had always been a sense of never having Dad to myself, and I was torn with that need as I gazed at thousands of people beginning to assemble for the public viewing. A raised platform supported a piano and an empty seat whereupon lay a black and silver jacket, a recognizable trademark to anyone who had seen one of Dad's performances. The spotlight had almost faded on a lifetime of memories upon a stage, and I had forever stood in the wings. It was a dream of mine to be on the stage with my father, but this was not the manner in which such a vision was held. I looked into the coffin; he looked so thin and emaciated. Both Raenee and I broke down and cried.

"Like I told myself at my mother's funeral," I said brokenly to Raenee, "the soul is free, this frame no longer capable of housing his spirit's flame."

We were escorted back to Raenee's and, once again, were in the dark regarding the arrangements of the next day's funeral. I had been treated like this frequently in federal prison: a need-to-know basis, informed only hours before the next transfer. It made me angry that those directing my father's funeral treated everybody like they were federal prisoners. Joe had hired feds. We, our father's blood, had not even yet been informed that we were on the list—the invitation-only list to our father's funeral. It was late that evening when we were finally put on notice that the limousines would once again escort us to the service.

The seating within the limousines had become standard; Paul and I were once again with Raenee and her family. The procession began in front of my father's office and studio. I thought of my last words to him: "I will be right there." The love Sandra Betts and God planted in me for my father was supernatural, far superior to the love any one of his employees, doctors, or nurses was capable of providing him—a spiritual love, a connection of the soul that superseded all relationships of business. The power of such love had been illustrated to me profoundly through my past, and I was convinced that, had I been with him before he passed, love would have healed and miraculously restored him to health. I felt guilty at allowing him to die.

Police and security surrounded the black limousines. The memory of being escorted in such a secured fashion was unavoidable, but the current chains that bound me were invisible to the eyes of man. *Well, Dad,* I thought, *this is it. No longer will I be able to wish and hope for the opportunity to feel your embrace, feel your arms about me, hear your voice whisper with your heart's truth, "I love you." Mom's love for you was something I could never understand. We fought for recognition from you in a manner that you could not answer as we needed, but I know you loved us all and continue to. In my heart, I know this to be true because God tells me it is so. Yet I cannot let go in a complete way. You were my daddy, and I don't know how to stop looking for you. I need to find you.*

I stared blankly through the limousine's window into the faces of hundreds of Dad's fans every block of the journey, thousands and thousands lined up on the sidewalk to say good-bye to someone they had only known through his music, his voice. I sought to understand it.

We exited into a tightly secured area with the rotor chop of police copters overhead. By anyone's standard, it was a production fueled by the presence of celebrity, photographers, secret service and L.A. police security. Throngs of people stood upon closed streets. Inside, we were seated in a grand cathedral, its ceiling vaulted one hundred feet into space overhead. An enormous mural commemorating Dad and his music spanned the wall behind the altar's stage. A large choir of fifty or more members dressed in blue, full-length robes assembled on four sets of risers at the back of the stage.

Clint Eastwood, the Reverend Jesse Jackson, Quincy Jones, Bill Cosby, Stevie Wonder, Willie Nelson, Wynton Marsalis, Cicely Tyson, and so many more public figures were present. Among hundreds of floral tributes surrounding the church, a huge wreath of white chrysanthemums formed the letters *RC*. Gazing at the coffin garlanded with flowers, I saw a large, shameless, and obtrusive red ribbon emblazoned with gold letters reading *EMMA AND JOE* draped across the display. It did not say *Loving Father and Grandfather*; it said *EMMA AND JOE!* I sat within a moment that cannot be adequately described, surrounded by members of my family to whom I had only recently been introduced, within an emotional contradiction, a perfectly balanced desire to cry uncontrollably and laugh hysterically. Staring at three letters on my father's coffin, *J-O-E*, I thought,

Where is one human being who does not have a horror story when it comes to Joe Adams? There must be someone, God, for you have shown me there is good in everyone. Forgive me, Father, for what I am feeling at this moment. God, help me find my peace.

Bobby, the Reverend Robert Robinson, opened the service with gracious words. "If you would do something for my family today, why don't you stand on your feet and give some praise? Because we're here to celebrate God today and thank God for this man." And as all immediately stood, I was filled with pride for my brother, thankful that he was permitted to do the opening invocation. "He's blessed us all; he's blessed us all," Bobby continued. "Say hallelujah; say hallelujah!"

The outpouring of emotion and heartfelt words delivered by numerous individuals who had known my father dwarfed me, but it was not until the sincerity within the music of Stevie Wonder's voice that I knew God had answered my prayer made but a moment earlier. His words resonated within my heart. Of my father, Stevie said, "I knew that his voice made me feel like I wanted to love deeper, to care more and reach out and embrace the world." At that moment, I began to cry uncontrollably, for never before had I truly understood this world and who Ray Charles and Sandra Betts were within it. To be delivered to the world as a little girl trembling in fear and darkness while living in the shadows of two giants was the source of the greatest confusion and pain. So deep the connection with my father's soul, so close to my own, that to hear him sing was the most painful of all experiences. But now I knew I could have him in a manner outside that pain, a source of the greatest joy and peace.

Upon conclusion of the service, we were once again inside limousines on our way to a private burial, stopping at Dad's recording studio where once a dream lived in me with my father. The beauty of the cemetery was remarkable, thousands of flowers of numerous varieties, tulips, roses, and wild flowers in every imaginable color. The people escorting us were exceptionally kind and encouraged us to pick flowers from outside the mausoleum where Dad would be entombed. We did, and so, too, we all clung to them as if they were a piece of him, holding the petals close to our hearts. That is how it always was for me, saving things as ridiculous as the peels from his orange, something to hold until the next time. Now there would be no next time.

Fully understanding I had no living parents on this earth, I began to cry. Paul was so present to my sadness, so loving. I was grateful for him, grateful for love. As we were walking, one could not help but notice a huge blotch of red painting in an area of the cemetery's ground—red shirts, red bandanas, red hats, red, red, red. I knew immediately it was the Bloods; there was a huge photo displayed of the young man who had been slain.

I turned to Paul and said, "God is no respecter of persons."

"Respecter of persons?" Paul sounded perplexed. "The gang member over there being put to rest. The loved ones so gathered to mourn him—their sense of loss is as great as my family's. Love knows no boundaries and is all-inclusive. It cuts through to the marrow, deeper than what the world thinks of you."

We entered the mausoleum with flowers. Others had pictures, jewelry, and personal items to leave. I was glad Dad would not be lowered down into the ground. Watching them slowly lower my mother's body down into the dirt had been more than I could bear. The choir sang, and, while a door to my father's resting place was sealed, another began to open in my heart. We were escorted back to Raenee's, changed our clothes, and went to a gathering of family and friends at the Radisson Hotel. Paul, Kevin, and Erica where allowed to attend, and I was once again eternally grateful for the presence of Stevie Wonder, who sang at length. Members of my family begged me to sing, but I did not feel comfortable enough. Joe showed up for a moment, long enough to inspect that they were serving drinks and cold cuts.

I told Raenee I needed time with my brother at his hotel, that Paul and I would rent a room for the night. She understood my need to be with him, and we parted with the promise she would pick me up at noon for a final brunch before our early evening flight.

We hung out in Kevin's room and learned they had watched Dad's funeral on television. The network had interrupted coverage of Ronald Reagan's funeral service to broadcast the service of my father's, the final shadow he would cast over Kevin and me, one that blanketed many lives outside of ours. But it was Kevin and I together inside the blanket woven by Sandra Betts and Ray Charles. It was fitting when Kevin told me, "During the coverage of the funeral, it was almost like the cameraman couldn't keep the camera off you, Sheila."

The embrace both Kevin and I received from my newfound family was thrilling, but that history was as new as the day at the break of dawn. I needed Kevin; he understood my struggle, my yesterday, so I may know the direction of tomorrow. Lee Roth was present. So often over the years, he had been there for us. He had heavily supported my mother's efforts and rescued us financially more than once. And Juice was as close to the family Mom created as anyone could be. I was comforted by the presence of these two great friends, but it was Kevin I needed at that moment. I was glad when everyone decided to retire and leave the two of us alone, one on one.

We looked at each other with knowledge of a past that had welded our destinies. Our mother's pain, his pain, and my pain all brewed and mixed together in the same pot down to the very last serving. It was time to finish with love what had been started in love. In an indescribable moment, we surveyed and stood witness to past behavior that made one question the sanity of the entire human race. Our lives had been spun within a web of love between Sandra Betts and Ray Charles, innumerable crisscrossed, intersecting fibers, the very definition of confusion. Yet there was something that rang true to this past that was undeniable, a love and bond that no human act could undo, a love for one another planted in our hearts by God and nurtured in the fields of human experience by the most remarkable of women—our mother, Sandra Betts.

"Mom and Dad are gone now, Kevin."

"I know, Sis. Let's finish it for them."

"Together," I said in his arms as we parted.

As promised, we met for brunch at Raenee's for the final day—Raenee's daughter and husband, Raeshan and Kevin; Raenee's mother, Mae, and sister, Robyn, along with Robyn's daughter and husband; the house crew. We reaffirmed our commitment to each other as family, a family bond formed by our Heavenly Father. Within Joe's arrogance, the ever-present thorn he provided did not weaken our commitment to one another; it did the very opposite. We, the children of Ray Charles, were about to make our mark on the world.

"Like it or not," I said to Raenee as I held her in my arms, "here we come."

For so long I thought myself unworthy, undeserving, and less than another—I was lost, hopeless, without identity, and I came to know others with the same sense of abandonment. Imprisoned within those pages the world tried to erase from the book of life, I have come to know that there is goodness within everyone, and beneath every heart pounds the rhythm of truth God alone directs.

Our flight left around seven. As we made our way to the airport to board the plane, I thought of my future. I knew the time had arrived for my brothers and sisters, for my children, and most important, for me—time to say farewell to a life behind the shades. It was time to fly.

Love's hello knows no good-bye

MORE GREAT READS
FROM VOX DEI

Run, River Currents **by Ginger Marcinkowski** (Religious Fiction) Determined to recover from the hands of a father who sexually abused her and an emotionally distant mother, Emily seeks the peace she'd lost in her youth. Will she ever let herself truly open up to the power of unconditional love?

The Button Legacy **by Ginger Marcinkowski** (Fiction - ebook only) Told through the eyes of a godly grandfather, The Button Legacy laces together the power of one man's prayers and offers a lesson of how God's grace can be seen even in the simplest thing—a button.

The Romance of Grace **by Jim McNeely III** (Christian Theology) What if God's main question is not how to make us moral but rather how to get us to fall in love with Him? Jim McNeely explores Bible passages that tell us what God's love really means.